BD21.H6 1959

W9-CRM-270

DISCARD

TYPES OF PHILOSOPHY

TYPES OF PHILOSOPHY

by

WILLIAM ERNEST HOCKING

with the collaboration of

RICHARD BOYLE O'REILLY HOCKING

THIRD
EDITION

CHARLES SCRIBNER'S SONS, *New York*

Copyright © 1959 Charles Scribner's Sons

Copyright 1929 Charles Scribner's Sons;
renewal copyright © 1957 William Ernest Hocking
Copyright 1939 Charles Scribner's Sons

This book published simultaneously in the United States
of America and in Canada—
Copyright under the Berne Convention.

All rights reserved. No part of this book
may be reproduced in any form without the
permission of Charles Scribner's Sons.

A—12.58[V]

PRINTED IN THE UNITED STATES OF AMERICA

Library of Congress Catalog Card Number 59-8019

PREFACE TO THE THIRD EDITION

WITH this second revision, more thoroughgoing than the earlier one (1939) the present text passes its quarter-century mark, and begins an auspicious collaboration with Professor Richard Hocking of Emory University.

What was previously said about the cherished incompleteness of the work still holds good. Its aim is not to present the full variety of the philosophical cornucopia past or present, but to offer the major clues for beginning its enjoyment and for discovering one's own mind.

In the nature of the idea of the Types, its message is relatively free from the demand for timeliness: it is an interpreter of all times. Its aim is to single out the strands, not the varying pattern; and these strands are found in every epoch of the reflective history of mankind. If there is a Perennial Philosophy toward which the mind gravitates at all times—and during the past fifteen years we have heard much of Philosophia Perennis—there are also perennial modes of deviation therefrom which are at the same time modes of dialectical approach thereto. And the symbolic tale of the endless quest will also contain the vision of a possible arrival.

I cannot personally doubt that there is a reality the same for all men to which all our thoughts and imaginings are drawn as to a magnet. There must be a *bent to truth* within the activity we call thinking, and therefore a bent to agreement. And since we live by truth and perish by error, what every man desires is to gain valid knowledge of that reality. In this sense every true thinker is by conviction a realist.

And if the reality toward which all such minds are drawn is in any sense discoverable, the total picture of human effort should, over a stretch of years, show some tendency to converge. If that is the case, the story of Types should reflect that movement. There should, at least, be a quiet mortality of phases of error. The period through which this book has been in publication is too brief to witness alterations of major scope. Even so, important changes are observable. Philosophic thinking, stirred to the depths by catastrophic events on a world scale, has become a public concern in a new sense. The rise of clear-marked ideologies, undertaking to align men in vast numbers behind a constellation of points-of-view which it would be unfair to call philosophies—unfair to philosophy, I mean— yet with philosophical groundwork, has compelled men the world over to take issues of truth with renewed seriousness. The disasters of war years, the accompanying revelations of depth of defection and heights of greatness of which human nature is capable, lend passion and impetus to the quest for bearings in a universe whose physical mysteries are opening with appalling speed. In the total aspect of the human attitude to this world, something like a general movement is discernible.

The nature of that general movement I should describe as a *passage beyond modernity*.

I call modernity the era of thought dominated by the two contrasting aspects of the philosophy of Descartes, the subjective certitude of one's own existence, and the objective certitude of a nature whose process lends itself exhaustively to mathematical expression. Seizing upon one or other of these two bases of experience, modern philosophies in the interest of unity inclined to make one or other of these two certitudes absorb its neighbor. The idealisms, inspired by the subjective revelation attempted to include the growing mass of scientific knowledge within the circle of I-think. The naturalisms, inspired by the vision of a calculable and lawful natural order attempted to include human nature, its feelings and purposes, within the wide net of "nature". The types became marked, and the issues sharply drawn. These issues remain, in sharpened form. But the present century has been the scene of their resolution, as a new empiricism has found its way to a stage of justice both to the particulars of existence and to the universals wherein being becomes one.

WILLIAM ERNEST HOCKING

Madison, New Hampshire
November, 1958

THERE are three serviceable ways of beginning the deliberate study of philosophy. First by reading the history of the subject. If one lights by good fortune upon the right guide to this great story, he discovers thought in its living context of biography and social change, and his own concern for truth is deepened by association with the motives which animated the heroes of human speculation. This way has its dangers; they arise chiefly from the plenitude of genius which has been poured into philosophy during two thousand years of reflection. There is a multitude, a growing multitude, of thinkers worthy of consideration. The mind becomes fatigued by its riches; and may gain the paradoxical impression of futility. It is hard for the beginner, especially if he reads dutifully, to take history in the right way: not as an obligation to know all that wise men have thought—no one achieves this—but as an opportunity to make a few durable and important intellectual companionships. If five out of forty great names light up with a personal allurement, one has found *his* friends among the philosophers, and his reading of history has been a success. The likelihood that an American student will achieve this is increased, I believe, if history is his second course rather than his first.

The second way is by direct attack upon the problems of philosophy: what is the mind? how is it related to the body? is the behavior of human beings a part of the machinery of nature? is there a soul? does it survive death? what are these qualities we call good and evil? what have we to do about it? how much, if anything, can we know beyond what we call science? The answers to these and other such questions constitute a man's philosophy: these are the things he wants to know.

*   *   *

The third way, our present way, is a union of both the historical and the systematic interest. By selecting certain types of world-view that recur in the history of thought, the appalling multiplicity of systems is reduced. One's primary interest is in the validity of the world-view, not in its historic rôle; we are, in fact, attacking the problems of philosophy for their own sakes. At the same time, we are becoming acquainted with representative thinkers; and under conditions which are, at least in one respect, more favorable than in the historical series. For we meet them when our own concern with a given philosophic problem is at its height, and their thought may most readily come to the aid of our own. It is hard, in an historical course, to get up steam on the problem, let us say of free will, as many times as there are philosophers who have had something to say on it. We have that, in general, to do but once.

*   *   *

From the PREFACE TO THE REVISED EDITION, 1939

*   *   *

During the ten years since the last edition was published the need for revision has not decreased; for, in spite of rumors to the contrary, philosophy does progress. There have been marked changes in the temper and position of philosophical discussion. There have been even more marked changes in the philosophical interest of the public.

In technical philosophy, the chief changes which ought to affect our statement of the Types seem to me to be these: the disintegration of modern realism as a school; the partial inheritance by "logical positivism" of that current of faith which, eviscerating metaphysics, stakes all on scrupulous care in definition and inference; the completed outline of Whitehead's metaphysics; the marked effort in the later thought of Dewey as well as of Whitehead to incorporate strands of idealism into naturalism.

There is evidently here a division of labor, which threatens to become a confusion of tongues, between those who believe (with the nineteenth century) that an improved logic and theory of knowledge must precede any advance in philosophy, and those who see that every theory of knowledge assumes a metaphysics, and who go directly about the substantial work of philosophy, that of guiding mankind in the judgment and ordering of life. Philosophy cannot do its work unless these two concerns are held in working accord; nor can it otherwise meet the change which I have mentioned in the philosophical interest of the public.

*   *   *

One quality, however, I stubbornly keep, though it is at least half a defect,—incompleteness. I decline to attempt an exhaustive review of extant (still less of historical) varieties of doctrine. I keep in mind the student who wants to see his way to truth, and who has first to make the main problems his own before he can achieve any appetite for the shades and half-shades of the "isms." With this principle, something less than justice is bound to be done to individual thinkers. Put it this way: all the types are one-sided; nobody's philosophy is one-sided; ergo, nobody's philosophy is a type; ergo, nobody's philosophy is here expounded (except my own)! For this I offer apology to my colleagues, as a failing inherent in the task, not in the unconcern of the author. It is a failing which I can count on their tolerance and humor to understand, especially since it offers them an invitation to expand at the point of their own choosing.

CONTENTS

PART I · METAPHYSICS

PART II · EPISTEMOLOGY

PART III · METAPHYSICS AND EPISTEMOLOGY

TYPE IV · DUALISM

TYPE V · IDEALISM

TYPE VI · REALISM

TYPE VII · MYSTICISM

PART IV · CONSPECTUS OF THE TYPES

PART I

METAPHYSICS

CHAPTERS 1–2

TYPE I · NATURALISM

CHAPTERS 3–7

CHAPTER 1: WHAT PHILOSOPHY IS

1.1. When in the vernacular we speak of a man's philosophy we mean simply the *sum of his beliefs*. In this sense, everybody or at least every mature person, necessarily has a philosophy, because nobody can manage a life without an equipment of beliefs.

We are speaking of "beliefs" now in the wide sense in which belief includes all those views about the world by which a man actually guides his actions. They need not necessarily be *debatable* opinions. A physician does not ordinarily debate nor try to prove that life is worth preserving: it is the belief he is living by, and he may take it for granted as a nearly self-evident truth. On the other hand, he may believe in the politics of the Liberal Party, or that the new school of painting is an inartistic outrage, while recognizing that his views are highly controversial. We mean by a man's beliefs all those judgments, from certainties or convictions at one extreme to mere impressions at the other, upon which he customarily acts. Beliefs are the opinions a man lives by, as distinct from those he merely entertains: in this sense they constitute his philosophy. And in this sense we can understand Chesterton's remark that "the most practical and important thing about a man is his view of the universe,"—his philosophy. The employee is at the mercy of the philosophy of his employer; and the employer stakes his business on the philosophy of his employees,—do they believe in doing an honest job, inspection or no inspection?

1.2. When we speak of philosophy as a science, however, we mean the *examination of belief*,—thinking one's way to a well-grounded set of beliefs.

And we refer, in general, to those beliefs which have the widest scope: such beliefs as enter into a religious creed (existence or non-existence of God, immortality or extinction of the self at death), a code of right and wrong (the Ten Commandments, lawyer's code of ethics, what constitutes fair competition), political convictions (democracy or benevolent dictatorship, equality or inequality of men, races and nations), the most general scientific principles (evolution, uniformity of nature, conservation of energy).

3

Thus philosophy differs from the special sciences in its range. Each science deals with a portion of the field of knowledge; philosophy attempts to frame a picture of the whole,—to establish a world-view, a *Weltanschauung*. Herbert Spencer proposes to define science as partially unified knowledge, philosophy as completely unified knowledge.[1] Does the name philosophy savor somewhat of pretentiousness, as of a science beyond science?

There is no doubt that this color, let us say of high mental ambition, adheres to the ordinary connotation of the word philosophy: the name "philosopher" in a special sense has been reserved for a few outstanding intellects among men. Plato and Aristotle themselves had to meet the criticism that they were aiming at a type of knowledge reserved for the gods. Their reply was in effect that they were *merely philosophers*, that is, in the literal sense, "lovers of wisdom"; to which Aristotle added this reflection, that the human reason is a divine element in man; [2] in justice to ourselves we cannot do less than live as if whole-knowledge were our rightful portion. There is nothing peculiarly overweening in seeking knowledge of the whole of things: it is not presumptuous for the artist to outline the whole of his pictures before putting in the details,—it is not a matter of choice but of necessity if the labor is not to run wild that some sense of the whole should accompany all of it. The whole is commonly sketched-in roughly and is held subject to change as the picture develops: philosophy likewise may have to be content with approximate answers, or as some have thought, though here I enter a caveat,[3] with purely hypothetical answers, subject to constant revision. But some sense of the whole we inevitably carry with us. Undertake to answer the simple question, Where are you? and you find that it involves some notion of the whole universe in space. (Try it.) Philosophy is not the peculiar business of the gods, nor of the specially endowed: it is human business; it is everyman's business.

Beliefs about the world as a whole, then, we must have; but can we reduce them, by logical examination, to a theoretical form without presuming too much upon our mental capacity?

1.3. We do not commonly acquire our major beliefs by a process of reasoning. They come to us first by way of authority or suggestion, the authority of parents and teachers, the suggestion of admired persons whose views are absorbed by the hero-worshipping mind of childhood, or of the social environment, especially of those more intimate groups whose views are simply accepted or taken over because they are the current and ap-

---

[1] *First Principles*, Part II, Ch. I.   [2] *Nichomachean Ethics*, Bk. X, Ch. 7.
[3] On this point, see the concluding chapter.

proved ways of looking at things in those groups or sets. Beliefs so gained and held without further examination may be called *prejudices*, not in the derogatory but in the literal sense of the word.

Literature and the drama are common and powerful sources of belief. The romance or the play conveys a silent invitation to accept a creed subtly recommended by the author through his characters.

All conversation tends to transmit philosophy, since no one can express an idea without conveying, if only by a flick of the eye or a gesture, something of his general temper and outlook, his optimism or pessimism, his belief in intangibles or his hard-headed practicality, his self-centred disdain or his liberal sympathy. And this process when it becomes that conversation between one generation and another which we call "tradition," from which every one selects what appeals to him as valid or fit, is the chief original source of belief in the form of prejudice.

1.4. There is something to be said in behalf of prejudice, as against the proposal of philosophic science that belief should be examined.

Digging around the roots of our beliefs in order to get reasons for them, good or bad, may kill a good healthy belief. Or, it may be simply a way of deceiving ourselves into the notion that we have "proved" or "established" a doctrine which we are really holding because it suits us to do so,—"rationalizing" our prejudices. "Metaphysics is the finding of bad reasons for what we believe upon instinct," said F. H. Bradley; [4] adding the remark "but to find these reasons is no less an instinct." Argumentation everybody instinctively distrusts; the reasons for our beliefs are commonly weaker, and less important, than the beliefs themselves. Hence we may refute all the reasons alleged for a belief without refuting the belief, or shaking the conviction of its holder.

Edmund Burke, appalled by the excesses of the French Revolution committed in the name of Reason, praised prejudice as the normal support of "the spirit of a gentleman and the spirit of religion" [5] which, he thinks, have made the civilization of Europe.

"You see, Sir, that in this enlightened age I am bold enough to confess that we are generally men of untaught feelings; that instead of casting away all our old prejudices, we cherish them to a very considerable degree, and, to take more shame to ourselves, we cherish them because they are prejudices; and the longer they have lasted, and the more generally they have prevailed, the more we cherish them. We are afraid to put men to live and trade each on his own private stock of reason; because we suspect that this stock in each man is small, and that the individuals would do better to avail themselves of the general bank and capital of nations and of ages. Many of our men

[4] *Appearance and Reality* (Oxford, 1930), p. xii.
[5] Burke, *Reflections on the Revolution in France*, Everyman Edition, p. 76.

of speculation, instead of exploding general prejudices, employ their sagacity to discover the latent wisdom which prevails in them. If they find what they seek, and they seldom fail, they think it more wise to continue the prejudice, with the reason involved, than to cast away the coat of prejudice, and to leave nothing but the naked reason; because prejudice, with its reason, has a motive to give action to that reason, and an affection which will give it permanence. Prejudice is of ready application in the emergency; it previously engages the mind in a steady course of wisdom and virtue, and does not leave the man hesitating in the moment of decision, sceptical, puzzled and unresolved. Prejudice renders a man's virtue his habit; and not a series of unconnected acts. Through just prejudice, his duty becomes a part of his nature." [6]

1.5. But let us be clear what philosophy proposes to do. It does not necessarily insist that every belief must be established by reason. It does not assert that we have no right to believe what we cannot prove. What it does is to inquire what the grounds are on which beliefs are held and *what grounds are good grounds*. It may find a normal place for prejudice, distinguishing justifiable from unjustifiable prejudice. It may, in some cases, sanction authority as a ground for belief, aiding us to discriminate between a good authority and a bad one. It may advise us, in other cases, to rely on intuition, offering some way of telling a true intuition from a false one. A large part of its business is to inquire what reason can do, and what it cannot do, in the way of supporting belief. This will be a part of our own study.[7] But in any case it holds that we cannot, as human beings, remain satisfied with dumb tenacity in holding our beliefs. So long as false beliefs are possible, and such false beliefs in vital matters are perilous luxuries, there can be no virtue in declining to *think* about the foundations of belief.

The idea that philosophy is presumptuous can only mean that it is too ambitious a thing to try living intelligently in so vast a universe; and that it is somehow more modest to go it blind! Surely it is extravagant to imagine that the capacity for thinking is an inherent vice. We cannot, even if we would, prevent ourselves from thinking about the frame and principles and destiny of our lives; and we believe that the right use of reason brings us nearer truth, not farther away from it. Thus philosophy itself may be said to be founded upon a belief, a belief expressed long ago by Socrates, that "the unexamined life is not worthy to be lived by a man." [8] The various beliefs with which philosophy is especially concerned fall into the following scheme of classification:

1.6. *Beliefs about reality:* the theme of metaphysics. It is a large part of the ordinary business of life to distinguish between "appearances" and the true state of the case,—the "reality." If it is a matter of life and death

---

[6] *Ibid.,* p. 84.   [7] See §1.8. Also Chs. 8–15.   [8] Plato, *Apology* 38.

for the fox to penetrate the cunning deceptions devised for him by the hunter, it is none the less vital for man to know when he is dealing with reality, and when with a mere semblance of reality. There is presumably no cosmic hunter intentionally luring him into traps; it is chiefly in the shams and fair showings which cover social hostilities and greeds that he gains his abundant experience in distinguishing the real from the unreal. Yet nature herself presents many a misleading appearance,—the fixity of the stars, the stable quiescence of the earth, the "firmament" of the sky, and a thousand others. The stick appears bent in the water; in "reality" it is straight. A piece of wood or metal appears solid substance; in "reality" it may be a shimmering dance of molecules, separated by proportionately vast spaces, while they in turn are composed of elements devoid of every vestige of tangible solidity. It is the business of experience and of physical science to find the realities which such appearances conceal.

But the physical world itself: is that as final and substantial as it seems? Death appears to be the end of the human personality: is that true? We seem to ourselves to be free agents: are we? The world appears to be an assemblage of many things of many kinds: is this the case, or are all things manifestations of a single hidden being? The search for reality here is the business of metaphysics. Reality is the ensemble of things as they are, after all error and illusion have been corrected. In one aspect, reality is called "substance," the underlying or original stuff whose various modifications explain the appearances of things.

There are two kinds of thing which we are likely to take as undoubtedly real. We take physical objects to be real, and we take states of mind to be real. We might say, anything is real if it is as real as a rock, or as real as a pain. Sometimes the rock appears to be more certainly real. Sometimes it appears easier to doubt the existence of the rocks themselves than to doubt the reality of the pain.

But there may be moments when it seems to us that the physical reality is the only true substance, and that the mental appearances can be explained by it. Or, it may seem that the mental reality is sufficient to account for the physical appearances: that the mind alone is genuinely real. The history of thought has been very largely controlled by the fact that to some men the rock is the impressive and sufficient type of reality, to others the feeling or "the mind." The former tend to become materialists, or *naturalists*, the latter tend to become *idealists*. To the former, mind is an appearance of physical reality; to the latter, nature is an appearance of mental reality. If we consider that whatever is metaphysically real necessarily endures, while the appearances are subject to change or to dis-appearance, the difference will not appear unimportant.

There are other logically possible alternatives. Mind and physical nature may be manifestations of some third substance which is neither the one nor the other. Or there may be two kinds of reality, the material and the mental—eternally distinct and irreducible—the belief of *dualism*. Are there still other alternatives?

Even though there were nothing to be done about it, one could hardly be accused of idle curiosity if he were concerned to reach an answer to such questions as these about the character of reality. There is a natural interest, not to say piety, in looking toward the origins of our own lives and of the rest of the life and consciousness in nature; there is a natural concern in looking toward the ultimate destiny of all this living world. And there is a natural wonder, not absorbed by the several sciences, which without further motive would drive us to metaphysical inquiry. The world is worth knowing about!

But philosophy also seeks wisdom in regard to the conduct of life: it would be hard to say which is the more primitive interest, the theoretical or the practical. Hence, in the second place:

1.7. *Beliefs about better and worse, right and wrong:* the theme of ethics. In some uses of the word, philosophy is identified with this practical interest. To "take a thing philosophically" is to take it without undue disturbance of mind,—without too much depression, if it is a misfortune, or without too much elation in the opposite case. And it is to take things this way not because one is insensitive, but because one has attained a just valuation of the various objects of life, of what is better and what is worse, and is prepared for sufficient reasons to consider tolerable the pains or losses which overwhelm more trivial judges.

It is the Stoics (Zeno of Citium, Epictetus, Marcus Aurelius and others) who are chiefly responsible for giving the phrase this color. It was their aim to attain equanimity, called by them "apathy," to become superior to remorse or anger, to "bear and forbear," to school themselves to a life of complete fearlessness through achieving a capacity to accept with perfect serenity whatever might occur whether through natural event, or through fortune, or through the consequences of doing their duty. Boëthius, who wrote *On the Consolation of Philosophy* in a Roman prison, had much to do with transmitting this meaning to English usage. For his work was translated into Anglo-Saxon by Alfred the Great, and into English prose by Chaucer and a series of successors.

The noble endurance of hardship is only an aspect, and a negative aspect, of the wise conduct of life. The fundamental question is, What can we make of existence? There are those who regard the conditions of human life as intrinsically bad. The array of desires with which nature has provided us, and which under the control of will and reason are apparently destined to serve as guides to pleasure, and perhaps to happiness, are to be distrusted. There is illusion for the will, as for the intellect, in the whole scheme of nature; and the wise man will keep his desires and hopes in check, finding his chief good first in contemplation and then in ultimate nescience. This outlook of *pessimism*, widespread in the Orient, in Brahmanism and the teachings of Buddha, has been given expression in the West by Schopenhauer, von Hartmann and others. Opposed to this is the prevalent temper of the affirmation of life, the temper of *optimism*, which believes that the world and man are so adjusted that the attainment of happiness is the normal order of things. The will and the environment in which it plays are attuned to each other: and we can wisely give ourselves to a study of the positive aims of action, whether for our own personal enjoyment (*egoism*) or for the sake of others (*altruism*).

We have been speaking of the pursuit of happiness or of the good. But what of "duty"? Is that the same as the general obligation to use discretion in the pursuit of good? Or are there rules which, like the rules of a game, give structure to our conduct without altering its objects, and qualify some ways of reaching our end as definitely right or wrong? If so, what is the source of these rules or standards of right and wrong?

And are these rules fixed in the nature of things, or do they change with the *mores*, or different stages of social usage? The pervasiveness of change is dinned into our ears. "Old rules of politics and law" we are reminded, "religion and sex, art and letters—the whole domain of culture— must yield or break before the inexorable pressure of science and the machine." Important, if true: and simplifying many difficult questions, if all that wisdom has to suggest is to yield at once to whatever science and the machine would like to do with us. But perhaps there are other sources of obligation, even more persistent than these; and perhaps there are certain principles of right and wrong, founded in the nature of things and in human nature, which, changing in their application from age to age, are yet permanent in their central meaning. Nothing would be better worth knowing at the present moment than the answer to this question.

Perhaps, too, there is something in duty which affects the ends we pursue, as well as the rules whereby we pursue them. As many of the wisest heads from Aristotle onward have seen the world, nature herself seems to be struggling toward a certain perfection, by way of what we to-day call evolution; and there is something laid upon us to fall in with that great effort. Such questions experience sets before every man sooner or later; and these are the questions which philosophy considers under the head of ethics.

1.8. *Beliefs about belief:* the theme of epistemology. Now consider: What are your more decided beliefs at the present moment? Distinguish your beliefs from your idler, non-working opinions. Take one of your major beliefs, whether in metaphysics or ethics, politics or religion, or science, for a brief examination. Ask yourself on what grounds you have been holding that belief. These grounds may fall under one or more headings of the following list or you may find that the grounds which have influenced you are not included here.

Authority:
  Prestige of elder persons or of tradition;
  Suggestion from social surroundings;
  Literary or dramatic suggestion.

Intuition:
  A feeling of certainty based on a personal experience of insight, as if one should say, I believe in free will because I am sometimes immediately conscious of freedom.

Good results:
  Holding to a belief because, on the whole, it works well to believe it, fits in well with one's scheme of thinking and living, makes existence more hopeful or otherwise satisfactory, or seems desirable for the good of mankind; this mode of judging belief is called *pragmatism.*

"Reason," an ambiguous term which may mean one or more of several different sort of ground, as:
  Self-evident truth, and deductions therefrom, as when one holds it to be a self-evident truth that all men are created equal, and deduces therefrom that men should share equally in the protection of law and the choice of rulers. Those who hold that our important beliefs can be and ought to be established in this way are called *rationalists.*
  Experience: that is to say, observation of facts, and generalization (or induction) from such observations, as when one who observes that the state of mind regularly changes with the state of the body infers that this will always be the case, and that the death of the body will therefore bring with it the death of the mind. Those who hold that there are no self-evident general truths (or none of importance), and

that our important beliefs are only well established when based on experience are called *empiricists*.

There are, of course, no rationalists who do not, like all human beings, learn much of their philosophy by the aid of experience. And there are no empiricists who do not, as in the illustration here given, make constant use of deduction. The only issue between them is whether there is *any* general truth which is not somehow born from experience. Empiricists and rationalists, being both committed to the use of reason, deductive or inductive or both, are sometimes loosely referred to as rationalists in a wider sense of the word.

The questions we have here raised about the foundations of your beliefs are questions which belong to a branch of philosophy called the theory of knowledge or *epistemology*. They arise after men have undertaken to examine their beliefs in metaphysics and ethics; have come to see the difficulty of attaining certainty; and have concluded to institute a careful preliminary inquiry about the possibility of getting certain knowledge in philosophy. Thus we build up a group of beliefs about belief, and its attainment.

We have now identified three main branches of philosophy: metaphysics, ethics, and the theory of knowledge. A completer scheme would include also logic, aesthetics, and psychology, and might be mapped out as follows:

Theoretical philosophy:
   Metaphysics: beliefs about reality;
   Epistemology: beliefs about belief;
   Logic: the technique of reasoning, sometimes included in
Practical philosophy, or the philosophy of values:
   Ethics: beliefs about the principles of conduct;
   Aesthetics: beliefs about the principles of beauty.
Psychology: a natural science of the mind bearing on all branches of
   philosophy, and borne upon by them.

1.9. *Types of philosophy.* Beliefs about reality are crucial beliefs in the sense that they usually bring other beliefs with them, beliefs in religion, ethics and other areas of thought. This is as it should be: for a man's arrangement of his practical principles can hardly fail to be governed to some extent by the kind of world he supposes he is dealing with. And vice versa, the sort of thing a man deals with successfully, whether rocks, colors, money, or men, will appear real to him and will affect his judgment about reality.

Our beliefs thus tend to form clusters, hanging from some significant stem-belief: such clusters we call types of philosophy. Naturalism and idealism are evidently two such types. They are *metaphysical* beliefs to begin with; but they carry with them different outlooks in ethics, psychology, aesthetics. They present the most fundamental contrast in the general outlook on life with which we have to deal.

Other clusters of belief are formed about the stems of the various *theories of knowledge,* that is to say, the various beliefs about how beliefs are reached and established. For evidently our ways of looking for truth will have some influence on what we find. Thus "rationalism" or "pragmatism" or "intuitionism," while they do not settle finally what conclusions a thinker will reach in metaphysics or ethics, have certain characteristic tendencies, and so deserve to be regarded as types of philosophy.

1.10. If we were going to set up a complete scheme of the types of philosophy, historical or possible, we should have to consider many shades and interconnections of thought which I am proposing to ignore.

It would be of great interest, for example, to take the practical side of philosophy as furnishing certain stem-beliefs, and see how far divergent attitudes of the *will* carried with them characteristic differences in metaphysics and theory of knowledge. For there is no doubt that the temper or set of will with which a man begins his thinking will affect the world-view he arrives at. There is at least so much truth in the caustic remark of Fichte

"What kind of a philosophy one chooses depends consequently upon what kind of man one is; for a philosophical system is not a piece of dead household furniture, which one can use or lay aside at pleasure, but is animated by the soul of the man who has it." [9]

William James thought that the splitting-place of opposing world-views lies in the contrast of temperaments: the "tender-minded" want an architecturally handsome, rationalistic and idealistic philosophy, while the "tough-minded" prefer a loose-ended, empirical, realistic view.[10] According to Karl Marx, it is not the ethical nor the esthetic, but the economic side of the will, the prudential and technical interests, which govern all the rest of our thinking. If these thinkers are right in finding the root of all philosophical differences in differences of the will, the most clearly marked types of philosophy ought to be those which are defined by such contrasts as optimism and pessimism, or Epicurean and Stoic, or pleasure-for-pleasure's sake and duty-for-duty's sake. I have been surprised to find how little

[9] Fichte, *First Introduction into the Science of Knowledge.* See Rand, *Modern Classical Philosophers* (Boston, 1936), p. 496.
[10] James, *Pragmatism* (New York, 1907), p. 12.

there is in the history of philosophy to bear this out. Ethical differences have followed metaphysical types far more clearly than metaphysical differences have followed ethical types.

Let me confess then at the outset that I am not interested in completeness: the idea of "types" is intended to preserve us from the unmanageable voluminousness and intricate interdistinctions of an "adequate survey,"—to my mind an enemy of thought, and one of the chief curses of American education. My aim is to present enough of the great and lasting issues so that students may recognize and place their own thoughts, be prepared to appreciate the greater thinkers of the race, be able to steer a steady course amid the confused currents of contemporary life, and work out a world-view for themselves. We want to consider, not all types of philosophy, but such types as are pre-eminently "natural,"—natural in the sense that strong voices in their favor will be found in all the great ages of human thought; and in the further sense that in *every individual human mind* there will be a tendency to look at things that way.

If you rightly understand the types, as we review them, you will find in yourself some inclination toward each one in turn: and this inclination will not be wholly mistaken. For we shall consider no type that has not an aspect of truth which the final view must contain. The types contend with one another throughout history, but do not kill each other off! In a sense, they educate one another.

When we have finished our review, we shall have to answer—and shall try to answer—the question, How these various partial truths can be set into a single consistent philosophy.

CHAPTER 2: THE ENDURING PRE-PHILOSOPHY: SPIRITUALISM

2.1. It belongs to the nature of the human animal to make some idea of the whole frame in which his life is set. On this account we are justified in saying that there never was a time when human societies were without a set of beliefs about the world they were living in. We should not be justified in calling these beliefs a philosophy. They were certainly not, in the earlier stages of human development, *examined*. To us, a belief is a separable, statable, definable view, held by an individual. In primitive societies, beliefs had a group-character, very likely tribal ways of looking at things; and they were usually tied in with group customs, sometimes as explanations of rites or sacraments considered important for the welfare of the group. Group-knowledge and group-magic were inseparable; and magic was a way of securing favorable, or avoiding unfavorable treatment from invisible powers, thought of as co-operating with the techniques of the daily or seasonal round of life.

We can hardly imagine that the ideas involved in these customs were singled out and discussed, still less subjected to criticism by individual free-thinkers! Doubt there must have been—for after all, thinking has always to be personal. (The notion of group-thought, as if a group could think, is something of a superstition, is it not?) And deviating ideas must always have been born in individual heads; they must occasionally have been expressed; and being expressed, they might win general response and survive in "group-memory," and in the most auspicious case enter into group "tradition." On the other hand, ideas that failed to impress were likely to receive no other criticism than that of being forgotten.[1] On this score alone, the infant-mortality of sporadic ideas must have been enormous,—it still is! But this type of criticism constitutes no "examination"

---

[1] An English writer, F. B. Jevons, has given attention to the difficult conditions under which in early societies ideas about what is sacred or taboo could be altered or improved. Where free discussions of ideas—very different from parleys about tribal action—could not exist, the notion of a "survival of the fittest" among competing ideas has no application. Change could occur only with the approval of authoritative persons,—medicine men, priests,—speaking in the name of their divine power. This would be, not a natural selection, but what Jevons calls a "supernatural selection." *Introduction to the History of Religion* (London, 1904). p. 95.

14

of belief. In a loose use of the word philosophy, traditional group-beliefs were the first form of philosophy; and since there is a certain family resemblance among the ideas of most primitive groups, the first philosophical type. But identifying philosophy as we do with the thoughtful examination of belief, these early beliefs are really pre-philosophical. The examination of beliefs belongs to a relatively late stage of history, is not more than three or four thousand years of age, so far as our arts of recovering long-buried thoughts have yet reached.

But pre-philosophical thought, as the background from which philosophy is born, deserves our attention, not because it was primeval, but because as I shall try to show *it continues to exist as a pre-philosophical background*. And from it, Types of Philosophy continue to be born!

Does it, in fact, seem to you that we ever get away from primitive views, or that we ought to? Whoever says yes must be able to think that a common human belief about an important concern can be *all wrong*. For one, I cannot believe it: wrongness seems to me, in such cases, to eat away the periphery, but to leave something central intact. Over the ages we have improved our mental operations, but we have not reversed them; and even the improvements have been made at some cost: what would we give for the memories or the powers of observation of some savages? We have developed a power of voluntary concentration of attention unknown to early man: and we have lost a certain sense of proportion in our general impression of the world that was quite native to him. We try sometimes to put aside our sophistication and see the world with the aboriginal simplicity of outlook: philosophers have been known to inquire, as an important bit of analysis, what it is that is "given" to us in experience, apart from all that our acquired knowledge intrudes upon it—somewhat like trying to obey the injunction to pass a half-hour without once thinking of the word "hippopotamus"! For pure freshness of outlook, we have to see things vicariously through the eyes of primitive man—or of infants. We are doubtless in a far better position for judging the world sanely than primitive man was. I am only saying that he was probably not all wrong, and therefore that we shall not be all right unless we have something in common with him. His views, in addition to their oddity and antiquarian interest, will always deserve our respect.

2.2. In all its variant forms, this pre-philosophy was contained in religion, that is, in what we call religion. But in the precritical ages, religion was not as with us a special outlook and mode of life which some members of the community adopted and others not: it was one of the normal aspects of community life. Religion, let us say, is the habitual reference of life to divine powers: to the primitive view these powers though invisible are indubitably there. They are the causes of many visible effects, and are to be reckoned with as part of ordinary prudence.

The most obvious part of religion is the *practical* reference of life to these powers, showing itself in observances and codes. There is magic as a technique, side by side with a primitive scientific technique, for securing luck. There is prayer, as an appeal to the powers, either by way of bargaining, or of securing something of their super-power in oneself, fortifying oneself for the crises of existence. There are special invocations and spells for times of trouble. There are the great ceremonies which celebrate death, marriage, birth, coronation, victory, public penance; and which bring communities together in devotion to an object of loyalty which, standing behind the ruler and behind the law, abets the power of both, and aids the early efforts for social cohesion.

But this practical and overt side of religion implies a *theoretical* reference of life to these powers,—a creed. It is the ideas of the creed which constitute the pre-philosophy whose meaning is embodied in the code and the ritual. Early creeds are seldom worked out in explicit formulas; they may be expressed in myth and poetry, or more dumbly, simply in the traditional observance. In any case, it is these ideas we are now concerned with. They constitute the background against which all human philosophizing takes place.

2.3. With the general cast of these ideas every one is familiar,—ideas of a supernatural realm peopled by superhuman agencies—spirits, souls, deities—distinct from the visible realm of nature and yet in active intercourse with it.

We shall ignore the vast variety of imaginative representation of that supernatural world which distinguishes the different religions and stages of religion,—all the lore of precivilized fancies, the polytheisms of antiquity, the emergence here and there of monotheism, the development of the great ethnic religions and of the universal religions of to-day. It will require something of a *tour de force* to say what is common to all this pre-philosophic multitude. Yet there are common elements. What would you think of the following as an attempt to summarize them?

There exists another world than this world shown us by the senses;

This other-world is somehow veiled from our ordinary perceptions; and yet it is continuous with nature, and of easy access in either direction if one has the right path;

It is the residence of powers or agencies which we distinguish as divine; they always know how to get at us; we are not so clear how to get at them;

This word "divine" indicates a superiority both in *power* (or reality) and in *worth*,—the human world, which may not last forever, being regarded as derived from that other world, which is eternal, as constantly dependent upon it, and as obligated to the deference of worship and obedience;

There are ways of living which are in harmony with the divine powers, and other ways which are strictly out of harmony; and these ways can be known;

The souls of men, or some of them, pass over at death into this other world.

This proto-philosophy, which in developed religion centers about the ideas of God and immortality, we shall call Spiritualism.

2.4. No one can be certain how these ideas arose originally; and from one point of view, it is an idle question. Historically there is evidently nothing to check the free play of speculation on this point, and speculation has taken full advantage of its liberty. Almost any one can explain the origin of religion, prior to having considered the question. But there are particular difficulties involved in trying to get some more or less sensible notions about the origins of religious ideas for the ideas themselves are elusive; the words we use, being taken from our experience of this world, do not precisely apply to the "other" world; the best clue to their meaning, if we could get it, would be the context of experience which gave birth to them.

The various theories which have been held and are held about these origins indicate to my mind that there is no one source of them, but a variety of roots which we may designate the speculative, the emotional and the ethical.

2.5. *The speculative root.* It is improbable that religious ideas arose (as Herbert Spencer in an unguarded moment suggests) as a "theory of original causation": we cannot picture early man as sitting down to meditate on where he and the world of nature came from. Wonder does not at first extend so far, but begins with more local exhibitions of power such as excite admiration or alarm. Nevertheless, as long as the human animal has been human there has been some free play of speculative inquiry: the mind has been prone to run out along the lines of natural phenomena to the edge of traceable causation and then to take the leap into the imperceptible. The mystery of the stars in their courses, and the miraculous rebirth of vegetation after its seasonal death, have left few races uninquisitive. And the oddities of fortune, the plays of good and bad luck, affect far more than primitive minds with a sense of mysterious luck-agents behind the scenes, needing somehow to be appeased or charmed.[2]

Dreams and hallucinations have been supposed to contribute something to the idea of another world in which souls may survive and enjoy unusual powers. Perhaps, something. But the divine powers are not all visualized by early man, still less by later man, however much they may use pictorial language. Mana, wakonda and the like are names for an impersonal energy, not for a quasi-human shape such as a dream might present. The gods of early man are powers of his waking as well as of his dreaming states. It is likely that certain ideas of divine power are derived from intense social experience; for the spirit of the human group does on occasion inspire and command its members and lift them beyond their ordinary selves.

But the imagery of the idea is less important than the conviction which the idea registers, and which seems to deepen with time, that just as the several things and events of the world cannot simply happen but imply some authorship, so the world itself and our presence in it raises a question of producership or responsibility which the human mind cannot abandon. There must be—so reason seems to say—a creator of the world, or a number of co-operating creators.

2.6. *The emotional root.* The divine is a power, and as such is a fact; but it is always more than a fact, namely, a *quality.* It is regarded as "holy" or "sacred." [3] Ideas of this sort are not products of our cooler states of reflection, but rather of feeling.

The old theory that "fear made the gods" is thus better than any theory which refers these ideas to pure speculation. But the emotion chiefly concerned can hardly have been fear. For while there is much evidence of an early fear of the spirits, the primitive language of religion is derived from expressions of admiration and wonder: the divine is the "excellent" or the "bright and shining," like the sun or like fire. Religion evidently had something in it (like the fear of ghosts) to make early man more timorous in the world than he would have been without it; and just as evidently it had something in it (like the guardian spirits, totems, fetiches) to give him greater confidence in the world than he would have had without it. The presumption is, then, that religion is due to some emotional experience in which man seemed to perceive that the powers which behind the veil of nature were actually controlling things, and which because of their

---

[2] How the fortunes of pioneering affected sober New England settlers is well pictured in Legrand Cannon's story, *Look to the Mountain.*
[3] Rudolph Otto, *The Idea of the Holy.*

greatness and their uncanny nature might well be dreaded, are really friendly or auspicious!

Now any such impression on the part of primitive man is at least noteworthy. For he had far less reason than we have to regard the world as friendly: he had fewer defenses against death, disease, or famine; he had, perhaps, less to live for; his struggle for bare existence was incessant, and physical nature often threatened to wipe him out. Yet he had a religion which consisted very largely in a systematic defiance of the pretense of nature to be his master. The great ceremony of early religion, if not of all religion, is the ceremony of putting away the dead: and that ceremony is an instituted denial of the sensibly obvious fact that nature has conquered. Almost universally there is some provision made—often at heavy material sacrifice—for the wayfaring soul which is alleged to have survived and to have taken its journey. How do you explain this belief in survival? Is it the result of our propensity to feign as true what we would like to believe? If so, the luxury has been a costly one. Or remembering that crises of feeling are also moments of intense mental activity may it have been the result of some change in the objective vista of things (corresponding to a revulsion of feeling) when under the influence of strong grief or resentment men of acuter insight perceived that nature is only a part of the universe, and that behind its cruel appearance there is a benign reality?

In either case the religious idea means a discovery (or "revelation") that there is a way of looking at things which turns the edge of the worst evils of experience, namely, by assuming a supernatural supplement in which the incompleteness of the present life is rounded out and our deepest values are conserved.

2.7. *The ethical root.* The friendliness, or potential friendliness, of the gods is only a part of their divine quality; another part is their severity as a source of moral requirement. The context in which this idea arises may be the circumstance that man has had to work out his life under a course of restraints and taboos which limit the free exercise of his instinctive impulse. No social life is possible at all without some curbing of native pugnacity, greed and sex-impulse: and no doubt the belief that the gods, with their "Thou shalt not's," are on the side of these demands for self-control has greatly aided the early stages of social evolution. But how did it come about that the gods were supposed to be on that side, or concerned about the matter at all?

There are two views. Some suppose that the connection was a man-made affair. Early leaders or rulers, having a responsibility for getting laws observed, would have a motive to appeal to the prestige of the supernatural already established. Most early codes of law have, in fact, come with a "Thus saith the Lord" as an introduction; Rousseau in his *Social Contract* points out how profoundly the great legislator needs this sort of backing,— "It would require gods," said this apostle of pure democracy, "to give laws to men." [4] The other view is that each individual realizes more or less dimly that the call for self-restraint is in the direction of his own growth, and would be there even if there were no artificial social requirement. There is something in personal affection which naturally limits selfishness and sensuality, apart from all lawgivers. The notion that this same control is due from us, beyond the small circle of affection, to all members of the community, or to all men, would suggest itself to the mind when trying for the wider view of things, including the natural and the supernatural.

In my opinion, the latter is the only reasonable view to take. Unless men were sensible that there was something in the eternal bent of the world summoning them toward decency and consideration of their neighbors, the political announcement of a "Thus saith the Lord" would have fallen on ears dull if not deaf. There is in every man a dim sense of obligation which refers outward, and naturally connects with his notions of the divine if he has them, or may even be strong enough to beget such notions. The "holy" is something beyond us, something real, before which we are constrained to humility, and it may be to penitence. Certainly those who represent these fundamental restraints as something which men would never observe without a politically exploited religion are blind to some of the plainest facts of human nature.

2.8. The roots of religious ideas are thus various, and these ideas are themselves various; only by a long and painful struggle do they find their way together in orderly creeds. Primitive religion collects, under a vague sense of supernature, all the exalting and exciting experiences of life, without much discrimination; and runs its ceremonial enthusiasms in the direction of high artistic and ethical achievement, the development of dance, drama, architecture, or in the direction of orgiastic excess, intoxication, war-frenzies, fanaticism and general degradation of human energy.

The theoretical clarifying of religion takes the direction of unifying the world of the gods, and working out the relations of God and the world, under the notions of creation, miracle, providence. Miracle, the occasional intervention of deity in natural affairs, tends to lose itself in the notion of providence: for when God does everything, nothing stands out as specifically supernatural. In primitive religions the divine action is local, but

---

[4] Rousseau, *The Social Contract*, Bk. II, Ch. VII.

there are myriads of such agencies, so that everything may be suspected of being the work of some spirit. In the most developed religions, this universal divine action is recovered; but it is the one God who is everywhere. His action is miraculous, but miraculously silent and unobtrusive.

It is in these ideas of miracle and providence that Spiritualism first encounters the hostile opposition of the early efforts toward systematic science.

2.9. It is in this systematic opposition to the ideas of the prevailing Spiritualism that philosophy proper is born. There could be no effective criticism, no examination of beliefs, until there was some glimpse of an alternative. Human thinking must first achieve not only courage and independence but also a sufficient body of coherent knowledge to propose a contrasting world-view. Then we may look for the emergence of philosophy, and of *types* of philosophy distinct from the matrix of Spiritualism and from each other. Each type will mature into the form of a deliberate and widely conducted examination of beliefs. When this examination has given to a body of beliefs *critical* statement, *explicit* logical organization sustained by *evidence*, a type of philosophy has made its appearance.

This achievement took place in the budding civilizations of China and Greece almost simultaneously, let us say in the seventh and sixth centuries B. C.[5] And with this event the existing tradition in each region was obliged to examine critically its own body of thought. Thereby it passed from the pre-philosophical to the philosophical stage; though its best-known defenders at this point were, as they had to be, its critics from within, Confucius, and Socrates, interpreters of the faith and reputed heretics. In a similar way and at nearly the same time in India, the markedly philosophical Buddhist reform arose in the environment of Brahmanic religion, stimulated in part by the critical attack of an Indian materialist doctrine known as the Carvaka philosophy.

In brief, Spiritualism does not become philosophical until it is confronted by an opposition. Hence our first truly philosophical Type, both historically and in the logic of the case, is not Spiritualism itself but its early, and constant, critic and stimulus-to-thought, Naturalism, based on the conviction that supernature is a superstition—that the world of nature is the whole world, sufficient to itself and to us. And herewith we define the primary division or polarity in belief, whose debate continues through the ages of human maturity. Why does it continue?

[5] There were earlier crises in religious thought in advancing civilization, probably many of them, as political intrigue sought aid in or opposed priestly prestige. Among these, the noted revolt in Egypt connected with the name of Ikhnaton, or Amenhotep IV, in mid-fourteenth century B. C., which substituted worship of the sun-disc for the worship of Amon. These, leaving no philosophic heritage, we pass by with the note that sparks of critical thought are visible long before philosophy emerges.

2.10. It continues chiefly because religion is not a philosophy. Its basis is more substantial and less vulnerable than the fabric of speculative ideas in which it seems to consist. Its beliefs, relating to an unseen world, appear to evade proof or disproof and therefore incur the distrust of scientific judgment which seeks its basis in "experience." What better foundation can any body of thought have than experience? But could it be that religion also has experience as a basis? May it be that the experience which science uses, experience through the senses of tangible and measurable events, is *not the whole of "experience"*? Is there an "inner experience" as well as "outward," even more irresistible than sight or touch? If so,—and remembering that experience itself, the grist for thought, is always pre-philosophical,—we can understand how Spiritualism, whatever the fortunes of debate, reverting to experience, continually renews its life.

The "inner experience" that sustains religion regards itself as an experience of rapport with powers that control nature at a deeper level than the "causes" operating within nature. If this affiliation with the Source of things led to a strategy of magic and charm for securing material results, to heal disease or ensure good crops, conflict with applied science was inevitable: the idea of natural law rejects the short-cut of miracle. Hippocrates, father of western medicine, was an early voice announcing the clash. In a treatise of about 400 B. C., in dealing with epilepsy, commonly called the sacred disease, he says,

> "As regards the disease called Sacred, to me it appears to be no more divine than other diseases, but to have a *physis* just like other diseases. Men regard its origin as divine from ignorance and wonder, since it is a peculiar condition and not readily understood. Yet if it be reckoned divine merely because wonderful, then instead of one there would be many sacred diseases. To me it appears that they who refer such conditions to the gods are but as certain charlatans who claim to be excessively religious and to know what is hidden from others." [6]

Our own sympathies here will be with Hippocrates; bearing in mind that in our day a certain mental therapy, especially in psychosomatic disorders, brings an important "inner" auxiliary to the resources of scentific medicine, without appeal to miracle. But we will further recall that this early experience of rapport with the Source brought products in self-mastery and hope, in dream and art, perhaps equally important, even in the dismaying task of mastering the economic necessities, with the technical skills flowing from the causal analysis.[7] The relation between the two modes of experience is not one of clear-cut exclusion; it constitutes a problem worthy of the age-long examination it has received.

[6] *Science, Religion and Reality*, ed. J. Needham (London, 1926), pp. 95 f.

[7] "Religion and art are older than agriculture and industry . . . man was a seer and an artist before he was a producer." Christopher Dawson, *Religion and Culture* (New York, 1948), p. 132.

And in working it out, Spiritualism has not been dependent wholly on external criticism for self-correction: no phase of thought has been more continuously self-critical. From its own inner spring of experience, the reform of religion has been in the main reform *by* religion. In fact, religion is the only agency that *can* reform religion, though spurred by interaction with all phases of advancing social life. Whatever is pure superstition and irresponsible myth will betray itself in absurdities and crudities falling athwart common sense. The mounting sacrifices called for in providing for the dead, the idleness of monkish multitudes, subtracted from social capital, the decadence of inturned otherwordliness, the losses of opportunity in waiting for the auguries before giving battle or launching a ship . . . all these incongruities of a misinterpreted Spiritualism provoke revolt from within, no less than from without. The pre-philosophic root lives on.

It expresses itself in no one philosophy; its life is in the developing religions of mankind. Hence Spiritualism cannot be a Type,—as an 'ism, it is simply a common character of the world-views of the various religions whose center is a belief in God. But it finds its philosophic expression in fragments among the great thinkers, few of whom are quite orthodox.

We have mentioned Socrates and Confucius, each of whom was concerned chiefly with the problem of right living and hesitated to engage in discussions of metaphysics. And each in word and act gave respect to the deeper pieties of his community. Socrates considered that the business of life must be conducted with the aid of three guides: the ordinary techniques of living should be guided by science, the ethical decisions by the discovery of principles through rational analysis of what we subconsciously know, but the major decisions by divine monitors and oracles. As he put it, "The gods have reserved to themselves the most important events." [8] Both Socrates and Confucius, in the crucial decisions involving their own life-or-death, gave convincing proof of their faith in the spiritual order of being. Socrates, before his judges and during his imprisonment, referred to his "voice" or *daemon* as the medium through which he learned of superhuman approval or disapproval of his conduct.[9] The word of Confucius, when he was rescued from a mob-attack, and remonstrated with by his disciples for placing his life in danger, is worth recalling. "T'*ien*, Heaven, has appointed me to teach this doctrine; and until I have done so, what can (the mob) do to me." For each, a human life lived, as if by the appointment of Heaven, had an imperative character and significance unavailable in a world of scientific fact alone.

But now we must turn to listen to the view of the Naturalist.

[8] Xenophon, *Memorabilia*, Bk. I, Ch. 1 (Bysshe transl.).
[9] See Plato's *Apology* and *Crito*.

CHAPTER 3: THE NATURALISTIC
VIEW OF THE WORLD

3.1. The word "nature" as it is used in philosophy summons up a wide perspective. It is not only the "nature" of forest, mountain, wild life. It is also the nature of astronomy in its vast reaches of space and time, and of physics and chemistry in their atomic and sub-atomic analyses. In this perspective, human life may appear a detail and relatively accidental; yet the term "nature" as we here use it is not set in contrast to man, his works, and his culture,—but includes them in a single undivided system of phenomena. The distinction we often make between physical and human nature has an obvious practical value, yet it does violence to the conception of nature which we are here building: for "nature" implies continuity among all phenomena, their interdependence on one another, their rise out of and passing into one another in a single system of events. Nature, in this sense, denotes the same object as "universe" or "world," but with a particular meaning of its own. It is the name we give to the universe, when we consider it as a *region of regularity*; it is the world as having a "nature," a *physis*, a way of behaving such as we learn to count upon. And it belongs especially to this picture of nature that its habit is *productive*: whatever the secret of its systematic processes may be, this activity has resulted in living beings, and eventually in ourselves. Nature is vast, enigmatic, relentless, apparently unconcerned, presenting formidable difficulties to life, occasional abundance; but in any case, it has made human existence and a slowly advancing human technique possible: in a stern and factual sense nature has been maternal. Nature is our permanent riddle, our permanent obstacle, our permanent storehouse; nature is our birthplace, our home, our lure, and perhaps the eternal tomb of our race and of all the life she has brought forth.

These are some of the innumerable aspects which nature presents with reference to ourselves and our interests. But what is nature in itself? An uncounted multitude of things involved in apparently incessant change and strewn throughout unfathomed space. However far we explore nature, we are still in the same space: and however far we trace the series of cosmic changes backward into the past or forward into the future we are still in the same time-order. In a literal sense, we may define nature as the sum of things and events in a single space and time, subject to a single system of causal laws.

Naturalism is the the type of philosophy which takes nature, in this sense, as the whole of reality. Naturalism denies the existence of anything beyond nature, behind nature, other-than-nature, such as the supernatural or other-worldly, or any unheralded intrusion into this system of new energy or new stuff, creation new or old, spontaneous beginning, "accident" in a literal sense. If there is anything in the world which inclines to set itself apart from nature, as independent of the causal laws, be it free decision of the human will, product of creative imagination, a poem, a song, human reason itself, naturalism declares that also to be a part of the scheme of nature: it is the "nature" of man to be artful, artistic, artificial. And if you ask, what causes nature itself, the answer is—nature *is* the total system of causes; each phase of the universe leads to and explains the next phase: hence nature as it now is is completely explained by nature as it has been. To ask for a cause of nature outside of nature, a "First Cause," a "God," is meaningless.[1]

There are different varieties of naturalism according to the differing conceptions of what these things in space and time, in the ultimate analysis, are. If, as was formerly the case, they are considered as atoms of matter in motion,—every phenomenon being in reality just that—we have classical *materialism*. If matter itself is regarded as a form of energy, and everything else is thought reducible to some form of energy, we have *energism* or *dynamism*. Or if we refrain from deciding what the ultimate stuff of the world is, but insist that everything that is real is linked up with other things in observable order, and therefore falls in the domain of one or another of the positive sciences, we have an approach to *positivism*, the pure form of which should be considered not as a metaphysics but as a theory of knowledge.[2]

In ordinary speech "materialism" is sometimes used as a general name for all such views as these, equivalent to naturalism. It implies simply the explanation of the crude phenomena of experience by the eternal flux of motions of the ultimate entities of the world in the impalpable medium of space. There is nothing "crass" about this view: these ultimate realities in any case are of inconceivable fineness, more like light rays in their essence than like the clod; and to their infinitely subtle pulsations mathematical enquiry is always relevant. For, at least in the traditional picture, there is an impeccable lawfulness in the minutest crevices of nature.

[1] J. H. Randall, "The Nature of Naturalism" (Epilogue), §I, in Y. H. Krikorian, ed., *Naturalism and the Human Spirit* (New York, 1944).
[2] See §8.10.

3.2. *The negations of naturalism.* The peculiar force of naturalism lies in what it denies. The imaginative fringe added to the field of sense-experience by religious speculation shrinks to the dimensions of what can, in principle, be measured and controlled; and the whole metaphysical horizon is at once limited and simplified.

The disappearance of the "other world" implies that there is no God (unless Nature itself or Humanity can serve as an object of worship). There is no immortality nor any sort of survival of death, unless the lasting effects of one's life and doings, or the cherishing of one's memory by later generations, can serve as a sort of immortality. There is nothing in the human being more than what he derives from the natural causes which have produced him. If we mean by "soul" something in man distinct from nature, there is no soul.

Since there is nothing to intrude upon the regular processes of nature, miracle and providence are excluded; and prayer becomes a meaningless performance, unless one keeps it up for aesthetic or disciplinary or therapeutic effect.

And there can be no "freedom of the will," if one means thereby a capacity in man of deviating from the line fixed by the causal processes which flow into him and out of him. Naturalism (typically) implies determinism. "The laws which govern man's behavior are the same as the laws of the movements of the stars and the atoms." You have the feeling of free decision, looking forward: you say, "I have not yet decided what I shall do." Your atoms have decided, together with the rest of the world: you will do what you must.

If freedom means doing as you choose, you are free. But, as Spencer reminds you, you always do as you please; you cannot do anything else. That is where nature has you: what you please to do is what nature has caused you to please. "You can do as you please; but you cannot please as you please." Your desire, your preference is the means whereby nature works her will in your behavior.

Finally, conscious reason is not one of the original and permanent facts of the world. The kind of mentality we have in human beings is a transitory feature of things, evolved out of lower organisms, and ultimately out of physical things which are presumably wholly inanimate. And, so far as we can see, reason will again flicker out into the inanimate. The enduring realities do not think or plan: there is neither reason nor purpose for the world as a whole.

3.3. *Naturalism and experience.* No one can escape a strong inclination to naturalism. Reality can be roughly defined as that which corrects our illusions. This is what the substantial facts of nature are always doing; they cure our excesses of fancy, and reduce the castles built by our subjective wishes. They do this work of sobering and correcting best when we are active. We may sit still in the desert and find no refutation of our mirage; but motion banishes the dream. During the course of the centuries, man has become increasingly mobile and aggressive; and increasingly, too, his thinking is done in close connection with his acting, and is thus healthily exposed to the constant battering of the factual reals. Our occupations always define for us some aspect of reality; whatever we are daily occupied with and can deal with successfully, making it respond to our wills,—that we regard as real. To the banker, the flimsy figures on his account sheet represent realities; to the artist, his colors and the things of beauty he can produce with them: and these may or may not seem to the banker as unreal as the abstractions of financial credit to the artist. But there is one universal occupation, the occupation with physical things, place and motion, food and shelter, physical labor, which fortunately no one wholly escapes. Hence these objects around which after preliminary defeats and corrections we build our successful habits become regarded as real not by special classes of men but by the race.

Then again no one escapes a constant reminder of how fragile the mind is, and how constantly dependent it is on the physical world. One may defy nature to the extent of reducing food to one meal a day instead of three, but not to none; reducing sleep to three hours, but not to none; prolonging life but not escaping death. Further, changes in food, temperature, energy or fatigue, condition, health affect the state of mind. The mind develops with the body, and old age brings decrepitude to both. Death ends our communication with the personality, and we have no tangible evidence that it, the conscious self, has escaped the fate of the body.

As for the forces at work in the world outside us, if there is any god among them his distinguishing effects are elusive. The ruling powers of the world appear indifferent alike to individual human interests and to the hopes of the race. If the relentless laws of nature are prevented from working cruelty as well as benefit it is only, so far as we can see, because some human will intervenes. There is no divine intervention to arrest calamity.

We ask ourselves, then, whether apart from our wishes and imaginations the coolly rational explanation of the world is not that of impersonal physical law, and the rational history of man his visible career on the planet—nothing else. Human life is mounted upon a sub-human pedestal, and must shift for itself alone in the heart of a silent and mindless universe. Life has its own justifications if we are among the fortunate ones, and if at the same time we can forget those many to whom it brings a balance of

suffering or defeat. It has also its own costly glories as human civilization
mounts its slow ascent. But there is nothing in "nature" to keep or to remember what has been so hardly won! In all likelihood, life on this planet
will some day pass, and all its traces be churned back into the cosmic
mill. We have the present, we have comradeship, we have the common
concern to increase good and diminish evil: the darkness of the end we
may recognize and forget. Naturalism is the philosophy of our disillusionment, perhaps also of our sober maturity.

3.4. *Naturalism and science.* The detailed material filling of the world-
picture of naturalism is the sum of all the truth that belongs to the field of
the natural sciences. But since there is no type of philosophy which calls
the truth of science into question this is not peculiar to naturalism.

The special sciences, such as physics, chemistry, biology, have nothing
to say for or against naturalism, inasmuch as they have nothing to say
about the world as a whole. Each of them deals with a partial province.
Neither singly nor all together do they constitute a philosophy. And none
of them makes any statement about the non-existence of objects outside
its domain; nor do they make any collective statement to the effect that
all of reality is included in what they survey. It is not science which adopts
naturalism: it is naturalism which adopts science as the metaphysical guide.
Science cannot be brought forward as a witness in favor of naturalism,—
not directly.

But scientific work carries with it a strong impression to the effect that
natural law rules all happenings without exception. It is not merely the
expanding success of "scientific method," a success beyond expectations,
in bringing one by one the supposedly inexplicable aspects of experience
into understandable and predictable control. It is also that, when we
consider the matter closely, we cannot mention any phenomenon which
we can safely say is out of reach of such explanation. "The admission of
the occurrence of any event," said Huxley, "which was not the logical
consequence of immediately antecedent events would be an act of self-
surrender on the part of science." The assumption that every event is the
consequence of a previous state of things is one the scientist is obliged to
make by the very nature of his work.

Thus science tends indirectly to favor naturalism by crowding the more-
than-natural out, leaving no room for it. The hypotheses of free will, vital
force, divine working are not only superfluous, from this point of view, but
positively in the way. If one must rest one's belief in supernature on the
regions of experience not yet scientifically explained, it is evident that that
belief rests on a rapidly narrowing base, and that science looking forward

can concede to it no place which must forever remain inexplicable. Can you suggest any such?

This completeness of the scope of scientific explanation is re-enforced by the incredible accuracy of the microscopic and sub-microscopic measurements which physics uses in tracing reality to its last hiding place. New discoveries in science to-day are commonly made by examining the infinitesimal residues which older explanations leave unaccounted for. Those minute remainders which have become so precious as cues to the investigator will certainly not be willingly surrendered by him to the "obscurantist" who desires them as support for an argument for a supernatural agent.

As a general principle of thinking, William of Occam (d. 1347) left to posterity the so-called Law of Parsimony, to the effect that "What is well explained in a science on fewer grounds is not to be explained again on more numerous grounds." Occam put it tersely: *Frustra fit per plura quod fieri potest per pauciora.*[3] This led to the rule: *Entia non sunt multiplicanda praeter necessitatem.* If then there is nothing which, in principle, natural causes cannot explain, supernatural causes may be dismissed.

3.5. *Naturalism and evolution.* The phenomena which have given the greatest difficulty to scientific explanation are life and mind. They seem to stand out from other things, so that their origin forms an exception to the general rule of nature that like always causes like. Theology has been ready to invoke for the explanation of their origin a divine creative act. It is true that, so far as experience has yet gone, living things are never produced by anything but by previous living things: though products of the laboratory are coming every year closer to the construction of a living cell. But if naturalism is right, the living and animate thing must somehow have come out of the non-living and inanimate. One who sees clearly the contrast between the living and the non-living can understand how generations of scientists who believed that the mechanics of the world could explain everything else, were still unprepared to resist the view that some divine act was necessary to produce the many species of organisms and the human soul.

For the student of philosophy to-day, however, the difficulty may be to get an adequate sense of the contrast. We are living in an era when sharp distinctions of this sort have been so obscured by newly devised intermediaries that many who are unable to think clearly see no difficulty whatever in a gradual transformation from the inorganic to the organic, and from the non-conscious to the conscious. Let us then first ask, What are the peculiarities of life and of mind?

[3] *Summa totius logice,* I, 12.

The most striking characteristics of living things can best be told by aid of the word "self": they are self-building, self-repairing, self-regulating, self-reproducing. There are machines which feed themselves; but there are none that grow by what they feed on. There are self-righting machines, automatic equilibrators, self-steering airplanes and the marvels of "automation." But no machines spontaneously repair their own injuries, or adjust themselves to an unlimited range of variable conditions. As for self-reproduction, there is no machine nor chemical product which develops within itself a germ containing the capacity to grow to another like the original, still less to produce within that other a germ having the same capacity, and so on forever, as if within one organism there were packed away, in cells within cells, an infinite series of completely specified mature individuals! The "self" of the living organism, to us who look on, means an identifiable outline through which there is a constant flow of matter and energy, its metabolism: it is the same individual from time to time without having in it the same stuff; when it acts, it acts as a whole, and as if it were trying to preserve its own existence and that of an endless series of individuals like itself. The activities of its life consist, in terms of Spencer's definition, in the "continuous adjustment of internal relations to external relations": if the outer world changes, the organism changes in response, and in such wise as to keep itself intact.

Now, how does "mind" differ from "life"? We have characterized life by its peculiar, but observable, functions or activities; we must characterize mind by an unobservable quality,—*feeling*. The living organism acts *as if* it were interested in itself; the mind (if the organism has a mind) adds the *fact of interest* to this appearance of interest. Characteristic of mind is that awareness of benefit or injury which we call pleasure or pain. It is not certain that there are any organisms without this awareness; life may always be accompanied by mind; it is not certain that the tree is indifferent to being cut down. But at least *some* organisms are "conscious." And man, in addition to being simply conscious, "*thinks*," i. e., forms ideas of objects, makes theories about his nature, conceives purposes and executes plans. The term "mind" includes this whole gamut of conscious and intentional activities.

Now the puzzle for naturalism is first, how a world of non-living things could have produced the living, self-preserving things; and second, how the fact of self-preservation becomes the awareness of self-preservation i. e., how mind enters. For there is all the difference in the world between an action and the consciousness of that action as being done by me. It is the difference, let us say, between an arrow mechanically driven to the target and a mythical arrow which should intend and try to reach the target, and experience satisfaction when lodged in the bull's eye. (Do these latter traits apply to the "self-directed" missiles of modern warfare?) There are those who feign to consider consciousness unimportant: it is not recorded that these persons decline anæsthetics under surgery. Since values and importances are the precise features of the world which are wiped out when consciousness is absent, it might fairly be said that consciousness is the most important single fact in the universe. Without it there is no perception, no judgment, no knowledge, no enjoyment. Its presence constitutes the major problem for naturalism; its meaning is the central problem of all philosophy.

This is the point at which the theory of evolution offers aid in the completion of the view of naturalism. It proposes to explain the origin of life and of mind. Darwin's theory made no such attempt: his work was limited to changes within the different forms of life,—the origin of species, the descent of man. He took life for granted, assuming that life always comes from life; but he broke down the lines between species and thus between lower forms of life and higher forms. It remained for a generalized theory of evolution to attempt the passage from non-living to living, and from non-mental to mental.

This generalized theory in its philosophical form we owe chiefly to Herbert Spencer. He assembled the scattered scientific work of his day into a picture so vast, and so impressive in its cumulation of details corroborating the universal law of development through "differentiation and integration," that it became much easier to believe that the remaining difficulties would eventually be resolved. The line between the non-living and the living was primarily for the biologists to deal with in conjunction with the chemists. All living matter is composed chiefly of five common elements, oxygen, hydrogen, nitrogen, carbon, sulphur: there is no element peculiar to living things; the presumption was that "life" consists in a pattern of arrangement, which might be artificially reconstructed. Since 1827, when Wöhler synthesized urea in his laboratory in Giessen, confidence had increased that the special processes of physiology can be understood as extensions of chemical law.[4] Grape sugar, oxalic acid, indigo, and other organic products can be manufactured. It could easily appear to Spencer that the difference between living and non-living had already become a matter of the degree of complexity of the molecule of protoplasm, and of the high instability of compounds of nitrogen. Whether these scientific researches take care of the peculiar self-reference of the activities of organic life, their tendency to preserve *a total individual*, through a peculiar assemblage of processes which one by one may be chemically commonplace, the

[4] For sketch of the salient points in discovering the chemical basis of physiology, see Joseph Needham, "Mechanistic Biology and the Religious Consciousness," *Science, Religion and Reality* (London, 1926); also J. A. Thompson, *Concerning Evolution* (New Haven, 1925), pp. 42–51.

student must carefully consider for himself.[5] We shall return to this question.[6]

As for the line between the non-mental and the mental, this caused Spencer much perplexity. He was at first inclined to regard consciousness as a form of energy,—one in the series of transformations which energy can undergo, as from heat to electricity, to light, to translatory motion. But mental energy does not seem to admit of measurement, as do all the other forms of energy, in terms of the mass and velocity of moving particles. Nor is there any evidence that the physical energy of brain action declines when mental energy increases.[7] For these and other reasons, he later considered consciousness as an *accompaniment* of changes in the brain, a rather inexplicable accompaniment which we have to accept as being there. (This amounts to giving the problem up.) The mind, he thought, could be understood as a highly complex system of minute feelings "similar in nature to those we know as nervous shocks": but he did not mean by this that a "nervous shock" (which is a physical fact) is identical with a feeling (which is a mental fact); so that it still remains a mystery how the mental elements happen to accompany these nervous events. Ernst Haeckel, in *The Riddle of the Universe*, solves the question by use of the convenient term "gradually": "Consciousness," he says, "has been gradually evolved from the psychic reflex activity," [8]—reflex activity being in his view "psychic" but not conscious, a distinction which it requires a certain agility to encompass. Whether you find yourself able, by the aid, perhaps, of current theories of the "subconscious," to make use of such a bridge from the inanimate to the animate, I cannot tell; but note that this is a critical point, perhaps *the* critical point, in any theory of evolution which offers itself as support to naturalism. Haeckel's word "riddle" implied that for him, as for Spencer, the solution was incomplete.

There can be no doubt that within the animal kingdom the mind, once it is present, has *evolved* along with the evolution of the body. Darwin offered important evidence for this fact; [9] and a series of able investigators in comparative psychology, George Romanes, Lloyd Morgan, Max Verworn, Jacques Loeb, Robert Yerkes and others have pressed the enquiry at what point in the organic series we can assume that consciousness arises, and what its primitive form is. These researches labor, as one can readily

---

[5] William Ritter and Hans Driesch maintain that in self-building, etc., the organism behaves as if *the whole* were acting for itself, and not as a mere combination of units. It is as though the whole preceded and selected its own parts, and were thus a separate entity. Ostwald, *Natural Philosophy*, has given some attention to this question, which most naturalists overlook. Jacques Loeb, *Physiology of the Brain*, traces the activities of the simpler organisms to "tropisms," direct reactions to light, heat pressure, salinity, etc. Walter Cannon, in *The Wisdom of the Body*, and L. J. Henderson, in his various studies of systems of equilibration in the blood, have contributed important data.

[6] See Ch. 7.   [7] See H. Bergson, *Mental Energy*.

[8] "Psychic Gradations," Ch. VII, *The Riddle of the Universe* (New York, 1900).

[9] See *Origin of Species*, Ch. VII; also *Expression of the Emotions*.

see, under the disadvantage that consciousness is invisible, and that the farther away we get from the human stage of mentality the less there is in the way of expression which we can safely interpret as evidence of the presence of mind. We can only say that if, as a matter of principle, we are satisfied that mind can arise out of the inanimate world, all such researches aid us in picturing the stages of its growth from its rudimentary beginnings,[10] which still remain speculative.

3.6. *Emergent evolution.* Since Darwin and Spencer wrote, many changes have been made in our views of the manner in which evolution takes place. The word "gradually," which was appropriate to a Darwinian era relying on the conservation of small variations by natural selection, has been submerged: many steps of development, it is now seen, have occurred abruptly, by "mutation." It is suggested that mind may have entered the scene in one of these saltations.

It has long been known that there are two kinds of effect in nature, which George Henry Lewes distinguished as "resultants" and "emergents." [11] The resultants are the effects which we are able to deduce from the causes; as when we say that the weight of salt is the sum of the weights of sodium and the chlorine that combine to produce it. The emergents are the unpredictable effects, which, so to speak, supervene together with the resultants; as the *taste* of the salt, its crystalline form and color, which lacking all resemblance to the properties of either sodium or chlorine seem to be something quite new and additional to the situation. Such emergent qualities appear to depend upon the way of arrangement or composition of the ingredients.

Now may it be that life and mind "emerge" in this abrupt way whenever in the rearrangements of physical elements the right kind of arrangement or pattern happens to be struck out? This is the suggestion of Lloyd Morgan.[12] Morgan himself is not a philosophical naturalist; he believes, rather, that in the universe at large there is some mental cause for the emergence of consciousness in connection with the animal organism. He regarded "emergent" as merely a word for the scientific observer, to mark the empirical fact that something new had occurred for whose explanation he had no further responsibility than to note the conditions under which it appears. But the word was a good one; there are so many cases of emergence in nature that it seemed to amount to a new law, namely, that under the right circumstances unpredictable qualities arise and continue to exist.

[10] See L. T. Hobhouse, *Mind in Evolution;* Lloyd Morgan, *Instinct and Experience,* Ch. IV.
[11] *Problems of Life and Mind,* p. 412. Quoted by C. Lloyd Morgan in *Journal of Philosophical Studies,* January, 1929, p. 23, in an article, "The Case for Emergent Evolution," which deserves careful study.
[12] See Lloyd Morgan, *Emergent Evolution.*

(Does this seem to the reader like making the absence of an explanation serve for an explanation, by providing it with a name, and finding numerous cases of it? It is some reply, not wholly satisfactory perhaps, to point out that most so-called laws of nature do that very thing. We do not understand any single case of gravitation; but when all bodies attract each other in the same unexplained way, which we can exactly formulate, we have a command of the How, if not of the Why, of the whole group of phenomena,—and with this How, modern science regards its work as finished.) Thus Morgan found his conception immediately put to the uses of naturalistic evolution, as in Alexander's *Space, Time, and Deity*.[13] Alexander considers life and consciousness to be "qualities" arising from underlying levels of less complex existence. Thus he writes:

"Mind is, according to our interpretation of the facts, an 'emergent' from life, and life an emergent from a lower physico-chemical level of existence." [14] "The higher quality emerges from the lower level of existence and has its roots therein, but it emerges therefrom, and it does not belong to that lower level, but constitutes its possessor a new order of existent with its special laws of behavior. The existence of the emergent qualities thus described is something to be noted, as some would say, under the compulsion of brute empirical fact, or, as I should prefer to say in less harsh terms, to be accepted with the 'natural piety' of the investigator. It admits of no explanation." [15]

Professor Sellars employs this same idea.

"We are confronted with *pluses*. Chemical properties are not the same as physical properties. There is a further plus when we examine the functioning of organic tissues. The older properties are transcended and included. And behaviorism is suggesting that a still more synthetic level is reached in the nervously controlled action of the whole organism." [16] He argues "that consciousness is not a new stuff in any metaphysical sense and that awareness and cognition are functions of the structure of consciousness and the activity of the organism. But while psychical contents are inseparable from cerebral states and are a literal part of their nature, they are novel just as these states are novel. They cannot be deduced nor foreseen." [17]

The picture of evolution thus presented restores the older conception of a series of *steps* in which life, mind, reason mark off clearly distinguished groups of phenomena. Is it possible that this way of arraying the facts of evolution surmounts the difficulty with which both Spencer and Haeckel struggled?

It has at least this advantage. The older conceptions conveyed the impression that whatever is evolved is composed of, and therefore in reality is, the more primitive thing out of which it came: Evolution is (as its ety-

---

[13] Published in 1920, and acknowledging indebtedness to earlier suggestions of Lloyd Morgan.
[14] S. Alexander, *Space, Time, and Deity*, II (London, 1920), p. 14. Quoted by permission of the publishers, Macmillan and Co. Ltd.
[15] *Ibid.*, pp. 46–47.
[16] R. W. Sellars, *Evolutionary Naturalism* (Chicago, 1922), p. 297.
[17] *Ibid.*, pp. 283–284.

mology suggests) an out-turning or unwinding of the contents of an original germ; the mind is nothing but the revealed inwardness of its ancestral capsule, the dust. To the emergent evolutionist, however, each new level of being is an arrival, to whose advent the whole surrounding figure of events has contributed. It is not "contained in" any earlier shape, and though not as real as the elements from whose arrangement it emerges, it cannot be reduced to them. The "nothing but" phrase ceases to be appropriate. Without being any the less a lawful and determined universe, the world is capable of giving birth to novelty, and in a sense of stepping *upward*.

3.7. *Naturalism and human nature.* The question of the evolution of mind is bound up with the question *what mind is* as we now find it. If naturalism can give a sufficient account of human nature as it is, there will be no final obstacle in determining how it came to be. The scientific account of human nature is usually called psychology: and psychology will necessarily test and be tested by every judgment we make of the mind and its place in the world. Psychology is and must be the chief battleground between naturalism and other views of the world.

Since the middle of the nineteenth century, psychology has been written largely from the standpoint of physiology. That is to say, the mind has been treated as a function of the brain, an organ in an organism, and subject like the rest of the body to the laws of cause and effect which include that body in the circuits of physical nature. At first the naturalist had one main instrument of explanation, the "reflex arc": the mind as an active affair was considered a phenomenon of stimulus and response. When the finger touches a hot iron there is an instant and mechanical withdrawal: the response takes that particular form because the nervous current is routed through the system, along an inborn path of least resistance. Instincts are more complicated sequences of behavior into whose composition a number of reflex arcs may enter; and instincts modified by experience constitute our habits, and thereby the character of the mature individual. Just how this simple scheme accounts for memory, anticipation, reasoning, and the higher mental process is naturally a matter for much careful enquiry.[18]

During recent years another instrument of explanation has become available, in the form of the chemistry of the blood as affected by the glands of internal secretion, the so-called endocrine glands. It had long been known—indeed, it was the basis of much ancient psychology—that the

[18] An ingeniously worked-out plan of human psychology strictly on the reflex-arc pattern may be found in Max Meyer, *Fundamental Laws of Human Behavior*. On the theory of instinct, see James, *Psychology*; McDougall, *Social Psychology*; Hocking, *Human Nature and Its Remaking*. See John B. Watson, *Psychology from the Standpoint of a Behaviorist*. The work of Pavlov on conditioned reflexes has thrown light on the processes of learning.

emotions are governed largely by visceral disturbances. Recent experimental work has brought to light how profoundly these changes in the body are affected by the pituitary, adrenal, interstitial, thyroid, and a number of other secretions. By proper administration of thyroid extract, for example, a cretin may be brought much nearer to normality; and by stopping the dosage he may be dropped back again. There is thus much justification for the view that the chemical balance of the body is immediately reflected in the temper and the tonus of personality.[19] There is rather less justification for the extravagant expectations which have been built on this discovery, as by Bertrand Russell and Trotsky. The latter once suggested that in time we should be able by proper chemical feeding to lift the level of the racial mentality so that all men will stand in a scale from Newton's level upward! Unfortunately no drug has yet been found which will raise human intelligence above its present normal, so that it will stay up.

But we cannot require of psychology that it change human nature: its first business is to understand human nature. And beyond doubt, as a result of the work of physiological psychology, many things about the mind are better understood. The visible proof of this is in the applications of psychology. Mental diseases are cured. Useful proposals are made to education, to industry, to advertising, to political life,—to every situation in which human beings can be *managed*. And if we can thus learn of the mind through the behavior which we can observe and measure, is it not reasonable to assume that the acting organism, with its marvellously sensitive nervous mechanism, is equivalent, for scientific purposes, to the mind itself? This is the position of behaviorism, the extreme development of naturalistic psychology. The organism can be observed; some laws of its behavior can be known; why worry about the "consciousness" which may or may not be present?

The question for us, however, is not whether psychology has thrown a great flood of light upon human nature. The question is simply whether the sort of psychology which investigates the mind solely as an object in nature, subject to laws of cause and effect, can tell *the whole truth* about the mind. Remembering that "the mind" is something of which each man has a specimen close at hand, do you accept this equation of your mentality with the mechanisms of your behavior?

3.8. *Naturalism explains religion.* Naturalism would not be so convincing as it is if it merely sat in the stronghold of natural law and declared all other outlooks on the universe superfluous. No one convinces his opponent simply by ruling him out of court. This is one reason for the comparative fruitlessness of much argumentation. To be convincing, one

[19] Dr. Berman's title, "The Glands Regulating Personality," states the case over-emphatically.

must step onto the mental ground of his opponent and show why it is that he thinks as he does, where he makes his mistake. The evidence for naturalism will not be wholly satisfying, therefore, unless it can explain why men have been religious, or have taken the spiritualistic view of the world. But this, by way of psychology, naturalism is quite prepared to do. Naturalistic psychology of religion explains religion as a natural—and for a time serviceable—human mistake.

The function of ideas (or of whatever corresponds to ideas in the nervous centres) is to guide behavior: they stand between stimulus and response. The perception of a red glow on the prairie arouses the idea of fire and guides for man and beast the response of flight. The true idea aids survival; the false idea leads to waste effort or to death. A belief being a complex group of ideas, we may say that animals whose brains produce true beliefs will tend to survive. And sometimes a mixture of truth and error will do this work of aiding survival, if the error is not operative. Thus, so long as men's journeys were of restricted range, the assumption that the earth is flat worked as well as the truer notion.

Now spiritualism has been useful in this way. It has offered *encouragement* at the time when man needed it most. The great mental task of early times, if man was to be markedly different from the animals, was that he should be able to see ahead, be interested in the future and plan for it: he could then begin to live by his dreams, using his creative imagination— perhaps his most distinctive faculty—with effect. Religion kept alive in him the hope that he could, by aid of the divine power, surmount his obstacles and work out a better order of life. It thus held him to the task of mastering nature until the great primary difficulties attending subsistence, shelter and the like had actually been mastered. It developed his imagination and confirmed the habit of devotion to an ideal.

It aided *social solidarity*, making possible that respect for custom which was necessary if men were to reach any common ground of social life. It sanctioned and idealized rulership, an essential first stage in state-building. Note that this idealizing of common things, which may seem so wild a departure from the cold facts, is often nearer the truth than the realistic description. When J. C. Gray describes the Supreme Court as "half a dozen elderly men, sitting on a platform behind a green or red cloth, with very probably not commanding wills or powerful physique . . . some of them, conceivably, of very limited intelligence," [20] he is intentionally omitting from the picture the powerful tradition of the public law of the land which operates through these men. Until humanity could recognize these intangible but actual elements of a working society it needed the schooling in deference to the unseen which religion supplied.

[20] *Nature and Sources of the Law* (New York, 1921), pp. 121, 84.

Further, religion created a *technique of enthusiasm*. Through its ritual excitements it trained the effusive emotionality of early man into relatively orderly channels. It is on this account that religion after much groping became the home of the infancy of all the fine arts,—though it is not altogether certain that this product of religion can pose as an aid to survival. It may be such an aid if the artist through his art reaches, and helps others to reach, a closer sympathy with the vital principle in nature.

But what is at first an aid may, in later stages of progress, become a hindrance, or even a poison. Encouragement may become a sort of coddling. Religion has been regarded by Freudian psychologists [21] as a belated moral infantilism, whereby in the maturity of the race, when we ought to be ready to face the problems of existence in all their harsh verity, men still persist in dreaming of a benevolent heavenly paternal roof, which personally shields them from the severest blows of fate. The support of custom may become (as it soon did become) a congealing of custom; so that the very agency for opening the future became a vice for fixing the bondage of the past. The interest in the ideal may become an indulgence in abstract contemplation, to the robbing of human life. And the arts, one by one, have had to claim liberation from their dominating parent. The secularization movements of history, ending with the still incomplete secularization of politics, indicate this phase of the warfare, not of science, but of the arts with religion. Thus religion takes its place in the program of naturalistic evolution, and we are invited to consider it not so much disproved as outgrown, with all due gratitude for its former beneficent rôle.

Auguste Comte (1798–1857), French positivist, has given a vivid expression to this view of the rôle of religion. He teaches [22] that men's views of the world naturally run through three stages. The first stage is theological: events are explained by referring them to divine powers. The second stage is metaphysical: events are explained by referring them to separate energies, life by a vital force, fire by a principle of heat, falling bodies by a heavy principle, and so on. The third stage is the "positive" stage: events are explained by referring them to causes, i. e., to previous events on which they follow according to definite rules or laws. This kind of explanation does not take us out of the field of observable and measurable facts, and is the highest stage of human intellect. The positive stage of thought does not destroy all that mankind has cherished under the name of religion; only, it substitutes for the supernatural being, whom no one can discover, the "Great Being," *le grand Etre*, with whom we have to do at all times, and whom we can loyally serve, Humanity.[23]

[21] See S. Freud, *The Future of an Illusion.*
[22] *Cours de philosophie positive*, 1830. Lects. I, II.
[23] See selections from Comte in Rand, *Modern Classical Philosophers*. Also John Stuart Mill, *Auguste Comte and Positivism* (London, 1907), pp. 1–32 and 124–148.

When any man judges his dreams to be dreams, he discards them, though regretfully, and girds himself to face the literal facts of the universe with sternness and courage. Thus, the idea of God is seen, by the eye schooled in the scientific temper, to be a visionary form of the permanently needful devotion to ideal social ends. The wish for immortality is seen as a projection of the impulse of youth for the affirmation of life. To perceive the psychology of our beliefs is to gain detachment from them.

3.9. In nothing of what has preceded has naturalism undertaken to prove its case. It has simply appealed to sober judgment. To summarize, it submits as in its favor:

a. Our common sense or intuition of the reality of physical things;

b. The tangible and measurable character of the objects it operates with in its explanations. (They give a definiteness and a clarity to language which contrast favorably with the often cloudy vagueness of the spiritualist. The materialist is peculiarly fortunate in this respect; for anybody can imagine an atom in the midst of space, if it is a solid particle of the Newtonian model. This clarity is an augury of good-faith and mental fraternity);

c. The completeness of its explanations, having in mind also the minute accuracy which has come with the quantitative phase of science;

d. In particular, its explanation of the human mind through a cause-and-effect psychology, and of the transitory function of religion in history. (The temper of naturalism was formerly arrogant and bitter; something of the scorn of the partisan fighting against entrenched bigotry appears in the work of Haeckel, and occasionally in the more genial writing of Huxley. But in Romanes and Spencer and later writers, one finds regretful acceptance of the bleaker view of the world which the evidence seems to them to require);

e. The simplicity and unity of the world-view, not cluttered up with supernatural intrusions and indefinite fringes. (It allows concentration on the human task. "It sternly implies the need for securing the finest conditions for human development in the world of here and now. Misery and want cannot be excused by considering them part of an inscrutable plan." Nor are we justified in deferring to another life the justice which it is our duty to create in this.)

3.10. *Naturalism in the history of thought.* As a tendency in every man's mind, naturalism would be expected to show itself in every period of history. It would gain clear expression wherever man had reached the sense of a reliable order of natural law.

For example, we find it in the Greek world, in the philosophy of

Democritus as a comprehensive atom theory. His Roman disciple, Lucretius, expressed the same doctrine in a great philosophical poem, *De rerum natura* (about 60 B. C.), a passionate appeal for a passionless view of the world.[24]

At the beginning of the modern era, Thomas Hobbes undertook to explain the mind as a case of matter in motion. Sensation is a direct effect of outer motions on the nerves; and as "motion produceth nothing but motion," sensation must be a kind of motion. Then imagination and memory are "decaying sense"; and reason a train of memories.[25]

Eighteenth-century France saw a striking development of naturalism in the spirit of classical materialism. René Descartes, often called the founder of modern philosophy, had already taught [26] that the body of an animal is an automatic mechanism, without consciousness. In consequence, as one historian comments, "For a long time it was fashionable among zealous Cartesians to torture animals in a frivolous spirit, in order to show that their theory was seriously meant." He thought that man was a machine so far as his body is concerned; but that the mind was a distinct substance, capable of acting on the body.[27] This reservation of the human mind was criticized by Lamettrie in a book entitled *l'Homme machine*, published in 1748 with the vast approval of Frederick the Great.[28]

But the great era of naturalism is, as one would expect, the century of Darwin and Spencer, when natural law was first applied with extraordinary success to the world of living organisms, and the principles of evolution in biology were extended to the history of the universe. The nineteenth century saw the notable works [29] of Herbert Spencer (1820–1903), Ludwig Büchner (1824–1899), Ernst Haeckel (1834–1919), T. H. Huxley (1825–1895), and Friedrich Nietzsche (1844–1900).

The most systematic expression of the philosophy of natural evolution is that of Herbert Spencer in *First Principles*. The beginner would do well to have the full text before him, sketching the chapters in Part II at the first reading, by omitting something of the vast bulk of illustration with which Spencer reinforces his argument, and paying particular attention to the last three chapters, Equilibration, Dissolution, Summary and Conclusion. Note carefully how Spencer brings the mind into the order of evolution. How Spencer deals with religion will be found in chapters i, ii, and v of Part I.

For a clear cut statement of materialism Büchner's *Force and Matter*, is a short book which can be gathered up in its main argument very quickly. The chapters worth most attention are those labelled Force and Matter, Creation, Purpose in Nature, Brain and Soul, Free Will, Conclusion.

Ernst Haeckel's *Riddle of the Universe*, chapters 1, 6, 10, 11, 12, 15, will outline the argument.

[24] See Bakewell, *Source Book in Ancient Philosophy*, selections from Munro's translation of Lucretius.
[25] See Hobbes, *Leviathan*, Part I, Chs. I–III, V.   [26] *Principles of Philosophy*, 1644.
[27] Descartes' views will be considered at greater length under the head of Dualism.
[28] See Lamettrie, *Man a Machine*.   [29] See Bibliography, p. 324.

Read also T. H. Huxley, *Lay Sermons*, on Descartes' "Discourse Touching the Method of Using One's Reason Rightly and of Seeking Scientific Truth"; *Life and Letters*, I.

Nietzsche's *Thus Spake Zarathustra* presents in the form of sermons the evolutionary view of man. See especially "Old and New Tables."

The nineteenth century seems to us now a period of naturalist classics. Physics aided by mathematics provided the ideal of an established scientific method; and the notion of a set of equations which should describe the law of the behavior of all atoms in all space throughout all time seemed not impossibly out of reach. The twentieth century has brought a profound revolution in our conception of the ultimate facts of physics. In the broadest sense, this makes no difference to naturalism, which is not committed to any particular physical doctrine but only to an acceptance of the physical universe, whatever it may prove to be, as the outline of reality. Twentieth-century naturalism is more complex, more varied, less typical, less confident. It frequently appears under the guise of realism,[30] a highly technical type of philosophy which we shall later consider.

Examples of naturalism in the twentieth century are:

Bertrand Russell's *Problems of Philosophy*; *Scientific Method in Philosophy*; *What I Believe*. Russell's writing has distinguished clarity, vigor and wit.

George Santayana's *Skepticism and Animal Faith*, a work of great charm and less lucidity by an eminent poet and master of expression.

R. W. Sellars, *Evolutionary Naturalism*, a textbook, solid, incisive, schematic.

John Dewey's writings, which, so far as they touch metaphysics, present a form of naturalism. See especially *Quest for Certainty*.

Irwin Edman's *Four Ways of Philosophy*, a truly eloquent defence of naturalism. See especially his fourth chapter, "Philosophy as Nature Understood." I know of no chapter in which the meaning of naturalism as we find it today is so adequately expressed, or where the skeleton which its universe conceals is so gracefully and kindly bedecked. Bertrand Russell's celebrated essay *A Free Man's Worship*, has to me a studied pathos; Walter Lippmann's *A Preface to Morals* is heavy with the awareness of Fate; but Edman's book has the true joy of the lover of nature, and his embrace of the negations of destiny rings sincere.

When the satisfaction in nature turns into an enthusiasm and offers scope for "natural piety," the mind finds itself imperceptibly attributing to nature as a whole a living quality, as when John Dewey is ready, under strictly specified understandings, to venture the use of the word "God." [31] Then naturalism is silently turning into something else.

[30] See Type VI.
[31] See Dewey, *A Common Faith* (New Haven, 1934), p. 51.

CHAPTER 4: THE LOGIC
OF NATURALISM

4.1. The foregoing arguments in favor of naturalism, I repeat, are not proofs. They are appeals to judgment.

In fact, there can be no proof of naturalism. How could one prove that nothing but nature exists? The only way in which anything can be proved non-existent is to show that it is impossible: thus a centaur is impossible, under conditions of terrestrial physiology, hence centaurs are non-existent on this earth. And there are certain kinds of god which may be shown impossible, at least under natural laws. But unless we assume that these natural laws rule the entire universe, which would be begging the question, we cannot prove that even the gods of Homer's Olympus are impossible everywhere. The non-existence of a spiritual God, or of another world, or of a future life, cannot be proved.

But there is a logical side to the case for naturalism. It consists in refuting the attempts which have been made in the past to prove that super-nature does exist.

4.2. What would you regard as the strongest grounds that could be given for a belief in God? Apart from intuitive and pragmatic reasons, there are three main grounds of a rational order, which have been elicited during the long defensive contest between spiritualism and naturalism, and which reappear in all arguments on this subject.

a. There is the argument that *nature requires an author*. As one student has put the matter, "There must be something all-powerful somewhere that created the universe in the first place." Another, "It seems required by reason that some great power is responsible for the existence of the universe, and since man has found no satisfactory explanation of the beginning of things in nature itself, I believe that power to be God." In brief, the world of nature is considered not self-sufficient: it shows signs of dependence not only among its parts mutually, but as a whole on something beyond itself. The dependent implies an independent being. That

42

independent and self-sufficient being is God. This argument, interested in origins, the first cause of things, creation, has been called the *cosmological argument*.

b. There is the argument that *the order and beauty of nature* could not be accidental, but *imply a mind* that appreciated them, and meant to bring them into existence. Thus one says, "The material universe, which always acts by fixed law, supposes a law-giver outside itself. No one can make a law unless he has intelligence. The creator is therefore an intelligent being." "Common-sense tells one that the beauty and co-ordination of Nature could no more have sprung into being by itself than a watch with its intricate parts scattered could spring into motion"; "Who but a god could have worked out the myriad laws of nature in all their exact perfection?" This argument, interested not so much in the bare facts of the world as in their value and fitness, has been called the *teleological argument*. It is the argument from the design to the designer.

c. A third ground more rarely comes to light. It is the argument that *the idea of God somehow guarantees its own truth*. "There seems to be something in the notion of a supreme being which cannot be false or illusory." "I cannot believe that the idea of God would have occurred to mankind if there had not been reality behind it." This argument also has received strong expression in the history of philosophy; but it has taken many forms, as if it were difficult to capture in logical terms, and were somehow more truly stated in the indefinite form. There is in the idea of God a peculiarity which sets it apart from all other ideas, and requires me to believe that its object is truly existent. What is that peculiarity?

Some mediæval schoolmen thought it "pure Being": God is pure Being, and pure Being necessarily exists.

Anselm of Canterbury (1033–1109) thought it "a being than which none greater can be conceived." He argued that the idea of such being (not "a" perfect being) necessarily involves the existence of that being. For if the idea is a mere idea or fancy it lacks something of that full perfection which it would attain if its object also existed; that is, we could conceive of a greater being. Hence we contradict ourselves if we think of the "being than which none greater can be conceived" as a mere idea. We must think of it as existing.

Spinoza (1632–1677) thought it "perfection." Perfection, he held, carries with it a power to exist; if we think of the absolute beginning or origin of things, perfection would assert its inherent power to be,—nothing could resist it. "The perfection of a thing does not annul its existence, but on the contrary asserts it. Imperfection, on the other hand, does annul it. Therefore we cannot be more certain of the existence of anything than of the existence of a being absolutely infinite or perfect—that is, of God." [1]

In these and other ways philosophers have tried to show that the idea of God contains our standard of reality; and we can never accept the suggestion that this standard may be "merely subjective," for it is only our standard of "objective reality" which could lead us to judge any idea as subjective. The idea of God then, by itself, requires belief in the existence of God. This has been called the *ontological argument*.

Do these three arguments exhaust what can be said in the way of attempting a rational proof of the existence of God?

4.3. Naturalism undertakes to show that all these arguments are fallacious. They have been criticised by many thinkers who are not naturalists. No one has attacked them more trenchantly than Kant.[2]

As for the last mentioned argument, the ontological, Kant voices the opinion of the majority when he judges that there is nothing in it. You have an idea of a perfect circle; that is, the definition of a circle: but this perfection is no guarantee of the existence of the perfect circle. On the contrary, the perfect is precisely what does not exist. Existence adds nothing to the perfection of an idea. Perfection is a quality: if a perfect rose could be translated from idea to actuality, its perfection would not be improved nor in any way changed. Has Kant met the ontological argument in its full strength?

The cosmological argument errs in making an illicit use of the idea of *cause*. The origins of things are their causes; and their causes are always in some previous state of nature. The origin of the hen is in the egg, and the origin of the egg is a preceding hen. Trace it back as far as you like, to the original protoplasmic slime, or to the original nebula: you are *never referred outside of nature* for your origin. The relation of cause to effect is the very essence of natural happening. We could never, therefore, be referred to a supernatural being for a cause of anything that happens. Nor yet for the cause of "all things,"—if that phrase has any assignable meaning.

Creation is a different matter, quite different from causation; for creation implies the production of the very stuff of the world. But clearly no argument from causality can help us in reaching the creative source of things, if there is any such source. For causality only plies between one state and another of existing things.

The wiser naturalists do not imagine that they have avoided all mental difficulty in thus rebuking the tendency of the mind to use the causal ladder to climb out of nature. If they insist that the ladder is really a chain

[1] *Ethics*, Proposition XI, note.
[2] Kant, "The Ideal of Pure Reason," in *Critique of Pure Reason*.

of causes leading backward into the past *ad infinitum*, they are asserting in effect that the world had *no beginning*. The demand that we believe in an actual infinitude of past time is a baffling one. An infinite series is one that never ends; but if there was no beginning, each present moment is the end of a finished infinite series. Is this conceivable? We have here a mental dilemma (or, as Kant called it, an *antinomy*): the world must have had a beginning, and it cannot have had a beginning. Whichever alternative we choose, we face the inconceivable.

Herbert Spencer fully recognizes this difficulty. He attributes it to the limitations of the human mind: the mind, he holds, is fitted for thinking in terms of relations, such as causality,—it can link one fragment of the world to another; but it is not fitted for thinking the whole. Our knowledge is relative, not absolute; it is scientific, not metaphysical. Hence, when we try to reach absolute beginnings, we are faced with "alternative impossibilities of thought." [3] There are only three alternatives possible for the origin of the world: it is self-existent, or self-caused, or caused by an external agency. And each of these alternatives is really without meaning to our minds. We cannot conceive that a thing exists in its own right without any source beyond itself; we cannot conceive self-creation, for that implies that the thing exists before it exists; and to refer it to an external creator merely defers the question. For we have to ask, Whence the creator? And that question, as Kant already recognized, is "the abyss of human reason."

If, then, the assumption of a God does not explain the origin of the world, the cosmological argument loses its entire point.

4.4. As for the teleological argument, which pretends to see in the order and fitness of nature a benevolent purpose, that argument has been under attack since the beginning of modern times. Lord Bacon exposed the fallacy of referring natural events and arrangements to "final causes," that is, to an assumed purpose. If we explain the good harvest by the will of a good God, it becomes inexplicable that the next harvest is a poor one. The hypothesis of purpose cannot be used to predict the future and is thus, as Bacon put it, "barren, like a virgin consecrated to God." And Spinoza termed it the "refuge of ignorance," [4] because of the idle habit of referring to the will of God whatever we cannot otherwise explain. Further, it was felt on all sides that the motives attributed to God by such explanations were paltry and unworthy. If the earth is not the centre of the universe, neither is man the centre of the value of the universe; and the fitness of the world for man, so far as it is fit, is not to be attributed to the supreme interest of God in the human being. Nor have we any right to forget the

---

[3] Spencer, *First Principles*, Part I.   [4] *Ethics*, Prop. XXVI, appendix.

degree of unfitness in the world; its evil, ugliness, and waste. If from the world as we find it, we try to infer an all-good designer, we are attempting to rise higher than our source. We are, as Kant pointed out, really attributing existence to our preconceived idea of God, that is, making unacknowledged use of the "ontological argument."

The appeals to design in the world of animal life, those admiring meditations which have always been excited by the marvellous structure of the eye and the other sense organs, the protective devices, and the instincts [5]— Darwin's great demonstration that the animal was fitted to the world and not the world to the animal, and that the fitting process could be understood by the ordinary operation of causal laws, more effectively banished these than the criticism of Kant had done.

But in any case, the teleological argument is not a real argument, for it fails to put forward a genuine hypothesis unless we have some conception of the process by which God, having designed the world, then brings it into being. Here we light upon the difficulties of the problem of origins which the cosmological argument brought to evidence, and are forced once more to face the limitations of the human intellect.

4.5. Unless there is something wrong with these criticisms, we should judge with naturalism that these arguments for the existence of God are not substantial. There may be other arguments. There may be grounds not capable of being put into argumentative form. There may be some aspects of supernature not dependent on the existence of God. The will might be free, the soul might be immortal, even if God did not exist. These questions deserve examination, and have been examined in the discussions of naturalistic writers. But since the belief in God is the kernel of all supernaturalism, we have before us the logic of naturalism at its best.

[5] See, for example, Fénélon, *The Existence of God*.

CHAPTER 5: NATURALISTIC ETHICS

5.1. If we cancel belief in God, and in the concern of an all-powerful and all-holy being for righteousness, what becomes of the standards of human morality?

Of course, for the naturalist, the horizon is rimmed by death, both for the individual and the race. But death is no more in the immediate foreground for him than for others. His idea of the wise conduct of life depends on what his reason shows him of cause and effect in producing happiness or misery. He has nothing to fear from the wrath of God; he has still to be mindful of the wrath of society and of his own nature.

His motives are obviously simplified; his conduct need not be essentially altered. He is not troubled to do anything for the glory of God nor for the love of God; and there is no reasonable sentiment in him of gratitude or loyalty to the physical universe which brought him forth, and will some day blot him out. But he cannot destroy the instinctive aspirations of his heredity. If he cares for science, he will still care for it. If his nature is sociable, he will still wish to please his fellow men. If he is sensitive to beauty and refinement, he will still cultivate harmony and decency in his behavior.

For as Plato (who was not a naturalist) long ago pointed out, moral rightness is simply mental health. Hence only the just man can be happy, for the unjust man, like the sick man, is incapable of the ordinary satisfactions of life.[1] The good life has its intrinsic recommendations in the nature of things, quite apart from rewards added by gods or men.

5.2. It is true that the first effect of abandoning a belief in God and the future life may be a sense of liberation. "God is dead," cries Nietzsche, "*alles ist erlaubt,*—everything is permitted!" Nature and natural impulse are not evil; away with shame and repression; away with discipline and restraint. The ethics of the free man will be the ethics of "self-expression."

Whoever takes this direction, or that of Omar Khayyam, the cult of self-centred joy and oblivion, is likely to incur the censure of other naturalists. They will point out to him, in terms not wholly different from Plato's,

[1] *Republic,* Book IV.

that there is a discipline which belongs to nature itself. Further, he cannot turn his back on the needs of humanity and be wholly satisfied with himself. Epicurus and Lucretius, with no remoter goal than the natural satisfaction of life, found the chief advantage of banishing the gods to an innocuous distance (they still professed a nominal belief in their existence) to be the fact that they had overcome the haunting fear of divine punishment and of death: their code of ethics we should call somewhat austere and ascetic, although the word "epicurean" has gained a very different connotation in our common speech. They believed that the undisturbing pleasures of life were the most satisfying, and that the more intense pleasures were deceptive, being both transitory and attended by pain and disgust. A life of leisure, in a small circle of friends, devoted to aesthetic cultivation, was to them the wise choice.[2]

5.3. Modern naturalists have made systematic attempts to apply their world-view to wise conduct. Herbert Spencer's *Data of Ethics* is one of the outstanding essays. Spencer argues that men can be happy only if they fall in with the evident trend of nature in evolution (we cannot say the "intention" of nature), and work with nature for the preservation and increase of life. This means care for one's health and for the development of one's mental powers to their highest capacity; it means trying to abolish war and all those conflicts which involve the subtraction of life and energy from both contestants; it means the replacement of a military society by an industrial society; it means free competition in that society, so that the best men come to the top; and it means the general growth of sympathy to such a point that one derives as much gratification from the pleasure of others as from his own pleasures, and egoism and altruism are reconciled.

5.4. Nietzsche draws from the same premises a very different picture. He finds Spencer's ideal too tame, ("a tea-table Elysium" as William James called it). Nature makes for evolution, it is true; but it does so by way of the destruction of the unfit. The strong and vital elements of society must assert themselves, though less for their own sakes than for the sake of the future. Christianity has been a detriment to the race by cultivating the amiable and sympathetic tempers. Instead of urging us to love others as we love ourselves, Nietzsche would urge us to be ruthless to ourselves as we should be to others. The Superman can only be brought forth by the *Untergang* of the less worthy; and if that less worthy be oneself, it is one's piety to yield to the better. Relentless self-mastery is the way of happiness. "*Geist ist das Leben, das selber ins Leben schneidet.*"

[2] See Bakewell, *Source Book in Ancient Philosophy* (New York, 1907), pp. 297-306.

5.5. Huxley [3] gives up the attempt to find a guide for ethics in the processes of sub-human nature. He finds that all civilization, like the work of the gardener, is a fight with the weeds. The social process cuts across the process of natural selection; and the social aspects of human nature must thrive, even in defiance of the method of struggle for survival. Huxley's essay is worth weighing in view of Nietzsche's powerful appeal for the Darwinian type of morals.

5.6. In sum, then, while the moral codes of naturalists differ, naturalism does not leave morals without support.[4] It does not necessarily turn mankind back to the jungle, nor reverse the direction of social advance. Only, its ethical outlook lacks the vista of eternity, and the resonance of a divine concern in its inward vitality.[5] We do not find here the sustaining motive of either a Socrates or a Confucius. We have rather man's gesture of heroism on the scaffold of a universe which will eventually write a cipher as the sum of all his works.[6]

---

[3] T. Huxley, *Evolution and Ethics.*   [4] We return to this question in Ch. 26.
[5] See George Herbert Palmer, *The Field of Ethics,* Ch. VI.
[6] See Bertrand Russell, *A Free Man's Worship.*

CHAPTER 6:
NATURALISM EXAMINED

6.1. Naturalism as a type of philosophy is now before us. Its case is undoubtedly a strong one. What is the strongest part of it? To my mind, it is the completeness of its program of explanation.

6.2. The advantage which naturalism enjoyed in the nineteenth century in clarity and imaginableness and the consistency of its scientific structure in all its parts,—that advantage has vanished. With the advent of a new outlook in physics, which we may date roughly from Roentgen's discovery of the X rays in 1895, a discovery which gave us the instrument for exploring the subatomic levels of the universe, physical conceptions have entered upon a period for which "transition" would be too tame a word. These changes, so far as they affect our world-picture, may be summed up roughly as follows:

a. The simple and unchangeable atom has shown itself to be a minute world of much internal complexity, capable of composition and decomposition, and of turning on occasion into some other kind of atom. The discoveries of the electron and other subatomic particles, and of radio-activity have revealed motion and change in what was formerly thought eternally stable.

b. The fixed difference between matter and energy is no longer clear. Nothing is more obvious to common sense and to nineteenth-century physics than that you can change the rate of motion of a body *ad libitum* without changing the mass of the body. In taking an inventory of the physical universe, you had always two quantities to consider, the amount of matter, and the amount of motion: these were independent facts. No matter could ever be created or destroyed. The same of energy, a function of mass, motion and position. There was a "conservation" of matter, and another "conservation" of energy. Now it appears that matter and radiant energy are convertible one into the other; and it is not inconceivable—or rather it is not physically impossible whether we can conceive it or not—that the substance of the physical world is being transported gradually from place to place, taking wings in the form of radiation, and being precipitated in remote regions as new-born atoms. By a sort of universal convection or gulf-streaming, the resources of the sidereal systems are forever redistributing themselves with the speed of light. If there is any conservation, it must be of some union of matter and energy rather than of either alone. To this theory of matter-energy, the school of Niels Bohr is adding a far-reaching doctrine of "complementarity," growing out of the quantum mechanics, and showing how far from common sense are the distinctions between position-and-momentum, experimenter-and-object, etc.

c. The law of continuity is in difficulties. There is hardly any principle of science of greater dignity than this law: *natura non facit saltum*. If a body is to get from one place to another, it must go through a continuous series of intermediate places, except in dreams and fairy tales. If a revolving fly-wheel is to increase or reduce its speed, it must do so by going through all intermediate speeds. But we are now asked (in such theories as Planck's theory of quanta, and by such facts as the Compton effect,) to consider that periodic motions may be "granular" or discontinuous like the series of whole numbers, that electrons may jump from one orbit to another without at any time being anywhere between, that radiant energy may go off into space in a series of distinct darts at once wave-wise and lump-wise. We are not asked to picture these events, we are simply warned that we may be required to believe them. Any *a priori* prejudices we may have in behalf of the continuity of all changes must be prepared to yield as gracefully as possible.

d. The independence of time and space is likewise under suspicion, —since the publication of Minkowski's memoir in 1908. Not that time is to be considered a form of space, or space a form of time; but that space and time have to be taken together for purposes of measurement, and that how much space and how much time are occupied by any given event are questions which cannot be answered independently of one another. The Einstein theory of relativity is to be regarded as a fundamental enquiry into the principles of physical measurements, rather than into the nature of space and time, that is to say, as a mechanics; but it has made clear that however distinct our ideas of space and time may be (can you think of time without space, or of space without time?) we must consider them one manifold for purposes of physical science. And further, we must take them together with the events which, as we say, occur "in" space and time: for apart from these events it is questionable whether space and time, as empty regions, would so much as exist.

When Herbert Spencer made up his list of "ultimate scientific ideas" he mentioned five,—space, time, matter, motion, force (to which he added consciousness, as another sort of thing),—and these five he regarded as alike inconceivable, if we ask what they are in themselves. He also held it to be unbelievable that these five are completely independent entities, and so proposed that the others are all manifestations of force, though how this could be he thought must remain unknowable. Physical science seems to be entering by necessity the region of these "inscrutable" relationships of ultimate ideas: and in so doing makes at least so much clear, that the apparent clarity of materialism was an illusory advantage. If we explain the world in terms of physical elements we are no longer explaining the unknown by the known, but the known by the unfamiliar and unpicturable, possibly even the unthinkable. Naturalism can no longer claim support from the human instinct to take the solid as the real.

6.3. Now do these puzzles of contemporary physics require radical changes in our metaphysics?

It is certainly too early to infer, as some have hastened to do, that these changes have made naturalism itself untenable. We need to remind ourselves time and again that the positive sciences do not of themselves constitute philosophy. However hard the physical world may be to understand, however disturbing to our established ways of formulating it, this difficulty has nothing to do with the *reality* of the physical world, nor with the ultimate question of naturalism, whether physical nature is all there is.

With this warning, however, we may say that the very existence of these puzzles has radically altered the question which the metaphysical Sphinx puts to the human mind to-day. The clear-cut finality of the physical object, which naturalism requires, is shaken. The classical atom-theory type of naturalism is now excluded from the possible alternatives by the progress of physics itself.

The near-positivism mentioned above [1] is also unsettled, if not excluded. Physicists are less ready to say, "We are not interested in what space and time and energy are; we are only interested in the order and connection of phenomena." For the order and connection of phenomena depend a good deal on what space and time and energy are. Physics to-day once more admits metaphysics into its counsels.

And in regard to the nature of space and time, the physicist no longer says with his former assurance, "We can settle the problems of physics without reference to *the mind*: the physical world can exist by itself, whether or not there are any minds there to observe it." For it has become an integral part of the theory of relativity that "the observer" must be taken into account before we can tell how much space or time or motion we are dealing with. This "observer," we should be careful to note, is for

[1] See §3.1.

the most part merely a recording instrument, a clock or a meter-stick. But if the facts depend on what such instruments show, and on the choice of them, the observing mind is brought into the reckoning; the boundaries between the objects, the apparatus and the experimenter begin to cause trouble. Thus if it is true, as Professor Bridgman says, that there is no geometry of pure space, but a geometry of meter sticks for near-by or "tactual" space and a geometry of light waves for astronomical or "optical" space,[2] then space loses its independent reality. And if "we must not talk about the age of a beam of light," nor "allow ourselves to think of events taking place in Arcturus *now* with all the connotation attached to events taking place *here* now," [3] then time ceases to have that objective reality which naturalism formerly took for granted. And if the amount and character of the physical universe are indeterminate apart from the operations of its mentally alive observers, the world prior to the entrance of the observing minds could only be given a vague, indescribable, pre-natal sort of existence!

Thus physics itself, we may justly say, has rendered naturalism less plausible and less self-confident.

But let no one suppose that the solution of the major metaphysical problems depends on the settlement of these intricate technical questions. Fortunately the great issues of life do not require all of us to become mathematical physicists. The merits of naturalism have, for the most part, to be determined on other and more accessible grounds.

If I am right in thinking that the strong side of naturalism is the completeness of its explanations, it becomes vulnerable at once if at any point its explanations are incomplete and *necessarily so*. Are there any such points? Consider three.

6.4. *Does naturalism explain qualities?* The world as we find it is full of colors, sounds, odors, tastes, touch-qualities, and the like. Causality as the eye perceives it operates between events full of these qualities: colored waves beat on colored rocks. But as scientific theory replaces crude observation, our understanding of the process changes. The color is merely our personal view of a certain vibration rate, and similarly with the sounds and other qualities which appeal to sense. In itself, the reality of nature is not colored, because it is the basis of color. Perhaps it is not even tangible, nor imaginable. The question, What does a proton look like, or feel like, has no answer. Diagrams of the atoms are confessedly mere symbols for possible spatial relationships. The thought of nature passes from the imaginable to the merely calculable. It is the totality of terms which are

[2] *The Logic of Modern Physics* (New York, 1948), pp. 67 f.   [3] *Ibid.*, p. 76.

to be introduced into certain analytical equations. It *abandons* qualities in order to *explain* qualities; and so, in itself, it approaches a pure quantity.

But the qualities are there; and if they are omitted from the idea of nature, can they really be explained?

Naturalism answers, the quality is the effect of a certain vibratory disturbance upon the nerves and brain of the organism. But the nerves and brain are themselves physical objects, and hence composed of the same ingredients as other physical bodies. If there is no color in the wave, neither is there any color in the eye or brain.

Quality cannot be denied to exist, and yet it seems to be strangely extruded from the naturalistic picture as a subjective superfluity which nature could very well get along without. This appalling and incredible loss of all quality from the conception of nature, which Fechner called the "night-view" of the world, modern realism tries to correct within the bounds of naturalism.[4]

6.5. *Does naturalism explain the mind?* If the brain has no quality, the brain is certainly not the mind. A motion in the brain may accompany the thinking process, but it is evident on consideration that a motion is one thing and a thought is something quite different. It is important to be clear on this point, for in common speech we often interchange the "brain" and the "mind."

If a materialist proposes, as Hobbes did, that a sensation is nothing but a form of motion, and a thought is nothing but a chain of dying sensations, hence a sequence of motions, the only possible answer is that the proposition is nonsense. When two objects are identical, you can substitute one for the other in every statement. But try to substitute for the mental proposition, "I hate you," the physical proposition, "There is in my nervous system and viscera a physico-chemical disturbance of a certain pattern. . . ." The microscopic inspection of a brain process, however perfect, would simply fail to discover any suggestion of what we mean by thought or feeling. We must hold to the clear insight of Descartes on this point: the essence of the mind is thinking, and thinking is not an event in space.

The only ground for materialism that is even worth considering is that the mind, though different from the body, is a *product* of the body, or an *inseparable accompaniment* of the body. If we say, with the French physician, Cabanis (1757–1808), that "the brain secretes thought as the liver secretes bile," we are obliged to take the word "secrete" in a Pick-

[4] See Ch. 29.

wickian sense: it is a secretion which has no chemical character. But it may be that when the brain acts in a certain way, *thought takes place,* as an effect of a non-spatial kind.

This is Büchner's position,—not that the brain and its operations *are* the mind, but that they are the producers of the mind: "that the brain is the *organ* of thought, and that these two, brain and thought, stand in such an immediate and necessary connection that neither can exist with-out the other." [5]

But this position evidently raises the question, How is it that, while everywhere else in nature motion produces motion and, as far as the physical account goes, nothing else, here in the brain motion produces sensation and thought?

Does naturalism really explain the mind, or does its explanation run a circuit which completes itself by cutting the mind out, just as it excluded the qualities which the mind perceives?

To make clear this contrast between the mind and the brain (or any other physical object), let us note certain specific points of difference.

a. The mind observes itself; the brain does not. This was the point of Pascal's observation of the greatness and littleness of the human being. As compared with the mountain, the man is minute; the mountain may crush him. But the man (in so far as he is a mind) has this point of superiority, that he knows he is being crushed, whereas the mountain does not know of its own superiority. As knower of the infinity of the universe of nature, man is the greater thing.[6]

b. The brain is in space; the mind is not. If this is not at once obvious, experiment with a few questions which imply that the mind is in space, such as these:

Where is it? Is it in the head? Is it out in front? What are its size and its shape? Is it harder to think of a long distance than of a short distance? Is it a longer thought? Is the thought of a cube a cubic thought? Are the several thoughts in the same mind at any one time above or below one another? Can they become crowded? Can the capacity of the mind become exhausted, so that no more ideas can be inserted? Does a great thought require more head-room than a petty one? No doubt the thought of an object is in some fashion *with* the object, and while, as an activity of thinking, it is quite different from the object, as comprehending or being with the object it is affected by the qualities of the object. Hence the thought of the universe, or of all of space, while not a spacious thought,

[5] Büchner, *Force and Matter*, Ch. 12 on "Brain and Soul."
[6] See Pascal, *Pensées*, §§72, 346–348 (Modern Library).

does imply by the instantaneous flash of understanding which grasps what is intended a certain infinitude in the reach of the mind. But in whatever sense the mind is related to space when space is thought of, it includes the whole of space in its intention, and is therefore not "in" space. In this sense, also, it is obviously far from being identical with the brain, which is one of the objects in space which we can think *about*, not only think *with*.

c. The brain is in the present only: the mind is extended in time to the past and the future.

When you try to explain memory by traces in the brain left by past experiences, you must consider that those traces are present traces. When they are aroused, you have an image of the past event. How does it differ from present impressions? It is fainter. Yes: but faintness is not pastness. For the brain, the past is gone. Nothing can locate an image in the past except a mind which holds the past before it. And so with the future.

d. The brain is a set of facts: the mind is a set of facts and their *meanings*.

A fact has a *meaning* when it stands for something else, as a vertical cross for addition. A fact *means* whatever it points to or leads to beyond itself. A news-stand means a chance for a paper; "a red sky at morning" means "sailor take warning"; a certain boat whistle means to the pilot passing to starboard; a certain animal track means to the hunter the recent neighborhood of his game. To Sherlock Holmes, every minute fact means something; intelligence might be measured by the amount of meaning facts have for the mind.

In the brain there are facts, but no meanings. What is a meaning for the mind is a *connection* for the brain: the five-o'clock whistle is connected (or "associated") with the muscular activities of quitting work. But a connection is not a meaning. The physical fact, to itself, is meaningless. To the mind, nothing is meaningless.

e. Among these meanings are the *qualities* we were speaking of [7] and in particular *pleasure and pain*.

We avoid the fire because fire *means* the pain of getting burned; we seek the mountains or the sea in summer because they *mean* certain types of pleasure. The brain *per se* cannot enjoy or suffer. The mind cannot escape joy and suffering: no experience is completely neutral. The mind is occupied with *values*. The brain is a system of facts.

In particular, the mind is occupied with *moral values*, judgments of right and wrong. It is there, perhaps, that we feel the difference between brain and mind most sharply. On its physical side what we call a crime

[7] §6.4.

may be a very simple operation, such as pulling a trigger. And if pulling that trigger is a mechanically necessary result of heredity and environment, the word crime and the meaning of moral reproach it carries are out of place. If we could regard the world simply as a set of facts, we should not so much as prefer virtue and its results to vice and its results. The Universal Robots could lose a hand or a limb without pain: they could be junked without crime.[8] Or if we could retain our preferences for some results rather than others, we might still regard the criminal as a disordered machine, and call the doctor rather than the judge.

Thus, one book on criminology has to say that "most crimes come about through disturbances of the ductless glands in the criminal or through mental defects caused by endocrine troubles in the criminal's mother."[9] Like the rest of us, on this theory, the criminal is devoid of free will; but he suffers from a "criminal imperative" which should relieve him from the moral reprobation we continue to feel toward each other, naturalists apparently sharing this feeling with the rest of mankind. In the case of the criminal, glandular medication should replace moral criticism and punishment.

But—not doubting that the mentally diseased criminal must have medical care—it is impossible for the sound human being to be morally neutral, just as it is impossible for him to ignore his sense of pleasure and pain. The brain is indifferent to right and wrong. To the mind, this is one of the most important of distinctions.

These differences between the mind and that physical object we call the brain and nervous system, or the entire functioning organism, suggest at every point that the mind is something not only different from the body, but *more than* the body. They emphasize the query whether naturalism can explain the mind as a product of nature, the greater by the less.[10]

6.6. *Does naturalism explain truth?* According to naturalism, a thought is an effect of some preceding cause. Change the cause and you change the thought. A man's philosophy would then be the result of the causes that act upon him, including his own inherited temperament. Hindu mysticism might be due, say, to the enervating effect of a hot climate; Schopenhauer's pessimism to a disordered liver.

But in this case, of what temperamental bias or atmospheric influence is naturalism the effect? What change of diet will turn the naturalist into

---

[8] See Karel Capek's play, *R.U.R.*

[9] M. G. Schlapp and E. H. Smith, *The New Criminology* (New York, 1928).

[10] For a development of this discussion of the peculiarities of the mind which make it irreducible to a function of the body, see Hocking, *The Self, Its Body and Freedom* (New Haven, 1928), pp. 28–49.

a mystic? If philosophy is the result of such causes, what is to guarantee its truth? If naturalism explains our thoughts in this cause-and-effect manner, does it not undermine its own case?

In a review of James Harvey Robinson's *Mind in the Making*, H. G. Wells has this to say:

> "I do not know who it was who first said that the human mind being a product of the struggle for existence was essentially a food-seeking system, and no more essentially a truth-finding apparatus than the snout of a pig. I believe it must have been Arthur Balfour, twenty-five or thirty years ago.[11]

> "It is upon the lines of this suggestion, it is upon a profound scepticism of the truth-testing instrument, that the new school of thought is going. Our minds, the most fundamental of our presuppositions, are as much a response to immediate necessities and as much the outcome of a process of trial, error, and adaptation as our bodies; they are as little to be relied on in new situations as our animal instincts. . . ."

Wells's inference from the naturalistic theory of mentality is quite legitimate. But this consequence is at variance with what we mean by truth. Truth does not vary with the climate; nor does our apprehension of it vary (consistently) with these variable causes. The multiplication table, the principles of logic, work in the same way for us at the equator and at the poles; what is true in physics and chemistry holds true for us whatever our state of health or temperament. Naturalism fails to account for the mind as a knower of truth. Reason is not a part of the chain of physical causes and effects.

Naturalistic psychology can give causal explanation of our errors: it is at home there. It cannot explain our reasonable deeds and thoughts.

> "Let a reasonable being make a mistake in his thinking, and his mistake immediately becomes a phenomenon for psychology. If I add two and two and get four, the result has nothing to do with the climate, the state of my nerves, or my personal idiosyncracies. It is no function of any *event* in heaven or earth. But if I should get five, an enquiry into these conditions would at once become relevant. There is no reason for going wrong; there is no cause for going right. Hence psychology is peculiarly interested in errors and illusions. It might almost be called the science of human fallibility." [12]

If we were completely causal beings, why should we feel it so much a matter of pride to be treated as rational? And why should we experience such deep resentment at being "managed"? Psychology, we were saying, can be applied to every situation in which human beings can be *managed*: but in what situations can this take place?

It is applied, for example, to advertising. But let me discover that the advertiser on the advice of the psychologist has artfully designed his picture of the family group assembled around the evening table for the

---

[11] Slander! W.E.H.   [12] Hocking, *Man and the State* (New Haven, 1926), p. 202.

sake of playing on my domestic instincts and inducing me to buy his lamp-shades, and my heart is at once hardened. When I find out that I am being managed, the causal series fails to work. Let me learn the trick of the dramatic play on my emotions, and I cease to be moved. But what kind of a science is that which ceases to be true when its laws are found out! It certainly does not work to treat the human being as if he were a thing of cause and effect, unless you can keep it from him as a dark secret that you are doing so. There must then be something false in the assumptions of the causal psychology. The human being is something more than a creature of cause and effect.

6.7. There are some features of the world which naturalism does not profess to explain: it regards them as inexplicable,—we must simply take them as given matters of fact.

If you explain an event by a law, that leaves the law unexplained. I see a steel rail buckled in the sun; and this is explained to me by the law that heat expands metals. But why does heat expand metals? This is explained by reference to a more general law of the collision of particles in motion. This law may in turn be explained by a wider law: but the last law in the series, while it explains all the others, is left unexplained.

Further, naturalism accepts the ingredients of the world, their quantity and proportion, and their arrangement, as given facts. They are here, and that is the end of it. We explain their rearrangements; we do not attempt to explain their presence. Hence the naturalist's rejection of the cosmo-logical argument.[13]

If we suggest that leaving these things unexplained casts a shadow on the completeness of the naturalistic philosophy, we are told that no one can do any better. In every philosophy, what exists must be taken as given. Our knowledge cannot penetrate into the secrets of absolute creation.

But before we accept this closing of the door to understanding, we have a further question to put. In the strictly naturalistic view, "efficient causes" have driven out "final causes," that is, to explain a thing by causal law excludes its explanation by purpose. Is this true? Can the two types of explanation exist together? This deserves a separate enquiry.

[13] §4.2.

CHAPTER 7:
THE NEWER TELEOLOGY

7.1. *Causality and purpose*. In ordinary language, we speak of the cause of an event as some other event (or group of events) which immediately preceded the given event and, as we suppose, required it to be. Causes precede and, as it were, push their effects into being. The blows of a maul upon a wedge drive the wedge into the wood, and heat the wedge. There is no question in our minds which is cause and which the effects. Causality we might roughly describe as the determining of events from behind in time. Purpose on the contrary is the determining of events from ahead in time. One who has a purpose sees ahead to a future state of things which he wishes to bring about, and works toward it. It is this picture of future and as yet non-existent things which animates his present action. It would not be wholly astray if we should say that causality works from the past into the present, and purpose from the future into the present; though evidently the event which is purposed as well as the event which is caused is moving in the direction of all temporal events from the present toward the future. All physical events, we believe, lie in some causal series. All mental events, we believe, lie in some purposive sequence; for there is no mind, so far as we know, which is devoid of preference or choice and the disposition to act for what it chooses. Now our question is, Are these two types of process mutually exclusive? If we have a world in which everything is in causal order, must we dismiss the notion that there is purpose in it?

In the case of a machine, no one doubts that it operates by mechanical causes. It is not the driver of an automobile who makes the car go. On the other hand, the assembling of the machine in the first place, and its guidance seem determined by the end in view, the purpose, Aristotle's "final cause." But the driver himself is in part a mechanism; and materialistic naturalism says altogether so.[1] In any case his purpose is a fact which cannot be abolished. He pictures himself, at a future moment, in some particular place; and that end, which seems to him to govern his actions, coexists with the mechanism of his body. It may be a good maxim for the

[1] §3.1.

scientific mind not to *fall back* on final causes when it is studying nature: but it is clearly a mistake to suppose that all purpose must be excluded. For there it is—a fact of experience. And it has found some way of living together with the mechanical or "efficient" causes.

7.2. Let us examine more carefully the working of causes and purposes.

Causal action cannot be observed. We observe only the sequence of events. The sun rises and the air becomes warm; we note the sequence, but we do not observe the sun's rays causing the warmth. The axe falls and the wood falls apart: we do not see the force of the wedge splitting the wood. The moving picture, or the stage blow, gives us an equally convincing spectacle of causality though there is no force at work in either case. Causation cannot be perceived. This is Hume's proposition.[2]

Why, then, are we so sure about causal laws? We *believe* that all events have a cause; and this belief leads us to try to fit events together. There must be some cause, we believe, for the gradual warming of the day; and as the sun is changing its position somewhat in proportion to the change of heat, we easily make the connection.

But what is the source of that belief that every event must have a cause?

Hume thought it a result of mental habit. When we observe often and without exception that event B follows event A, we expect every A to be followed by a B. Repeated confirmation of such expectations in a great variety of instances of sequence induces the generalized belief that for every event a cause can be found. The real force of the belief in causality lies in the strength of our expectation. If Hume is right, it is only probable, not certain, that every event has a cause. There is no way to prove it.

Without attempting to pass judgment on Hume's argument, we must give him credit for having called attention (of Kant among others) to the great difficulty of vindicating even what used to be called the "causal axiom,"—that every event must have a cause, and a sufficient cause. Causality is *imputed to* the world-order, rather than seen in it.

Now the perception of purposes is in very much the same case. We do not see purposes: we impute them. Here is a train at the station, and here a man running toward it and boarding it. We seem to have seen the man running *for the train*; but we have seen only the sequence of events,—the purpose is inserted by our conjecture.

We read purposes (or motives) into human conduct at a well-known risk: the "imputing of motives" is notoriously liable to error. The risk is

[2] Hume, *An Enquiry Concerning the Human Understanding*, Sections IV and VII.

greater when we impute motives to animals. If we venture beyond the animal realm into the world at large, we take still greater risks.

Yet, as we can neither prove that every event has a cause nor disprove it, so we can neither prove nor disprove that *every event has a purpose*. The failure to find a cause does not disprove its existence: no more does the failure to find a purpose disprove its existence.

It is logically possible that every event has *both a cause and a purpose* or meaning.

7.3. And it is also logically possible that those features of the world which causality leaves unexplained, such as the highest natural law, as well as the amount, proportion, distribution of the matter and motion of the world, have a meaning and thus a possible purpose.

Purpose may be appealed to to explain *quantities*. Thus, the bow of William the Conqueror: Why is it just so large? There is no mechanical answer, but purpose explains it at once. It must be stout enough to defy all other arms: it must be not so stout as to defy his own. The quantities of the world may have a meaning.

7.4. Note that we are only talking about logical possibilities. All we say, so far, is that even if we could explain every event by its causes, there would still be room for explaining the same events by their purposes. But we should not be justified in asserting such purposes unless we had some positive ground for doing so.

When have we such ground? Evidently, in the first place, the result must have *some assignable value*. The waves wash the sand up and wash it out again; our ideas of purpose find here nothing to light on. The production of an oak-tree or of the vertebrate animals or of man or of a sunset, however, seems to have some worth, and our thoughts pause to enquire whether that value could have been intended. But, in the second place, there must be some evidence that the process *tends to preserve* what it has produced. And there is no evidence that anything tends to retain the sunset. Organic bodies are in a different case: they are produced, and preserved by the processes of nature. But even yet, we would hardly have enough ground to assert purpose unless we could see that *the means* by which the result was brought about were somehow *selected* from many other possible sets of causes, and not merely random combinations of events.

Is there any evidence of this sort that nature, or any of the features of nature, may be regarded as results of purpose, at the same time that they are results of causality?

7.5. Now the several steps of "emergent evolution"—taking the step from inorganic to organic forms, then from the non-mental to the mental, then from the sub-rational to the rational as the chief of such events—seem to our judgment to have brought forth something of value, and also to have preserved what has been brought forth, at least to the present time. But is there any evidence of the selection of means?

The naturalistic believer in emergence relies on causality alone; and in doing so he makes use of an *unavowed assumption,* namely, that changes of form being implied in the constant motion of the ingredients of the world, *given sufficient time all possible forms must be arrived at, all possible arrangements of the ultimate units of the world,* so that eventually organisms were bound to happen. Let us examine this very common and plausible assumption.

Create an imaginary universe. Let it consist of four particles set at the four corners of an exact square; and endowed with gravitative attraction for each other, and with perfect elasticity. The history of this universe can be precisely foretold through all eternity. The four particles will first move toward each other along the diagonals of the square. They will click together at the same instant, and being elastic will return to the exact point of departure (supposing we gave them no initial velocity); they will then repeat the cycle and continue without variation forever.

Now create another universe like the former, with a single difference. Let one particle be slightly off the corner of the square. Can you now predict the history? They will move toward one another as before; but they will not click at the same instant. The rebound will be irregular, and none of them will arrive precisely at the point of departure. The subsequent journeys will show an increase of irregularity for a time depending on the degree of the original malformation. But one thing we may say with entire certainty: at no time will the four particles of this second universe form a perfect square.

And since the particles of our first universe are never in any other relation than that of a perfect square, we may say with equal certainty that throughout eternity the particles of the two universes never fall into the same figure. In general, an original symmetry will always give symmetrical configurations; and an original asymmetry will always beget asymmetry.

It is evidently false then to assume that any given universe must run through all the possible configurations of its particles if we give it time enough. And if this is true of the picayune universes we have been experimenting with; how much more is it the case of the actual universe, that its entire history is a unique series of configurations, from which an infinitude of possible configurations of those same particles are forever excluded as unrealized. The common belief that in infinite time the stuff of the world must arrange itself in every possible way, therefore in this present way, is one of the few errors of which we may conservatively say that it is infinitely wide of the mark!

We may then assert that the assumption on which the naturalistic emergentist relies is unfounded: *form has no inherent tendency to rise.* If it does rise, it is as if the series of shapes which constitute the causal history of the universe were selected from an infinite number of possible other shapes. And the grounds required for applying the idea of purpose are present. Emergent evolution is as if it were the result of intention.

7.6. This is a generalized form of what L. J. Henderson undertakes to show in a highly concrete manner in his book, *The Fitness of the Environment.* The result in which he is interested is the production of organisms. They are results worth producing. But it is easy to imagine universes with slightly different proportions of these same materials—let us say a little more nitrogen and a little less carbon or oxygen—which would have rendered not only such organisms as we know but any organisms at all impossible.[3] Of all the possible universes (with ingredients like these) the present one is nearly the fittest for the production of organisms. It is thus reasonable to call it *biocentric.* There is, it appears, a principle of teleology in the structure of the universe—or a possible principle of this sort—which the criticism of the teleological argument cannot exclude.

Professor Henderson avoids the word purpose; he leaves the nature of the end-reaching tendency for metaphysics to decide. He does not allow that this tendency ever interferes with the perfect mechanism of nature. It does all its work "at the very origin of things, just before mechanism begins to act."[4] Whether in the course of evolution life arose from dead matter, Henderson does not try to decide; but if it did, "that is surely the crowning and most wonderful instance of teleology in the whole universe."

To summarize the argument in its total effect: If we regard organic life as something worth the labor of a universe to produce, it *cannot be excluded as a possibility* that the entire configuration of this particular universe represents an original choice, or loading of the dice, with that end in view. And if this were the case, the purpose or aim thus expressed would be prior to, and something else than, the "nature" it has chosen. To

---

[3] At this point, note a logical weakness in Henderson's argument which the argument of §7.5. avoids. The change in the proportions of ingredients would render organisms impossible only if the *laws* of physics and biology remain constant. But why, if we are altering the universe, not consider the laws as altered also? And so altered that organisms could flourish?

[4] Henderson, *The Fitness of the Environment* (New York, 1913), p. 308.

understand nature, we must then go beyond nature, and into the region of mental things; to this extent, naturalism yields to spiritualism—as a conceivable view of the world.

To estimate the force of this argument we should have to judge the proportion of the number of possible configurations that would admit living beings to the number that would exclude them. How would you calculate this proportion? Consider that moving any original particle out of its original place, by any amount however small, would on naturalist assumptions entail a different world through all time; and consider that the number of such particles is very large, perhaps of the order of the entire series of whole numbers; then the number of different possible universes would be, let us say conservatively, infinitely infinite. I judge that an infinite number of these would admit life; but that the ratio of this infinitude to the infinitude of total possibility is less than $1/\infty$. In other words, if the configuration of the given particles were a random cast, the chances for life would be nearly zero.

But why assume just those given particles?

If we are at liberty to suppose a purpose capable of determining the arrangement of particles, there is no assignable reason to deny it the capacity to determine the particles themselves. And with this supposition, we would conclude that everything that occurs in the universe,—not only the existence of organisms in general, but the existence of each particular organism, each person, of John Smith and Richard Roe, is a purposed result of the world-churning through measureless time. Also the undesirable aspects of the world, with the desirable aspects. Does the liberty of hypothesizing load upon the assumed purpose *too much?*

We must press this reflection to the end. The decisive matter is this: that nothing is important, nothing whatever, except to a conscious being. If there is no consciousness in the universe, the universe has no importance, absolutely none. To produce the tiniest squeak of consciousness, anywhere at any time, would be to make all the difference between meaninglessness and importance, for the whole affair. It is only then that the question, Is the labor worth while? could arise. From this point of view, any person is justified in regarding his own existence as an end, worth the labor of the cosmos to achieve. For whatever being is able to raise the question of worth does by his existence answer the question in the affirmative.

But is the hypothesis that a purpose determined the configuration and the particles configured—is that hypothesis genuine? Not unless we can conceive *how purpose could so operate.* Here the argument ciphers. It has no suggestion to offer, as to how purpose could effect or affect these aboriginal data. It is, in fact, an invitation to imagine the unimaginable. As an hypothesis, it fails not partially but absolutely.

We now see why it is that our two opposing metaphysical views,—what we have called "the primary division or polarity in belief" [5]—continue their debate through the ages. Neither one, on the grounds we have so far found, can exclude the other as a possibility. Each, through its criticism of the other, provokes an evolution in that other which strengthens its statement and appeal. The elements of Spiritualism in Plato, in Aristotle, in Plotinus are firmer than those in Socrates. The elements of Naturalism in Epicurus and Lucretius are firmer than those in Democritus. And in the immense advances of thought in the sixteenth and seventeenth centuries in Europe, when in the short space of a hundred years, from Copernicus (1473–1543) to Galileo (1564–1642) the work which gave natural science its freedom was in principle accomplished, and the Newtonian world-view given a three-century lease of life, both Naturalism and Theism (as the central form of Spiritualism) reached new heights of clarity and completeness.

But a standing opposition, without resolution, is a condition which human thought unwillingly entertains forever. It stirs up a new question, how can we decide? how can we know? It requires a new phase of philosophy, an enquiry into the ways human beings *think*, and whether there are limits to what we can know and understand. Are there perhaps permanent riddles before which we halt as man before the eternal Sphinx? Herewith we are impelled to take up Epistemology, the problem of Knowledge.

[5] Above, §4.3.

PART II

EPISTEMOLOGY

CHAPTER 8

TYPE II · PRAGMATISM
CHAPTERS 9–10

TYPE III · INTUITIONISM
CHAPTERS 11–15

CHAPTER 8:
MISGIVINGS ABOUT REASON

8.1. *What can we know?* Having considered one type of world-view, naturalism, against the background of another, spiritualism, we have gained some experience of the difficulty of reaching *certainty* in metaphysics.

Naturalism, as a rule, has been an expression of great confidence in human reason. Its case has often been presented as a case of reason against faith. Yet anything like a strict proof of its case has not been forthcoming: it is extraordinarily difficult to prove that something—whether black swans or supernature—does *not* exist. And naturalism has led by its own logic, strangely enough, to a doubt about the capacity of reason in metaphysics: if reasoning is *caused*, and caused by the unreasoning energies of nature, it has no guarantee of working true.

We are therefore ready for a review of the question, What we human beings are fitted to know, and Whether there are limits definite or indefinite to the successful use of reason. The history of philosophy includes in its records many outspoken critics of the philosophic enterprise (a clear-headed critic of philosophy must be a philosopher).[1] There are the sceptics, who doubt the validity of reason everywhere, the agnostics and strict positivists who doubt its validity in the special field of metaphysics, and a series of "anti-intellectualists" who claim that we can indeed reach metaphysical truth, but by the aid of some organ other than the intellect or logical reason. Such anti-intellectualists are the pragmatists and the intuitionists. We shall consider in turn each of these "ways of knowing," giving especial attention to the two last named. We must begin with a fair look at our natural confidence in reason.

8.2. *Pre-philosophical rationalism.* Men naturally trust their reasoning power. Or rather, it does not naturally occur to them to distrust it. We reason, as we breathe, without being aware that we are doing it, and hence without calling into question our power to do it successfully. Our attention is given not to the act of thinking, but to the object thought about: it

---

[1] As Pascal put it, "Se moquer de la philosophie, c'est vraiment philosopher."

hardly occurs to us that we are using a special tool or instrument which may fail or mislead us. It is a part of our animal self-confidence that we assume we can think successfully, and get a true view of our environment. In this sense, we are born *rationalists*. But what is this "reason" that we so spontaneously trust?

Since we are unaware of effort in exercising what we call common sense, the moment-by-moment use of reason, we are pleasantly unconscious of employing any logical technique. If we hear a dull roar overhead, and judge "an airplane, flying low," are we using induction, or deduction, or both? For our self-awareness, neither one; yet presumably both processes are present, and in close conjunction. For consider:

Suppose yourself stepping on ice for the first time; suppose a slip and a fall. Suppose then your next step taken with a newly acquired caution. A thinking process has swiftly intervened. The psychologist's report is likely to be that your perception of this hard, shiny surface recognized as "ice" has now "associated" with it a new quality, "slippery." The logician's report, as analytical, has to be more detailed: he says that from a single instance you have generalized, "ice is slippery," an induction. Thereupon, you have immediately used this generality as premiss for a deduction: "Since ice (meaning all ice) is slippery; and since (as minor premiss) my next step is also on ice, that too will present slipperiness, i. e., the possibility of a fall." Hence your caution. The simplest case of "learning from experience" has thus its internal complexity: the psychologist's "association" is the logician's "induction-and-deduction." Each report is valid for its own special interests: we accept them both.

Experience has the repute of being an eminent teacher. Growing to maturity consists in part in acquiring through experience a store of generalities sufficient to guide, by deduction, all usual occasions of decision. Are we wrong, or "hasty" when we thus generalize from single cases? On the contrary, we have no choice; for we can only learn from experience if we live in a world in which single things and events exhibit universal traits. *This* generality we cannot learn from experience, for only by assuming it is such learning a reasonable process. Our "reason" then contains some generalities not taught by experience, but—as the phrase is— *a priori*.

Every event thus carries its generality; it is easy, however, to make a wrong generalization. "Ice is firm," another sweeping induction, is perhaps valid in January, possibly not so in May. The accuracy of induction is not supplied by the event: *experience, as a set of observed events, teaches nothing*: it is we who make the induction, and in doing so we must "use judgment,"—we must have some inkling as to why and under what conditions ice is firm. *Intelligence,* human or animal, is *primarily good judgment,* extracting from the rill of experience the right inductions; and drawing from what we thus know, the right deductions. Good judgment, as a presiding sense of the whole situation and its internal necessities, cannot be formulated, and in consequence logicians and psychologists have given it too little notice. It is a third factor of our natural reasoning processes.

I have spoken of our spontaneous trust in reason as an "animal self-confidence." For though man has been defined as "the reasoning animal," in the behavior of many animals we must recognize the same processes of induction and deduction, guided by judgment. Let me, for example, recommend the red squirrel. Try to hang a box for bird-food in such wise that red squirrel cannot get into it. Hang it from the under side of porch rafters; cover the slanting roof of the bird-box with aluminum flashing, such as no squirrel has ever encountered. Squirrel will try it, and will probably have a fall. He will retire to the grape vine for meditation, with due chattering. He has made the necessary induction about aluminum surfaces, but his judgment suggests the possibility of sliding to a corner support of the box. He comes up with a new idea, defined as a "plan of action." In any such contest between squirrel wit and human wit, it is commonly safe to bet on the squirrel, at least for a time.

And obviously, the arts of domesticating animals, and of hunting, fishing, trapping, depend for success on giving the animal full credit for that more-than-mechanical intelligence, able to adjust itself to new and artificial conditions. The ingenious experiments of Robert Yerkes in measuring animal intelligence have reached many surprising results, ranking crow and pig, for example, high in problem-solving capacity in the scale with his favorite subject, the chimpanzee. He found the lowly earthworm capable of learning to avoid a path on which an open electric circuit could administer a shock. I incline to the hazardous generalization that to be alive as an animal is to be, to some extent, conscious; and that to be conscious is in some degree to reason.

If I am right in my own induction from such instances, *all animals reason;* and reasoning has everywhere the same structure.[2] But man alone *knows* that he reasons; man alone expresses his inductions in language and records them; man alone begets a logic, making a conscious art of his thinking. And man alone, in reflecting about his reasoning, is able to find himself doubting the competence of reason to master all the truth into which his questionings enquire. Man's distinction from the animals, then, is not in the fact of his reasoning and his spontaneous confidence in it; it is in his capacity to doubt his reason, and to set up a "critique" thereof.

And man achieves such doubt only when he is obliged to recognize a kind of failure in the results of his thinking that he must trace to the na-

[2] In what we speak of as animal "instinct" (of which the human genus is not devoid), the relation of "stimulus" to "response" acts as an acquired generalization, the stimulus being the "sign" (or minor premiss) for the conclusion. See our discussion of instinct, pp. 114 f. In this connection, consult Hume, *An Enquiry Concerning Human Understanding,* Section IX, "Of the Reason of Animals." Hume credits men and animals alike with the power of "experimental reasoning" carried along on the basis of "custom" or habit. The deliberately reflective "process of argument" he denies to animals, and indeed attributes to men only at a high level of self-consciousness.

ture of reasoning itself. Failure in practical adjustments has no such implication; such failure calls for more and better reasoning. But where thinking results in absurdity, or wide disagreement, or a misfit between the thinker and the world he tries to master through thinking, he has reason to doubt his reasoning. Primitive world-views, the prephilosophical spiritualisms, seldom lead to this embarrassment, because they evade direct encounter with experience. They generally leave intact the equally prephilosophical confidence in reason, until the early naturalisms (like Thales' attempt to derive everything from water) set up rival views, and call for decision. Philosophical rationalism, as a reasoned affirmation of reason, cannot arrive until there has been a reasoned doubt of reason. It will come as an answer to scepticism; we shall therefore have to follow the course of this natural trust to and through its encounter with the difficulties that compel its self-review.

8.3. No doubt, ever since the animal mind conceived the idea of an unknown whole, that is, ever since the evolving creature became human, he has been aware that there is *a beyond*—a region within the whole, but beyond his perceptive grasp. He has judged that this beyond contains "secrets" whose penetration is difficult. And he has been to this extent modest about his own powers of reason, that he has deferred his judgment on these beyond-matters to special persons of his group who appeared to be more conversant with the region, or better qualified for solving the deeper riddles, than others. Hence the primitive philosophy, in religious form, was handed down from the skilled knowers to the unskilled masses authoritatively; philosophy was a privileged knowledge, a "revelation" which could be taken as true, and ought to be so taken, without the critical checking-up of individual judgment. Thus the majority got their philosophy, if not entirely without thinking, yet without other thinking than that required to understand more or less vaguely what they were told. This way of getting a philosophy had one advantage; it enabled whole tribes, perhaps nations, to believe together, and so to act on a common faith.

But vigorous brain-power can never have been a complete monopoly of the officially learned, the medicine-men, the Brahmins, the monks, the priests. Although we cannot say that in mentality all men are created equal, still, as Hobbes shrewdly remarks, there is one sign of approximate equality, that "each is content with his share!" [3] Any lively society, with a spark of science in it, will beget its independent thinkers who will work out a

---

[3] See also Descartes, *Discourse on Method*, Part I: "Good sense is of all things in the world the most equally distributed, for everybody thinks himself so abundantly provided with it, that even those most difficult to please in all other matters do not commonly desire more of it than they already possess."

world-view for themselves which may or may not coincide with the traditional view. When this happens, the day of undisputed authority, and also of philosophic agreement, is past. In addition to the generally received creed, we have here and there "a philosophy," i. e., some notable thinker's special creation, identified with his name, and bringing together as many minds as he can persuade to think like himself.

We are not to think of these early philosophies as made by lone thinkers of great personal daring, in hostility to prevailing religious ideas. Very likely many of them arose in groups of alert-minded friends, who worked out their views together, in conversation; their aim being not so much to dissent from tradition as to get a literal grasp of its vaguely poetic or symbolic language. The early philosophers of Greece were often prominent members of groups or "schools" of active minds, much occupied with the scientific and political interests of their day. One of the most interesting of them, Pythagoras (c. 572–497 B. C.) was at once a mathematician, a philosopher, and founder of a fraternity aiming at the moral reformation of society. It is no accident that the same age which brought forth the first democracies, showing in politics its confidence in the general ability of the human crowd to *think*, also brought forth the first secular *philosophies* of the western world.

Naturalism, as we noted, is one of the early results of this independent rationalism; and throughout the history of human thought it has usually been, as the most thoroughly anti-theological type of philosophy, the product of an unusually sturdy confidence in human reason. The word "rationalist" was once equivalent, in English usage, to the "free-thinker" who had renounced his faith in the supernatural. Thomas Paine's *Age of Reason* is an American echo of the spirit of the French "Enlightenment" which, in giving birth to the Revolution, found it fitting to crown Reason as its goddess. Probably no subsequent age has been so confident of the sufficiency of reason to solve the riddles of the universe.

If, then, naturalism leads, as we saw, to the logical consequence that reason is a defective instrument for getting philosophic truth, this result is somewhat of a blow to the temper in which naturalism itself was begotten. Nevertheless, there are many considerations independent of naturalism which conspire to this same conclusion—distrust of the power of reason; some of them have led thoughtful men to scepticism ever since serious philosophic effort began.

8.4. *Sophistry.* One of these considerations is the simple fact of *philosophical disagreement*. If the results of independent reasoning are out of accord with tradition, they are also very quickly out of accord with each other, and we have a succession of differing "schools" of philosophy. Each philosopher, with a sense of final discovery, adds a new opinion to the now long list of world-views; and the history of philosophy may well appear as a gallery of ambitious failures. These individual philosophies do not appear to fuse into a growing body of established truth, as do the results of natural science; and the suspicion lies near that the philosophic undertaking is somehow less natural than the scientific,—may be beyond the natural scope of human reason.

The more anemic and easily discouraged minds have been inclined, from ancient days, to counsel retreat; to give up the effort of possessing beliefs and take one's mental and moral ease in superficial living. They become the "misologists" [4] or malcontents of reason described by Socrates in the *Phædo*. Socrates speaks as one who has gone through this trouble himself, and simply admonishes his friends not to indulge in a peevish blaming of "reason," when the proper object of blame is the *reasoner*, i. e., our own stupidity. Socrates probably had in mind the Sophists of his time, the professional teachers of the art of rhetoric and debate, some of whom, assuming that truth is out of reach, counselled their students, as the best equipment for success in public life, to be ready to take *any side* of an argument. This breed is not yet entirely extinct.

8.5. *Scepticism and its limits.* Others, of a greater mental vigor, seeing reason caught in difficulties, try to find a reason for those difficulties, thus bringing reason to the diagnosis of its own disease. They may reach something like a reasoned proof that reason is incompetent, as one may prove in mechanics that perpetual motion is impossible, or in mathematics that the circle cannot be squared. They then become, in the technical sense, "sceptics," like Gorgias and Pyrrho among the ancient Greeks, or Hume in modern times.[5]

The Greek sceptics had before them a peculiarly interesting case of the opposition of philosophical results. Their predecessors had agreed that the senses are deceitful, and that reason is given us to correct their false reports. But as to what our senses tell us and our reason, opposite opinions had been taught. One school, that of the Eleatics, had contended that the senses show us things as perpetually changing and passing away, whereas reason discovers that reality is permanent and unchanging. Another school, that of Heracleitus, had taught that the senses show us things as stable, whereas reason, looking deeper, discerns that "all things flow." Under

---

[4] Misology: hatred and despair of reason.

[5] See the Platonic dialogue, *Gorgias*; Diogenes Laërtius, *Lives*, IX, 61, Loeb Classical Library (London and New York, 1925); David Hume, *An Inquiry Concerning Human Understanding*, Sec. XII, and his *Treatise on Human Nature*, Bk. I, Ch. IV.

these circumstances, argued the sceptics, how can we trust either sense or reason? The trouble seemed to be that our ideas fit the facts of experience so loosely that opposite judgments may be made with equal justification. Zeno, the Eleatic, had given a certain notoriety to the work of reason by propounding his famous paradoxes [6] in order to show that our ideas of number, rest and motion could not be strictly applied without entangling us in contradictions. Gorgias and Pyrrho carried a similar logic into all the work of reason, and concluded that it is not the part of wisdom to hold any conviction firmly, but rather to maintain an easy reserve toward every belief, and keep the mind serenely free—from fanaticism, of course, but also from those commitments which attend all clear decision in belief.

This counsel, if one could carry it out, would lead to an ideal poise, indifference, and practical uselessness such as no living man has ever attained. But if one could be sceptical enough to be moderate also about his scepticism (as Pyrrho proposed) this attitude might lend an easy urbanity to the manners, and a supple opportunism to the character, which would allow a man to float genially with a noble superiority to all earnest purpose in a society whose hard work was done by others. The most attractive examples of this type are to be found in men of the world who, having reached that philosophy which consists in a contempt of philosophy, a graceful and sophisticated aloofness of mind, cherish the sentiment of Montaigne, "How kindly and healthful a cushion are ignorance and incuriousness for a well-conducted head."

In so far as scepticism results from unusually keen mental criticism, it is of the utmost use in philosophy. Our mental workshop must be able to stand the severest inspection, especially inspection by reason itself. The sceptic may be the most idle of thinkers; but he may also be the most earnest,—being sceptical because he desires to entrust his life to nothing short of a completely certain foundation.

Thus the good faith of philosophy is shown in its welcoming the sincere sceptic, including him among the philosophers, and attempting by his aid to reach a just estimate of the powers of reason. The development of philosophy is largely due to this scrupulous consideration of every legitimate doubt. Socrates himself was not less cautious than the keenest Sophist. He was aware of his own ignorance; he was puzzled when the Delphic

---

[6] See esp. the paradoxes of Achilles and the Tortoise and of the Moving Arrow. A statement of these paradoxes follows: (1) If the tortoise is ahead of Achilles, Achilles can never catch it. For when Achilles reaches the place where the tortoise was, the tortoise is at some distance farther on; when Achilles reaches this farther point, the tortoise has gone still farther. And so on, ad infinitum. (2) The arrow must move either where it is or where it is not. But it cannot move where it is not. Nor yet can it move where it is; for to be where it is is not to move. Hence it cannot move at all. There are eight of these paradoxes, some of which appear to us as verbal subtleties; nevertheless, easier to dismiss than to analyze.

oracle said that no man in Athens was wiser than he; his solution of this puzzle was his reflection (the nerve of the Socratic "irony") that to know that one does not know is a highly important kind of knowledge. For this knowledge separates one by a wide gulf from the self-confident ignoramus who is unaware of his own deficiency; and, further, it starts one on the right road to gain genuine knowledge.[7] At the threshold of the modern era, Nicolas of Cusa in the same spirit wrote a treatise *On the Instructed Ignorance*.[8] Descartes (1596–1650) deliberately adopted the method of trying to push doubt to its extremest point, in order to find at least one proposition which could not be doubted. In his *Meditations on First Philosophy*, he imagines himself supposing

"that all the things I see are fictitious; that none of the objects my memory represents ever existed; that I have no real sense of an outer world: that body with its shape, extension, motion or position, is but a fiction of my mind. What, then, can be held to as true? Perhaps only this, that there is nothing certainly true. . . . But if, with the other bodies, I thus doubt the existence of my own body, does not this carry with it a suspicion that I myself do not exist? Hardly so, since it is I who do the suspecting! But may there not be some malignant Being of supreme power and cunning who is carrying an ingenious deception into the very centre of my life? Even then, if I am deceived, I must exist. No deception can bring it about that I am nothing, so long as I am aware of myself as a conscious being. Then this proposition, I am, is necessarily true, every time I frame it." [9]

The best doubter cannot doubt that he is doubting, and in doubting, he is thinking, acting, therefore necessarily *existing: cogito ergo sum.*

The effort to doubt everything thus leads to the discovery that there is something which cannot be doubted: a perfectly universal scepticism is impossible. The criticism of our knowing power must recognize at least one spot in which knowledge is successful. This spot, "I exist," may not appear momentous; yet, as setting a decisive boundary to scepticism its consequences might be—and were—the making of an epoch in human thought, modernity.

8.6. *Rationalism.* Taking Descartes strictly at his word, his one and only certitude was his "I exist," meaning, of course, "I, René Descartes, exist." On this purely solitary assurance of a purely solitary existence what could be built but a purely private philosophy? Descartes' actual intention went far beyond this: he intended to establish a point of beginning for *all philosophy*. He took his experience, rightly or not, as representative: his doubt was everyman's doubt; his certitude everyman's certitude. In sum,

---

[7] Read Socrates' defense of his way of life in Plato's *Apology*.
[8] *De docta ignorantia,* 1440.
[9] The whole of this memorable passage should be read by every student of philosophy. See *Meditation,* II, in *Meditations on First Philosophy,* published in 1641.

he considered his private experience as somehow universal, apparently without noting that especially he, Descartes, needed to establish his right to do so. Free from second thoughts on that score, he published to the world his personal discovery! In 1637, in the town of Leyden where he had studied, appeared his first book A *Discourse on Method*.[10]

His unavowed faith was amply vindicated by the outcome: his work was quickly and widely noted. It is common to date the beginning of "the modern period" in philosophy from his early writings: his course of doubt spoke to a widespread need. (What, after all, is the philosopher but the person who takes upon himself the burden of the world's doubt? As Socrates for antiquity, so Descartes for the arriving modern world). A widespread need, for apart from the confident young scientific movement (Galileo was still living) the Renaissance was going out in intellectual confusion.[11] Its "humanistic" side, trusting human reason for human ends, found the new cosmologies (Copernicus, 1473–1543, Bruno, 1548–1600, and successors) and the innovating logics (Peter Ramus and followers) fit ferments for discrediting the magnificent thought-systems handed down by the great theological doctors. Theology was lively in response, but its contemporary doctors were at variance among themselves: the church was rent. If semi-serious sceptics like Montaigne or Sanchez gained a wide hearing it is because among thoughtful men there existed a sense of philosophical futility.

It was this general malaise of thought that penetrated to young Descartes as a student at the Jesuit school at La Flèche. He first found relief through his initiation into mathematics. It was only later that he came to his *cogito ergo sum*, by way of seeking a certitude "equal to that of the demonstrations of arithmetic and geometry." It is in this ideal of demonstration, rather than in the certitude of I-exist, that the spirit of Rationalism is found. Descartes' *Discourse* carried an appendix on Geometry; in that appendix the principles of what we commonly term analytic geometry were first announced.

The first effect of the discussions over Descartes' work—and remembering that Sir Francis Bacon had published *Novum Organum* (1620) proposing a logic of induction—was to compel attention to the question, What can we know, and how? From this time forward for a century and a half, philosophers were disposed to put the epistemological question first: metaphysical enquiry had to show its credentials. Thus John Locke (1632–1704), center of a group of friends concerned over religion, begins with An *Essay concerning Human Understanding* (1690). Kant's *Critique of*

---

[10] *Discours de la méthode pour bien conduire sa raison.* The autobiographical element reveals itself in the *"sa"*: it is his own reason whose conduct he is explaining.

[11] See Etienne Gilson, *The Unity of Philosophical Experience,* Ch. IV.

Pure Reason (1781)—a perfect title—marks the culmination of this trend.

It is evident that the certitude on which Descartes proposed to build all philosophy was twofold, not single. The certitude, I-exist, was factual, empirical, *subjective*. The certitude of mathematics was logical; and if mathematics is the form of nature, the certitude of mathematics-in-nature could fairly be called *objective*. Descartes made it his life work to set up a system of objective sciences on the pattern of his geometry, with his metaphysics of God and the world at the summit. What is the pattern of his geometry?

Analytic geometry is in effect an applied algebra. Like all geometry, it operates not with the shapes we meet in experience, but with shapes ideally perfect. It considers these shapes, however, not solely as finished facts but as generated by sizeless points moving in paths defined by algebraic equations.[12] It is in this generating process that we take command of the perfection. Thus, experience presents us "round" objects in plenty; and we can produce "wheels" as nearly circular as technique may require. But *where is the true "circle"* to which these approximations approximate? We never find it; and we know that it cannot be found. It is produced by an ideal "point" in motion; and if we know what we mean by a "point," (do we?) we know it to be wholly unobservable. The standard "point" and the standard "circle," then, are *ours*; they are "ideas," and not from experience. Such ideas, Descartes held, are "innate," meaning mind-born (not birth-born). And each of the concrete sciences, together with philosophy, is built about certain "clear and distinct" innate ideas of this sort.

In any natural science, for example, our thought is guided by a notion of "causality,"—we assume that the events we are examining have causes. Or to put the matter negatively there is nothing that "just happens," *ex nihilo nihil*. And this conviction that there are causes, the finding of which is the chief business of science, we do not require to learn from experience. For every striking event, be it no more than a sudden noise, any intelligent being, babe or man, instinctively seeks some prior event or agent,—a "cause." As to the nature of these antecedents, our guesses easily go wild; yet the guessing itself betrays the assumption of causality. And quite without instruction, we incline to assume a certain *fitness* between "effect" and "cause," a likeness of kind (motion causing motion), an adjacency, an equivalence in amount: if a tree falls, no one suspects the zephyrs nor the birds. During Descartes' youth, not only were "final causes" being excluded from nature, as we have seen,[13] but astronomy and physics were

---

[12] Algebra in this case is simply a notation for the exact description of the "locus," the path of the moving point. Thus, if I write the equation $x^2 + y^2 = r^2$, r being a constant while x and y are variables, I have defined a perfect circle of radius r, centered on the origin of co-ordinates, x and y. The equation is simply the *law* of the generating point.

[13] Above, pp. 28, 45, 59, 60 ff.

sharpening the conception of "true causes" (Kepler's *verae causae*); a conviction of the mathematical integrity of nature's processes was becoming firm, and lending force to the naturalistic world-view. To Descartes the implication was quite different. It was but specifying and confirming the "innate idea" of causality, a necessity at once of thought and of actual happening;[14] it constitutes nature a perfect field for reason, human or divine,—deductive reason first, and inductive afterward;[15] and it offers a clean separation of the world of material masses, moving in space, from the subjective world of the I-think,—of material substance from mental substance. Philosophy must be the original witness-bearer of this inherent rationality of the universe. A philosophic *Rationalism*, based on science, is born.

8.7. *Empiricism*. While the Cartesian rationalism was moving on to its chief fruits,—the systems of Spinoza and Leibniz, the most effective criticism of it was ripening on British soil, not in the name of scepticism but of a different technique of reason, one based on "experience" and making use of inductive logic for its generalities. John Locke, who had sojourned in Holland, took explicit issue with Descartes: he was not charmed by the mathematical ideal for philosophy, and as for the innate ideas, he found none. (Nor could he, looking for them as he did in the wrong place, in conscious thought rather than in tacit assumptions.)

Locke's affirmative theory of knowledge in any case excluded innateness. Our individual concepts (Locke's "ideas") depend on simple elements arising either in physical sensation or in that inner sense he called "reflection." And since all knowledge expresses itself in propositions, and propositions connect two or more ideas, knowledge can grow only as ideas grow,—from zero (the *tabula rasa*[16]) upward. Experience shows connectedness among ideas (grapes-purple-ripe) but not necessity; through induction we may achieve generality, but only with probability.

What Descartes sought was certitude: "we reject," he said, "all merely probable knowledge, and make it a rule to trust only what is completely known and incapable of being doubted." Herewith the modern cultivators of reason, which in its natural operation we have seen to be a continuous union of inductive and deductive operations, divide on an issue which becomes a party label. The issue concerns *the source of our generalities, and their degree of necessity*. The party which holds to "induction only" and "probability only" sets itself off as "Empiricism." The party of Rationalism

---

[14] *Principles of First Philosophy*, I.

[15] Descartes was especially engaged with mechanics and biology; but he carried his deductions to medicine itself. He was also an active experimenter, especially in anatomy.

[16] This expression conveys the picture of a mind as a "blank tablet" upon which nothing is written until experience does the writing.

then defines itself by contrast: *some* generalities, and they the most important ones, are *a priori* and necessary.

It is important to note that the issue is not between induction and deduction: for both empiricist and rationalist must use both modes of reasoning. The empiricist must use his generalities as a basis for deduction; that, in the main, is what generalities are for. And when, by induction, one reaches an hypothesis, it is by applying the hypothesis to special cases, i. e., by deduction, that it is tested. The rationalist, for his part, must rely on the empirical methods for mastering the factual side of experience: no one questions that our great store of scientific knowledge—the laws of natural happening—is inductive. The issue is simply whether *any objective-and-general knowledge whatever* is *a priori*; or as Kant put it, whether there are any "synthetic *a priori* judgments." To this question the empiricist says No. Yet it is not without significance that John Locke is one source of the theory—and to some extent of the very words—of Thomas Jefferson's birth-born and self-evident rights of man,—in Locke's list, the rights of life, liberty, and property. It is presumable that the *a priori*, if it exists at all, lives in us as a presupposition, or presuppositions, ordinarily transparent and unverbalized, hence easily overlooked.

To this relatively invisible (or subconscious) store belongs what we have called the pre-philosophical rationalism of the human mind. As a boy "cutting corners" is using a judgment wholly unformulated, to the effect that there is a "shortest distance" from point to point which he will later identify as a "straight line," so any creature that, as a proper empiricist, "learns from experience" is assuming that once he has recognized a cause-effect sequence he has ground for expecting its repetition whenever the cause recurs, or can be made to recur. He has found a particular with a "universal" character. He assumes a *reliability* of nature such as experience cannot teach, because it is the presupposition of all possible teaching and learning.[17] Without this assumption no habits, human or animal, could be formed, and in so far as life is dependent on habits which grow to competence by inductive learning, life would perish. As our study proceeds, we may find that the *a priori* in some form is as unalienable as animal instinct, or what Santayana calls animal faith; and that induction itself is capable after all of eliciting not only the probable, but the necessary. The issue is currently being pressed. A circumspect rationalism may yet rejoin a self-critical empiricism.

---

[17] The debate on the scope of induction later reaches a certain culmination in the work of John Stuart Mill (1806–1873). Mill was entirely clear that the "uniformity of nature" is a generality presupposed in all ordinary generalizing. Yet he maintains, with a determination which suggests to me the urgency of an *a priori* theory in straits, that this also is an induction of the highest or most general degree. (*System of Inductive and Deductive Logic*, I, iii, Ch. 2.) The problem of induction continues, with new intensity and new light, into our own days; we shall meet it again.

During the centuries following Descartes, dominated by the rivalry of the two parties in epistemology, a large part of the destiny of modern philosophy was given its outline. The rationalists were dominant on the Continent, the empiricists chiefly in the British world. Kant attempted a synthesis of rationalism and empiricism allowing an *a priori* order of experience but vastly curbing the scope of "pure reason." To the rationalists we owe the most architecturally imposing metaphysical systems of modern times, notably those of Spinoza and Leibniz.

8.8. *Reason limited by reason: "Criticism."* It cannot be said that these great systems have failed. Whether or not any one of them can now stand as a whole in our judgment, each of us must accept the guidance of these hardy adventurers until he catches their vision. They will show us at least this, that Descartes' audacious hope of bringing the rational certitude of mathematics into philosophy was much more than a private dream: the fire spread. It continued through the modern period to inspire thinkers averse to dogmatic metaphysics, desirous of welding science and philosophy into a unit,—men of commanding and scrupulous intellect, pioneers in other fields of thought, contributing like Leibniz and Newton to the advancement of mathematics and physics.

What has to be said is that these system-makers were not in that complete accord with one another which their premises would require, an accord like that which enabled the new physical science to begin the march of corporate and cumulative building that is one of the glories of modernity. In contrast, the philosophers differed among themselves both as to their supposedly self-evident beginnings and as to their conclusions. Spinoza, for example, found the universe a necessary unity, a single Substance which we may call Nature or God, whereas Leibniz found it a necessary plurality of "monads" whose solitary experiences unfold simultaneously in "pre-established harmony." Such divergences where—if an identical reason is an original source of truth—perfect agreement ought to prevail, conspired with the sharpening shafts of the empiricists to beget a doubt whether mathematical science is a wholly suitable model for philosophy. The ideal perfection of measurement and of theory proper to mathematical science could seem to lend an inappropriate rigidity to our thoughts about the wider universe. This doubt, with others, led to various efforts to find a *via media*, perhaps a synthesis,—attempts to *define by reason definite limits for the valid operation of reason.*

Hume had pressed the logic of empiricism with a laudably thorough energy. He had arrived at a scepticism which sapped the foundations of science itself; for if causality is but a mental habit, the supposed "laws of nature" waver in a psychological haze. His sharp-witted analysis appeared to be taking empiricism seriously; yet its conclusions were not wholly convincing even in his own sober judgment. For, as he himself put the case, "A true sceptic will be diffident in his philosophical doubts, as well as in his philosophical conviction"; and he was wont to recover from the malaise of his own scepticism by "being merry with his friends." [18] It was necessary to meet Hume's analysis, and with at least an equally keen blade; to discard premisses incompetent to appreciate scientific method; and at the same time to avoid futile aspirations of metaphysics "to outsoar the atmosphere"—as Kant put the matter—"in which it floats."

At the close of the eighteenth century, it was generally felt that the term "experience," given further examination, might furnish a clue to the problem. This term had been the hall-mark of empirical *method*. It was now drawn into service to indicate the *domain* of legitimate reasoning. "Within experience" we may reason empirically or rationalistically as the case requires; "beyond experience" there can be no legitimate use of reason, whether empiricist or rationalist. We must not expect the successes of science to be carried over into metaphysics.

This distinction of domain is common to various schools of thought: it is present in Kant's "Criticism," in the "Positivism" of Comte and his present-day successors, in the "Agnosticism" of T. H. Huxley, and in certain of the Pragmatists, whose way of thinking we shall later examine in some detail. Meantime, without regard to the order of time, let John Dewey speak for the common element in these several attempts to set a rational limit to the use of reason. He writes:

"But in the sense that 'metaphysical' means that which is outside of experience, over and beyond it, all human beings are metaphysical when they occupy themselves with problems which do not arise out of experience and for which solutions are sought outside experience. Men are metaphysical not only in technical philosophy but in many of their beliefs and habits of thought in religion, morals, and politics. The waste of energy that results is serious enough. But this is slight compared with that which is wrought by artificial problems and solutions in preventing, deflecting, and distorting the development of the scientific attitude which is the proper career of intelligence." [19]

But while all of these several schools undertook to maintain the validity of "the scientific attitude" and method, one alone at the close of the 18th century, in full view of Hume's analysis, maintained that this attitude must include a set of *a priori* certitudes; that the empirical tools of science—observation, experiment, induction, verification in experience—are not enough, without foundations in universal and necessary conceptions. The

---

[18] *A Treatise of Human Nature*, in Edition of *Works of David Hume*, I, ed. Green and Grose, pp. 548, 552.
[19] *International Encyclopedia of Unified Science*, I, No. 1, p. 32.

work of Immanuel Kant (1724–1804) was inspired like that of Descartes with the ideal of rigorous logical procedure: he felt obliged to show *why* the limits he set for the use of reason were rationally necessary. Since he was prescribing the limits of scientific method, he could not, with Dewey, call his method "scientific"; he would venture the formidable term "transcendental." Or more simply, it is "Criticism,"—roughly defined as an enquiry into the *presuppositions* of all empirical knowledge. His typical question is, *"How is experience possible?"* As experiencers, taking experience for granted, our difficulty is to see how such a question is possible! or what kind of answer could be given. Kant's argument, while strictly concerned with experience, does indeed call for an unusual from-above attitude toward experience, and doubtless deserves its reputation for severity. Its main themes and principles, however, are wholly within our reach.

Kant had read Hume; had been deeply stirred by him. Hume had destroyed Kant's easy acceptance of the self-evident "truths of reason" on which the then-dominant Leibnizian tradition was founded. In Kant's phrase, Hume "wakened him from his dogmatic slumber." Why "dogmatic"? Because whatever is taken as self-evident must deprecate all requests for proof or evidence as unnecessary and impossible of response: the allegation of self-evidence *has to be* dogmatic (recall the Declaration of Independence!). The position appears strong; but there is a danger in "axioms." Quite apart from the logical and mathematical explorations of recent years, or the paradoxes of quantum mechanics, or the elusiveness of space-time measures in physical relativity,—apart from all this, the confident security of the "self-evident" begets a certain uneasiness. The "axiom" induces us to play too safe. The original treasury of "innate" truth savors too much of a costless store of unchanging wisdom in a world in which the pursuit of truth is, and perhaps ought to be, an endless adventure. If there be any such thing as an *a priori*, it cannot stand as its own justification: it *must present its credentials*.

This is the great distinction of Kant's work. He offers the credentials. He says nothing of self-evidence. He *derives* the *a priori* elements by a strict rational procedure. He identifies a whole system of such elements as involved in the foundations of science, morals, law, esthetics,—"pure reason" he calls them; he derives them systematically from the universal conditions of experience. An example or two will illustrate his procedure.

We must first single out the elements of "pure reason" from the empirical ingredients with which they are involved, such as the "general ideas" derived from observing and classing objects and events. If you know the difference in the forest between hard woods and soft woods, and among soft woods between the firs and the spruces, you have a set of general ideas, class-ideas, derived from experience,—your own or others': your knowledge is empirical. But your ideas of "space" and "time" are quite different. They furnish a non-intrusive background for the forest and all that goes on in it. They are definitely *not general ideas*. As Kant points out, we have but one example of each; and without prior exploration we know each to be infinite,—a rather surprising command of entities so intangible! Further, we perceive neither the one nor the other by the senses. Things-in-space we see, they reflect light to the eye: space itself can reflect no light. It is a condition of all seeing, itself unseeable. Similarly with time (work out the parallel): it is a condition of all events, itself no event. There is something radically wrong with an empiricism that holds our ideas of space and time to be empirical, as if generalized from sense-experiences: they must be *ready from the beginning*, as schemes of order for arranging the incoming flood of sense-data. In brief,—as a partial answer to Kant's "critical" question,—they *make experience possible*. They are thus necessarily *a priori*; and the sciences of geometry and arithmetic which unravel their properties are equally *a priori* and universally valid,—the same everywhere.

Space and time are relatively abstract,—Kant calls them formal conditions of perception: "causality" and "substance" are relatively concrete,—always mixed with empirical stuff,—yet again, they too are not general ideas; and we have *no sense-experience* of either. To this we may be less ready to agree than in the case of space and time: we see the hammer strike the nail; we see the nail sink; do we not see causality at work? Definitely not: we see the two events, contiguous and immediately successive: we do not see the compulsion. A moving picture of a carpenter at work would give us the same impression of causality. Experience offers us the sequence, often the repeated sequence; the necessity is a contribution of our interpreting mind.[20] It was this that Hume convincingly showed Kant. But Hume said, the compulsion that carries our mind from cause to effect is mental habit; whereas Kant saw that it preceded the possibility of habit-forming. The concept of necessary sequence is a *key with which we approach* the mixed happenings of the day's sense-reports and "make sense" of them. The causal concept contributes to "make experience possible" as an orderly pattern of events.

Likewise with the idea of "substance" as a durable substratum maintaining the identity of objects (and persons) as their qualities change. The melted iron is still the same substance; the man is the same individual as the child from whom he grew—altered qualities, identical substance. We spontaneously recognize, or impute, this enduring substratum in the case of persons; it is the continuing selfhood, sometimes called the "soul,"

[20] See above, pp. 61–62.

the "mental substance" of Descartes. The physical substratum is more elusive,—once the atom, then a conserved quantity of energy in "conservative systems," then energy plus mass,—in any case a totality self-sufficient and permanent, nature's reliable, indestructible substance. Underlying all change there is a *that which* admits change without itself changing. The difficulty is, we never observe this "that which"; we observe only the qualities and their changes. In Locke's candid eyes, "substance" becomes an enigma, a *"je ne sais quoi."* And Berkeley makes the audacious proposal that material substance, so far from being the real, *par excellence*, is precisely that which does *not* exist.[21] (It is remarkable that in the period from Locke to Hume it is the empiricists who undermine the bases of that common-sense empiricism whose building-blocks are places and times and causes and durable objects). The emergency was one for empiricism quite as much as for rationalism. Kant was prepared for it. He could welcome the fact that cause, substance, etc., are not given by experience; he alone perceived that this circumstance might indicate their essential function in the original or *a priori structure* of all experience. Substance cannot be given *by* experience, for it indicates the factor of durability or persistence (Kant's *Beharrlichkeit*) without which change, and time itself, lose their basis of reckoning. It thus contributes to *make experience possible*, as an intelligible procession of events.

So far, Kant is affirmative. He upholds a rationalist theory of knowledge *for experience*. With Newton's physics as his background, he supplies a justification for the *a priori* premises of the then-existing sciences of nature. Here his affirmation ends. Beyond experience, there is no ground for science; there can be no rational theology,[22] no rational metaphysics. If the whole sense and function of our *a priori* knowledge is to make experience possible, then to attempt its use beyond experience is to misuse reason, and to involve ourselves in insoluble riddles.[23] To many minds of his day, this negative force of Kant's Criticism was its most impressive aspect; he was termed "the All-crushing One", *"der Alles-zermalmende."* And it was possible for later thinkers who had little sympathy for his deed of rescue of the *a priori* factors of science to cite Kant in support of their rejection of scientific metaphysics; among them Auguste Comte, founder of Positivism.[24]

8.9. *Reason limited by reason: Positivism, Agnosticism.* As the name Positivism indicates, Comte was far from resting his thought solely upon a negation. Its affirmative element is its insistence, in common with empiri-

[21] Below, pp. 162 f.   [22] See Chapter 4, above.   [23] See pp. 170–171.
[24] Weber and Perry, in *History of Philosophy* (New York, 1925), p. 384, quote a letter from Comte to Gustave d'Eichthal, in which he says that he has always considered Kant as the thinker "who most closely approximates the positive philosophy." See also pp. 38–39, above.

cism, on *what we positively have in hand* as the basis of all knowledge, the "given" data of inner and outer sense. Kant had much to say of "phenomena," that is, of what appears to us, with the implication that behind the phenomena there are *noumena,* or things-in-themselves, of which we can have no knowledge. Comte, however, would regard the assumption of things-in-themselves as a lingering remnant of metaphysics, together with the concept of inherent causes. Our concern is solely with the discoverable, regular, lawful *relations* among phenomena ("relations constantes de succession ou de similitude" [25]). He thus strongly abets the movement in physical science which ceases to talk about "causes" and "forces," and confines attention to the observable and measurable connections among the always accessible phenomena. He prepares the way for an Ernst Mach,[26] for whom the concept of "substance" is so far superfluous that the distinction between mind and body may be reduced to a difference between two modes of connection among sense-properties both of which exist: colors, sounds, etc. are "mental" when they are considered in their contexts of memory and purpose; they are "physical" when they are considered as members of stable groups we term "things" or "objects."

If human thought could succeed in banishing the notion of some substance or "reality" behind the phenomena, the path of knowledge would be clear. There would be a hierarchy of positive sciences, with physics at the base, and sociology at the summit; and philosophy would be the compendium or unity of the whole. The distinction between what is within experience and what is beyond experience would cease to concern us. But another distinction intrudes itself, only partly coincident with the distinction of domain, namely, that between *the relative and the absolute.*

Positivism, while disposed to accept sense-data at their face value, is still obliged to recognize a degree of "relativity" in our experience of sensequalities. Long before the rise of the doctrine of Relativity in 20th century physics, the "personal equation" was recognized as a factor in scientific observation. The work of science had succeeded in overcoming much of this psychological and positional relativity. But if it is the proper business of science to show us the *relations* of phenomena, an element of relativity remains in the very process of knowing. If scientific explanation consists in referring an event to some law or pattern of event-sequences, explaining is relating: a doctrine of the "relativity of all knowledge" presents itself. The highest success of scientific explanation would be to find a single law unifying all types of event-sequence: that law, itself, could then have no explanation. *Absolute explanation becomes a contradiction in terms.* With

[25] *Cours de philosophie positive,* I.
[26] Ernst Mach (1838–1916) wrote *The Science of Mechanics,* 1893.

this doctrine of relativity, therefore, there enters into Positivism itself a confession of the Unknown,—perhaps of the Unknowable.

And with it, an unwelcome negation enters the soul of the positive philosophy. If there is an Absolute Being, the nominal goal of philosophical enquiry, we can know nothing of it. Such is the position of Herbert Spencer whose thought, adding the evolutionary picture, is closely akin to that of Comte and of T. H. Huxley who coined the word "Agnostic."

Huxley writes thus of his own view of knowledge:

"When I reached intellectual maturity and began to ask myself whether I was an atheist, a theist or a pantheist, a materialist or an idealist, a Christian or a freethinker, I found that the more I learned and reflected, the less ready was the answer. The one thing on which most of these good people were agreed was the one thing wherein I differed from them. They were quite sure they had attained a certain 'gnosis'—had more or less successfully solved the problem of existence: while I was sure I had not, and had a pretty strong opinion that the problem was insoluble. This was my situation when I had the good fortune to find a place among the members of the Metaphysical Society. Every variety of opinion was represented there; most of my colleagues were -ists of one sort or another; and I, the man without a rag of belief to cover himself with, could not fail to have some of the uneasy feelings which must have beset the historical fox when, after leaving the trap in which his tail remained, he presented himself to his normally elongated companions. So I took thought and invented what I conceived to be the appropriate title of 'agnostic.' " [27]

It begins to appear that the doctrine of the relativity of knowledge contains an admission damaging to pure Positivism. If we know knowledge to be relative, must we not know what we mean by non-relative knowledge, i. e., absolute knowledge? Just as, beneath the phenomena there creeps the shadow of the noumena, so beneath the relative, there creeps the shadow of the absolute, as necessary to give the idea of relativity its meaning. The agnostic as an offshoot of the positivist reveals a weakness in the traditional positivist position: the only ground for the negative turn in the term "agnosticism" is the implication that there is an absolute, though one is denied knowledge about it. Herbert Spencer, while insisting on the principle of relativity, accepts this inference. And while he declares the inscrutable character of the "ultimate scientific ideas" themselves—among which he counts space, time, matter, motion, force, consciousness—he asserts an underlying unity, an Unknowable Power, toward which it is reasonable to maintain a sentiment of reverence.

To this extent, he becomes definitely metaphysical; and indeed he approaches the rationalist camp more closely than either a strict positivist or a strict naturalist ought to do. For having found an inductive formula for the general process of cosmological evolution, he proceeds to confirm

[27] *Collected Essays*, V (New York, 1898), pp. 237 f. See also Leslie Stephen, *Agnostic's Apology*.

his induction by a hazardous deductive excursus from such principles as "The Instability of the Homogeneous," "The Multiplication of Effects" etc., which fall a trifle short of being self-evident, but do tend to knit the impressive picture together!

In the nineteenth century Albert Lange, Ernst Mach, and Henri Poincaré were truer to the strict ideal of positivist outlook. Our present century has seen a renewed attempt to give it a position and rendering based on a securer logical analysis.

8.10. In recent years it is *logical positivism* which has furnished us with a refined and precise logical discipline for clarifying both the scientific and the non-scientific uses of language in such a way as to avoid metaphysics. We may properly recognize this aspect of logical positivism as an expression of the newer agnosticism. We shall not undertake to develop the position as a distinct type of philosophy, though one might readily expand the discussion, at this point, into a type under our general heading of Epistemology. In any case, it is important to be familiar with this current vocabulary of technical restraint upon the scope of philosophical ambition, akin to agnosticism, but taking the affirmative form of securing the empirical basis of all legitimate knowledge—hence "positivism."

The following propositions are characteristic of the general point of view:

a. *The unity of science can and should be achieved without relying on metaphysics or theology.* Scientific effort tends toward a purely empirical harmony among the parts of our knowledge, justifying the ideal of a new sort of intellectual encyclopedia. Otto Neurath writes,

"An encyclopedia and not a system is the genuine model of science as a whole . . . such encyclopedism is the expression of a certain skepticism which objects not only to metaphysical speculations but also to overstatements within the field of empirical sentences." [28]

A philosophical "system," such as Aristotle's, for example, must be regarded as anti-scientific in its fundamental character, because it fails to adhere to the logical positivist's "strict disavowal of the metaphor language of metaphysics." [29] It is inevitably tinged with speculative "overstatement."

b. *The decisive source of knowledge concerning matters of fact is the empirically verifiable report of the natural and social scientists.* All statements which are unverifiable are declared neither true nor false, and hence meaningless for scientific purposes. All verifiable statements are held

[28] Otto Neurath, "Unified Science as Encyclopedic Integration," *International Encyclopedia of Unified Science* (Chicago, 1938), I, pp. 20–21. Quoted by permission of the publishers, University of Chicago Press.
[29] H. Reichenbach, *Experience and Prediction* (Chicago, 1938), p. v.

tentatively, as probably true or probably false. Their probability may be very high, but it never reaches certainty. The criterion of "verifiability" requires very careful definition. For most logical positivists the process of verification of a scientific statement requires that it be brought to some sort of test by sensory observation. It is furthermore usually *assumed* that sensory observation furnishes "the republic of the sciences" [30] with public and common data. A. J. Ayer writes of the criterion of verifiability:

"We say that a sentence is factually significant to any given person, if, and only if, he knows how to verify the proposition which it purports to express—that is, if he knows what observations would lead him, under certain conditions, to accept the proposition as being true, or reject it as being false. If, on the other hand, the putative proposition is of such a character that the assumption of its truth, or falsehood, is consistent with any assumption whatsoever concerning the nature of his future experience, then, as far as he is concerned it is, if not a tautology, a mere pseudo-proposition." [31]

c. *The task which falls to the philosophers is the logic of science.* This reduces philosophy to a modest minimum. Philosophy may not contain statements of matters of fact; it may contain only statements about the scientists' statements of matters of fact. R. Carnap even adds the further caution:

"But it is possible to abstract in an analysis of the statements of science from the persons asserting the statements and from the psychological and sociological conditions of such assertions. The analysis of the linguistic expressions of science under such an abstraction is *logic of science.*" [32]

This work of language analysis, which comprises philosophy on this view, is divided into two parts. The analysis of the language of science which confines itself to the structure of the language, without reference to the things or objects which the scientists claim to know, is called *logical syntax.* The further analysis of the language of science with a view to the cognitive relations between the language and the things or objects designated by the language is called *semantics.*[33] Philosophy consists of logical syntax and semantics.

When we compare the conception of philosophy implied by these three propositions with the more traditional scheme of the branches of philosophy mentioned in our opening chapter,[34] we can readily take the measure of the agnosticism of the logical positivist. Epistemology is merged with

---

[30] Otto Neurath, "Foundations of the Social Sciences," *International Encyclopedia of Unified Science,* II, No. 1.

[31] A. J. Ayer, *Language, Truth and Logic* (London, 1936), pp. 20–21. Reprinted through permission by Victor Gollancz Ltd. and Dover Publications, Inc., New York 10, N.Y.

[32] R. Carnap, "Logical Foundations of the Unity of Science," *International Encyclopedia of Unified Science,* I, No. 1 (Chicago, 1938), p. 43. Quoted by permission of the publishers, University of Chicago Press.

[33] *Ibid.,* pp. 43–44.   [34] See §1.8.

Logic. Metaphysics is removed from the scene entirely (sometimes re-classified as a confused subform of poetry). Ethics and Aesthetics, insofar as these claim to furnish normative *truths*, are likewise removed from philosophy, while any non-normative, or matter-of-fact, statements they may contain are merged with the social sciences and scientific psychology. Ethics and Aesthetics, as parts of philosophy in the strict sense, tend to become analyses of the language we employ in making ethical and aesthetical statements of value. And finally, psychology, as "behavioristics," purged of introspection as a source of data, takes its place with the natural and social sciences.

Logical positivism appears to narrow unduly the scope of our rightful will to know the nature of the world we live in,—metaphysics. Yet the love of exactitude and stability in building our structure of truth is an essential motive, too precious to be slightly regarded. There is an admirable severity, perhaps a sort of asceticism, in the self-discipline imposed by this school upon its members, an asceticism which showed itself in the early days of the Vienna Circle by hanging a placard bearing the scarlet letter—M for *Metaphysik*—over the neck of any member who by chance fell into the forbidden area of thought. (That there were such members is perhaps a comforting reflection.) Indeed, someone has characterized the movement as a "Calvinism of the Intellect," thinking perhaps of a certain vehemence, characteristic of the prophetic stage of hopeful reforms, in denouncing sins of the mind. Their equivalent for damnation, lavishly applied, was "nonsense." As a technical term referring to any proposition not verifiable by sense-experience, this could be used with entire accuracy, sweeping aside at a stroke, for example, all expressions of value-judgment, such as "murder is wrong,"—obvious nonsense, is it not?

It is only just to recall that some changes have occurred in this respect. Philipp Franck has recently remarked that while moral judgments are strictly "non-scientific," they may be "all the more important," inasmuch as "importance" itself is an unscientific term.

Let me suggest in the briefest terms what seems to me the Achilles heel of this position. The saving word in knowledge for the logical positivist is "verification." If one can establish without doubt the process of verification, the scope of verifiable, and so of meaningful, knowledge follows. If verification always consists in referring a proposition directly or indirectly to a sensory experience, it follows that a proposition whose intention contains or implies no sensory reference cannot be verified and is therefore meaningless. But how can we be sure that this definition of verification is valid? Does it, as a definition, submit itself to verification—sensory verification? And if not, is it arbitrary? Might you or I, for example, set up another definition? He who dogmatizes at this point brings his conclusions with him into his original definition. His conclusions are therefore circular, and can have only linguistic interest.

Logical Positivism, as a school of thought in the theory of knowledge, reached this country chiefly from Vienna. Its careful work has been paralleled by that of a kindred school in Great Britain which tends to call its chief concern "Philosophical Analysis." The two movements of thought are alike in giving close attention to the rules of linguistic precision, or let us say generally to the analysis of sentences as used in science or otherwise. Philosophical Analysis, as carried on in Great Britain, has tended to be more sensitive than the Vienna school of positivism to the everyday usages of common speech. It has been guided more by the notion that after all most of our persistent philosophical problems reach their first expression in the common speech of all of us. This being the case, it is upon the customs and usages of common speech that analysis should operate with the aim of freeing our non-technical expression of thought and feeling as far as possible from ambiguities and other obstructions of language. This is a more flexible as well as a more concrete conception of a program of clarification of language than is represented by the austere ideal of logical positivism.[35] One of the guiding spirits of the British school of analysis has surely been for many years G. E. Moore who "has insisted over a long period that the common usage of the ordinary person . . . is not to be *lightly* declared rough, vague, ambiguous, and so on." [36]

By way of simple summary, the program of analysis, in the narrower form of logical positivism and even in its ampler form, represents a sharpening and also a restricting of previous empiricisms. In consequence, it is running the risk of becoming untrue to experience. For there is such a thing as "inner experience," entering into social experience, moral experience, legal experience, aesthetic experience, etc. The swing of the twentieth century is in the opposite direction—toward broadening its empiricism, as in the work of Husserl, of which we shall speak. This new empiricism will be, in its scope, the best answer to the restrictions of logical positivism and linguistic analysis generally, from whose careful clarifications philosophy draws permanent profit.

8.11. *Envoi.* We now speak of a "post-Kantian" era in philosophy, in quiet recognition of his achievement marked as much by integrity as by mental power; in reading Kant, and returning again and again, one feels

---

[35] A helpful outline of these intimately related movements is to be found in the published series of radio talks, *The Revolution in Philosophy* (London, 1957), which opens with an Introduction by Gilbert Ryle, p. 67.

[36] *Ibid.,* p. 67. See also the lecture entitled "Construction and Analysis."

at every point the deeply penetrating, but also the simply veracious mind. Where he negates, it is because he must; when he shuts the door on the advance of reason, it is because the clean-cutting tool of his "Criticism" demands it. The post-Kantian era keeps Hume in mind as well, as an indispensable revealer of the universal fallacies of naïve judgment, with the gift of a caustic humor, not a part of Kant's quiver. The barrier against rationalistic metaphysics set by these two great thinkers remains as a dominant presumption of our present age, the background for its recurrent essays in positivism and analysis.

Yet in the immediate context of Kant's work, the obvious question was put, how reason can set limits to reason without implying some knowledge of that which it professes to exclude. Hegel suggested that epistemology itself implies a metaphysics, and that the plausible proposal that we must first examine our faculty of knowledge before proceeding to know is self-criticizing: it is not clearly easier to know knowing than to know objects,— the chances of error may be at least as great! The difficulty of the agnostic in remaining a clean blank in regard to the forbidden territory becomes a part of our common philosophical experience.

How, indeed, can we keep ourselves to a vacuum of belief about any object we regard as "the Real," central to our own being, as well as to that of the outer world? We have noted Herbert Spencer's inconsistency at this point: he goes so far as to say of the "Unknowable Power" that while we cannot regard it as personal, the choice is between personality and something greater, not something less! If, as Kant and Schopenhauer alike maintain, the human mind cannot refrain from asking questions about what lies beyond experience, then these questions must be pertinent; and if they mean something, they must be capable of an intelligible answer.

We are urged by the more zealous agnostics, as a matter of intellectual duty, to keep our judgment in suspense about matters on which we have no evidence. "If a belief has been accepted on insufficient evidence, the pleasure is a stolen one. . . . It is sinful because it is stolen in defiance of our duty to mankind." [37] But what if the active man cannot do without some metaphysical belief? And what if this "suspense of judgment" is, in effect, *judgment in the negative*, really a pretense of knowledge and not a "suspense"? Spencer's agnosticism, we have said, is equivalent to acting as if God does not exist. If scepticism is a luxury for the idle, agnosticism, and with it strict positivism, is a mental attempt to lock one's mind in prison from the outside. If reason cannot establish our beliefs—so far as these beliefs are answers, pro or con, to legitimate, perhaps irrepressible, questions—we shall find ourselves reaching convictions in some other way: we

[37] W. K. Clifford, quoted by William James in *The Will to Believe*.

may become *"pragmatists."* In simplest terms, pragmatism is that type of philosophy which *calls upon the will* to supplement the intellect in deciding questions of belief. This way of knowing has assumed a large influence, and though its original proponents here, Charles Peirce, William James, John Dewey, have passed from the scene, its position has deeply and permanently affected the thinking of our civilization, as expressing universal tendencies of the human mind. We shall study it as our second type.

CHAPTER 9: WHAT PRAGMATISM IS

9.1. Pragmatism accepts the agnostic's judgment of the incompetence of "pure reason" in metaphysics: the most important of our questions about the universe cannot be answered by way of proof or disproof; and there are no fixed axioms or *a priori* truths to serve as a firm base of certainty. But suspense of judgment is not alone a painful inner restraint: it is in some cases a practical impossibility, since one must act on some belief or other, and in other cases an impoverishment of life. May not the decision then be handed over to some court capable of reaching a verdict: what the contemplative intellect cannot do, may not the will or the active self accomplish? Pragmatism we may roughly define as *an appeal to the will* to achieve conclusions in vital matters of belief, or to aid in achieving them.

Pragmatism reminds us that thinking does not take place in a vacuum, or apart from the rest of life. It is itself a form of action; it may fairly be called a vital function; it has its part to play in securing survival, and also in securing all the rest of the good life that lifts us above the plane of mere existence. We think in order to live. Then our ideas, our beliefs, are to be regarded as working tools in this business of living well. What then is the function of philosophy in a man's life? Is it to produce some accurate picture of an inaccessible realm, whether of supernature or of the hidden forces that manifest themselves in phenomena? But this, we are assured, is beyond the reach of our intellects. Then let us give up that picturing enterprise. Let us not, however, stop at that point, as the agnostic does. Let us take belief in its total sense as something to live by;[1] and let us accept and use those beliefs which, by the test of personal and social experience, conduce to better living, meaning by "better" more helpful, effective, resolute. Such beliefs we have a right to regard as true, though they cannot be established by any process of pure reason.

This is the general idea of pragmatism. In our own philosophic community it has divided into two main streams, according to what its exponents are chiefly *opposed to.*

Some are chiefly *opposed to rationalism.* They want first of all to get away from what they regard its deadening fixity, its formality, its support

[1] §1.1.

of dogmatic conventionality and a dumbly tenacious conservatism. They are all with the agnostics in the insistence that there are no eternal and *a priori* truths. But they add that if we are willing to hold everything flexible in the domain of philosophic principle we may work out a thoroughly adequate set of beliefs by simply extending and enlarging the well-tried methods of empirical science. We may become *experimentalists* in our beliefs, take them as working hypotheses, and hold them not as absolute and final verities, but as judgments to be freely modified by the tests of common experience. This is the variety whose acknowledged leader was John Dewey.

Others are chiefly *opposed to agnosticism*. They reject its life-laming indecisiveness. They are repelled by the essentially dogmatic and dog-in-the-manger attitude of those who would set up the sign *Eingang verboten* at all belief which cannot be proved. Such thinkers are likely to take the direction of *voluntarism*, pleading the right of the active self to reach out for a positive metaphysics. They are more interested in the sources of belief than in the methods for testing belief. This is the variety whose leader in this country was William James.

These two branches, with their different interests, are likely to reach quite different metaphysical conclusions. So far as the theory of knowledge is concerned, there is nothing essentially incompatible between the two in the primary matters of principle. But in our own exposition, we shall lean toward the latter variety of pragmatism, chiefly on the ground that it is a more distinctive type. The former variety is in its chief contentions a quite natural development of empiricism, and is frequently designated *experimentalism* or *instrumentalism* rather than pragmatism. We shall, however, keep both types in mind.

9.2. *A new name for some old ways of thinking.* This way of reaching beliefs is far more wide-spread than the name; most men are influenced in favor of the beliefs they regard as valuable for practical purposes, or as helpful to human order and progress, or as suited to their general temper. Thus if one adopts a belief in God, not because there is conclusive evidence for it, but because it appears to him to add to the meaning of life, to dispel pessimism, or to encourage morality, he is so far a pragmatist. He has not reasoned his belief out, he has *chosen* it; and choice is an act of will. As Whiting Williams has well put it, "We live our way into our thinking, rather than think our way into our living."—More likely we do both.

There was a strand of pragmatism in Tolstoi's philosophy.[2] Mussolini acknowledged that he owed much to Nietzsche and William James for his method of reaching his political beliefs. They led him to discard "pure

[2] See Tolstoi's *My Confession*, Ch. XII.

reason" or "*a priori* principles," and to adopt those policies which work out best in practice: the true policies are the expedient policies: this is political pragmatism.

Nietzsche goes so far as to say that a falsehood, if life-preserving, may be preferable to the truth. "The falseness of an opinion is not for us any objection to it. The question is, how far an opinion is life-furthering, life-preserving, species-preserving, perhaps species-rearing." This is merely Nietzsche's violent way of saying that belief, even in the form of prejudice, imagination, ideal, quite apart from the possibility of otherwise testing its truth, is a necessary condition of successful living. We men, both as individuals and societies, live best under the influence of a *myth* of some sort, a vision of the future which lures us on, making effort and sacrifice appear not only reasonable but exalting, whether or not these visions are even possible. A Nietzschean might call myths the Christian's Heaven, the Marxian Socialist's Ultimate Revolution, the Syndicalist's General Strike, the patriot's triumph of Liberty, the pacifist's warless world, all the various Utopias that have inspired history. William James would not subscribe to this doctrine of myth; he would not allow that we are justified in believing falsehoods or demonstrable fictions. He admits the will never as against reason, but only to tip a wavering scale, to finish what reason fails to effect. Only in such cases is it his view that the life-preserving proposition is the *true one*.

9.3. Pragmatism is often regarded as "the American philosophy." Ruggiero, a contemporary Italian historian of philosophy, says, "Pragmatism was born in America, the country of business, and is, par excellence, the philosophy of the business man." But this view is mistaken. Just as there has been scepticism in all ages, so in all ages there has been a tendency to resort to the voluntary cast of belief as a relief from the negations of sceptical and agnostic views.[3]

It is true that the name pragmatism (or pragmaticism, as Charles Peirce preferred to call it) was given vogue by William James; and that the pragmatic way of knowing was given a vigorous impetus by these and by John Dewey, all American writers. But Arthur Balfour in England [4] and Hans Vaihinger in Germany,[5] as well as Friedrich Nietzsche and F. C. S. Schiller of Oxford, were bringing forward similar ideas at about the same time. William James described pragmatism as "a new name for some old ways of thinking." Immanuel Kant and his great successor J. G. Fichte (1762–1814) had struck into the pragmatic groove long before any of these writers.

---

[3] *Cf.* St. Augustine's injunction of Christian faith, *crede ut intelligas*, believe in order to understand.

[4] *Foundations of Belief*, 1895.   [5] *Philosophy of the As-If*, 1911.

9.4. *The pragmatism of Kant.* As an example of the predecessors of contemporary pragmatism, it is worth considering how Immanuel Kant emerged from the agnostic conclusions of the *Critique of Pure Reason* to the positive beliefs of the *Critique of Practical Reason.*

In the *Critique of Pure Reason,* Kant had come to the conclusion that we cannot prove the immortality of the soul, the freedom of the will, the existence of God.[6] In the *Critique of Practical Reason,* he argues as follows:

We cannot escape the fact of conscience. At least as certain as the fact that I exist, which Descartes had taken as the central certainty of experience, is the fact of obligation or duty. Whether other animals have a moral sense may be open to question; but man recognizes the meaning of the word "ought." To every man there is a clear difference between "I want to," "I must," and "I ought," though they may all apply to the same act.

Now if conscience is a fact, we must regard it as either valid or invalid. It is possible to regard it as inherited prejudice, or transmitted racial experience.[7] In that case it has no more authority than the experience of our ancestors can have for a world in which conditions are constantly changing. But the evolutionary account of conscience is defective. Mental traits that come down to us from antiquity grow weaker as we recede from the source, whereas conscience, like the aesthetic sense, grows more sensitive, and gives rise from time to time to men of moral genius, who develop new ethical ideas. There is no doubt a fund of inherited feeling which attends certain moral requirements which are deep rooted in the race, such as the revulsion against murder, unchastity, and perhaps theft. But conscience itself moves ahead of ancestral requirements, and hence cannot be explained away as a mere biological inheritance.[8]

We may, therefore, regard conscience as valid. Indeed, since the idea of "ought" has arrived in the mind, it is impossible to escape it except by using it. For if conscience is invalid, we ought not to be governed by it: that is, we appeal to the "ought" to overcome the "ought."

It is at this point that Kant stands. To him conscience is the one point of experience in which we touch absolute reality. Conscience is a token of something in man above nature, for it calls upon him to rule his own natural impulses. Nature appears in human nature in the form of instinct, impulse, desire and aversion: conscience recognizes these facts and calls on the individual man to take control, to govern them rather than to be governed by them. George Herbert Palmer defined conscience as the "call of the

---

[6] *Critique of Pure Reason,* Transcendental Dialectic.

[7] For example, see Herbert Spencer, *The Data of Ethics,* §6.5.

[8] This paragraph is not part of Kant's discussion; it is a retrospective defense of Kant's starting-point, the validity of conscience.

whole to the part." To Kant, it is the call of reality to the will, within the individual mind.

And if conscience is valid, then we are bound to believe whatever is necessary to make it valid, that is, significant and binding.

9.5. In the first place, if nature ruled man, it would be mockery to call upon him to rule nature. There is no sense in "I ought" unless "I can." The moral law is invalid unless man is free. As Kant puts it, "I ought, therefore I can." If duty is required, freedom is required; that is, *freedom* is a "postulate" of conscience.

Again, the moral law requires not alone this act and that: It is concerned with what we are. It is not satisfied with anything short of perfection. For how could conscience acquiesce in imperfection? So long as I find that my duty is contrary to my inclination, I am not perfect. I cannot change duty: I may change my inclination. But to reach perfection, or holiness, will require infinite time, Kant argues. It will certainly require more than one lifetime. Hence, either the moral law requires the impossible, and so is invalid, or else we must have the necessary time to fulfil its demands. *Immortality* is thus a second "postulate of practical reason."

Finally, while the individual is called upon to do his duty without regard to his own inclination, pleasure, fortune, happiness, so that the material rewards of existence are frequently to the corrupt or the compromising rather than to the dutiful, nevertheless, if this were the final truth of the matter, no one could quite regard the universe as *just*. If conscience is rooted in reality, and not in illusion, then reality must be a *moral order*: and it must therefore bring about an agreement between morality and happiness. But the only power capable of doing this would be a power controlling the whole course of experience in this world and the next. That power is what men call God. Thus *God* is a third postulate of practical reason.

In brief, Kant argues, if I accept conscience as a genuine call of the universe to my individual self,—and duty begins in this acknowledgment of duty,—I must also accept the beliefs in God, freedom, and immortality. The moral will establishes what the intellect leaves in doubt.[9]

9.6. *Contemporary pragmatism.* Contemporary pragmatism differs from Kant's position in the following ways:

a. Kant insists on the *necessity* of belief. Recent pragmatism emphasizes the rôle of *choice* in belief. This is a result of the fact that Kant

[9] For this great argument of Kant, see *Critique of Practical Reason*, Bk. II, Ch. II, "The Summum Bonum."

believes that we can *reason* from the needs of our moral nature to the beliefs which alone can support it. We do not require to wait for experience to show us what we must believe. Contemporary pragmatism takes its instruction from experience.

b. Kant allows only *moral interests* to determine metaphysical belief, because he regards the moral sense as the only clue we have to reality. Recent pragmatism allows a *wide range of interests* to govern belief; in fact, no human interest is held irrelevant to belief.

c. Kant appeals to the will to establish only these three ideas which belong to the *sphere of religion*. Contemporary pragmatism points out that fundamental *scientific beliefs* have the same foundation. We cannot prove, for example, that all events have a cause. We *postulate* this, in the interest of scientific knowledge.

The position of contemporary pragmatism is that we are employing all the time, not a few beliefs, but many beliefs which cannot be proved by pure reason. The scientist like the rest of us is "living by faith" in objects which cannot be directly observed nor discovered, "inaccessible objects" like gravity, electrons, energy, cosmic constants. Such beliefs can only be judged by their effect in guiding action: if they give us the right direction, they are true beliefs.

The same is true of our ethical and political beliefs. To Kant, the law of duty was the fixed point in the whole structure of belief; and specific moral laws, such as keeping promises, telling truth, respecting life, could be deduced from this unchanging law, the "categorical imperative." To the contemporary pragmatist, moral principles are neither immediately certain nor provable *a priori*, but must be judged by their fruits in experience. Justice, chastity, democracy,—these principles are no more secure in reason than they are in traditional authority: they must be tried out. The good must be good *for something*, and must not attempt to shine by its own light. Here the pragmatist is inclined to join hands with the utilitarian and the naturalist in morals.[10]

9.7. *What ideas mean.* American pragmatism begins in an attempt to move from the question, Is a belief true? to the prior question, What does it mean?

In 1878, Charles Peirce published a paper in *Popular Science Monthly* entitled "How to Make Our Ideas Clear." He was impressed, as Spencer had been, with the fact that many of the ideas or terms with which our beliefs are concerned, such as force, free will, God, have no pictorial or otherwise

[10] See John Stuart Mill, *Utilitarianism;* Herbert Spencer, *Data of Ethics,* Chs. III and IV; Dewey and Tufts, *Ethics* (New York, 1908), pp. 346–363.

sense-graspable meaning. So far as mental images are concerned, they are simply "inconceivable." If that which we cannot imagine is meaningless, we can save ourselves the trouble of asking whether God exists, by noting that the alleged idea of God is a meaningless word. But Spencer had already seen that the unpicturable idea may nevertheless have a very definite meaning if it leads us to make predictions which can be verified. We cannot picture electricity; yet we can calculate how electricity will behave: electricity *means* the agent of these effects,—electricity is what electricity does. Charles Peirce extends this principle. The meaning of every idea which has no direct sense-imagery in it may be discovered—if it has any meaning—in the sense-effects it leads to. He writes:

"Let us next seek a clear idea of Weight. This is another very easy case. To say that a body is heavy means simply that, in the absence of opposing force, it will fall. This (neglecting certain specifications of how it will fall, etc., which exist in the mind of the physicist who uses the word) is evidently the whole conception of weight." [11]

Such a method relieves us at once of many puzzles in our perhaps forever fruitless efforts to guess what Weight may be *in itself,* or force in general, or free will, or God. Consider simply what effects these entities have in experience. If they have no effects, they have no meaning. If two such entities have the same effects, they have the same meaning, though they have different names. Thus Charles Peirce thinks there is no real difference of opinion between Catholics and Protestants in regard to the substance of the sacrament of the Lord's Supper. To say that the wine and bread *are* the body and blood of Christ, and to say that they are mere symbols thereof, must mean precisely the same thing, so long as (and if) the bread and wine have precisely the same qualities in each case and if the rite has the same emotional import.

As a matter of fact, many of our ideas which *have* a kernel of sense-imagery in their meaning, tend to reduce to directions for action. A certain bell means "Get up and go to breakfast"; its sound is forgotten, its "pragmatic meaning" remains. The red and green lights on the railroad are not thought of by the engineer as colors, but as directions for his conduct. The notes on the musician's score mean certain deeds with the bow or the fingers. Charles Peirce defines an idea as a "plan of action." And a belief giving some idea or other a definite status in the world,—"establishes in our nature a rule of action, or, say for short, a *habit.*" What I believe about gravitation, for example, *means* the establishment of certain habits in handling things, in lifting, piling, building, walking, carrying, and so on.

[11] Charles S. Peirce, "How to Make Our Ideas Clear," §3, *Collected Papers,* V, (Cambridge, 1931 f.), pp. 261 ff.

9.8. *The test of truth.* From this doctrine about what ideas and beliefs *mean,* it is but a step—though a momentous step—to the doctrine of William James about when a belief is *true:* namely, that a belief is true if it guides us to success, or establishes valuable habits. It is false if it leads us astray or establishes destructive habits.[12]

It is evident that the theory of evolution would lend a certain support to this theory of truth. For evolution makes the intellect an organ in the struggle for existence: the mind must be an aid in survival, otherwise it would not exist. The value of a thought, then, would not lie in any pictorial resemblance to external things but solely in its leading to the fittest possible response to the environment. In themselves apart from the eye, physical things have no color; apart from the ear no sound. But for the purposes of successful action it is not necessary that the ripe apple should be red nor the unripe apple green: it is only necessary that this vitally important difference in the quality of the apple should be reported to the mind by *some* sign,—a color is as good as another sign. If life is "the adjustment of internal relations to external relations," of differences of behavior to differences of external fact, then the mind which has some *sign* for an external difference can be of service to life, even though its total picture of the world is nothing like the world as it is itself. Truth is the service of survival, in the first place, and then of all higher well being. The true is what "works" in this way.

Building on this biological view of the mind, John Dewey calls his type of pragmatism "Instrumentalism." By this he means that thought is to be considered simply as an instrument for promoting life, not as an organ for reaching a knowledge of things as they are in themselves. And F. C. S. Schiller calls his brand "Humanism," to indicate that whatever is true for the human being must serve human interests through human agencies, and should not serve the interests of any superhuman being, nor involve superhuman aid.

9.9. In this recent pragmatism, the broad formula, "A belief is true if it works," needs to be made more definite. For the term "working" means different things in different situations. It means:

a. "Cash-value." That is, to work is to lead to, or arrive at the actual facts of sensation, pleasure and pain, which the belief predicts.

Thus, the belief that the world is flat would lead me to think that if Springfield is west of Boston, and Albany west of Springfield, then Albany is west of Boston, and my shortest distance to Albany would be westward. This

---

[12] Witnessing the new developments of pragmatism with some concern, Peirce commented that they were "lively," whereas "in order to be deep it is requisite to be dull! I make my pragmatism to be a mere maxim of logic, instead of a sublime principle of speculative philosophy."

can be verified in the actual sense-experience of the journey, the cash-value of the belief, which is, so far, true. If I should argue that Pekin is west of Boston and London west of Pekin, and hence the shortest way to London is westward, the belief would encounter a negative cash-value, and would be proved false. When a scientific hypothesis can be verified by actual observation of conclusions drawn from it, this, its cash-value, establishes, or as some pragmatists would say, *is* its truth.

This is the empirical element in pragmatism. The truth of every belief must be found in its report in the experience of the concrete observer, so far as it is capable of such test.

b. Harmony with other propositions. We cannot take our beliefs simply one by one. It will not do to believe in one kind of an atom in physics, and in another kind in chemistry, though each belief works in its own field. If we accept inconsistent beliefs of this sort—and science has sometimes found itself doing so, even compelled to do so, as in quantum theory and wave theory for light—it is with the understanding that they must be brought to agreement eventually.

A new belief about the world which is out of harmony with old beliefs, as, for example, Copernicus' astronomy was out of harmony with Ptolemy's, will either have to yield to the old, or make over the old on its own pattern. The total result must be consistent. And where, as in this case, either view is justifiable by its cash-value, the choice may be made on the ground of *simplicity*.

Thus the body of truth is continually changing. Each separate belief can be said to "work" only when it complies with both conditions: it must have its own "cash-value," and it must cohere with the other things we believe.[13]

c. Higher values. Besides the effects of a belief in guiding the physical actions of our bodies, there are effects on feeling and attitude toward the world. A belief may give comfort or anxiety, stability or uncertainty, stimulus or repose, moral resolve or moral laxity. Whenever, as in the case of religious beliefs, there is little or no sensory cash-value and they may be made to harmonize with other beliefs, these higher values may be the deciding factor. Thus, other things equal, a belief making for optimism rather than pessimism would be judged true. But note particularly that no pragmatist, unless with Nietzsche he recommends "vital lies," holds himself justified in choosing a belief on the score of these higher values if the two earlier tests decide its fate in the negative.

9.10. On the ground of these three tests of truth, the truth for one man would tend to resemble, but not necessarily to be identical with, the truth

13 William James, *Pragmatism* (New York, 1907), p. 61.

WHAT PRAGMATISM IS   103

for another. Thus, the amount of risk in the world which would stimulate one man might discourage another: it might work for the former to believe in a world of chance, and for the latter to believe in a world of divine providence.

Taken literally, pragmatism would encourage each man to adopt the belief which works best for him, regardless of its agreement with any other person's belief. It would thus accept a thorough-going *relativity* of truth; and a man's philosophy would quite rightly depend on his temperament and circumstances.

But evidently it does not altogether work to be out of accord with one's neighbor, any more than to be out of accord with oneself. To work perfectly, a belief must be in harmony with other propositions (the second test); but it must also be in harmony with the beliefs of other people.

Hence "individual pragmatism" tends to give way to "social pragmatism," which holds that belief to be true which works for the great majority of men, and ultimately for all men, in the long run. The truth of a belief would then only be determined by a long course of *social experiment*.

The social form is the prevailing type of pragmatism in America to-day. Just as Dean Pound's "sociological jurisprudence" judges those laws to be right which are shown to lead to the maximum realization of interests, all interests being considered and weighed, so Dewey's instrumentalist school judges those beliefs true in religion, ethics, metaphysics, which experience shows to promote the welfare of the human community after long trial. Dewey himself would add that nothing transcendental or other-worldly can satisfy these conditions. Here he differs from William James who thought that some form of theism is requisite for human happiness.[14] In Dewey's judgment, the other-worldly character of traditional religion "operates to distract energy" from the practical tasks of social advance. The effort of human intelligence should be held to its proper work which is to master the always-hazardous, always-uncertain environment of our present lives. "Ideas are worthless except as they pass into actions which rearrange and reconstruct in some way, be it little or large, the world in which we live." [15] A "revolution in science" is here proclaimed. Experimental science shall not consist of mere common sense beliefs put in logical order, but rather of active rebuilding of the social environment through the instrumentality of ideas many of which are so technical as to be very far from common sense. As a result, our common sense beliefs become pliable and undergo indirect change by way of the progressive reconstruction of our environment.[16]

---

[14] See William James, "Reflex Action and Theism," in *The Will to Believe and Other Essays.*
[15] John Dewey, *The Quest for Certainty* (New York, 1929), p. 138.
[16] See John Dewey, *Logic: The Theory of Inquiry*, Ch. V.

One development of the social form of pragmatism gives especially scrupulous attention to the above-mentioned factor of harmony among propositions. This form has been called "conceptual pragmatism." It keeps alive the relationship between Kant and the modern pragmatic movement, while also drawing upon the analytic discipline of modern logic.[17] As thinking grows more scientific, it becomes apparent that concepts and propositions take on increasingly the form of conceptual systems. We speak of alternative geometrical systems. We can regard the Ptolemaic and Copernican astronomies as distinct conceptual systems, each having its own internal logical harmony. The more definitely our analytical thinking proffers alternative conceptual systems of any field of knowledge, the more clearly it becomes a pragmatic matter which one of these systems is to be applied in that field of our experience.[18] It is in the choosing and applying of a conceptual system that the pragmatic element enters, and it is the conceptual system, not the empirical stuff of experience, which is pragmatically tested. Such thought-systems arise through the cooperation of individuals, and are decidedly social products.

[17] See §8.8 and §8.9.
[18] See C. I. Lewis, *Mind and the World Order*, especially Ch. VIII.

CHAPTER 10:
PRAGMATISM EXAMINED

10.1. We can best make sure that we understand pragmatism by trying it on a number of beliefs.

Mussolini made a pragmatic judgment that democracy is a failure, that is, a false belief. It was not working in Italy. Was he right? Had democracy been tried? Has monarchy been tried? Has any form of government been tried *enough?*

Can we judge Christianity pragmatically? When the world wars broke out, it was said on many sides, Christianity has failed. The judgment was pragmatic, based on the assumption that Christianity has been tried. But *has* it been tried?

Can history yield a pragmatic test of any belief?

Take a simpler belief, that in immortality. How shall we judge the truth of this on pragmatic grounds? Kant saw but one aspect of this belief: it allows room for moral perfection. May it also allow room for eternal degradation? It may promise eternal bliss, or eternal pain, remorse, ennui. It may stimulate to high effort, or lead to loitering, since there is eternity for every task. According to the *kind* of future life, and not merely the fact of future life, will be its influence on this life. In the past, associated with the belief in rewards and punishments, it has upheld law and ecclesiastical authority. It has held societies together, and strengthened the arm of war. Can we sum up the good and the evil and strike the balance? And is this the way to judge the truth of the case?

10.2. To determine whether pragmatism meets our idea of the way to determine truth, take the following test-cases:

a. *The lost trace.* Which of the two propositions is true: There was a man named Homer, There was not a man named Homer? Ordinary logic and common sense require that one or the other must be true. But suppose that no evidence can be found for or against either proposition, all traces being lost. Then neither proposition has any cash-value in terms of facts; and neither has any advantage in terms of harmony with other beliefs, or of meeting our higher needs and wishes. Then, by the pragmatic method, neither is true and neither is false; but having no consequences and "making no difference" both are devoid of meaning. If we continue to believe that one must be true and the other false, we have some other than the pragmatic idea of truth.

The liar is the person who endeavors to exploit lost traces. For the actual course of past events, he substitutes a fictitious course which will fit in with all the facts other people know, and so "work" for them, while working vastly better for himself. The cross-examination of a witness is an effort to discover whether his story does fit all the facts known by others, and most liars fail somewhere by this pragmatic test. But suppose there were a super-liar, a perfect liar: then would his story be true? This case leads naturally to the second test-case—

b. *The perfect imitation.* There are in practice few perfect imitations. But one coin is very nearly a duplicate of another. Suppose, then, that two men at the bank receive in exactly similar bags the same number of new coins; and suppose that, without knowing it, each takes the other's bag. Pragmatically, there is nothing to shake the belief that each has the bag that was intended for him. Are these beliefs then true? If not, we must get some other definition of truth.

In this case, nothing hangs on the identity of the two bags, and one is not forced to reach an opinion. But there are cases in which identity is highly valued. The perfect copy of a Rembrandt successfully marketed would lose almost all of its value if it were known to be merely a perfect imitation. This is illustrated by the story of the collector whose enemy, instead of stealing his priceless old painting, drove him to a deeper despair by making so exact a duplicate of it that the collector was unable to tell which was the original. When the interest is in individual identity, a pragmatic equivalence fails to satisfy.

c. *The multiconsistent universe.* It is conceivable that there are several hypotheses about the nature of things which work equally well, all of them being consistent with all the facts. Fichte thought that there were two systems of philosophy of this sort: Spinoza's system of rigid determinism, and the idealistic system of freedom. Your choice between them would depend on what kind of person you are.[1] Suppose that there are many such consistent views, such that one works best for one man, another for another. Are they all true? The person who makes such an hypothesis cannot maintain that they are all true; for to him the truth is that character of the world which allows it to assume these various appearances. The truth about the color of the chameleon is not any one of its colors, but that quality which enables it to vary.

[1] Fichte, *First Introduction into the Science of Knowledge.* See above, §9.3. Also §1.10.

It is evident that the human mind aims at a kind of truth that is independent of its wishes, and even beyond its power of testing.

10.3. The central trouble with pragmatism seems to be that when we choose our belief, it ceases to be our belief.

The suspicion that our will has tipped the balance of evidence brands for us the chosen hypothesis as *subjective*; but a belief is the reference of the mind to an object assumed real, independent, objective. The suspicion of subjectivity therefore destroys belief.

The logical error of pragmatism may be stated as a "false conversion" of "All true propositions work" into "All propositions that work are true." This conversion is not logically allowable. From All crows are black birds, it does not follow that All black birds are crows. It only follows that No bird which is not black is a crow. Or in the present case, No proposition which does not work is true. Thus a *negative pragmatism* is of use in detecting the presence of error, though positive pragmatism cannot establish truth.[2]

There is a type of situation in which it is allowable to convert a proposition. "All equilateral triangles are equiangular" and also "All equiangular triangles are equilateral." This is so because the classes named in the subject and the predicate coincide in extent. Similarly if the "true" propositions and the "working" propositions were identical, we could take working as a test of truth. Now *if* we could assume that the universe is entirely benevolent, as we understand benevolence, or entirely fit for our existence, the true beliefs would be at the same time life-promoting, comforting, etc., and the pragmatic test would be approximately valid. The value of pragmatism would then depend on an antecedent piety, not piety on pragmatism. The original belief in the fitness of the world could not be pragmatically established; for it must be used to establish pragmatism.

Ultimately, then, pragmatism requires a non-pragmatic truth. It fails by its own test.[3] Let use see how these considerations apply to each of the three fields, ethics, science, religion.

10.4. In ethics,[4] pragmatism attempts to judge what is right by what works well, as making for "the greatest good of the greatest number," or some other measure of welfare. Now no one would hold a mode of action to be right which made for the extermination of the race, excepting perhaps an avowed pessimist like Schopenhauer. But we cannot judge what is right by what promotes welfare or survival or happiness, because we can only

---

[2] Hocking, *The Meaning of God in Human Experience* (New Haven, 1912), p. xiii.
[3] *Ibid.*, p. 206.   [4] See §9.2.

determine what promotes welfare, or survival or happiness, by first enquiring what is right.

Since the first world war, we have been increasingly conscious of the necessity of "morale" in industry, politics, and all group action, as a precondition of all social welfare. And morale is a state of the will of the members of a social group in which each is willing to act in good faith for the objects which the group is pursuing. But men will not identify themselves in this way with their groups unless they are persuaded of the justice of the group, its good faith with them. The only prosperous group is one in which the leaders and the members first take upon themselves something like the Kantian law of duty. This law, then, is not contrary to welfare, but *prior* to welfare.

The existence of such a law of right is exceedingly fortunate for the conduct of life, if only because the calculation of the effects of action is impossible; both because of the infinite series of effects, and because of the qualitative difference of effects,[5] and because there is no way to weigh pleasures against pains.[6]

10.5. In science, it is important to make the distinction between verifying an hypothesis by the test of facts [7] and choosing an hypothesis because we like or approve of it. There is no real reason for claiming the process of verification as peculiar to pragmatism. An hypothesis is verified by finding out what facts would follow from it, and then looking to the facts to see whether they are as the hypothesis demands. The procedure is one of strict logical deduction and observation, from which the human equation is excluded as rigorously as possible.

Of course, science bears the mark of human interest: the truths it enquires into are the truths it concerns us to know. Our interest motivates the questions; but it does not determine the answers. The unfavorable answer is taken as well as the favorable one. It is the part of science to tell us the worst as well as the best about the world. And the principle of scientific truth is that no human interest, however great, can outweigh any item of evidence, however small.

It is probable that our interest in natural laws and the regular order of nature is due to the practical advantage of operating in a reliable environment. It is also probable that our ideas of atoms, electrons and the more recently discovered particles are worked out so persistently, because our practical interest in recombining the things of the world requires us to know the elements. The assumption that there *are* laws and elements may have

[5] See J. S. Mill, *Utilitarianism*.   [6] See W. E. H. Lecky, *History of European Morals*, Ch. I.
[7] I. e. cash-value, as in §9.9. above.

a practical motive. But this assumption does not control what we find: it does not make the regularity we discover, nor exclude the irregularity which we may be obliged to admit. The whole significance of the effort to *know* the "laws" and the "things" of nature lies in their indifference to our wishes.

Pragmatism, therefore, can claim no support from the ordinary procedures of scientific method; and in so far as Instrumentalism is an extension of scientific method it is not peculiarly pragmatic.

10.6. The pragmatic element in Instrumentalism is its substitution of a plastic set of ideas to be experimentally verified for the stable truths of rationalism; its recognition that transition, change, invades the most permanent of our intellectual properties. Now observe: we all believe in the pervasiveness of change; and we all believe in experimentation. If Instrumentalism meant simply the growth of the experimental spirit in thought and in life, everybody would be an Instrumentalist. But the question is, *How much?* Does everything pass, and does everything change at once? Is *all* that I believe true to-day liable to be false to-morrow; and on that account shall I hold nothing as certain?

If this is the position, then we must part company with Instrumentalism, for the very idea of an experiment itself requires that something does *not* move, namely the conditions which make the experiment significant. The x which the mathematician uses in his equation must keep the same value throughout the problem,—otherwise the operations become meaningless. The mind which experiments must remain the same, and mean the same by its enquiry when it ends as when it began; otherwise the experiment is irresponsible. And in so far as some problems remain throughout the life of the individual and of the race, there must be some *constants* in the life of men and of society. To make every habit and foundation tentative, and every standard provisional, would be like living in a house which was sliding in its place and melting over our heads. Further, all experiment has for its object to *establish* something, to learn something which will stay learned, once we have it. Truth must be cumulative in the race; but to accumulate, there must be an element of permanence in what is gained. If what we learn by experiment is to be at once unlearned, the motive to learn it is destroyed at its root.

And to experiment with experimentalism, we find that in casting away all stability of principle, we are obliged to introduce into our living stability of another sort. The political dictator, for example, who abandons the fixity of political principles, resorts typically to another absolutism, that of the particular I-will. And yet, ironically, stability of principle instead of stability of force has the pragmatic advantage that it allows flexibility and growth. The experimental ideal itself requires a non-experimental background.[8]

10.7. In religion and metaphysics generally pragmatism may seem to have its strongest claim, because of the difficulty of finding any other ground of belief. The claim is strengthened by the close alliance between religion and poetry. For we may conceive art generally, and poetry in particular, as a region of release from the sordidness of facts in a certain play of perfection, in which case a religious belief would be a higher form of art. So Santayana interprets it.[9] Or else we might regard it as a presentation of a non-existent ideal to be realized in action, and so a desirable support to the will to achieve, as well as to the will to be moral. But the history of religion opposes this view. The advance of religion is an advance out of poetry into literality.

It is particularly in religion that the objective truth is the only thing that can set us free. For religion is the orientation of the human self to what it regards as the most real thing in the world. God is nothing if not that on which we depend. But every chosen belief, every man-made idea of God too palpably depends on us. We cannot swing up a rope which is attached only to our own belt. If we can get no evidence in religious matters, we must go without religious belief; for here most of all the possibility of a negative answer to our hopes must be kept open. Here most of all a chosen belief ceases to be a belief, and so fails to "work."

10.8. Pragmatism, we conclude, is not the final answer to the question, how we are to get our beliefs. It is not, on that account, without value.

It has called attention to the fact that truth is an enterprise which requires active effort, not passive waiting to be convinced. The surgeon, not knowing whether an operation will save a life, will never find out by "suspending judgment": he must adopt a working hypothesis, and act on it. Only, we must distinguish between the will to reach truth, and the will to decide truth. Our decision does not make the truth true.

Again, it has called attention to the fact that there is a great region of the world which is unfinished and plastic wherein our action changes the facts. Treating a man as if he were an enemy may make him an enemy; treating him as a friend may make him such. In such cases the subjective factor of will makes the difference between one truth and another. "Is this enterprise a success or a failure?" It is neither the one nor the other until

---

[8] See further §40.7.   [9] See *Interpretations of Poetry and Religion.*

you act: your will to believe it a success may decide the issue. Here prag-matism has its rightful field.

But for the rest, where the character of the universe is in question, we must always distinguish between our working hypotheses and our beliefs. Action often cannot wait, and must seize on the best hypotheses available: the will to believe is a precept for exigencies of action, but not for thought. For thought has all of time in which to test its hypotheses, while using the certitudes implied in all testing.

This age-long effort we have no right to relinquish in despair. Prag-matism acquiesces too easily in the agnostic view of metaphysical truth. The presumption is that whatever in the universe can affect us is con-nected with us by lines which our knowledge can trace. *There is no in-accessible truth.*

CHAPTER 11: FEELING
AS AN ORGAN OF KNOWLEDGE

11.1. The agnostic, the pragmatist and the intuitionist agree in one thing: they distrust the capacity of the intellect to reach metaphysical truth. But while the agnostic in this situation proposes to get along without a metaphysical belief, and the pragmatist, seeing that some such belief is inescapable, chooses one for its life-serving value, the intuitionist points out that we have other resources for knowledge than the intellect. He resorts not to will but to what is sometimes vaguely called "feeling." In order to see what intuition is, it will be well to consider the nature of feeling.

11.2. Feeling is an ambiguous term. It is some times used as an equivalent for emotion and sensibility: "the feeling of grief or joy," "to hurt a person's feelings." It is also used to indicate a kind of knowledge, belonging to touch or akin to touch: "the surface feels rough," "he felt that their attitude was unfriendly." This ambiguity arises from the fact that intellect and will are developed from a more primitive type of mentality in which these two functions are not clearly separated. Feeling is a fit name for this primitive mentality.

Its place in the mind can be seen by considering certain differences between the human mind and the minds of animals which are revealed by their respective languages.

11.3 Animals have language: they communicate by signs, and in the gregarious species these signs may be intricate and subtle. We are by no means sure we know all about them. But in general we may say that the language of animals is a language of *interjections*. There is a call which implies "Danger"; a call which implies "Food," and so on. An interjection or exclamation gives a total meaning in a single sign.

Human language establishes signs for *fragments* of meaning. A word is a sign for an object which, in general, only serves to make up a complete meaning when set with other words. The units of human language are combined and recombined in various ways to make sentences. And the declarative sentence itself is not, for action, a complete meaning. The proposition, "The prairie is on fire," strongly suggests action, but does not define it. It leaves open the possible question, "What to do," and thus a possible variety of suggestions and a clash of judgment. Thus the exclamation "Fire!" conveys a more complete meaning than the sentence; for it assumes an appropriate action and intends to summon it. The declarative sentence, so far as I can judge, has no existence in animal language. Human language is analytical; it allows the poise of intellect in the abeyance of action. Animal language is total: in it knowledge and active-attitude are unseparate. It directs the communal operations of instinct: it is at once announcement and command. In brief, it is the language of feeling; and feeling thus appears as *undifferentiated mentality*.

Psychologists have for some time been critical of that division of mental powers which treated intellect, feeling, and will as three distinct and coördinate functions. They have pointed out that feeling, as emotional disturbance, is the beginning of action, and so *merges with will*. This is seen with especial clearness in the case of those feelings which are closely associated with instincts. The feeling of fear is the early stage of those reactions which lead to flight or concealment. The feeling of anger is the incipient form of hostility. But it is equally true that these feelings emerge insensibly from the *cognition* or knowledge which (as the "stimulus") calls for the reaction. Fear and anger contain a keen and heightened awareness of unfavorable situations. We cannot therefore hand over the feelings to the active phase of the mind to the exclusion of the cognitive or knowing phase. Feeling partakes of both characters: it is a disturbing *knowledge*; it is a recognition that the world is unbalanced and calls for action; it is an idea moving toward an act of will. Feeling, then, we shall regard as neither coördinate with intellect and will, nor merged with will, but as the simpler state of mind from which intellect and will are differentiated:

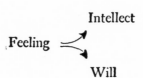

Intellect

Feeling

Will

11.4. We do not, of course, say that animals are devoid of intellect. Still less do we say that human beings are comparatively weak in feeling. On the contrary, in spite of the fact that intellect and will play a proportionately larger rôle in human life than in animal life, feeling is a large factor in every man's conduct,—in some, perhaps the chief factor. And the character of feeling which now concerns us is stated in the thesis:

wherever there is feeling, there is cognition,

that is to say, some knowledge or judgment about the objective world.

The truth of this we have just noticed with regard to fear and anger, as feelings closely connected with instinct. Both fear and anger may be based on fictitious or imaginary grounds. But the point is that whoever experiences these emotions believes certain judgments to be true; destroy the belief and you destroy the emotion. One has to *know* something to be angry,—to recognize something as an injury, a menace, an affront: a man may be too wise to be angry, he may also be too stupid. Anger contains knowledge of some sort. The same is true of more general feelings, such as melancholy, laughter, sympathy.

Laughter is highly cognitive: it is impossible unless there is a certain rapid concentration of knowledge, as in "seeing the point" of a joke. Laughter engages one's entire view of the world; but to excite laughter this view must work instantaneously and unlaboriously. Hence satire—an unlabored application of philosophy—is often the most effective form of criticism; and Shaftesbury wisely demanded that all good things should be able to endure the "test of ridicule" and come through unhurt. If America has any peculiar philosophy of the method of knowledge, it is not pragmatism: it is rather the belief that insight is better than argument; and that insight can be condensed in wit. Wit is finding the shortest way to the point; and laughter is the joy of release.

Sympathy, as feeling with another, contains the true knowledge of the other's state of mind. The unsympathetic person is blind to some of the important facts of the world. If intellect is "cold" it is not merely because it lacks emotional color: it is because it lacks truth. The cold or unfeeling individual is somewhere stupid or dense.

In sum, feeling appears to contain some essential element of truth, needful in our adjustment to reality.

11.5. *The advantage of feeling.* Now we are concerned with possible sources of metaphysical knowledge. Why, then, turn back to that primitive type of knowledge contained in feeling which man has in common with lower animals? Intellect, as the capacity for analysis and invention, no doubt represents an advance. But feeling, as the total response to the total situation, may have its advantages which *ought not to be lost* in this advance.

We know that the instincts of animals—without indulging in any superstitious wonder about them—often show an extraordinary keenness in sensing the environment: their perceptions frequently surpass our own and leave us puzzled as to "how they know." Bergson's interest was attracted by the canny conduct of the insect world.[1] Animals presumably have no theories; but in the feeling-knowledge which accompanies instinct there must be a prevailingly true sense of situations—otherwise the instinctive life would not be successful.[2] "L'action ne saurait se mouvoir dans l'irréel."

Now each separate instinct, as food-getting, nest-building, migrating, is occupied not with the whole environment, but with some fraction of it. But all the specific instincts are branches of a total instinct, the orientation of the animal toward its life-task. This total or root-instinct may be called, with Schopenhauer, the will to live: it may better be called the will to do one's living well, to realize the idea of the species in one's own career.[3] To this instinct there corresponds a feeling of the total environment of life: it may properly be called the sense of reality.

Is it possible that this feeling, presumably very vague in the animal world, and yet definite enough to sustain the vital effort of the creature, may become in the human being a valuable organ of knowledge? May it be that this "total response to the total situation" ought to accompany and supplement all the efforts of the intellect? It is this that intuitionists believe.

[1] See his discussion of instinct and intelligence in *Creative Evolution*, Ch. II, in which he quotes from Fabre, Peckham on Wasps, and others.

[2] Bergson, *L'évolution créatrice* (Paris, 1913), p. iv.

[3] On the unity of instinct, see Hocking, *Human Nature and Its Remaking*, Chs. IX–XI.

CHAPTER 12:
THE APPEAL TO INTUITION

12.1 Reliance on intuition in metaphysics is more ancient than reliance on intellect. The earliest sages announce to mankind not what they are ready to prove, but what they see. As "seers," their teachings are dogmatic. Confucius sees, and states dogmatically, that "The good man forms a triad with Heaven and Earth"; Buddha sees, and states dogmatically, that "the craving for individuality is the source of suffering." Religious "revelation" is the dogmatic statement of what the prophet has caught sight of: it is his "vision."

And the beginnings of non-religious metaphysical thought are of the same sort: the effort to "think," or to contemplate, is often simply an effort to see, i. e., to adjust the instrument, to get rid of distraction, to concentrate the mind, so that seeing takes place. The famous doctrine of Thales in which Greek philosophy takes its beginning, that all things are manifestations of one thing, and that one thing is like water,[1] was presumably an announcement of an intuition, rather than a result of demonstration such as Thales used in geometry. It was the vision of a thinking mind, but none the less an intuition.

Since intuition is the oldest source of metaphysics, it is natural that as philosophy became more and more a matter of intellect and reason, any dissatisfaction with reason should provoke a resort to intuition. An age of scepticism, we said, is likely to bring about some expression of pragmatism: it is still more likely to evoke the intuitionist. And it frequently happens in the history of philosophy that a thinker, after having gone as far as his reason will take him, relies on intuition for his final reach of truth. Thus Plato[2] regards the "dialectic" as a progressive rational enquiry destined to usher the mind to a direct vision of reality.

12.2. *Faith.* In the Middle Ages, the chief source of metaphysical truth was commonly defined as *faith*; and philosophy, as a work of the intellect, was frequently regarded as an auxiliary support to faith, and the "handmaid of theology." This faith is a direct apprehension of truth, whether on the part of the one who originally receives the authoritative revelation, or on the part of the believer who appropriates it; it is a form of intuition.

---

[1] Aristotle, *Metaphysics*, Bk. I, Ch. 3.   [2] *Symposium*, 211; *Republic*, 515, 532–535.

It is true—as pragmatists have pointed out—that faith is regarded as a virtue, and so implies an act of will: one must have the loyal resolve to accept the truth and act upon it, else he will not find it. But it is also true that what this faithful will seeks is not a *resolve*: it is a perception or insight. "Faith is the substance of things hoped for, the becoming evident of things not seen (with the physical eye)." Faith is thus an intuition; and while its discoveries can never be contrary to reason, they may well be *beyond reason*.

12.3. If distrust of reason leads to an appeal to intuition, an excessive confidence in reason will provoke the same appeal by way of protest.

Never was "Reason" more generally and enthusiastically trusted than in the France of the Enlightenment. And it was this very Age of Reason which gave birth to Rousseau, the apostle of feeling. Repelled by the prevalent mechanical account of human nature as a physically regulated procession of ideas, he rejected the method of thought which solemnly brought forward such a caricature as a true portrait. The feeling of individuality within us, he thought, would give us a better truth: intuition shows us our own minds not as fabrics of ideas spun out on a loom of necessity, but as spontaneous and unitary agents of sentiment and will.

Germany also had its apostle of intuition, during this same period, in the person of F. H. Jacobi (1743–1819), sometimes called the "faith-philosopher." He was stirred to protest by the philosophy of Spinoza, the purest of rationalists. It seemed to him that the unaided intellect must necessarily lead to atheism and fatalism, because in its own nature it can only deal with finite and partial objects, putting them into systematic connection, but is unable to get the raw material of truth, particularly the truth about the whole of things. A God who could be proved would be no God at all: for intellectual knowledge is a sort of mastery or taking possession, and the supreme being cannot be thus mastered. Metaphysical truth must be reached, not by the "mediate" knowledge of ideas, but by immediate perception. Jacobi called this direct knowledge faith (*Glaube*). It is what we mean by intuition. Thus by his criticism of Spinoza, he was prepared to meet the agnosticism of Kant's first Critique by recommending the intuitive way of knowing in metaphysics.

12.4. But Kant himself came very near to recognizing what Jacobi meant by faith, and what we mean by intuition. In his second Critique [3] he had touched the vein of pragmatism,—belief by the necessity of the moral will. In his third and in many ways his greatest Critique [4] he comes to a view that belief may be grounded on the necessities of *feeling*.

[3] *Critique of Practical Reason.* 1788.   [4] *Critique of Judgment.* 1790.

But here, as usual, Kant strikes a new note. For the feelings he has in mind are our *aesthetic* feelings, our sense of the beautiful and the fit. And his proposition is that these feelings are a form of "judgment" (*Urteilskraft*): they imply some knowledge or discernment, which it is the business of his study to ferret out. He comes to the conclusion that our feeling of the fit and worthful in nature is due to the presence of *organic life*, which we can only think of as a product of some teleological principle.[5] So Kant asserts that our feeling of deference to and regard for living nature is a dim recognition of some metaphysical background of life, which we might term God.

But Kant hesitates to give free rein to this intuition. He speculates [6] on the possibility that some higher type of mind might possess an "intellectual perception" which, so far from confirming this teleological judgment, would dispense with it! He admits feeling into metaphysics only to shut it out again. But he had let fall a suggestion eagerly adopted by some of his successors, notably Schelling and Schopenhauer.

12.5. Schopenhauer's (1788–1860) system of philosophy rests on the belief that while the scientific intellect presents us only with the surface of things,—appearances, phenomena, set in an understandable connection with each other, we have an immediate or intuitive knowledge of reality in our own minds, and know this reality to be of the nature of will. He taught, furthermore, that by a discipline of art, altruism, and ascetic self-sacrifice, the mind of the race might eventually be brought to the ultimate intuition of the vanity of existence and reabsorption into the original nothingness.[7]

But it is Schelling (1775–1854) who most completely grasped and used the Kantian suggestion that our aesthetic sense may contain a perception of the ultimate truth of things, that the genius of the artist is a gateway to metaphysical knowledge, and "art the organon of philosophy." [8]

Unfortunately, Schelling's views on this point were neglected, and Schopenhauer's pessimism attracted greater interest than his doctrine of intuition. The nineteenth century, under the spell of an advancing naturalism, was inclined to see in intuition nothing but another name for uncontrolled imagination. Its alliance with art was generally regarded as an alliance with irresponsible literary dilettantism in philosophy. Schelling was one of the Romanticists. It is only through the work of Bergson in our own day that the method of intuition once more receives a respectful hearing. For Bergson unites in himself the scientific care of the student of mathematics with the sensibility of poetic insight.

[5] *Critique of Teleological Judgment*   [6] *Ibid.*, §77.
[7] *The World as Will and Idea*, Bk. II, §§17–18; Bk. IV, §68.
[8] *System of Transcendental Idealism*, Introduction to Idealism, Section IV.

CHAPTER 13: BERGSON

13.1 Henri Bergson (1859–1941) conceived in his student days at the École Normale at Paris an ambition to reach an accurate understanding of the fundamental concepts of physics,—time, space, matter, motion, force, energy. He was led, in the pursuit of this aim, to a discovery which turned the current of his life, namely, that the *time* which enters into physical equations is not real time; and that real time is to be known, not by the measuring and standardizing intellect, but by a direct perception of the passage of our inner life. This direct perception he afterward gave the name of intuition.

This was an intellectual conversion for him, because it meant an escape from naturalism. It appeared to him, as it had appeared to Jacobi, that naturalism and determinism are results of intellectual method; but that something is missed by this method. Real time is missed. And the real self is also missed; for the real self lives in the flow of time: its states are not strung along in causal succession, but interpenetrate, carry their past with them in such wise that each one involves the whole self. The life of the self is thus not mechanically determined. This important result Bergson announced in his first book.[1] This emancipation Bergson has been able to communicate to many others. One commentator says of him that he is the first to make an effective breach in the defences of naturalism. His weapon is the generalized method of intuition.

13.2. The importance of Bergson lies in the fact that he tries to give an exact definition to the elusive method of intuition and to indicate the wide range of objects to which it applies.[2] He makes it clear that intuition is not the "feeling sure" of some proposition or other. It is perception of an actually present object. It is an extension of "sense perception" to the region beyond sense: it might be called simply perception of what is invisible and intangible but nevertheless actual. Thus, time cannot be perceived by the senses; yet time, according to Bergson, can be perceived by intuition.

---

[1] *Time and Free Will*, the French title being *Les données immédiates de la conscience* (1889).
[2] He states his view of intuition best in an article published in 1903, which is translated as *An Introduction to Metaphysics*.

What objects, then, can intuition perceive? Motion and all forms of change; for time enters into their constitution. The self. Living beings beyond self, animals, other persons,—whatever can be an object of "sympathetic intelligence." Further, fragments of life that have life in them, and products of life; books, characters of drama, acts of skill. Even, as a rare and extreme achievement, the central pulse of the life of the world in its unity,—for Bergson believes that there is such a thing, the vital impetus or *élan vital*.

Can we give a general definition of these objects? They must be objects which have an "inside" and an "outside": for intuition perceives them inwardly, while intellect judges them outwardly. They must be objects which have a complex aspect and a simple aspect: for intellect analyzes them, while intuition grasps them simply and as a unit. They are all objects, then, which have some organic character, binding a manifold into a unity; and conversely, all such objects can be known by intuition.

13.3. But what are the defects of the intellect which prevent it from attaining an adequate knowledge of these objects? They have been touched upon from time to time: let us assemble them.

a. Intellectual knowledge is *external*.

The intellect approaches an object from outside, i. e., from other objects, and considers it as like these others or different from them. I see a palm for the first time: I am undecided whether it is a tree or a vegetable; in either case I am trying to think of it in terms of other objects I am acquainted with. I will end by classifying it, knowing it by its resemblance to other trees, bringing it under the *concept*, tree. The concept is the typical achievement of intellectual knowledge. But evidently one can see likenesses, and make concepts, without getting any intimate sense of the life of the tree.

b. Intellectual knowledge is *relative*.

To know a thing by way of its likeness to something else is to know it in relation to that other thing. It is also to know it in relation to *the interest* which led me to see that likeness. I am interested in foliage; and so I observe that a palm, having foliage, is like other trees. But if I am a woodcutter or a lumber merchant, I am more likely to class the palm with the vegetables, for I can make no wood of it. Every concept or class thus represents a "point of view," a particular interest. Like a publisher's concept of a book as a commodity having a good or bad sale, it does not claim to know the book *as it is*, but only in relation to a certain interest. It is thus a relative and not an absolute knowledge.

When the interest is practical, the resulting knowledge may be said to be pragmatic. The book is to the publisher what it does for him; and his idea is true in the pragmatic sense if it works. To Bergson, the whole of physical science has a practical motive: we consider the world with the question, how can I move in it, construct and control things in it: hence the concepts of physical science are pragmatic. This explains why Bergson is sometimes counted among the pragmatists; but it is evident that this is not the characteristic aspect of his philosophy.

c. Intellectual knowledge is *abstract* and *partial*. Any point of view is one among an indefinite number of possible points of view; and the truth that can be got from any one of them is but a part of the whole truth.

I may conceive the cherry as a fruit, from the point of view of a botanist or of a cook. From that of a painter, it may be a bit of still life or of decoration. To a small boy, it may be classed among the projectiles or the pigments. It is all of these things, and more. Any one of these concepts gives a ruinously incomplete knowledge of the cherry.

In another sense the very outlining of the object is an abstraction: for the living cherry can only be understood as a part of the life of the cherry-tree. As conceived it is cut out, *découpée*, from the environment in which alone it is itself.

d. Intellectual knowledge represents its objects as *static* and therefore *dead*.

It is essential to the concept that it remain the same forever. A meaning cannot change its meaning without becoming some other meaning; that is, it cannot change. Trees may change, but the idea of a tree is permanent. The concept therefore cannot do justice to the changing thing. To comprehend motion, it tries to assemble states of rest. To comprehend life, it tries to catch fixed units and laws. It must fail. "Tous les cadres craquent." [3]

e. In sum, intellect *analyzes*, and cannot recompose. It can dismember the organism, but it cannot from the parts restore the living whole.

13.4. In all these respects, intuition is the precise counterpart of intellect. It therefore succeeds where intellect fails. In particular, it is the specific answer to the troubles arising from the "relativity of knowledge"; for it dispenses with points of view, comparisons, special interests, and seeks an immediate rapport with the object in its own being. Its knowledge may therefore be described as immediate and absolute.

Intuition also promises to settle the dispute between the empiricist and the rationalist. For both of these employ the intellectual method. The

[3] *L'Evolution créatrice*, p. ii.

empiricist in studying a living thing, for example the human self, reports it as made up of a multitude of "states": he thinks he is reporting pure observation, but he is the victim of his analytical intelligence. The rationalist asserts the unity of the self: but unity as an idea of reason is merely an abstract numerical quality which the self would have in common with a post or a stone. Both are relative truths; and both can only contribute to a true knowledge of the self when they yield to intuition, which alone is capable of getting beneath these generalities to what is *unique* in the living individual.

So far, the doctrine of intuition, especially in Bergson's formulation of it. We have now to test it.

CHAPTER 14:
INTUITIONISM EXAMINED

14.1. *Self-knowledge.* The question which intuitionism puts to us is plain: Can we human beings have a direct perception of anything beyond what the senses show us: and if so, how much? Let us test the claim of the intuitionist in two cases: knowledge of the self, and knowledge of continuity.

Self-knowledge is perhaps the best case for intuition. For we certainly do not perceive our minds by the bodily senses. And yet it seems evident that we do perceive them. To Descartes the most certain of all knowledge is the knowledge "I exist": for if I try to doubt my existence, I must know that I doubt; and to doubt, I must exist. Knowledge of myself seems to be present with all knowledge of other objects. If I observe "the clock ticks," a completer statement of my experience would be "I hear the clock ticking": I am aware of the clock, but also aware of my hearing, and aware of myself as the being who hears.

But just this direct self-knowledge has been subject to searching question. Hume, seeking for an abiding "self," cannot find it, but only a stream of impressions: and Kant so far corroborates his report as to say that the self, as the subject of knowledge, can never be an object. If I say, "I perceive myself," I claim to be at once the observer and the object observed: but the self must be always the observer, and what is observed must be something else. The self, thinks Kant, is a logically necessary centre of reference for the various experiences of the same person: for he can always annex to those experiences the phrase "I think," "I hear," "I see," and the various grammatical subjects refer to the same Ego. But while the Ego thus infers the existence of the Ego (and here Hume was wrong), the Ego never catches sight of the Ego. Hume's difficulty was, as one critic remarked, the natural one of a man who goes out of his house, and looking in at the window, reports that he cannot find himself at home. It is not in the nature of the self to perceive itself.

These doubts have been elaborated in our own time by various thinkers, among them Charles Peirce and Josiah Royce.[1] Royce puts the case radically: "Never do I observe myself"; "Common sense does not in the least know, when it appeals to the self, whom it is addressing." [2] Royce bases his judgment on the perplexities of experience in trying to judge ourselves; in knowing the boundaries of our self,—where the self stops and the not-self begins; in knowing what kind we are,—for our friends often know us better than ourselves, and we get our self-estimates largely through reflection from their opinions of us; in knowing our own identity other than through external things such as places and duties. Royce believes that just as we reach a knowledge of other persons by interpreting the signs they give us, so we reach a knowledge of ourselves, reading a thousand signs that come to us, chiefly through social experience, showing what sort of person we are.

14.2. Just self-judgment is difficult; and few achieve it. But it is possible to be entirely sure that an object exists, and to be aware of it, without being able to describe accurately its qualities and limits. The uncertainties we suffer from in regard to ourselves are largely doubts about how we should be classed or measured with reference to others: Do we rate as clever or stupid, as industrious or lazy, as reliable or shifty?—these are questions of comparison, of "concepts," the business of the intellect, not of intuition. The fact that the intellect is in difficulties should not be held to discredit the immediate sense of our own being.

Those who doubt self-knowledge indirectly confirm it. Any one who asserts that the knower is different from the object known must know both of them in order to be sure of the distinction, and must therefore know the knower. Any one who says we may be mistaken in judging our own quality must have some standard of judging the mistake. He is like some one who says a translation is in error, but that nobody knows the original: he refutes his own statement. Any one who asserts that the self is not the same from day to day and from company to company asserts that *it* grows and changes; and thereby confesses that he can identify it as the same self.[3]

We hold that the intuitionist is right, so far as the self is concerned: we have a direct knowledge of our own Ego—in spite of the miracle by which knower and known are the same—and this knowledge is the original by which all false judgments must be corrected. The final authority on one's own likes and dislikes, pleasures and pains, is *oneself!*

[1] See Josiah Royce, *The World and the Individual*, II (New York, 1901), pp. 253 ff.; *The Problem of Christianity*, II (New York, 1913), pp. 61 ff., 138 f.
[2] *The World and the Individual*, II, p. 265.
[3] Bennett, C. A., "Bergson's Doctrine of Intuition," *The Philosophical Review*, January, 1916.

14.3. *Continuous change.* We accept the positive doctrine of the intuitionist,—intuition exists: it gives us a certain amount of necessary knowledge; just how much it gives us besides self-knowledge we have still to enquire. But how is it with his negative doctrine,—the doctrine that the intellect cannot know these two things? To test it let us take the case of *continuous change.*

Bergson holds that change, like time itself, is broken up by the intellect into discontinuous parts; and that these cannot be fused by the intellect into the original whole, which only intuition can give us. His favorite illustration is that of motion and the cinematograph. I think we may understand this best by enquiring how we know *continuity* in general, the kind of continuity that is illustrated by a continuous straight line or an unbroken surface as well as by an unremitting motion.

When we undertake to say what we mean by describing a line A——B as continuous, we are apt to speak in negatives: there are no gaps in it. To describe it positively, we may imagine a point moving from A to B: and then if we ask what we mean by saying that its motion is continuous, we return to the line and say that it covers in its journey all the points on the line. To the intellect, the continuity of the line is to be defined in terms of its points, of which there are an infinite number; and the question is, how shall we describe the setting of those points, each of which occupies a zero length of the line, so that together they will constitute the whole line.

Suppose that we fill the line in this way: set a point C midway between A and B; and then midway between each of the two new pairs, set another; and continue, according to the rule that midway between every pair of points there shall be one other point. This will evidently define an indefinite number of points; and the line might appear to be filled. But it is not.

To show this, take another line A'——B' whose length is the diagonal of the square on AB; and for every point set between A and B, set a point on A'B', in the same proportionate position. There will then be an infinitude of points on A'B'. Now if AB is superimposed on A'B', with A on A', *none of the other points on AB will touch any of the points on A'B'.* That is, we have found an infinitude of points not included in AB which already has an infinitude of points in it. And we could find other infinitudes by taking other lines whose ratio to the original line is some irrational number.

We must therefore try other modes of defining the series of points. Mathematicians have tried this; Dedekind and Cantor have found ways of defining series of points in such wise that there are no gaps in the line,

no chance to cut it *between* the points. We need not follow these defini-
tions.[4] But we have to ask the question, How does the mathematician
know when he has succeeded? It can only be because he knows what he
means by a continuum, namely, "all the points on the line." He must
have a *concept* of continuity, quite as much as he has a concept of a point:
it may even be that the concept of the continuum is the simpler of the
two.

In the same way, if we attempt to analyze continuous motion, and discover that an infinite series of states of rest does not agree with what we
mean, it can only be because we have a concept of continuous motion as
a standard.

14.4. We conclude that the intellect cannot be excluded from the
knowledge of change. Verbs and adverbs are "concepts" in the same right
as nouns and adjectives. "Running" is the concept of a certain kind of motion; "melting" of a certain kind of change: these are general ideas with
many instances and varieties.

The concept is changeless in the sense that running must always mean
running and not walking, creeping, flying . . . but it is not the less the
concept of a change, and the permanence of the concept does not make
our idea of change "static" or inadequate to the living fact.

14.5. The intuitionist is mistaken in trying to define a region into
which the intellect cannot come. For in defining that region, he makes a
concept of it, and the intellect has already entered it.

After all, the intellect is not a separate organ of the mind. Both intuition and the intellect are the mind in action: intuition recognizing the
presence of objects, intellect defining what they are. They are inseparable.
They constitute a working-pair.

They might be distinguished as perception of whole and perception of
parts; perception of the object for itself and perception of its relations;
perception of the unique in the object, and perception of the qualities it
has in common with others. And since we are likely to forget the whole in
attending to the parts, it is needful, from time to time, to be recalled to
our intuitions.

But normally speaking, we do not forget the whole when we consider
the parts; and therefore our analyses need not present us with dead objects which we cannot restore to life. A scientific knowledge of the world is

---

[4] Bertrand Russell, *Introduction to Mathematical Philosophy*. Ch. X gives a brief outline of the
subject.

not hostile to the growth of poetry; nor does a knowledge of anatomy detract from the painter's intuitive appreciation of the living body. The artist is the better, not the worse, for his science and his analyses. In every one, the art of living consists in keeping intuition and intellect together.

CHAPTER 15:
ESTIMATE OF INTUITIONISM

15.1. The great achievement of intuitionism is that it restores our confidence in our power to know the real nature of the world we live in. It answers agnosticism.

Agnosticism and pragmatism agree negatively in withholding judgment about a reality behind the appearances. Intuitionism holds that even if reality is in some sense "behind" the appearances, as life may be said to be behind the manifestations of life, yet there is *nothing essentially concealed* from us by the "relativity of knowledge": we may have direct perception of reality as it is, in "sympathetic intelligence" or intuition.

This is evidently an immense claim,—a long stride from the cautious curbing of knowledge in Hume, Kant, Spencer and their like. Has intuition, then, any metaphysical results to its credit? Has it anything to report about the nature of reality?

Perception, of course, is an individual matter. And different individuals may perceive different things about the world: the intuitions of different minds need not be identical. We cannot, therefore, say that intuition, as a way of knowing, carries with it any specific metaphysical doctrine, any more than pragmatism carries with it a specific doctrine.

But inasmuch as certain intuitionists, and Bergson in particular, have given a fairly full conceptual account of their results, we may take these results as illustrative of what the intuition of other observers may be able to verify.

15.2. Bergson has, in the first place, something to report about the *creativity of life.*

It is the nature of life to "endure," that is, to carry its past along with it, to remember. This is a peculiar use of the word endure; for it would not apply to rocks and atoms, because they do not carry their past with them. Life thus accumulates with time, like a snowball; and accordingly it meets every succeeding moment with a different self. On this account, for a living being there can be no repetition of "the same thing": the second appearance of the event is met with the memory of the first and is therefore something different. The second experience may be better (as when we hear a piece of music for the second time) or worse (as when the repetition of some drama, the plot being known, loses the element of suspense): in any case it is something new. Life confers novelty on all its facts. The very laws of history cease to be true on being known. And the new meaning brings a new reaction, an experiment. Life is thus in its own nature *creative:* and evolution itself may be considered the result of an experimental vital impulse.[1]

15.3. It is implied in the above, as a second result, that life is *free*, not mechanically determined. The will is free. Likewise, everything that has life in it is free, in the sense that what it does from moment to moment is determined from within, by its own spontaneous and novel activity, and not from outside, by the necessity expressed in physical laws.

A mechanical law can apply only to repeatable events: when the cause happens, the effect follows,—when the temperature falls, water freezes, and the like. Then whatever in the nature of the case is unique, unlike anything that ever happened before, and unrepeatable, gives "law" no foothold. Further, a law, "when the cause happens, the effect follows," requires that we can clearly distinguish cause and effect: the fall of the axe is one event, the splitting of the wood a subsequent and clearly different event. But in life, and particularly in mental life, there is no such clear separation of past and present: the past remains with the present, the so-called mental "states" interpenetrate, and causality loses its meaning.[2]

There are, of course, psychological "laws" in the sense that there are some tendencies to regularity in the way our minds work. Much of this regularity is created by the mind itself, in the form of *habit*. Habit may be called an acquired mechanism. And evidently, if a mind becomes a "slave of habit" it may fall a victim to the mechanisms it has itself created. But the purpose of habit is to get a mechanical way of responding to a mechanical situation, as in walking, the daily routine, and all technique; so that the mind is left free to deal with whatever is not mechanical in the world, in its own novel way. Thus life fights mechanical nature with mechanical weapons in the interest of greater freedom.

15.4. Finally, Bergson suggests that *reality in its whole extent is living.* We have been speaking as if the world were divided into two parts, the living and the mechanical; and as if these were distinct and somewhat hostile principles. This is a form of "dualism." [3] The naturalist tends to

---

[1] Bergson, *Creative Evolution*, Ch. I.   [2] Bergson, *Time and Free Will*, Ch. III.
[3] To be considered as Type IV.

reduce this dualism to a monism by deriving life from the physical. Bergson reduces it to a monism by the opposite route: he *derives the physical from life.*

How can the physical world be derived from life? We have seen that habit—which is mechanical—is derived from life. Imagine this process extended to the background of space, matter and natural law which habit assumes as existing. [4] All free action requires a material to which it imparts form: the painter requires his canvas and colors, having their own reliable natures or "habits"; the poet requires his words and his alphabet. It is impossible that the letters and words should assemble themselves by natural laws to make a poem, or that the colors and canvas should combine themselves into a picture. These products are created forms, products of freedom, like any act of the will. But once made, they leave a certain amount of new matter behind them, in the sense that the poet develops a new word, line, meter, or the painter a new method, which becomes a part of the material resource of his successors. By extending this rude analogy, it is possible to consider the entire material cosmos as a deposit of universal life, a record, so to speak, of growing intelligence.

In trying the difficult task of showing *how* the physical world is derived from life, Bergson is, of course, going beyond what intuition can give him, and entering the realm of intellectual explanation. All that intuition could give would be the simple dogma: Life is the reality behind matter; matter depends on life. The theory of how matter can be imagined to originate is, after all, less important than this intuition, which, if it is true, is the refutation of naturalism.

15.5. It appears, then, that intuition is or promises to be fertile in philosophical results: indeed, it may set up a good claim to be our most important mode of knowledge in every aspect of experience. For if everything that has life in it must be known by intuition; and if everything that exists has to be traced to life as its ultimate reality; then *nothing can be truly known until it is known intuitively.*

Let us set up a few concluding propositions about the place of intuition in knowledge, supplementing those of the foregoing chapter. We recognized that intuition and intellect always go together. We must now recognize that they are mixed in very different proportions in different parts of our knowledge, and that intuition has a certain initiative of its own which is indispensable to good judgment.

Knowledge begins with intuition; and intuition is always ahead.

[4] *Creative Evolution,* Ch. III.

We do not know living things, persons, by beginning (as empiricism suggests) with the parts and building up the whole: we perceive the whole from the beginning. Knowledge grows in detail; and the detail can be placed because the frame of the whole is there to place it. Here intuitionism corrects a more rational empiricism.[5]

It is true that many of our intuitions are *acquired*. We ought to distinguish between original intuitions, as of time, and the self, and acquired intuitions, as of tricks of skill, connoisseurship, "knowing horses" and the like. The latter are of the nature of induction: they consist in *being admitted* to an inner knowledge of things after what Bergson calls a long acquaintance with their superficial manifestations. They are a winning of simplicity after much complexity. But these acquired intuitions are based on original intuitions, and could not exist without them.

Intuition is *always ahead* of intellect, in the sense that living things, persons, social situations, human causes and interests, are always inexhaustible. A person may be intuitively perceived, but is never completely known, analyzed, or described in conceptual terms. Mental tests, depending on analysis, always leave out something important. There is no chart of personality in which men can be classified and graded. Psychologies which depend on analyzing the mind can give us true knowledge, but never complete knowledge; and perhaps the most important knowledge is that which eludes scientific treatment. In business, the gift of intuition is an indispensable element of foresight. In the movement of history, the prophet, the artist, the poet,—that is, the true ones,—see farther ahead than the plotters of historical curves. Philosophy is expressed in poetry and dogma long before it can be expressed in rational systems.

But intuition is always in danger of getting lost.

This is a simple corollary of the general rule that attention to the parts tends to obscure the whole. Details of law may blind the skilled jurist to the intuition of human justice. And this may be so prevalent an occupational defect that the common citizen may come to dread the courts of law, as places in which justice only occasionally emerges, as it were, by accident from beneath the mass of technicalities. The scholar may be buried in the meticulous, through zeal for his subject; and spend his life in adding one more to the list of Latin subjunctives, which the young Roman absorbed in the run of conversation. A friendship founded on intuitive perception or liking, a true intuition, may have to undergo a stage of criticism, —the mutual criticism of personal defects which intelligent acquaintance reveals: and a legal attitude to these defects may easily obscure the intuition

[5] See §8.5. above.

and destroy the friendship. Every day's work, by sharpening attention to detail, lowers the level of intuition, until fatigue brings with it a certain mechanical rigidity of outlook.

In all such cases, there must be some way of recovering intuition, gaining fresh views of the whole: and this usually occurs in the normal rhythm of living, the alternation of work and play, of waking and sleeping, of the secular life and the life of worship (which is deliberate attention to affairs in their wholeness), of science and philosophy. These swings back to wholeness of view must be resorted to whenever it appears that more effort of the same kind does no good, but more litigation, more analysis, more distinctions, only sink us deeper in our defective apprehension.

As intuition is helpless without intellect, it must always be *accompanied and followed by conceptual thinking.*

Intuition, if it tries to set itself up as a sufficient way of knowing, has three defects. It cannot define *what* it perceives; for a definition makes use of a concept. It cannot *communicate* what it perceives; for language is made of the common coin of concepts. It cannot *defend its truth, nor distinguish true from false interpretation,* without the aid and criticism of the intellect.

There is always in the living facts of experience a unique quality which concepts, depending as they do on likenesses and other relationships, never do justice to, which only intuition grasps, and which—at any moment—cannot be communicated. But there is nothing which in its nature *excludes the effort* to define, analyze, communicate: there is nothing so unique that it has not in it the universal quality which makes it susceptible to conception, to thought.

The truth of intuitionism is thus no charter for laxity of thinking, or reliance on uncontrolled inspiration. Genius does not consist solely in the capacity for profound intuition: it consists in the capacity to express, i. e., to push the grasp of conceptual thought a stage farther into the elusive substance of life. Intuition is not wisdom; and intellect is not wisdom: wisdom is the union of intuition and intellect.

We said that wherever there is feeling, there is cognition. We now add, more specifically, *wherever there is intuition, there must be thought.* We turn once more to types of metaphysics which are based at once on intuition and reason.

PART III
METAPHYSICS
AND EPISTEMOLOGY

CHAPTER 16: DUALISM

16.1. *The quest of unity.* Bergson has presented reason in the rôle of an analyst, while intuition grasps wholeness or unity. What are we to make, then, of the often repeated statement that reason "seeks unity"? Is it possible that reason *does both?*

Consider reason at work in classifying things, one of the first stages in getting scientific command of the world. We put together things that are alike; and call them by the same name. Presumably this is "seeking unity"? We bring cattle, deer, camels, sheep, goats, antelopes and various other animal groups together under the class-name ruminant: one idea comprehends them all. However, what is the ground of this grouping? Some single trait common to all these animals. They all have complex stomachs and chew the cud. But this observation sounds like the result of analysis. Must we analyze *in order to unify?*

Or consider reason at work in explaining events. Explaining is in some respects like classing; we bring many events under the same formula. Thus the release of energy in the body is explained as being the same sort of event as the burning of fuel; they are both forms of oxidation. Oxidation in turn is one of many forms of the flow of energy whose laws in various fields may presumably be brought under a single law, the vastest generalization of science. In terms of this single law, all particular physical happenings would be explained. This is surely "seeking unity." But in order to bring, let us say, the laws of heat and the laws of motion together, it is necessary to conceive heat as the motion of molecules. We are driven to smaller and smaller units in order to conceive all happenings as *their* behavior. Again we must analyze in order to unite. Reason does both; it is no mere analyst for the sake of analyzing: it certainly seeks unity. Its goal would be attained if some one law could be found which would explain all events; and some one substance could be found of which all things are various forms. Or rather, its goal would require that the substance and the law were themselves united in a single ultimate reality.

16.2. But is there any guarantee that the world is such as to satisfy this aspiration of reason? Perhaps there is no one reality which explains everything. After our best efforts, is not the world a grouping of several distinct kinds of thing?

The strict materialist would say: everything is *matter*. But does he not require, in addition, the *space* in which his matter exists, the *motion* it has, and the *time* through which this motion takes place? Herbert Spencer, as we have noticed, used five "ultimate scientific ideas,"—space, time, matter, motion, force,—and adds consciousness as an awkward something else. He speculated that all of these may be manifestations of one reality, whose best name is force, energy, power; but how this one reality accounts for space and time and consciousness remained obscure. Spencer aspires to a monism, but he only achieves a pluralism with a faint hope of unity in the unknown!

To many minds—and some of them among the greatest—our best efforts to understand things rationally arrive not at one reality, but at an ultimate pair of contrasting realities, such as mind and matter,—not at a monism, but at a dualism.

16.3. Perhaps the oldest of all extant traditions, that which lies behind the great philosophies of China, thinks of the world in this way. Experience is a struggle between opposing principles, light against darkness, heat against cold, dry against wet, good against evil: of these several pairs, the beneficent elements, these remote thinkers believed, were united in one principle, the Yang; the maleficent elements were united in one principle, the Yin. It appears ungracious but it is also a fact of history that the Yang and the Yin were further contrasted as masculine and feminine. And these two principles, mingled in different proportions in every existent thing, explain not alone the forms which things assume but also the endless strife and inner conflict of the world.

In the ancient religion of Persia as reformed by Zarathustra this conflict takes on cosmic proportions. The universe is the scene of war between Ahriman, deity of evil and of darkness, and Ahura Mazda (Ormuzd), deity of goodness and light, worshipped under the symbol of fire. The earth, created by the joint action of both, is a mixed realm; man is called upon to take sides in this cosmic struggle, the righteous coming to the aid of Ahura Mazda. In fact, this warfare is carried on chiefly within the wills of men, and their free choices of good and evil incline the scales now one way and now another. Most ancient religions had their spirits of evil; but the Persian religion most clearly unified all evil and all good in these two figures, divided all the rest of reality between them, and hung the history of the universe on a moral issue. The Persian Ahriman became the prototype of the Jewish Satan and of the Christian Devil.

16.4. It was the Greek genius which was first able to look at the world with a clear intellectual interest, in which ethical and religious motives though not absent were not dominating. Their great thinkers were meta-physicians of a pure stock; and when, in Plato, they came to a definite dualism, it was a division of the world not between the good and the evil, but between the material and the immaterial.

The earlier Greek thinkers had begun by being naïve materialists—monists of a sort: "All things are water," said Thales; "All things are air, or fire," said others. Matter is at first so obvious, the mind so intangible and out-of-the-foreground, that mind had to be *discovered* for metaphysics, —not, of course, for pre-philosophical spiritualism—as a part of reality omitted by these theories of the first look. The honor of this discovery must be shared between Heracleitus (540–475 B. C.) and Anaxagoras (500–428 B. C.); Heracleitus teaching that there is a principle of universal Reason (*logos*) which like an infinitely subtle flame pervades all the processes of the eternal Flux; while Anaxagoras believed in a cosmic Mind as an abiding principle of order (*nous*) instigating the evolution of the world from chaos, sorting out the well-mixed germs of things, itself unmixed, bringing objects and living beings into distinctness from each other and into classes or species. Though Anaxagoras still imagined the Mind a very fine and diapha-nous substance disseminated throughout limitless space, he came close to realizing its distinction from all physical objects, and thus stood on the verge of dualism.

Plato (427–347 B. C.) sees the world as a system of immaterial beings, the "ideas," which appear to be "embodied" in the particular shapes we see by becoming as it were entrapped in matter, and compromised by asso-ciation therewith, but which in reality remain unsullied in their own un-changeable realm. The ideas are perfect and eternal; their visible images are defective and passing. There is a type tiger; actual tigers are more or less good specimens of this type; the ideal specimen does not exist in the realm of change. Nevertheless, the ideal, the type or prototype of all actual tigers, is the *real* tiger. It is what our knowledge, when it is true, seizes as the essence of all members of that class at all times, the unchanging pattern of the species. It is the business of thought to discern these ideas, in the midst of their defective images of sense; and especially the most general ideas, as of Being, of Virtue, of Beauty, of the Good. The material principle in man, present in his consciousness as sensation and sense-desire, tends to obscure his perception of the ideas; thought is most perfect when the dis-turbing avenues of sensation are shut off; the soul is enmeshed in the body as in a prison, and may attain a purer vision of the ideas after death,—as it presumably had before birth, since the new discernment of an idea in life is attended with strange tingling as of reminiscence. So Plato separates the immaterial ideas which are real and eternal, from the material substance which is a sort of eternal non-being to which experience owes its defective and transitory forms. Plato's dualism puts the ideal over against the material, the universal over against the particular, the perfect over against the imperfect, the absolute over against the relative; and the aspiring spirit must strain toward the immaterial Good against the leashes of the body.[1]

Wherever dualism has recurred in the history of thought it has been due to some new perception of the unique quality of the mind. Thus Descartes, whose philosophy is the very type of modern dualisms, felt bound to separate this self of his, this I-think of which he was so unshakably certain, from the physical world; mental substance is that which thinks, *res cogitans*; physical substance is *res extensa*. And Kant, with an even intenser perception of mentality, regarding Descartes' field of extension as a property or function of the mind itself, still left room for the belief that there is an unknowable reality outside the mind at whose incentive the materials of sensation appear to us.

16.5. The great dualistic systems of history have thus dichotomized the world *in different places*; but they have all insisted on the reality and independence of some mental or spiritual being. If we were to classify the great thinkers as the great disturbers of thought and the great finishers or settlers of thought, we may say that the great disturbers of thought have frequently been dualists. Plato, Descartes and Kant were great disturbers; their greatness consisted very largely in the fact that they stimulated a series of equally great efforts to resolve the antitheses which they made evident. Bergson also is to be numbered among the disturbers: he again seized with intense vigor the uniqueness of Life as over against Mechanism; his dualism has challenged the complacencies of a satisfied evolutionary naturalism. We have now to consider dualism on its merits.

[1] Read the great myth in the *Phaedrus* depicting this struggle.

CHAPTER 17: DUALISM EXAMINED

17.1. Ancient dualism was chiefly occupied with a rift in the cosmos, of which the dual nature of man is a sort of echo; modern dualism is chiefly concerned with the mind-and-body problem, and interprets the cosmos in the light of that domestic division. We shall begin by examining the relations of mind and body.

At the outset let us be cautioned about the pitfalls of language, and particularly language concerning mind and body. In a recent book Prof. G. Ryle has voiced this caution with great nicety.[1] As a warning example of the incorrect use of words, he considers Descartes' difficulties with the mind-and-body problem. Descartes is rather like a guest who, having met each member of his host's family, asks then to meet "the family"; he has made a linguistic mistake, a "category-mistake." With regard to mind and body, Descartes stumbles from seeing that the mind is not a *mechanical* thing, like the body, into supposing that the mind is a *thing* which is not mechanical. He should have considered the possibility that the word "mind" may not stand for a thing at all, but for a way of organization like the word "family." This line of criticism illustrates an approach to a metaphysical problem through modern linguistic analysis.[2] Its lesson is salutary as we turn to the inductive report of experience.

17.2. Agreeing that we know what we mean by mind and by body, and agreeing with our savage ancestors that these words mean different things, so that our imagination may even conceive the mind or soul as a temporary guest in the body, how is this intimate union possible? A union so close that when I act,—let us say, take a walk,—it never occurs to me to go without my body, never occurs to me that there is any other self to go walking than the entire "person,"—the mind-body partnership!

If mind and body are two different realities, what theories can we form of this association?

There are two, technically called the theories of *parallelism* and *interactionism*. Both of them invite us to think of mind and body as two *processes* rather than as two substances: they ask, What have these events which make up our mental history to do with these other events which make up the history of the brain? Parallelism asserts that (certain) brain-events and mind-events run along in perfect correspondence each to each,

---

[1] "Descartes' Myth," Ch. I, in *The Concept of Mind.*   [2] See §8.9.

without interference from either side. Interactionism holds that brain-events affect mind-events, and that mind-events affect brain-events. Inasmuch as these two series either do or do not affect each other, there are for dualism no other alternatives.

17.3. *Parallelism.* Both theories are interested in the position of the imaginary physiologist who is supposed to be investigating brain-events while the living person is carrying on his train of ideas. Suppose him to be armed with every conceivable instrument of physical and chemical knowledge, capable of minutest measurements. It is agreed that he cannot observe the thoughts. The question is whether he can see anything which will betray the existence of this unique union of thought and brain. Will the brain use some of its energy in producing thought or emotion?—in which case, some physical energy will appear to vanish! Or will the mind, in deciding to move a muscle, impart some impulse to a brain-event which the previous brain-events do not account for?—in which case physical energy will appear to be created! The traditional methods of the physiologist would be distinctly upset if he were obliged to make such allowances as these; and while he would probably not "abandon science," as some have feared, there is no doubt that his prejudices (for scientific workers sometimes have them) protest against such a situation as undesirable, and perhaps inconceivable.

Parallelism gives this imaginary physiologist his own way. There is nothing in the brain-events constituting any exception to the laws of physical nature; no passing back and forth of energy from the physical to the mental realm. The brain behaves precisely as the naturalist would expect. But the brain is not the mind. The mind follows its own laws with equal cleanness. It knows nothing of the physiologist nor of the brain; its world is coherent on the basis of its own principles of connection, namely, the principles of *meaning.* And since we have two perfectly consistent series of events, they may form an harmonious composition.

17.4. This theory would be more plausible if it were not dualistic. If we have two independent realities, mind and body, each going its own way, the perfect attunement which this theory requires becomes the extremest improbability. It is only believable if we can consider the mind and the body as two different aspects of the same thing, so that we have really but one series of events which appear to the inner observer as the events of his mind, and to the outer observer, the physiologist, as the events of a brain. We are then not dualists, but monists: and Spinoza, the first great parallelist, was such a monist, holding that thought and extension are but two ways in which we apprehend the underlying substance of the world.

But again, if our parallelism is dualistic it is necessarily *deterministic*; for at least the physical side of the event is following the demands of the physical order in its separation from the mental; and if the physical finger in obedience to physical law pulls a physical trigger, it is not evident how the mental event corresponding to this can be other than a will to shoot!

Now if the mind really makes no difference to the series of physical events by its presence, it is not quite clear why from the point of view of Darwinian evolution, the mind should have come to exist. Or if the mind can go on through the same set of experiences whether the body is there or not, why is not the physical world superfluous? How has creation come to duplicate its history in these alternate versions? Parallelism hardly fits the credibilities of the situation.

17.5. *The theory of interaction* has the great initial advantage of accepting what appear to be the obvious facts of experience, namely, that the body affects the mind and the mind affects the body. It restores to the mind that sense of usefulness of which parallelism robbed it; the conscious intelligence of the human mind has some value in the struggle for existence; our thinking does something which the physiology of the brain could not accomplish. If the theory of parallelism were true, it might still, perhaps, be worth while to be conscious, even though our physical machinery did all the work, merely for the sake of enjoying the panorama of existence. But this version of our mental life is strangely out of accord with our belief that we are agents, not spectators only, and that our wills can make changes in the world, including the world of nature; the belief, for example, that when I dig a ditch, my mind is using my muscles to alter the physical facts of the universe.

17.6. Now what is it, precisely, that the mind does which the body with its nerves and brain could not do? It is the neo-vitalists, holding to a distinct vital principle, who have given the most definite answer to this question. A "vitalist" is, be it noted, necessarily a dualist and an interactionist. For he comes by his vitalism through discovering that there is something in the behavior of living organisms which the resources of mechanics and chemistry cannot explain.

We ordinarily have no difficulty in distinguishing a living body from a machine. The living body operates itself, whereas the machine is operated; the living body is flexible and various in its movements, the machine follows a limited series of motions; the living body *moves to a purpose*, so that we who look on can "understand" what it is up to, whereas the machine moves to the purpose of some controller, not to its own. When I step on a log and find it to be an alligator, the change in my judgment is due to a kind of motion in the alligator which logs do not present, a flexible motion which appears to come from within and to aim at self-preservation, possibly continuing that aim through a variety of postures. As William James put the matter, the outer signs of mental life are "the pursuit of ends with the choice of means." An engine may appear to pursue an end; but if balked by an obstacle, it does not devise some other way around. The utility of the mind lies in its *inventiveness*, after adopting the welfare of the body as a part of its purpose.

Further, the mind is persistent, and can continue to do its work after interruption, and in various orders. A machine must grind out its songs always in the same way; or if, perchance, it can say its alphabet backward, it cannot mix up the order of its letters unless a provision for randomness has been mechanically prearranged. A spider whose web is partly destroyed can begin anywhere and mend it; a bird whose nest-building is interrupted may start again, and finish it in any one of several different orders. Mind is of use by *keeping the end in view*, and fitting the action, through all sorts of new and unexpected situations, to that end.

Perhaps the word *guidance* will express what, in all these cases, the mind contributes to the machine. When Hans Driesch finds that he can cut a star-fish embryo into pieces in every direction at random, and that these pieces, if not too minute, will develop into complete adults, he infers that the growth is *guided* by some vital principle. When Bergson finds that the molluscs in the order of evolution proceed by steady steps to develop an eye, which astonishingly resembles the eye developed by the independent line of vertebrates, he infers that these two series have been *guided* by a common vital impetus to this useful end. When McDougall considers the "instinct" by which pigeons or bees find their way home, under changing conditions of appearance and lighting and odor, he infers that their behavior is *guided*, not by uniform "stimuli" acting on nerve-machines, but by a mind which has an "idea" of location and a "purpose" to get home.

17.7. Another point at which mechanical explanations seem to fail is in that kind of behavior which responds, not to what things are, but to what they mean. A child can be made to cry by a spanking: the response to that stimulus may very well be as mechanical as the stimulus. But if the cry is caused by a reproof or threat or sign of dislike or fancy of neglect, the mechanical explanation is in difficulties: a machine can respond to a sensation, but how can it respond to an idea or *meaning*?

An instinct is a mechanism which is to be set off by the appropriate

stimulus; and in a good machine the same stimulus would naturally produce always the same response. Now consider the instinct of curiosity;
what will stimulate that instinct? Anything strange, let us say. But what is
strange to-day is not strange to-morrow. The same stimulus does not produce the same effect. Curiosity, then, is not a mechanism: it is aroused not
by what objects are but by what they mean to the observer. This sort of
response to meaning, the vitalist urges, requires a mind.[3]

Thus the vitalist answers the question, What do the mind and the
body do to each other, as follows: The body, through sensation, presents
the mind with a report of the facts of its situation; the mind, acting on the
motor regions of the brain, substitutes an intelligent reaction for the mechanical reaction which would otherwise have taken place,—an intelligent
reaction being one which grasps the meaning of the facts, as well as the
the bare facts themselves, and which is inventive and persistent in guiding
the organism to a desirable end. *Ideas* are inserted into the reflex arc.

17.8. If now we ask our dualist to come a little closer to the actual
events, and explain where and how body acts on mind and mind on body,
we may acknowledge that this question is hard to answer. The physiologist's
perplexity as an external observer we have noted. Our own perplexity as self-
observers is hardly less; for we do not discover our sensations coming in
from the body,—they are simply there; and we do not discover our volitions
acting on the brain,—we are sublimely unaware of the existence of that
organ by any direct experience. The dualist may say that it is not necessary
to explain how these mutual effects take place, so long as it is evident that
they do take place.

But do they take place? We do not observe their taking place. And furthermore, is it possible or conceivable that mind and body should affect
each other? If so, it is a case of anomalous causation. Everywhere else in
the world, cause and effect are alike in kind and equal in quantity; but
how can a volition be equal in quantity to an energy-change in the cortex?
As Clifford put it, we might as well expect "a goods train to be held together by the sentiment of amity between the stoker and the guard." This
difficulty, so formidable as to drive many thinkers back to parallelism, has
required the more responsible dualists to offer some theory of the process of
interaction.

17.9. Descartes' attempt to identify the point of interaction is famous.
He lighted upon a mysterious and minute glandular body in the midst of

[3] For more detailed discussion of these points, see Hocking, "The Dilemma in the Conception
of Instinct," *Journal of Abnormal Psychology and Social Psychology*, June–Sept., 1921. Reprinted
as Appendix I in *Human Nature and Its Remaking*.

the brain, the pineal body, as the place where the thoughts may meet the vital spirits and, because of a great delicacy of physical poise in that organ, deflect their course by an infinitesimal impulse. This speculation was regarded as signally unfortunate even in his own day, though no one could then have suspected that the "pineal gland" is a degenerate middle eye, clearly marked in certain reptiles!

Recent theories have been more ingenious and discreet. That of Driesch is most carefully worked out.[4] Mindful of the principle of the conservation of energy, he inserts between the mind and the body an intermediate, non-mechanical principle, purposive in its nature (which he calls, after Aristotle, *entelechy*), having the capacity to *delay* incipient changes in the brain, and so, without changing their amount, to alter their outcome.

All such attempts indicate the good faith of the vitalist, and yet are sure to suffer from excess of ingenuity. There appears to be no valid reason for sparing the conservation of energy; for if the mind is to change the course of nature in any way, it must do some work which would otherwise be done by a physical force. Hence various dualists boldly reject the physical law of conservation in this case, and regard the mind as a source of energy.[5] And some of them point out that the causal principle itself has no sanctity other than as a description of what sort of events we find actually tied together in the order of nature. Any sort of thing, for aught we know, may be the cause of any other sort of thing; and we cannot dismiss *a priori* the possibility that mind may act on matter, and *vice versa*, merely because elsewhere in nature there is likeness of kind between cause and effect.

17.10. The real difficulty with interactionism, however, does not lie in the circumstance that some physical laws would be interfered with. It lies in the fact that it is—while seeming to be in accord with experience— radically *out of accord with experience*. Neither the body nor the mind can accept the rôle which it assigns to them.

The mind is called upon to do only what cannot be explained by physiological machinery; and inasmuch as physiology explains almost everything, that leaves the mind very little to do. I am pursued by a wild beast in the forest; the instinct of fear takes possession of my bodily mechanism and I find my body running away—with my full consent; whereas I, the mind, as guide in the affair have nothing to do but dodge the trees! This is not the way I should describe my experience; I never consciously make this division of labor between mind and body; I, the mind, do not consider my-

---

[4] Hans Driesch, *Science and Philosophy of the Organism.*
[5] McDougall, *Body and Mind;* Bergson, *Mind-Energy;* Pratt, *Matter and Spirit.*

self as doing a *part* of the operation; if it is a conscious operation at all, I do all of it:

What my body, as a whole, does, *I do.*

It is I who perform all of my voluntary acts, however the mechanism of instinct or other bodily processes may take part in them. From the standpoint of experience, then, the body is not something else than the mind: it is an organ of the mind, and so far, a part of the mind itself.[6]

Ponder this idea: it may rectify some mistaken notions about what you mean by "the mind." The intuition of self, as we said, is a bit of pure certainty; but this intuition is not infallible about how far the self extends.

17.11. But the body also has reason to protest the place assigned to it by dualism. For as set apart from the mind, it suffers by the contrast. Its work is of a lower order; it is "merely" mechanical. There would then be some justification for Plato's assumption that knowledge proceeds better when the body is shut-off; and for the moral dualism which has frequently gone with the metaphysical dualism, according to which the body, in the form of sense-pleasure and desire, is to be overcome.

Now there is nothing greater or truer in the whole field of ethics than the demand that "the world, the flesh, and the devil" are to be overcome: there is a moral *direction*, and it pulls away from that sensuality and moral materialism to which the easy will perpetually gravitates. No one has grasped this moral direction more nobly than Plato. But what we have to fight against is materiality of the "mere" variety. It is when the body sets up as moral authority, and demands that *its* needs, *its* instincts, *its* complexes and libidos, shall be attended to as separate and sufficient goods that we have to rebuke its presumptions in the name of something higher and more complete, our moral direction. That higher thing cannot be a life of the mind in defiance of or apart from the body. (Our materialisms are frequently the revenge of an unduly despised physical existence.) Rather, it is a life of the mind which appropriates and absorbs the body into its own currents of meaning,—makes it mean what *I* mean, instead of taking my cue from it. It is not the ascetic rejection, but the "sublimation" of sense-pleasure: it is what Plato with his immortal sanity and profound psychological insight described in the *Symposium*. The *Symposium* is the completion of the *Phaedrus*, and the answer in advance to an excessive mediæval *contemptus mundi*.[7] (Do not confuse such sublimation with the popularly abused notion derived from psychoanalysis which assures sensual-

---

[6] For an elaboration of this argument, read Hocking, *The Self, Its Body, and Freedom.*

[7] Read Paulsen's memorable chapter on Christianity in his *System of Ethics*, Book I, Ch. II.

ists on scientific grounds that it is unhealthy for them not to do about as they please. This is another "mere" materiality in disguise.)

17.12. If dualism will not work in the mind-body relation, we are committed to some kind of monism,—the human person must be one reality. What are the alternatives?

Naturalistic monism would say that this reality is the physical organism: mind is a sort of luminous (and ineffective) accompaniment—an "epiphenomenon"—of the real process, the life of the body. That view we have rejected.

It may be that mind and body are both appearances of some third reality, which is neither: that they work together as "parallel" phenomena because they are two aspects of this underlying neutral substance. This as we have seen is Spinoza's view.

Or it may be that the mind itself is the one reality; and that the body acts with it (from each person's own point of view) as a part of it, and (from the point of view of other selves) as a visible image or expression of that whole person. This is the view of idealism, which we shall shortly consider.

CHAPTER 18: COSMIC DUALISM

18.1. It becomes evident why the great dualists are disturbers of thought. They have recognized a real distinction in the world; and they have made so much of it as to leave us with a set of unsolved problems,— How can these unlike and independent beings co-operate? and How, if really independent, have they found themselves together in the first place?

These questions are somewhat more embarrassing for the mind-and-body dualism than for the cosmic dualism, which begins by recognizing the universe at large as a scene of the mixture or conflict of two contrasting principles. For mind and the body are so inseparably fused in the human personality that Aristotle could fairly reply to Plato: the soul is not something else than the body, it is the very "form" of the body, the inner life of the body, fitting it as the hand the glove. In the macrocosmos, contrast or even hostility of opposites can more fairly represent the whole situation. Yet here also dualism must explain the relation between the opposing beings, and answer the question whether they are really independent of each other in origin and substance.

18.2. In considering these cosmic dualisms, it may appear slightly ominous at the outset that they have divided the world in different places, one healing over what another had breached. The moral dualisms of good and evil are to some extent effaced by the metaphysical dualisms of idea and matter, or form and stuff. Yet never entirely effaced,—the metaphysical cleavage becomes a source of moral direction, as in Plato, and in Bergson.[1] Let us consider them on their merits.

18.3. There is an evident reason why religious feeling, if it has a strong ethical quality, should tend to dualism. For dualism relieves the divine principle of the responsibility of having created the evil principle which it is engaged in fighting.

But when God is so divested of responsibility he becomes a finite and limited being; and his significance as creator is lost, for there is something else in the world which can exist by its own right as well as he. In such a

---

[1] Bergson, *Two Sources of Morality and Religion*.

view, the Good is simply not the supreme being—there is no supreme being; and our thought seeks some more ultimate reality which may account for the existence and mutual contact of both.

Hence religious dualisms have seldom been either enduring or consistent. One is likely to find in the background a belief in some mysterious ultimate unity. In the Chinese tradition, Tao, the unknown Law, is above the Yang and the Yin. In Persia, the two deities are the twin sons of Time, Zervana Akarana, and are destined at last to be absorbed into Time again.

18.4. On purely logical grounds, it is evident that the opposite members of a contrast, such as light and dark, cold and heat, have a strong family-likeness. Cold and heat are both degrees of temperature; they are contrasted only with reference to our sensibility and to each other. Can the same be said of good and evil, or of spirit and matter?

Of the evil, one may certainly say that it must contain good in order to be effective as evil. Lucifer can fight Heaven only because he is also of angelic fibre. If we could effect a clean cut separation of good from evil, evil would vanish; and the question has been raised whether good would not vanish also, i. e., whether some element of contrast is not necessary to give good its quality. Of that we shall have more to say; but at least so much is clear,—because of the meaninglessness of pure evil, good and evil cannot be independent realities.

18.5. Of spirit and matter, it is not so evident that either requires the other in order to exist. They appeared to Descartes to be two distinct substances: for "two substances are said to be distinguished really when each can exist of itself apart from the other." [2] We can form a clear and distinct idea of space and of matter without thinking of mind: this was sufficient to convince Descartes that matter could exist without mind. It seemed to him also that we could form a clear and distinct idea of "I think" without contemplating space or matter; and therefore that mind could exist without a physical world. What is your own judgment of this?

18.6. Most of us, I suspect, believe that we can think of matter without thinking of mind at all: we can imagine a time when the world in its lonely evolution had no vestige of consciousness in it; we can think of space empty of things, and empty of persons who think about it. When Whitehead said, in his book on the *Concept of Nature*, that "nature is closed to mind," he meant just that,—that we can and do consider the facts of physics without dragging the mind into the picture. And this constitutes a pretty fair argu-

[2] Spinoza, *Principles of Descartes' Philosophy*, Part I, Def. X.

ment—at least for those who believe with Descartes that our thought is a good criterion of reality—that the stuff of nature is an independent reality.

On the other hand, most of us would say that there is some difficulty in thinking of mind without matter. When we think, we think *of* something; and that something nearly always, perhaps always, has sense-imagery in it. Nature is an indispensable raw-material for experience, which is the basis of all thinking. Then mind needs matter in order to exist?

But consider more carefully. Does mind need matter, or does it need *simply the thought of matter?* And could this thought exist without the real existence of the matter as an independent substance? If you see the point of these questions you have the key to the movement of philosophy from Descartes onward.

18.7. Spinoza said: it is evident that mind and matter belong together, —our thoughts are first of all thoughts about matter; but when we think of matter, we think of it as a trait or "attribute" of the ultimate reality itself, —and this thought is true. Likewise when we think of the mind; that also appears to us as part of the very essence of reality,—and this appearance is likewise true. But if both are true, there can be but one ultimate reality or substance, of which matter and mind (extension and thought) are two quite complete and equivalent modes of expression of the same being, as it were in different languages. We must, he argues, return from dualism to monism: and this one ultimate substance, we may call Nature or God,—one being, perfect, self-caused, and the ground of everything that appears in experience.

Leibniz hazarded a bolder suggestion: perhaps the *thought* of matter is sufficient, without the real existence of any corresponding outer substance. The thought of nature is, after all, just what we have. When we say that the mind needs nature as raw material for thinking, perhaps we have told the truth and the whole truth about what nature is. This leads the way to another sort of monism, in which the reality of nature is absorbed in the reality of the mind. This is called technically "idealism."

Idealism appears historically as the type of philosophy to which dualism has naturally led the course of thought. For as dualism has arisen each time because of an exceptionally vivid intuition of what the mind is, the meaning of that intuition cannot be realized by resigning the mind once more to inclusion within nature,—one of its own objects; but rather by achieving a new and revolutionary monism in which the mind takes nature into itself.

Naturalistic monism we have judged on its merits, and have found it unsatisfactory. There are then only two alternatives. Either a monism like Spinoza's which would absorb both mind and matter into a single substance whose ultimate being is not so much neutral as unknowable. Or else the precise counterpart of naturalism,—a monism which would absorb nature somehow into mind. How can that be? We must turn to the idealistic world-view for an answer.

18.8. Meanwhile, a remark on the inferences from the history of thought. It is historically true in the Occident that every dualism has given way to a monism which has brought together what dualism had put asunder. The later dualism of Kant was immediately displaced by the monism of Fichte and his successors. This circumstance does not of itself refute the dualist. For it may be said with equal truth that after every synthesis of the cosmic opposition, the fundamental struggle and restlessness of the world have led some new thinker to hazard another form of duality in metaphysics. No monism can be finally satisfactory which does not account for the drag and resistance which the spiritual principle of the world encounters both in its effort to know the world and in its moral *élan*.

CHAPTER 19: WHAT IDEALISM IS

19.1. Idealism is the philosophy which holds that reality is of the nature of mind.

It is not, like pragmatism and intuitionism, primarily a way of knowing, with incidental metaphysical results. It is primarily a metaphysics, a world-view which may be reached by various ways of knowing. Thus pragmatism and intuitionism have commonly led their adherents to idealism, or in the direction of idealism.

Bergson, in so far as he foreshadows a monistic world-view, tends, as we saw, toward idealism. But he stops in an interesting intermediate position. If we should set up a scale of being,

Matter-energy . . . Life . . . Mind,

naturalism interprets the whole scale by the first term, idealism interprets the whole scale by the last term, while Bergson tries to interpret both ends by the middle term. His doctrine might be termed bio-ism. The idealist would comment that Bergson, in order to make his interpretation intelligible, is obliged to credit "life" with the qualities of mind, such as memory and inventiveness. The idealist believes that our alternatives are really but two: *we must either explain mind by physical nature, or we must explain physical nature by mind.* And since we have found the former to be impossible,[1] we must adopt the latter.[2]

19.2. The idealist's position may be expressed in two propositions, one negative and one positive:

First, *the apparent self-sufficiency of nature is illusory:* nature appears to be independent, to go its own course, to operate its own laws, to be eternal, to require no creator or other ground outside of itself; but in truth, nature does depend on something else. (Idealism decidedly does not say that "nature is illusory," as it is sometimes supposed to say.)

Second, *that upon which nature depends is Mind* (Spirit, Idea). The word Idealism is not particularly fortunate to express what this positive

---

[1] Recall the argument of Ch. 6.
[2] See Fichte, *First Introduction into the Science of Knowledge.*

proposition means. In the first place it ought not to suggest ideals (as though it had any monopoly of ideals) but *ideas*, the "I" having entered the word for euphony rather than for sense: idea-ism would be more to the point. In the second place, the stem "idea" is an historical accident, due to the fact that John Locke and his idealistic successor, Berkeley, regarded experience as made up of *ideas*, which are, at best, fragments of mentality. Mentalism or spiritualism would be more accurate names, but they have been drafted to other uses. We shall therefore adhere to the word Idealism, taking it to signify simply that whatever is ultimately real in the universe is such stuff as ideas are made of rather than such stuff as stones and metals are made of. That is, if we are looking for the substance of things, the ultimate being which explains all other beings, we shall find it to be mental in nature,—the thinker and his thought, the will and its doings, the self and its self-expression. And whatever appears initially to be other than this, independent of it or hostile to it, as matter, or force or space and time, will be found to depend on the mind for its very existence.

19.3. Intuition is not a sufficient foundation for any philosophy; but we are not likely to achieve any true philosophy without it. Idealism has its first sources in intuitions, very ancient in the race. Indeed, philosophical idealism as a matter of history might be described as *an attempt to bring reason into the spiritual intuitions of mankind.*

And since these spiritual intuitions were first embodied in religion, idealism has often appeared as a philosophical outgrowth of religion. Thus, in India, Brahmanism gave rise to the Vedanta [3] philosophy which is a form of idealism. In China, Lao Tze's philosophy, built on the ancient Chinese Tao doctrine, is akin to idealism. Northern Buddhism produced an idealism in its metaphysics, and in this form exercised a wide influence in China and Japan. Judaism, with the aid of the immortal Greeks, has given birth to the theistic doctrines of Philo and Maimonides. Christianity, likewise with Greek aid, gave rise to Augustine, Thomas Aquinas, Bonaventure, and many more, whose theistic systems, like those of Plato and Aristotle before them, waver between dualism (or pluralism) and idealism.

In modern times, idealism has taken on a new growth in independence of the religious consciousness, based largely on a *new intuition* which appears in Descartes, Leibniz, Malebranche, Berkeley, and their successors. The first step in the understanding of idealism will be an attempt to achieve for oneself the fundamental intuitions which have given rise to it in the history of human thought.

[3] Paul Deussen, *System of the Vedanta.*

CHAPTER 20:
THE INTUITIONS OF IDEALISM

20.1. The ancient intuitions of the race are convictions or insights which at some time or other come to every man, more or less clearly, without argument: one "sees things that way." Our business at present is not to defend idealism, but to get its point of view, by achieving each one for himself these intuitions. I shall state four of these dogmatically and then give a fuller account of what each means. The force of these unargued convictions varies much from person to person and from time to time. The questions one has to ask himself at each point are: Can I entertain the proposition at all as *possibly true?* Can I see things that way, i. e., so that this proposition *must be true?* To grasp an intuition, at least enough to understand the state of mind of those who have it, is usually a matter of getting the right focus.

20.2. *The real things will not be among the obvious and superficial things; the obvious and superficial things will not be real in their own right.*

The plausibility of naturalism lies in the fact that it takes the things offered in perception as its patterns of reality: the physical things—earth, air, stars—are real; and whatever ultimate reality is, it will be of the same stuff. Our intuition casts doubt on this plausibility, or rather reverses it: because naturalism is plausible, it is improbable. The ultimate and controlling factors of the world are not on the surface; they have to be sought. Hence any view of the first look is an unlikely view.

Now a sober naturalism accepts this conviction part way. It has abandoned the idea that the world is made of water (fluid-stuff, Thales), æther (Chu Hsi), fire (*cf.* Stoicism, and the god Agni of India), or permanent and impervious atoms: the naturalism of to-day has for the most part abandoned literal materialism. At least the laws of nature have to be taken into the reckoning as part of the real, and they are certainly not "material": they have to be *thought.* After perhaps half a million years of human thinking on the planet we have in hand some pieces of the puzzle, but we do not yet know how they fit together—i. e., we do not know the reality within physical nature. Why should we suppose that the wider reality—including

153

mental and physical—should be easier to find? If it is "perfectly obvious" that "the brain secretes thought as the liver secretes bile," or that thinking is some other simple function of brain-action, that very obviousness arouses an intuitive doubt of these propositions.

20.3. *The ease with which we can imagine the world of experience an illusion disproves its finality.*

We do not believe the world of experience to be illusory, nor does idealism teach that it is an illusion. But we can imagine it to be such. Indeed, we can hardly doubt that for most persons the standard world of experience is visual, ergo, with a slight shift of expression, a *vision!* And the point is that if this world which is present to us were self-explaining, real in its own right, necessarily there, imagination would balk at the effort to consider it an illusion.

Literature is full of invitations to think of the world as vanishing, or as a dream from which we can awaken. The lighter play of fable which presents the physical appearance as a disguise which some magic word can alter, the more serious play of allegory, in which physical events become for us the language of an higher purpose (as chained lions set to test human mettle) or the still more serious play of cosmological poetry such as we have in the great epics, in Dante or Milton, and in that speculative poetry which interprets nature as the "garment of God," that total disguise which is the Sphinx-riddle set for our discerning,—all this indicates how often nature has appeared to human fancy as a pretence or an aspect of truth which is alterable, not finally real. Fancies of this sort are not intuitions; but there is intuition at their root: they are the more or less playful form in which men have expressed the intuition of non-finality.

20.4. *At least some natural happenings are purposive.*

Here is the assertion of our impulsive animism. Animism is the belief in mental agencies as the explanation of striking natural phenomena. It is commonly considered, especially since the time of Auguste Comte,[1] as a primitive mode of philosophy, a stage in the evolution of culture which the race gradually outgrows. It is one of the props of aboriginal spiritualism. The science of anthropology is concerned to give it its proper definition and setting. (The student of philosophy will find the literature of anthropology full of instruction presumably about primitive people, but he will be a poor philosopher if it does not greatly enlighten him about himself.) [2]

---

[1] See Comte, *The Positive Philosophy,* Ch. I.

[2] See E. B. Tylor whose works on animism, *Primitive Culture* and *Anthropology,* have set the theme for all subsequent scholars to revise.

Animism is not a pure antiquity. It is a universal human disposition. It easily runs to excess, and produces a sufficient crop of absurdities: it provides a realm of "final causes" against which we have seen modern natural and social science waging its most prolonged campaign. Our concern must be to see whether the disposition has to be eradicated or to be controlled, and (as a prior question) how and why we become animists.

We are disposed to animate any event which affects us in an important way. Our anger animates trivially the obstacle which refuses to yield to our first efforts; and the emotion releases additional energy to reduce its obstinacy. Profound or continued ill-fortune leaves few people wholly "philosophical"; we are tempted to believe in "ill luck," or to feel a touch of resentment toward circumstances,—but resentment has already attributed malignity to the source of these events,—a form of animism.

I have known people stunned by some heavy experience of defeat, loss, or injustice to say with a touch of bitterness that they refuse to believe in a god who could permit such things to happen: the bitterness itself carried with it an impulsive personification of the cause of the calamity. Fear has been said to be the source of the god-idea;[3] but fear does not "make the gods" unless the feared object is felt as personal, and therefore capable of entertaining an appeal. If prayer, as William James says, is instinctive in all people, it is because of a prevalent intuition that nature is a manifestation of will. The positive emotions are equally fertile in impulses to animate. The enjoyment of natural beauty is seldom without a touch of something resembling gratitude, directed nowhere,—but lighting upon the unknown reality as if this pleasing result had been intended. Thus animism is a close companion of our emotional life.

And its pertinence lies in the fact that since no purpose is perceptible, and since some events are surely purposive, at the very least the behavior of other living beings, we are obliged to be animistic somewhere if we are to have any social life whatever. It is only by "impulsive animism" that a babe interprets a given physical shape as its mother, or that any man has a companion or friend. Further, we are left to draw our own lines between the living and the non-living. How do we know what is living? Only by its behavior, which shows signs of "pursuit of ends with the choice of means" —is there any other sign? How do we know what is not living? Only by the fact that we do not see the signs of purpose, and are unable to converse with the object,—is there any other evidence? But such evidence is not conclusive: it shows our limitation, not necessarily the absence of life. When we learn to consider purpose not as running counter to causality,

[3] See §2.6.

but as accompanying and using causality,[4] the scientific opposition loses its necessity, and we are free to consider the possibility of universal animation.[5] This hypothesis appears in many modern thinkers as offering an escape from the awkward alternative of the evolution of life from the lifeless, and many go so far as to assume that every integral unit of physical being has its mental as well as its physical aspect.[6] My own belief is that this hypothesis errs by excess in animating the world. But what we have to note is that it is a possible hypothesis. Life is not seen, it is attributed or imputed to objects; and this imputing process is justified in principle. We still seek a theory which will mark out its limits. Meantime, while its application to the world in piecemeal is always doubtful, and thunder no longer means the voice of Zeus, its application to the world as a whole may be less open to criticism: we may be right in feeling the world to be the manifestation of a single life.

This intuition is liable to come to clearness at first only in times of extreme emotion; as when in death, illness, and other crises, the claim of nature to supremacy over the human spirit is defied. But it sometimes appears as a purely cognitive sense that matter, motion, energy, must have some mental sponsorship; that nothing could exist eternally, if no mind in all the universe either knew it, or knew why it existed.

20.5. *I may doubt the reality of everything else: I cannot doubt the reality of myself.*

This is the intuition which has become so much the characteristic of modern times that we may regard it as a new insight. It is the discovery most graphically expressed by Descartes, that the *self* is the most certain of all things, the primary thing absolutely certain. Whether or not Descartes correctly described the thing of which he was so sure has been much debated since he wrote; but the main point remains, the locus of supreme certitude is somewhere in the self-awareness of the thinking subject.[7] In this, Descartes was but the spokesman of the modern era, which is an era of heightened self-consciousness, repeating in its own way what the sages of ancient India had long ago discerned, namely, that the Atman or self is the central principle of being.

The new phase of this ancient intuition is the place which the world takes in reference to the self. The earlier intuitions perceived *the self as behind the world*, independent of the world, more real than the world. The Indian sage found that in the practice of his *yoga* he could leave the consciousness of things and emphasize the awareness of self until this self-

---

[4] See Ch. 7.   [5] Names for such a view are "hylozoism" and "panpsychism."
[6] See the writings of Fechner, Haeckel, Verworn, Paulsen, Whitehead.   [7] See §8.6.

consciousness was the whole of consciousness. The newer intuition may be regarded as a discovery of the *world within the self*. For in its own self-certainty nothing of "the world" is excluded: it is kept as "object of consciousness."

When, for example, I see and smell a rose, what is it of which I am most certain? May the rose be a clever artificial flower, and the scent a product of synthetic chemistry? Let my imagination run through all the possibilities of my own error and of the most radical deceptions of art,—and add to these the suppositious deceptions of a magic capable of substituting hypnotic imagery for my own sense-data: what is there which still I cannot doubt nor dissemble? It is the "I see" and the "I smell,"—the experience which now is "mine." Nor can any power, deity or demon, expunge from the universe this fact, that I do now have this experience of sight and smell. This is unbanishable actuality. And within it is the rose as seen and smelt.

And what is true of the rose is true of any other object perceived or thought of: the seeing, hearing, feeling, tasting, thinking are always there and are always the unshakable factors of the situation, whereas the "object" just because it is other than myself can be imagined manipulated or transubstantiated from within its (to me inaccessible) self, and so be other than I think it, or nothing at all! I am sure of these "contents of consciousness" and of my awareness of them: they are within me, and their sum, the world, is within me. "The world is my representation,"—so said Schopenhauer in opening his great work *The World as Will and Idea*.

It is important to be able to see the world through the eyes of this intuition of the self, as containing, by way of its sensations and ideas, the whole of experience. Modern philosophy becomes unintelligible unless one can, at least dramatically, assume this point of view. The mind is a little thing, a mere item in an infinite universe; the mind is itself an infinite thing, the whole universe is mirrored within it. It is this paradox which gives idealism its modern form.

Idealism does not dispute the paradox. In showing us the world within the self, it does not deny that in another sense the self is within the world. To hold that "the whole world in space and time is within myself as I now am" is a "subjectivism" which can hardly be the whole truth. We must however do justice to the truth it has.

20.6. When A. N. Whitehead published his *Science and the Modern World* (1925) he mentioned the intuitions which led him to reject subjectivism. They were in effect these: that I am in the world and not the world in me; that the world existed before me and will exist after me; that my action intends to make changes in a reality distinct from myself. When he published *Nature and Life* (1934) he wrote "We are in the world and the world is in us."

If the two opposing intuitions, "I am in the world" and "The world is in me" are to stand as being equally legitimate, we have a dualism which is only saved from being a contradiction by discriminating different senses of the word "within." It requires at least that something be left outside of my mind, however completely I include in my thought everything I think of! On account of this there are many halfway idealists in modern philosophy. Descartes and Kant are the chief examples. Spinoza and Schelling tried to hold an even hand between the two, and so ended in a metaphysics of neutrality. It is in Leibniz, Berkeley, Fichte and Hegel that idealism comes out with full clarity. We turn to a consideration of Berkeley's thought in more detail.

CHAPTER 21: BERKELEY

21.1. George Berkeley (1685–1753) found that our metaphysical difficulties are made by ourselves: "We have first raised a dust, and then
complain we cannot see." We look at our world and see shapes and colors:
then we mentally add something to the scene which is not there—"physical substance." Why do we project "physical substance" into the picture?
Because we think there must be something to possess these qualities, keep
them together, and enable them to continue in existence when we are
not looking. Thus gold is a substance which "has" the properties of yellow-
ness, heaviness, malleability, metallic lustre, and the rest. This "substance"
is the seat of the capacity which we suppose natural objects have for
independent being. We *impute* substance to things: but we never *find* it:
we find only the qualities. The world would look the same, behave the
same, have the same worth if it were omitted. *Let us omit it!*

Berkeley tried the experiment and found the whole metaphysical outlook instantly simplified. Physical substance is a superfluous puzzle. Qualities like shape and color are "ideas": if they inhere in anything they inhere
in the mind which perceives them; they are produced in us, not by "physical substance" but by another mind which acts directly upon us, the mind
of God. Physical substance may be dismissed: and with immense relief
and illumination.

This clarifying intuition came to Berkeley while he was still a student
at Trinity College, Dublin. His leading ideas were published while he was
still in his twenties.[1] He has so striking a gift of straightforward and persuasive writing that he leads his readers, almost too painlessly, to view
the world with him as a world of perceivers and their perceptions, a world
in which apart from consciousness there is nothing, absolutely nothing,—
and hence no purely physical nature whatever.[2]

In his own day his views were labelled "immaterialism"; his observation was precise and his reasonings were cogent, yet he seemed to destroy

---

[1] *A New Theory of Vision*, 1709; *The Principles of Human Knowledge*, 1710; *Dialogues between Hylas and Philonous*, 1713.
[2] I assume that every student will read something of Berkeley. And since nothing is less needful
than to clarify the clear, our own discussion in the text may be limited to aiding entrance to
Berkeley's world of ideas.

the heart of the substantial world of nature; his position appeared to many of the learned an "irrefutable absurdity."

21.2. Berkeley begins his public argument by an examination of the sense of sight. This is a useful beginning, because almost every one thinks of the real world as the world his eyes reveal to him. Few stop to inquire what it is precisely that we see, and what it is that we believe or construe on the basis of what we see.

Yet every one who draws, paints, makes a photograph, looks at a moving picture is reminded of one striking fact: three dimensions can be represented in two dimensions. There is a line from the eye to each point in the landscape, a ray of light from each point of the landscape to the eye: a plane surface held before the eye would intercept all of these lines: if these rays of light had their origin in that plane instead of in the distant objects, and had precisely the same color-rate, intensity, etc., the eye would see the same scene—how could it help it? Then distance is not something we see?

This is Berkeley's first thesis. We seem to see things at a distance, and for that matter at a graduated scale of distance. We make more or less accurate and instantaneous estimates of distance—otherwise our ordinary operations of reaching, walking, jumping, throwing, shooting, catching would never become skillful. The physical world is there before us in three dimensions, not two. Yet since the flat picture may present the illusion of depth, it is clear that distance is not seen but judged. It is inferred from certain signs. It is a mental fact which we add to the data given by the eye.

What are the signs of distance?

Not the lines and angles of the optical diagrams; for they are not directly felt. But we do feel the "turn of the eyes," the convergence of the optic axes when objects are brought near. We also perceive the confusion in the outline of objects if they are brought too near, and, we may add, the dimness if they are too far away. Also a certain strain of the eye when we try to focus on near objects, and another strain, if we try to make distinct something far away. Further, assuming objects to keep their same sizes, we judge them near if they look large, and far if they look small. Berkeley was not familiar with the stereoscopic effect of the different images on the two retinas. But he had enough to convince him that there are signs in the flat spread of color-spots which enable us to *think* distance; and the distance means to us the measure of effort we have to make to reach or to travel to the point. The eye has to provide us with the prophecies of successful action, contact, escape. Our third dimension of space is an interpretation, not a direct datum of sense: we take as an outward fact what is really the work of the mind.

21.3. Berkeley infers from his own analysis that a person born blind would not, if he suddenly received his sight, at once perceive three dimensions; he would have to learn to co-ordinate visual signs with his muscular habits; he would find difficulty in judging from the picture presented to his eye the solid shapes of objects, such as cubes and spheres.

Consider a test case. There have been various cases of the surgical opening of sight to persons born partially blind. One of them was carefully studied by the psychologist, Professor Latta.[3] John Carruth's eyes were completely cataractous from birth. His hearing was acute and he was able to run about without fear in the small Scotch country town of his birth. He was able to work as florist's assistant, and could make up bouquets by touch. He could dimly distinguish shades of light, could judge the direction of a light, and could tell night from day. At the age of thirty his cataracts were removed. The first object he saw was the face of the surgeon; he judged it to be a face by the mouth movements which accompanied the voice; he felt his own face with his hand while he looked. Some one thought to bring him a ball and a toy brick. He moved his hands as if feeling the objects, and then rightly named the round one and the square-cornered one. He said that the process of handling things had given him a "notion in his mind" of their form and of the meaning of form names. His new estimates of distance were uncertain. He lost his former confidence in moving about in the dark and, transferring the guidance of his movements from the sense of hearing to the new sense of sight, became afraid to move about without his eyes open. This case suggests that sight alone does not give the *amount* of distance; and that the idea of a third dimension which may be present in germ requires to be developed by aid of the experiences of touch and action. To this extent Berkeley is corroborated in his thesis that our visual perception of distance is an interpretation, not a direct datum.

21.4. This is a modest beginning of Berkeley's thesis: it amounts to a point of principle, namely, that what we think of as a property of the object (in this case the third dimension) may be contributed by the mind, even when the mind is unaware of doing so. The apparent independent existence of objects,—independent of their being observed,—may be illusory.

This principle had already been generally admitted prior to Berkeley's time in respect to other aspects of nature, the colors, sounds, tastes, smells, which ancient observation had seen to be different with different observers, and therefore not to be objective fact. Modern thought was coming to the view that our perceptions of color were to be considered as stimulated in the mind by uncolored emanations of some sort from the object—colors

[3] *British Journal of Psychology,* I, No. 2, June, 1904.

are "mental" not physical. Locke had attempted to distinguish the properties which are "mental" in this sense from those which are in the object.
Admitting that unless there are minds-and-eyes to see there are no colors,
without minds-and-ears to hear no sounds, surely, even in the absence of
all mentality, the physical object has its position, shape, size, motion,
solidity. These are what Locke had called the "primary qualities." They
are the qualities with which physics calculates; they are used in the explanation of the outer causes of sensation, as we have just seen in the case
of vision, and we cannot imagine them non-existent.[4]

It is here that Berkeley's meditation about the third dimension begins
to break down the distinction between the primary and the secondary
qualities—there is something mental about distance and position. On
further reflection, all the rest of space must follow! Nature cannot be
divided into two parts, one of which is mental and the other nonmental.
If color is mental, then the space and shape occupied by the color must
be mental likewise. And if space is mental, all the other "primary qualities," motion, solidity, and the others, must follow it into the mind.

Berkeley is thus revolting against what Whitehead called the "bifurcation of nature." Nature is all of a piece—the colors of the sunset belong
with the sunset, and conversely, the sunset belongs with its colors. It is
then either all external to the observer, or else it is all within the observer's
perception. Berkeley takes the latter alternative.

21.5. Having shown all the qualities or properties of objects to be
mental, Berkeley has then to deal with that "substance" which had acted
as their anchor, holding them all securely external to the perceiver.

The conclusion of his argument (developed in *The Principles of
Human Knowledge*) was stated at the head of this chapter. He has no
difficulty in showing that the supposed material "substance" of things is
not utilized either in science or in common life. The chemist can always
determine whether the object before him is gold; but he never does so by
inspecting its "substance," he reaches his conclusions solely on the basis of
its properties—its solubility in different acids, its combining proportions
and weights: these are all he has to work with, and they are all he needs.
Is not the "substance" of gold a mere name for the fact of experience that
these properties belong together?

21.6. We may summarize Berkeley's argument. The human mind is
forever forgetting its own part in making its experience. It fails to recognize color and sound as its own work. It has to learn that space is its

---

[4] Locke, *Essay concerning Human Understanding*, Bk. II, Ch. VIII.

"idea." It seems to perceive things as on their own, as having "substance," forgetting that "substance" is one of its own ideas (or attempts at an idea) by which it generously tries to endow its experience with an existence independent of itself! This effort necessarily fails. The mind cannot set a stake beyond the mind. Nor can it detach its experiences, its "ideas," from itself.

It is convenient to treat physical objects as if they could exist by themselves—we need not remind ourselves at every point that they are our perceptions. Hence, when we say that a thing exists we mentally endow it with independence: we treat it as if "to exist is to be independent." When we wish to emphasize this capacity of the object to continue its character and operations in our absence, we assume that "to exist is to be physical substance." But when we remember ourselves and the truth that an object is always an object of consciousness, of mind, we say that "to exist is to be perceived." This is Berkeley's formula, "*Esse est percipi.*" To which he added the clause "*aut percipere,*" since the perceivers also exist. The sum of all reality consists of perceivers and perceptions, thinkers and their thoughts.

The doctrine that to be is to be perceived enters into a contemporary philosophical movement known as *Existenz-philosophie.* According to these thinkers, among them Professor Heidegger and Professor Jaspers, the most concrete being is not physical, but the physical-held-in-mind; and the mind is most concrete not when it inspects, as an observer, but when it passionately cares about what is before it. If we seek reality we shall find it in experience, deeply and anxiously felt.

21.7. Berkeley is not averse to criticism; he invites those who doubt his argument to state where it is at fault. He anticipates our objections, and answers them. The most persistent of these difficulties are perhaps these: that he seems to destroy the difference between reality and illusion; and that he fails to account for the existence of objects when no mind perceives them.

Professor G. E. Moore wrote in 1903 a notable essay, "The Refutation of Idealism." He is a founder of the New Realism.[5] He pressed against Berkeley a keen logical analysis, maintaining that it was a plain error to propose that "to be" is "to be perceived." Consider, he argues, an object like "blue" and the sensation of that object, the "sensation of blue." We may claim that they are (a) identical, or (b) inseparable. (a) In identifying them, we fall into the contradiction of equating a part with the whole of which it is a part. (b) In claiming that they cannot be separated, we claim either too much or too little to help Berkeley's case. We claim too much if we say the separation is unthinkable, because it obviously is thinkable. We claim too little if we say only that

[5] See Type VI, Realism.

the object and the sensation of it in fact happen always to go together, because this leaves open the possibility that the object might exist unaccompanied by the sensation of it.[6]

This critique sets Berkeley's position in sharp relief. Whenever we abstract an aspect of a thing from the whole, as the color of a surface from its shape and size, we rightly remind ourselves of the abstraction by saying that "to have color is to have shape and size also." Berkeley's point is that the phrase "to exist" is such an abstraction. We complete the fact when we say "to exist is to be an object; to be an object is to be perceived."

21.8. Does Berkeley's idealism destroy the difference between reality and illusion?

Berkeley believed to the contrary.[7] In denying material substance, he denied only what no man ever really thought, because it has no empirical meaning. He felt himself upholding the cause of common sense against the artifice of the intellect which devises the abstraction of "material substance." He is prepared to state in definite terms what the difference between reality and illusion is.

When we discover an illusion to be an illusion, as when we recover from a mirage or from the mistake of thinking a bit of sky seen through trees to be a body of water, it is always experience that replaces experience, a more reliable experience replacing a less reliable. The "reality" is the kind of experience that maintains itself in all subsequent judgment. It is therefore not something outside of experience or, in Berkeley's terms, outside of idea. The marks of the real as distinct from the illusory experience are as follows:

Reality is (a) vivid, strong, lively, distinct; it (b) has order and coherence, we can trace it out in minute detail and it never vanishes under our hand, as dreams do; in particular it (c) has biological consequences,—it causes pleasure and pain, the real fire burns, the real food sustains us, the real rock displays its habitual inertia. The more violently you encounter "reality"—if you take the direction of Doctor Johnson's toe-stubbing refutation, the more certainly you play into Berkeley's hands. For nobody supposes the pain of a stubbed toe to be out of consciousness, and here the pain and the resistance are found together. When we "learn from experience" it is reality which teaches us; but what we learn is that x leads to y, fire leads to burning,—we learn the connections between our experiences— and these laws of connection, as objects of thought, are part of our perception of the world. The real remains within experience.

Might we add to these marks of "reality" (d) that it is external to us? Physical reality is for the most part external to our body; and this "ex-

---

[6] A kindred analysis is to be found in W. P. Montague, *The Ways of Knowing*, Ch. X, part iv.
[7] See *The Principles of Human Knowledge*, §§29, 30, 33, 34.

ternality" is the source of much of the resistance to Berkeley's argument. But "external to the body" or "outside of the head" or "in front of the eyes" does not mean external to the mind. Body, head, eyes, are all spatial objects, and they with all other physical things are external to the mind in the sense that they are objects and not the mind itself. But space and all its contents Berkeley has shown to be mental: none of these objects is beyond the mind; they are all qualities of *experience*, they are not outside experience.

All this indicates that reality is simply *standard experience,* and illusion is experience which fails to come up to standard in some one or more respects. Hence the world retains under Berkeley's view all the reality that it can have in the mind of any man who is not misled by abstract ideas.

We have, however, omitted one characteristic of reality which seems to stand apart. It is (*e*) active or a product of external action. I do not make it. I have no choice what I shall see when I open my eyes. This means, to Berkeley, that it is produced in us by the only active thing we know, namely, a living spirit outside ourselves, certainly not by an inert material substance.

21.9. *Does Berkeley's idealism leave absent or unperceivable objects out of account,* such objects as atoms, or unknown stars, or the unobserved and partly unknown forces with which physics reckons? Or even the furniture in houses at night, the unobserved interior of the earth, the continuing processes within us and without us which follow their courses without our knowledge and maintain the perfect march of the world's aging?

Berkeley's reply here is complete also.[8] The fragmentary world of direct perception is made, by scientific thought, into a complete and continuous whole. Of this supplement to perception, it is obviously in the first place, for us, an object of *thought;* and thoughts are not out of mind. Science does not use "substance": it only uses *law,*—the rule by which experiences follow one another, depend on one another, and so are always supplementing one another to make up a complete world picture.

When we say, then, that nature exists when no man perceives it, and that it existed before man existed to perceive it, we can only mean that the laws continue to hold, backward as well as forward without limit in time or space; and this may be true since there exists an eternal mind to think them. The mind of God is the guarantee, and the only guarantee, for the eternal endurance and order of nature.

[8] *Ibid.,* §§62, 65, 66.

CHAPTER 22:
SUBJECTIVE IDEALISM

22.1. We wish now to consider the argument of idealism in independence of Berkeley's line of thought.

The negative proposition of idealism is that nature is not *independently* real. It is real in the sense defined by Berkeley: it has an internal standard which corrects illusion. But it is not real as an independent, self-sufficient being: its reality is derived from the life sustaining it.

The illusion of nature's independence comes very largely from the belief that the objects which we perceive are the *causes* of our perceiving them, in other words, that there is in nature a genuine and original activity which can affect the mind, and which does in fact produce our sensations.

This impression can be shown conclusively to be mistaken by an argument independent of Berkeley's. The argument consists in assuming that the theory of physically caused perception is true, and observing that it leads to self-contradiction.

22.2. Simply stated, the argument requires chiefly that we be able to count two, and remember which of the items we have counted was which. It runs thus: if physical things are *causes* of our perceptions as the naturalist holds, they are not our perceptions; and our perceptions, as their effects, are not these physical things: but our perceptions are what we have of the world, hence we do not have the world itself before us, but only a subjective mental representation of it. But this result is contradictory to the assumption of naturalism, that we have the real world before us.

This statement may be too brief to be easily followed: I will therefore give the argument a fuller and more carefully ticketed form. Take any object in nature (N) and any observer (S), and follow the naturalistic explanation of how S comes to know N.

Let N be a candle, for example, and let us trace the course of the physical action of the light through the eye to the retina and the brain. The event in the brain is not itself luminous, nor candle-shaped; but on the basis of that brain-event, and at the same time with it, the mind (S) has an impression of the candle. Designate the impression as n to distinguish

166

it from the real candle, N. It is the effect; the candle-light is the cause: cause and effect are obviously not identical.

We have now to reflect that we who follow this process are ourselves observers of the candle, and are *in the same position* toward the object in which S stands. Let me take myself as an example, and designate myself as S^1.

My impression of the candle, n^1, will then be different from the candle itself, N.

But now, which is the impression and which is the candle? I cannot disown my impression: the impression is *what I have*, just as for S, the impression n is what he has. But what I have is just what I have been calling N. N must be my impression, then, and not the real candle. The real cause has slipped away from me; and I am left with a world composed of n's, a world of my impressions.

Thus, beginning with naturalism, which gives full credit to the appearance of nature before me as being the real thing with which I have to do, we end in subjective idealism, which contradicts that beginning.

This does not prove subjective idealism to be true. It proves my original assumption of common sense naturalism to be wrong. If subjective idealism is true, it needs further evidence.

22.3. Further evidences for the inclusion of the objects of experience in the mind:

a. There is no jar nor break nor discernible line between perception and memory. Can any one locate in his own experience the point at which a sound ceases to be heard and begins to be remembered? In the hearing of a word of several syllables, the syllable just past seems to be there with the syllable just now being uttered. But the past exists only in the mind. Therefore the present presumably exists in the same manner.

b. What is included in the word mind? A mind would not be complete without its thoughts and its sensations. But the objects of nature are contents either of thought or of sensation or of both. And neither thinking nor sensing can exist without contents. Hence there is nothing in nature which is not an integral part of what we mean by mind.

c. When we think of nature as other than mind, we think of its "externality" or its "objectivity." The question is *what we mean* by externality or objectivity. Whatever the answer, objectivity must be something I mean or think. And the effort *by thought* to get beyond the mind is evidently doomed from the start to failure: The mind may always say,

"When me they fly, I am the wings."

It is true that thought always brings us nearer to reality; but it is also true that the more we think, the more thoroughly the object is a thought-object, i. e., the more completely it is "taken up into the subject." Kant's *Critique of Pure Reason* is an attempt to show that not only space and time as the empty framework of nature, but also the ideas of substance and causation and interaction, of quantity and relation, all of which go to make up the physical objects with which science deals, are *thoughts*, or thought-forms, into which the mind receives the raw material of experience, and thus shapes experience.[1]

22.4. Immanuel Kant is a writer whose thought we have earlier met with, as setting limits to the use of reason in metaphysics [2]—and shall meet again, for there is no phase of philosophy on which Kant has not left a durable impression. We are here concerned with the affirmative aspect of his view of knowledge, namely, that certain fundamental characters of nature are the *work of the mind*, so that the physical world which we observe as outside of us, is in some sense within us. "Outwardness" is itself a form of thought.

Like Berkeley, Kant begins his *Critique of Pure Reason* with reflections on the nature of *space*. But he joins *time* with space: they must be taken together in stretching the measure of the world-room in which the universe is spread. Let us carry farther our previous meditations on space and time:

Each is endless; for if we try to set a boundary, there is always more beyond. Each is intangible; for if we encounter any *thing* in space, or any *event* in time, we at once distinguish it from the space or time it "occupies,"—two distinguishable forms of emptiness. They are, as it were, two kinds of nothing, which would be an absurdity unless it were also true that each kind of nothing has its own structure. Space is a manifold of positions, each position perfectly distinct from every other; time is a manifold of dates, each distinct from every other. If space and time have a grain, it is so fine that there is no limit to the possibility of making minute separations of position. They are both "continuous"—there is no gap in either, for if there were a gap it would be a space-or-time gap: there can be no holes in space for a hole is a space. Each lends itself to mathematical treatment. Kant thought that geometry was peculiarly applicable to space and arithmetic to time. But a generalized geometry of intervals applies to both; and arithmetic applies to both, for there can be no geometry without distinctions, and no distinctions without number and measure. And

---

[1] *Critique of Pure Reason,* Transcendental Analytic, Bk. II, Ch. II.
[2] Above, pp. 83–85.

further: every continuum requires for its description those extensions of number-theory which deal with infinite collections.

Space and time present mysteries for any view of the world. Naturalism is peculiarly embarrassed by the fact that they are apart from all natural happening. They have no evolution; they are changeless; they could have had *no* beginning. For all beginnings are *in* time; and time, therefore, is before and after every beginning. Time measures all change; but for that reason, the time-order itself cannot change.

In view of the enigmas which lie in the nature of space and time, Herbert Spencer calls them "inconceivable." Kant offers a different account of them.

Kant's interest is taken by the question how we know space and time. We can hardly say we perceive them by the senses for they are themselves imperceptible, and they extend beyond the limits of sensation. We know, for example, that space is behind us as well as in front of us. As Kant puts it, space is "not given by experience" because there could be no experience of things unless space were "ready" to place such experience. We cannot think space away though we can imagine all its contents to disappear. (This involves an exercise of imagination which one should try with some care. As you annihilate the last object in space, is space left intact?) This implies that it is not given to us in the same way as its contents. If it is an insuppressible notion, even when there are no objects of sense, must it not be a product of the mind's own action?

And there is one further, and to Kant conclusive, evidence that we are admitted into the very origin of space, namely that geometry is taken to be valid for all parts of it, however remote, without the necessity of testing it from place to place. The conclusion drawn by Kant is that space is a form or *order of arrangement* of the stuff of sensation, which order is the work of the mind itself. He calls it an *a priori* form of perception. Our geometry is a universal geometry because the objects to which it applies are our own construction, based upon this *a priori* form of perception, and therefore uniform everywhere. A corresponding argument for time leads to the conclusion that time is the *a priori* form of our perception of the succession of our own mental states. The science of number, based on this succession, is thus *a priori*; and the general principles of the science of motion, kinematics, which unites considerations of number with space and time, are likewise *a priori*.

The developments since Kant's time of non-Euclidean geometries, and of the physics of relativity, have led to modifications of the Newtonian views of space with which Kant was familiar. But Kant's contribution is not thereby cancelled,—a view to which Einstein definitely subscribes.[3] And it will be well for the reader to remember that much of the language of recent physical theory is in flux: its negations are themselves "relative," making use of common terms with altered meanings. For example, when "curved space" is referred to in physics, the curvature must apply to an assumed physical medium occupying space, not to purely mathematical space alone.

If space and time are the work of the mind, then the entire phenomenal world will share that character in respect to its extent and the relations of its parts. For this reason, questions about the beginning and end of the world will lead to mental confusion, if we assume that the extent of the world is a fixed external fact. We find that we can give plausible reasons for supposing that the world has no beginning in time and no limit in space; we find that we can give equally good reasons for thinking that the world must have had a beginning in time [4] and a limit in space. The logical situation is an "antinomy": both propositions appear inescapable, both cannot be true. Likewise for the divisibility of things—they must be and cannot be infinitely divisible. These antinomies had very early impressed the mind of Kant, and had led him, quite apart from his observations on space and time above reviewed, to the belief that these characters of the world are not objective, and that the question whether the world has or has not a beginning does not admit of an objective answer. Wherever we go, we carry space-time order with us; there is therefore no limit to the extent to which we can *trace* history backward, or the stellar universe outward, or the minute structure of things inward. But in itself, the world has no spatial-temporal aspect; hence there is no pertinence to the enquiry after such.

So far, Kant's thought has dealt with the formal order of experience. But what of its stuff? Strangely enough, while mankind was more nearly ready to accept the stuff of sensation (the "secondary qualities") as subjective than to think of space and time as subjective, Kant takes the reverse position: this sense-stuff is the given "manifold" which we do not

[3] "The following, however, appears to me to be correct in Kant's statement of the problem: in thinking we use, with a certain 'right,' concepts to which there is no access from the materials of sensory experience, if the situation is viewed from the logical point of view . . . I am convinced that even much more is to be asserted: the concepts which arise in our thought and in our linguistic expressions are all—when viewed logically—the free creations of thought which cannot inductively be gained from sense-experience." (Albert Einstein in Schilpp, *The Philosophy of Bertrand Russell*, Evanston, 1946, p. 287.) Arthur H. Compton has said, "In fact, one may question whether without Kant's analysis of . . . space and time, such a development as Einstein's theory of relativity could have occurred." (*Proceedings of the American Philosophical Society*, August 31, 1956, pp. 296 f.)

[4] For example, an infinite series is one which cannot be completed; but if we assume an infinite past, we must assert that the series of time-moments has *arrived* at the Now, its present terminus.

ourselves beget, and which definitely betokens outer activity. It is pre-supposed in all the ordering work of the mind.

Upon the space-time arrangement there is built the structure of our concepts of substance, causal relationship, world system. Of these ideas, or "categories," Kant has to say as he said of space and time: [5] that they are not given in experience (which is the reason Locke, Berkeley, and Hume cannot find them there); that they make experience possible, for without them the reliable connection and association of quality with quality could not be so much as stated; and that they are therefore the work of the mind, and *a priori* necessary. It is not accurate, then, to say with Berkeley that there is no physical substance, nor with Hume that there is no objective causality: if there is any nature at all, or any intelligible experience, sub-stance and cause are in the constitution of it. But without the mind there would be no order of nature, nothing but the unknowable, unspatial, un-temporal, uncausal source of the manifold stuff.

When we attempt to grasp the world of nature as a whole as an ob-jective fact we find not alone the puzzles of substance with which Berkeley and Hume wrestled, but further antinomies regarding causality and the totality of things. If we have causes at all there must be somewhere first causes, free origination such as we presume to be in the free will; and yet there cannot be first causes, because any origination must have its own reason or prior cause. So also the world has its totality, we can think of it as a whole; and yet the world cannot have any totality, for it cannot be enclosed or finished. These antinomies resolve themselves when we recog-nize that causality and the very idea of "world" cannot be attributed to objects apart from the mind. The categories apply only to "experience"; and all the confusions of metaphysics arise from trying to apply them to things as they are in themselves. There can be no scientific metaphysics.

Kant's system of thought may be taken as a powerful technical elabora-tion of the thesis that the mind is a factor in constituting the world which it seems to observe as an independent, external, and self-operating object. In beholding and thinking the world, the mind is recovering awareness of itself.

[5] See also the discussion of Kant, p. 84, above.

CHAPTER 23:
SUBJECTIVE IDEALISM EXAMINED

23.1. Subjective idealism in its pure form is not found in Berkeley or Kant. Each leaves for the individual mind some link with an outer world. Yet each uses arguments which would justify a complete subjectivism: "The world is my representation." This position is approximated by Leibniz, for whom each self is a "monad," a completely closed universe of experience, spontaneously unrolling its own panorama in perfect independence of, but also in perfect synchronism with, that of every other monad.[1] It is the logical conclusion of the principle that whatever I perceive or think of is "in my mind." For whatever be the object of my thought, even though it be the whole world or the whole of past or future history, still I can always prefix the clause "I think," and this at once exhibits the object as my idea. The "I think" is but the acknowledgment of the latent or subconscious tie of possession which moors all my objects to me, and gathers them within what I call my self.

We feel this philosophy extravagant. It is literally a cosmic egoism. It was most violently asserted, with the ethical consequences which might be supposed to follow from thinking of all my objects, including fellow human beings, as mere images before me, by Max Stirner in *Der Einzige und sein Eigentum.* Our present task is to define our uneasiness about extreme subjectivism and to see whither it leads. The idealistic insight is too deep founded to be essentially wrong. The form of it before us is too self-enclosed to be entirely right.

23.2. The defects of subjective idealism will become apparent by carrying certain of its theses to their full consequences. Consider three difficult corollaries which would seem to follow consistently from subjective idealism.

a. *The plurality of independent worlds.*

If my world is made of my ideas, and my ideas are products of my activity,—and if each person is, as he seems to be, distinct from every other,— then for each thinker there must be a separate space-time order with a separate nature in it. There will be as many worlds as there are minds. This

[1] Leibniz, *The Monadology.*

conclusion is accepted by Leibniz, each monad being a complete micro-cosm to itself.

Accepting this pluralistic tendency in idealism, Leibniz developed one of the major systems of philosophy. In summary, his doctrine was that God's power sustains a universe made up of an infinity of living units of consciousness, the higher ones called minds, all the lower ones "corresponding somewhat to souls." Each such real unit is a unit of action, continuously aware of the universe from its unique point of view, guided entirely from within by its own law of operation. So each living unit includes within itself a complete world picture or "perspective." It is evident then that we cannot think of monads as strewn about *in space.* Spatial order and temporal order are, rather, in each monad,—thought more clearly in human minds, sensed more confusedly in inferior monads. None of these units really exerts an influence on the others. All spontaneously act in harmony, through God's creative power.

Closely allied with the "monadic idealism" of Leibniz is the modern movement, Personalism, the doctrine that the universe is a plurality of persons.[2] It also is con-cerned to do justice to the pluralistic element in idealism.

b. *Solipsism.*

I cannot forget that my neighbors are parts of my world, and that I have ideas of them also. I must accept the logic of "my having ideas" as ap-plying to them. Then in dealing with what I take to be these other selves, I shall be dealing with objects of my own thought. Consequently I have no real conversation with other original sources of thought; no really social life. Love and hate become pantomimic. Each person is shut up to himself alone, *solus ipse.*

Leibniz was willing to accept this conclusion also: the monads, he said, "have no windows." And not a few thinkers have felt that the conclusion is logically inescapable; and that we can rescue ourselves from it only by a wrench of faith which is pragmatically, but not rationally, justified. Quite apart from the argument of subjectivism, it appears to other thinkers ob-vious that we do not *perceive* other minds than our own; but that we have good reasons for asserting their existence: we *infer* the existence of per-sons not ourselves. But an inference is, of course, a thought: and the thought of other conscious beings is not their actual presence. I cannot by inference escape the circle of my own subjectivity.

c. *God as an idea.*

Both Descartes and Berkeley appeal to God to escape from the magic circle of the self. Berkeley, for instance, regards the knowledge of passivity in sensation as the sign of the outer reality of God who acts upon us. But is not the sense of being acted upon also an "idea"? I have the idea of my passivity, and the idea that this implies an agent. But these again are my thoughts. God as the assumed cause of the stuff of experience becomes an

[2] See E. S. Brightman, *Person and Reality.*

hypothesis, an object within my mind and made by mind. Is there any better reason for believing in God than for believing in matter, or in other minds? Or rather, as objects of belief, must not God and other minds alike be taken within my own mind?

23.3. These disturbing consequences do not constitute a disproof of subjective idealism. They do not appear to contradict it. It is conceivable that one might accept them all as results of theoretical analysis, while reserving, as Hume did, the freedom to believe otherwise when in the company of his friends the rigors of intellect were off duty.

But subjectivism meets also the vigorous opposition of certain intuitions which must be set side by side with the intuitions leading to idealism. We have an intuition that we are not alone, and that the figures we deal with are real and present persons. We also have an intuition that the space and time of *our* experience are identically the same as *their* space and time; and that the world of nature is therefore one and not many.

These intuitions, especially the first, are so strong that many have taken it as sufficient disproof of any philosophy to show that solipsism is one of its consequences.

But we are bound, if we believe in reason, to turn these intuitions also into conceptual form, and not leave them as simple dogmas. When intuition clashes with intuition, that is the specific occasion for thinking! It will not do to refute solipsism by merely refusing to believe it.

23.4. Professor R. B. Perry gives a rational diagnosis of subjective idealism, by pointing out and labelling its fallacies. Chief among them is the fallacy of argument from the "ego-centric predicament." [3] Our situation is admittedly "ego-centric," i. e., everything we think of is our thought: we cannot get away from the "I think," which binds all objects within the self. But this situation Professor Perry regards as a "predicament" as well, because it prevents us from knowing objects which we neither perceive nor think of, although, he holds, *there may be such objects*. It is fallacious, he argues, to generalize about what exists on the basis of what we ego-centric beings can find, as if a person with blue glasses on should say there is nothing red in the world! The statement "I *can find* nothing but my ideas" does not imply that "*Nothing exists* but my ideas"; for the "predicament" simply prevents me from finding the negative instances, the things which exist beyond my perception and thought. [4]

This criticism is indeed pointed, and yet it does not reach to the root of the matter. It appears that in pleading for the possibly unperceived and

[3] R. B. Perry, *Present Philosophical Tendencies* (New York, 1912), pp. 129–132.
[4] Compare with §21.7. See also Type VI, Realism.

unthought negative instances, one is to think that he in his non-egocentric capacity, can think of objects which he, in his ego-centric capacity, cannot think of. Unluckily, the subjectivist has already thought of them. The trouble with subjective idealism is not a fear that there may exist objects which, because of our ego-prison, we do not find; the trouble is that this idealism seems to dispute what we *do find*—the other person here present and the singleness of the world we have in common. It is to these findings or intuitions that we must do justice.

23.5. We come nearer to the heart of the difficulty when we observe that, just as Berkeley could show that real and unreal are distinctions within experience, so self and not-self are distinctions within experience. That is to say, each self is self-conscious, has an awareness of itself, an idea of itself; and precisely because every idea is in contrast with what it is not, each self has also an idea of what is not itself.

Solipsism is a self-refuting position.

Whoever says "I can know only my ideas" makes a tacit admission: in imagining himself as *confined* to his own ideas, he confesses a fancy that he might know something else, otherwise his proposition has no significance. He is like Professor Perry, who thinks that there may be objects the egocentric self does not think of. His assertion therefore avows a wider horizon than "only his ideas." Ironically, he must mentally get out of himself in order to assert that he is confined to himself. Just so Leibniz, as philosopher, when he asserts that the monads have no windows, is placing himself outside them all; and knowing them to be plural and different from his own monad, is ascribing to this, his monad, an ample window— perhaps a complete absence of walls.

Now it would be impossible for me to think of what is not myself or beyond my ideas unless experience were providing material for proposing to me the conceptions of self and not-self simultaneously.

The error of subjectivism, and *a fortiori* of solipsism, lies in supposing that an idea of what is not self is a contradiction in terms, whereas the contradiction lies in asserting that the self is confined to ideas of self.

But subjectivism persists in its question, How can there be an idea of anything beyond myself? The answer to this question is a crucial point in philosophy.

23.6. It is the nature of knowledge to lay hold on what is not myself. An idea is, generally speaking, an idea of something not identical with the thinker. To perceive is to appropriate, to make my own what is being "given": my idea of the object is my degree of possession, shown in my degree of capacity to reproduce in imagination and ultimately in fact.

Empirical knowing is an *entering into* my idea, not the mere thereness of idea: its first stage is my contact with what is not myself.

The truth of subjective idealism is that whatever I know or have an idea of *becomes* mine. I remember it, take mental possession of it, use it in imagination and dream, reproduce it in a thousand ways. There is nothing we perceive which we cannot reproduce; and indeed, by retaining, we immediately proceed to reproduce every incoming impression. The world *becomes* my idea. But in its first presentation it is not mine. And while Kant and Leibniz are right, that sensation itself is an active process in which the mind is interpreting its received material by means of its own thoughts, they are wrong when they suppose that, because of this activity, we are not also passive or receptive. Kant insisted that we receive the stuff of experience, but create the form: the truer view is that we *receive both stuff and form,* and re-create both. Experience does come in to us from outside.

The real question, then, is as to the *nature of this outside and active reality.*

23.7. Here the naturalist wishes us to go back to the position that this not-self consists of matter or energy. But this we cannot do, since the position has been shown untenable in reason; [5] just as Bergson has shown it untenable in intuition. The true philosophy must preserve all that is true in subjective idealism; the destruction of the conception of material inanimate substance considered as a rootage of all physical beings in a completely self-sufficient, inanimate reality, the independent world of nature,— this negative proposition of idealism cannot be undone. There can be no going back to naturalism.

Also, the positive proposition stands, that reality is of the nature of mind. The error lies solely in the possessive "my." There is something beyond self, as real as myself; but that outer reality is not matter, it is other mind. That which acts upon me in sense-experience is some mind other than my own.

For the only thing that can limit or act upon a self is another self. Self is like space: it can only be limited by something of its own kind. Reality is what corrects our errors; but what is that? When I rectify a mistake, it is because a false judgment is displaced, not by a dead fact, but by a true judgment. The true judgment is what is forced upon me. But a judgment belongs to a judging mind. The world of reality, therefore, which is the world of truth, is the world of a universal and final judgment, a universal self.

[5] See §22.2.

We thus pass from subjective idealism to *objective idealism*.

We shall proceed to consider the position of objective idealism both from the point of view of nature, and from that of our social world.

23.8. Let us first re-phrase the discussion to this point.

Idealism has too long been identified by its critics with the subjective theory of knowledge: it is time for a fairer statement of its position, and so for a better understanding among contemporary schools of philosophy, all of which have learned from the century of debate.

Solipsism tends to vanish as a theory of knowledge. It is generally agreed that experience involves knowing a reality not ourselves. We have never been shut up to ourselves. The question is, What is that other thing? Idealism does not answer idly, My thought. It answers, Some conscious life exhibiting itself to my thought. Experiencing is intercourse with a not-self; but it is not staring across, as over a chasm; it is a passing across, and an adoption. The epistemology of realism, as we have touched upon it, tends to be a static congealing of the first stage of knowing: true, but purely cross-sectional.

The subjective intuition itself we fail to estimate at its legitimate value, because too much has been built upon it. It continues to impress us as an epistemological trick; and we are satisfied, when we have "refuted" it or bluntly rejected it, that we have disposed of it, root and branch. Finding that it is not the complete solution of the world-riddle, we fail to see in it a *partial indication of world-structure*. The latent "I think" is not to be ignored: [6] to affect to regard it as unimportant is to elevate into a principle the forgetfulness-of-self which is appropriate to specific action. There is no full account of reality which abstracts from the reach of selfhood into all its pores, and not only of the observing self, also of the self that wills and cares. The subjective argument has amply shown that the factuality of things is not their essence: in some way, their being is what they mean.

Finally, some of the results of the subjective analyses are discounted because they have so thoroughly gone into our life blood. Classical materialism is dead.[7] What we have is "experience." And as preliminary analyses of experience, if not as finalities, Hume's distinctions, the phenomenological point of view, the descriptive methods of Mach, Pearson, Poincaré, the new subjectivism of physics, modern realism itself, have become possible.

On these results, the philosophical world should be prepared to agree.

---

[6] The continuing influence of E. Husserl and his renewal of the Cartesian insight is evidence of this.

[7] Dialectical materialism is not to be confused with classical materialism.

CHAPTER 24: OBJECTIVE IDEALISM

24.1. Objective idealism meets half-way the feeling of naturalism that nature does not belong to me, the private self, but existed before me and will exist after me.

It also retains all that is valid in subjective idealism. Subjective idealism has shown beyond question that classical materialism is an impossible philosophy. And it has given strong support to the view that reality is mental, by showing the genuine creative power of the mind. For though the experience of nature is first given to us by an outside agency, we at once proceed to interpret and reproduce what is given us: we are first passive and then active. It is the extraordinary extent and power of this silent activity which alone justifies the audacious hypothesis of objective idealism that a mind *could* create nature, that the reality behind and within nature *could* be mental.

24.2. We can best appreciate what mental activity can do by considering the process of dreaming: for in sleep the intrusions of outer reality are—not abolished, but reduced to a minimum. The vivid dream has all the concreteness of experience. It often exceeds reality, both in the direction of realizing wishes and ambitions—for it is most completely in dreams that our "dreams come true"—and in the opposite direction of giving actual shape to our chief fears and dreads. We seem passive to our dreams as to our waking experience; the conscious self has little power to control the course of the dream event. Yet the dream must be, in all pictorial detail, the product of our minds, our subjective imagination.

Now in waking hours, the mind is similarly active, though its activity is partly overborne, like stars in daylight, by the superior vividness of what we call the "real" world. But it is not wholly overborne: it is easy to demonstrate that we are contributing every moment to the fabric of what we perceive. We hear a sound; we immediately interpret it as a "step," a "bell," an "auto horn," adding a visual image to the sound. Even in direct vision we see very largely what we expect to see rather than what is there,—otherwise the professional magicians would find it harder to deceive us and proof-readers would more certainly see the mistakes in spelling. Some of the arts depend on this mental supplementation of fact. A "two-color" process in coloring moving pictures uses only reds and greens; but the observer sees a much fuller gamut of color, supplying the blues and yellows from his own resources, and enjoying the picture as though they were there. In such pictures, continuity of motion, distance, and some elements of color are all supplied by the observer. Thus the very stuff of sensation, which even Kant assumed to be imported into the mind, is to some extent the product of the mind.

All this activity of ours is, of course, secondary: its materials are derived from some previous experience, for the most part. But what it shows is that there is nothing given in experience which we are not *capable* of reproducing. We are not the original creators of our world, but we are apprentices in creativity: we are learning how to produce a world out of our own store. Just as, when we read history, there is nothing there recorded which is not of the nature of ourselves,[1] so, as we apprehend nature, there is nothing in its fabric which remains alien to our powers of reproduction.

It is the reality of this creative power of the human mind which gives substance to the hypothesis of objective idealism: we have in our own being something like in kind to the activity which produces nature and presents it to us.

24.3. The supreme mind producing nature would indeed differ from our own, and not merely in greatness: it would also be different in quality. Our minds can only create after they have learned from experience: but the world-mind must bring forth the qualities of experience from itself, without previous pattern: it must therefore be wholly active, not partly passive—"pure act" as the scholastic theologians put it. Further, in its deliberate thought of the world, which is the creation of the world, it presents the world not alone to itself but to us; and this process of *communicating* the world-perception to other minds is evidently a different process from that of simply imagining an object for oneself.[2] Thus the world-mind, while sharing with our minds the essential elements of thought and will which justify the term "mind," is profoundly different from our minds.

But these differences do not affect the main hypothesis: that the reality of nature consists in its being willed (and therefore thought) by a creative mind.

[1] See Ralph Waldo Emerson's essay on *History*.

[2] Our own existence, as minds distinct from the world-mind, has also to be accounted for. As an example of an objective idealist inquiring into these problems, see Josiah Royce, *The World and the Individual*, especially Vol. II.

24.4. It has sometimes been taken as a sufficient proof of objective idealism that it avoids the difficulties of both naturalism and subjective idealism, while satisfying the idealistic intuitions of the race. It is the hypothesis to which we are naturally led when we try to combine what is true in subjectivism with what is true in naturalism. It is, in short, a "synthesis" of these two incomplete and imperfect views.

This is sometimes called a *dialectical* proof: the "thesis" (naturalism) leads to the "antithesis" (subjective idealism); and these in turn lead to the synthesis.

But all we can fairly say of such a synthesis is that it is a better theory than either of the two earlier theories: it accounts for all the truth so far brought to light. It may, in turn, be superseded, unless every effort to depart from it brings us back to it. It would thus be in order to seek other evidence that nature depends upon a creative mind. Let me mention some of this evidence, not by way of proof but by way of indication:

24.5. *As life comes only from life, so mind comes only from mind.*

Pasteur made it a probable hypothesis that under present terrestial conditions, living organisms come only from preceding living organisms. Bergson, in *Creative Evolution,* may be said to have generalized this doctrine in his view that all life in the cosmos comes from a single source, *l'élan vital.* There is reason to believe that "life," as Bergson meant it, is mental in nature; and that the doctrine can be further specified in the form, "mind only comes from mind." When mind seems to "emerge" from something non-mental, the particular arrangements of matter, nerve-cells or brains, which serve as its physical organs, become organs of *mind* only if mind is already present in the universe.[3]

24.6. *Causality is purposive.*

In our chapter on "The Newer Teleology" [4] we showed that causality is compatible with purpose. We brought out no positive evidence that the causal energy of nature *is* purposive. But what is energy? Is it mere mathematics?

Schopenhauer believed that at one point we have an inner view of energy, namely in our own will. The energy which appears in the brain as chemical or electrical appears in the mind as will-energy; and this is its true nature. Spencer only carries this idea from the brain into the outer world when he argues that in lifting a weight the pull down must be equal in quantity to the pull up when the weight is held in equilibrium; and things can be equal in quantity only when they are alike in kind: the feel of the up-pull must then be some clue to the nature of the down-pull.

---

[3] See Lloyd Morgan, *Emergent Evolution;* L. T. Hobhouse, *Development and Purpose.* S. Alexander, in *Space, Time and Deity,* however, takes an opposing view.
[4] Ch. 7.

But there are certain signs, too, in the way in which scientists have treated the *laws* of energy, that they have intuitively assigned to nature a certain moral quality. In his experiments on the law of falling bodies, Galileo, hampered by poor technical facilities for exact measurement, had to retard the fall by rolling the body down an inclined plane. In doing so, he made the assumption that the velocity of the ball at the foot of the plane would be the same no matter what the slope of the plane. What was the idea that led to this assumption? He reasoned that if we could vary the final speed of the ball by varying the slope of the plane, it would be possible to combine different slopes in such wise that by rolling the ball down the slope giving greater speed and then back again over the slope giving lesser speed, the ball could be made to rise higher than its source. And this he held to be impossible, on grounds which we should to-day recognize as the principle of the conservation of energy; but which to Galileo meant simply an unproved conviction that there was a certain integrity in nature's operations which never encouraged the wish to get something for nothing. Nature he felt to have something of the character of a just judge, implacable, perhaps, but reliable, invariable, impartial.

The laws of nature have sometimes been likened to the *habits* of living beings: [5] certainly they are arrangements to which the habits of living things within nature respond. The above considerations suggest that the laws of nature may have a rational meaning; and that the events of nature —though not expressing, like our own deeds, so many separate impulses of will—may express a consistent will animating the whole cosmic order.

24.7. *Law is an expression of intelligence.*

Indeed, the very notion of *law* in nature is baffling when we try to exclude mind from nature. We commonly take physical laws for granted, as descriptive summaries of the regular sequences of events: when x happens, y follows. That is, the appearance of x constitutes a sort of signal for the appearance of y. Now we know well enough what it means for a mind to perceive a signal and make the appropriate response. But we have not the slightest idea what a signal might mean in a perfectly inanimate world.

Take one of the simplest of laws, Newton's conception of gravitation: this implies that the motion of every particle in the universe is continuously and instantly responsive to the position and mass of every other particle in the universe. How is such a thing possible! It is one of the tremendous assumptions we make, and legitimately, when we are concerned only with the description of what happens. But it is none the less staggering; and for philosophy the question, "How?" will not down.

---

[5] See J. Royce, *The World and the Individual,* II (New York, 1901), p. 226. Also C S. Peirce and A. N. Whitehead.

Francis Bacon was prepared to credit material bodies with a sort of apprehension, though not a conscious perception, of each other. Hermann Lotze (1817–1881) [6] was not ready to attribute this degree of sensitivity to each particle. He pointed out that the many changes of the universe can be regarded as *one change,* a vast equilibrium constantly disturbed and constantly restored. And he proposed that this type of change implies a single mind, within which every partial change is instantly adjusted to every other partial change.

We readily grant, as Lotze points out, that human law only exists when it is thought of: if all citizens were asleep, the laws of the state could only in a Pickwickian sense be said to "exist." How, then, do the laws of nature exist? Only in the sense that events occur "according to" them: they are "observed" if not "obeyed." And this would seem to imply *knowledge,* if not in the parts of nature, then in the whole. For a law, a way of acting, is a generality, a "universal": and a generality can only be apprehended by a mind. Such is Lotze's thought.

24.8. If these indications are true, we should be justified in regarding the order of nature as the literal presence of a Reason in nature. The cosmological argument for the existence of God [7] drew an inference from nature as an effect to an intelligent Creator as a cause: this Creator was regarded as substantially distinct from the created world. The view of objective idealism would be that the world-mind is *within* the processes of nature: that those processes are the very reasonings of that mind; the passage from cause to effect is its *drawing* of consequences, its consistency of thought and steadfastness of purpose. The progress of science would be, not in a figurative but in a literal sense, the tracing of the paths of the divine thought. And the fact that science *can* think the world, that successful hypotheses can be found, would be understood by the fact that the world is nothing else in its fabric than the object of an eternal thought.

The teleological argument, likewise,[8] would be reinstated on a different footing. It is not that the world as a finished result is to be ascribed to a beneficent Deity as an external designer. But rather, the very march of nature, the *change* of the world as well as its being, is the working of an eternally present cosmic purpose within the frame of events. Nature is moving not only out of the past but toward the future; and, whether we can discern it or not, there is meaning and value in what now is, and in its motion, and in that toward which it moves.

[6] R. B. Perry, *Philosophy of the Recent Past* (New York, 1926), pp. 90–91.
[7] See §4.2.   [8] See §4.2.

CHAPTER 25: WHY NATURE EXISTS

25.1. For many people, perhaps for most people, the sticking point in philosophy is in what we are to think of nature, physical nature. In its great spread through space and time, is it inanimate, with a spot of life and consciousness here and there; or is it all alive? Has the whole thing any meaning, or are "meaning" and "purpose" a temporary specialty of the human episode within an infinite succession of meaningless cosmic changes going no-whither?

It used to be said that "Nature abhors a vacuum": it might also be said that human nature abhors a vacuum of meaning. The notion of an infinite senseless grind on such a majestic scale is so revolting that the mind finds itself imputing purpose to nature's performance, quite apart from any philosophy. Naturalism reminds us that this is an unjustified anthropomorphism, and would school us out of such provincial self-projection. Idealism declares the impulse legitimate in principle if not in extent: nature has a meaning.

But what does it mean? Why, if the world is a world of spirit, does nature exist at all?

Idealism might reply that it is more certain *that* the whole scene has a meaning than it is of just *what* the meaning is. It might quite reasonably say that the discovery of why nature exists could be left to the future. Nevertheless, its case would be much strengthened if it could throw some light on the subject. It has in fact something to say.

25.2. It is not enough to point to "signs of purpose" here and there. There are patches of perfection which everyone finds, and on which the poetic impulse seizes as tokens of the quality of the whole. There are the widely scattered beauties and sublimities of the world (striking because they blaze out from a setting of dullness or of confusion); there are harmonies we discover and also the deeper and undiscovered harmonies which the mind suspects or faintly discerns; there are the living things which show what nature contains of *possibility*; and there is the prevailing will-to-live of these myriad creatures, even if not their happiness.

But these inklings are too fragmentary to constitute *the* meaning of

183

nature though the poet is inclined to take them as cues to the whole. When Emily Dickinson was struck with a bit of nature's beauty, she was seized with "awe," as if called on to witness the inner animus of things. Yet against them must be set an endless amount of what to our eyes at least is ugliness, inertia, emptiness, waste, and cruelty. The impression made on the judicial mind is rather one of mixture, as if a trend toward meaning were struggling against a pull downward. Dualism suits the face of the facts better than an idealism which is committed to a purpose for the whole. It will aid our perspective if we recur briefly to the thought of the Greeks about nature.

25.3. The great Greek thinkers moved toward idealism, without reaching it. They ran hard against the fact of "matter," which appeared as a clog or hindrance to the soul of man, but also to the realization of meaning in things.

For Plato, the originals of meaning are in the eternal Ideas, for what is an Idea but a rationally outlined fragment of meaning? and the material factor is a source of defect from the perfection of ideas; for Ideas, as we have seen, become "embodied" in things, no one of which realizes the full meaning and glory of the pure type. The moral life of man is a conflict with less than rational impulses that hail from the body. The soul's rational love of the Ideas is degraded into physical desire and particular affections; its thinking is disturbed by the intrusions of sensation; its aspiration is toward release from the body, the partial release of trained meditation and even the complete release of death, when it will be freed from this impediment and at last qualified to contemplate the Idea of the Good, which is God, in its full beauty.[1]

Plato's view of matter as a mysterious slag, a receptive but recalcitrant principle over against all that is of the nature of thought and spirit, continued in modified form in the more Augustinian strain of thought in the Middle Ages and Reformation. It continues still throughout our literature.

Even for Plato, however, there persisted the premonition that "embodiment" is not altogether a blemish. To exist in physical form has its advantages: the souls released for a time by death return to life. Matter is the apparently indispensable medium of existence in time: and there must be some meaning in the enduring association between the undying Ideas, and an equally unperishing matter.

One of the differences between Plato and his great pupil, Aristotle, lay in their judgment of matter. Aristotle gives it a more honorable place.

---

[1] Following here the *Republic*, latter part of Bk. VI. But see also *Timaeus* for another expression of Plato's theology.

It is, to be sure, the counterpart of "form" as the intelligible and dignify-ing principle. In all physical beings, by which Aristotle meant all beings composite of form and matter—stones, plants and animals, human selves and the heavenly bodies—matter is the principle of possibility of altered form. The material must undergo the effective influence of an agent in order that its potentiality may be actualized. So raw marble becomes actu-ally statue; the egg becomes actually chick; the child becomes actually scientist. All natural things tend toward the achievement of their "proper" forms, and these give meaning to their material ingredient. But without matter there would be nothing for the spirit to inform; without the body, no human mind. Consequently, Aristotle thought that there can be no individual soul separating itself at death and living by itself, for the soul is the form, or life, of the body—this is its definition,—it is, we might say, the body's chart of activity, the function of unifying all its functions to the achievement of rational happiness. Distinct from physical beings, and the first cause of all their change, is the exceptional being of God, the one pure form of all forms. There is a tantalizingly undeveloped sugges-tion that human "active reason" might survive the death of individual human bodies. Further, Aristotle thus thinks of matter as the residence of "possibilities"—for possibilities cannot be nothing—they are an im-portant feature of the world—and since the possibilities of the future are contained in the present in some way, it is natural to assume that they pertain to the as yet unformed but formable stuff, the material element. And this is its meaning.

For these two thinkers of Greek antiquity, changeable nature repre-sents an ambiguous, disturbing, bedevilling passage way—for Aristotle a necessary passage way, in the effort of the world toward pure spirituality. Physical nature was at best a means, at the worst a hindrance and a fall.

25.4. The post-Kantian idealists must be credited with seeing that the full scope of their problem had to do justice to all these aspects of nature which made Plato and Aristotle philosophers of duality.

They were confronted in addition, with the sharp opposition between material substance and mental substance which Descartes had given the modern world: matter is precisely what mind is not, extension versus thought. They made these very difficulties the beginning of their solution. The fact that physical nature is the polar opposite of mind,—spatial, quan-titative, unfeeling,—that it resists, thwarts, opposes us,—it is this very hos-tility and deadness of material nature which they seize upon as revealing its primary purpose. For it is of *just such opposition that mind has the deepest need.*

Thus Fichte. Fichte took the essence of mind to be will: will must express itself in action: action means the forming of stuff, or the overcoming of obstacles. There must be stuff, obstacle, or else no will and no mind. In "work" man wins his first moral victories, and learns his first moral lessons,—industry, truth to fact, perseverance, foresight, courage. In order that man should be moral, there must be a material world: nature is "the material for our duty, made sensible." If, then, we can conceive a world mind entertaining as one of its aims the development of a free moral being, a "person," we can see that the production of a natural environment having in it plenty of hardship, reluctance, peril would be a suitable means to the end.

For Kant, duty was the gateway to belief in the supernatural;[2] for Fichte, duty is the gateway to the understanding of nature. Without effort, no morality; without opposition, no effort; without a world of stubborn physical facts, no opposition. Nature exists because it is a necessary condition of the moral life of finite minds.

25.5. In Schelling and Hegel we find a further meaning in this opposite-of-mind which we call nature. Nature is necessary in order that mind shall attain *self-conscious self-possession*.

There are two stages of knowledge of one's own land, for example, or of one's own language: the knowledge one has by living in the land or using the language, and the knowledge one has when after travelling in foreign lands one returns home. It has been said that he who knows only one language knows none: it is by comparison with something else that one appreciates the *meaning* of a thing.

In a similar way, Hegel suggests, mind must, as it were, abrogate itself in order to appreciate itself; it must wander in a world alien to its nature and come to itself again. Nature is this foreign land; nature is the "otherness of the spirit." Out of nature comes the mind, because nature is the mind in disguise. Emerging from nature, mind begins with ignorance and gains knowledge; thus it appreciates knowledge. As many a gifted person wastes his gifts because they are to him not gifts, but simply natural perception,—he lacks the appreciation of his own power; so even perfect intelligence would be an incomplete and imperfect thing without that self-measurement born of the journey from ignorance to knowledge. Morally also a state of mind wholly unaware of evil is incomplete, as if lacking one of its dimensions: the contemplation of sin must enter, if not sin itself, in order that any will shall come to the clearheaded rejection of sin which we call virtue. With these truths in view, we grasp the general

[2] See §9.4.

meaning of Hegel, when he describes the development of life and mind out of nature as the Odyssey of the spirit (*Geist*) coming to itself.

The ultimate law of the world Hegel declares is the paradox, Die to live: He that loseth his life shall save it. There is a "dialectic" in the structure of the world and of history. The thesis (abstract idea or abstract perfection) must take shape in its antithesis (fragmentary, imperfect, shattered, plural, material existence) in order to win the synthesis (concrete or incarnate perfection). So reason enters nature to become spirit; innocence by sin is driven from the garden, but achieves (as the snake truly promised) the knowledge of good and evil and the eventual redemption of a self-knowing rightness of heart. The infinite which excluded the finite is an incomplete or "bad infinite" (typified by the straight line). The infinite must also be able to appear in the form of the finite, if it is to make wholly good its claim to infinity: the "good infinite," like the circle, is the union of the finite and the infinite. The deepest truth of the world is the "incarnation" of the universal in the particular, of the world-spirit in the facts of sense.

25.6. These genial conceptions intrigue the imagination, and lure the mind toward a sense of initiation into the mystery of the cosmos,—a sense which some thinkers trust, while the more literal shrink from so much speculative boldness.

At their root lies a simpler consideration capable of entirely literal statement. An empty mind is no mind at all. To be a mind and to be occupied with objects are one and the same thing. Now a purely contemplative mind might be imagined which would be occupied solely with abstractions, such as numbers. But in order that the mind should have character or personality, there must be a difference between contemplation and concrete action. It must be possible to think first and act afterward. Now action means that a thought enters a world of sense, with infinite interconnections. Thus the world of sense is an essential part of what we mean by "will." *Nature is necessary in order that mind may qualify as will.*[3]

Thus nature is not only useful to mind: it is necessary in order that mind should exist, as a concrete and active reality. We cannot have nature *and* mind, as if mind could be something by itself. Nature is so essential to the very notion of mind, that if mind cannot be a product of nature, nature must be a function of mind.

---

[3] See Hocking, *The Self, Its Body and Freedom* (New Haven, 1928), pp. 81 ff.

CHAPTER 26: DIRECT EVIDENCE

26.1. Idealism as a theory is supported by the degree to which it can explain the existence of nature. It has gone far in this direction. Naturalism has done nothing, because in its view there is nothing to do: nature exists, and there's the end of it; to ask a reason for its being here is nonsense. Naturalism snubs at the outset all inquiry into the meaning of things: idealism encourages the quest, and gets on with it.[1]

But after all, what idealism so far offers us is simply a theory: it proposes an hypothetical source of phenomena, behind the phenomena, inaccessible to us. It may be a good theory; but is there any direct evidence of its truth? Must the world-spirit be like electricity, something we acknowledge because of its effects, but of whose nature we are and shall remain ignorant?

Metaphysics remains unsatisfying so long as it offers only theories of unknown powers, even though these views may be reached by a compelling logic. In my own judgment, this is an incomplete sort of metaphysics; for the Reality, whatever it is, is that with which we are dealing all the time; it is around us and in us. If idealism is true we should be able to find some direct evidence of the creative action of Mind.

I shall now inquire whether experience presents any such evidence. As a preliminary step, I ask how we know that any other mind than our own exists in the world.

26.2. We are sure of the presence of other minds about us. We are so sure, that solipsism is enough to condemn without further argument any philosophy that leads to it.[2] We are so instinctively sure, that it is only within the last two centuries that the question, How do we know these other minds? has impressed men enough to excite serious discussion. It proves to be one of the most baffling of the problems of knowledge.

[1] Note that Naturalism in the sense of Type I resists "teleology." The sense in which some thinkers call Aristotle's philosophy a Naturalism is quite distinct, since, as we have seen, it is fundamentally a teleology.

[2] Subjective idealism, as we saw, taken literally, ends in solipsism. We found solipsism self-refuting (§§23.1, 23.5). Our present inquiry should furnish a positive answer to solipsism, rather than a mere rebuttal.

It is a form of the problem of substance which Aristotle held to be the central task of metaphysics. Solipsism is simply an application to social experience of the same logic by which Berkeley dismissed material substance.

In this context one should be cognizant of the philosophy of Personalism, of which a much fuller account could fairly be given. It is a form of objective idealism which is more pluralistic than the one we have presented. It is a "monadic" idealism in a sense which can be traced back to Leibniz.[3] Personalism furnishes an alternative approach to the problem now before us of the knowledge of other minds. It holds to the thesis that "substance is person," and that the universe consists of a plurality of persons controlled by the "cosmic Person," God. As objective idealism in monadic form, Personalism shares with the form presented in the foregoing chapters the emphasis on experience and upon the teleological character of world order. A consideration of points of contrast would lead to the problems of personal interaction and of the nature of individuality.

We have no organ for the perception of these other minds. Our sense organs present us with sense qualities, such as we learn to attribute to physical things; but another mind can be no object of sight, hearing, touch. We are said to be able to perceive our*selves* directly in "self-consciousness," though psychologists often deny any such perception: we know our own states of mind by "reflection" (Locke) or "enjoyment" (Alexander) or "intuition" (Bergson). But here again, no manner of introspection could provide us direct knowledge of another mind.

Is our knowledge of this group of other selves, with which we appear to deal so directly, simply a theory or supposition, so abundantly verified in a million rapid and successful acts of social intercourse that it would be foolish to doubt it? If this is true, the solipsist is at least half right. We do not *perceive* other selves, we only *think* them.

But if this is the case, as almost all theories of knowledge take for granted, is it not extraordinary that such a surmise, as that there may be other minds in the world, is ever thought of by the self-enclosed mind? How did the idea arise? If one has as yet no idea of a neighboring mind, there is nothing in experience, by this view, to compel him to frame such an idea. This point deserves meditation.

26.3. We shall be aided by putting ourselves as far as possible into the position of the beginner in social exchanges. How does the infant first find his social environment?

Certainly not by arguing from the analogy between his own body and that of others. This is the explanation which almost everyone tries to fall back upon: "we see other bodies like our own; our bodies are animated by a self; ergo the similar bodies of others are so animated." But the infant

[3] See especially E. S. Brightman, *Person and Reality.* Also B. P. Bowne, *Metaphysics,* and R. T. Flewelling, *The Person.* And §23.2.

is a social animal long before he has seen his own body. And we adults also, we never wait for analogy before accepting mentality as present: if a tin horn began operating itself, we should pay attention. The analogy of body to body helps, no doubt, once we are socially minded,—when we want to know how an animal feels, a crab for example, we try to find his face: but analogy is worthless to explain how we first became conscious of a social environment.

Does the infant perhaps think of other minds on account of some peculiarity of the behavior of living as against non-living things, something like spontaneous motion which could not be explained by mechanical causes? This is most improbable: first because the infant does not appear to wait for a course of reasoning before he recognizes fellow persons; second, because he makes at first no clear distinction between the living and the non-living; third, because it is not altogether certain that any one can define what the outer sign of that difference is! William James thought, as we have noted, that the working sign of conscious life might be "The pursuit of ends, with the choice of means." This formula would enable us to distinguish an animated frog from an inanimate locomotive, but it would hardly help us to tell whether a moth were more alive than a self-steering torpedo, or whether either were conscious.

Language is a good sign of mentality, no doubt the most usable of all signs: we can hardly avoid attributing intelligence to a parrot or a well-devised "talking" robot. But our question must again be addressed to the beginner: how does the infant know that there is such a thing as language in the world? For unless there are other minds, there are among all the world's noises, no *words!* Before he can begin to listen for language, he must already be a social being.

This is the difficulty with the criterion of "response," appealed to by Royce, though response is prior to any other language. The infant's cry is responded to by aid; the infant attributes good will to the comforting effect—he is a primitive animist! Yes: but in order to reason in this way—if he does—his cry must have been regarded by himself as addressed to an outside hearer, and the idea of the other mind must have been already present!

All these theories make the primitive social experience much more a matter of reasoning than it really is. It does not appear true to the facts of observation that the human infant is first an unsocial individual, and then, by some course of thought, comes to the conclusion that there are other minds in the world. From the first he appears to deal with the surrounding world as though he believed it animated and ready to respond: he issues demands at random and complains if attention is not forthcoming.

He takes so kindly and promptly to behavior which implies that other minds are about, that one is inclined to refer his conduct to a "social instinct" or a "consciousness of kind" which is set off by subtle smells and tactual sensations. However, this "social instinct"—a notion which may be quite valid as a description of behavior—evades our particular question. Proposing, in effect, that gregarious animals are *born with the idea* of other minds, and never have to learn it, this appeal to instinct takes for granted that minds can have "innate ideas" without any experience to provoke them. We prefer not to beg the question to this extent. We shall have therefore to examine more carefully how experience can have such a very simple, unhesitant, unargued social quality.

26.4. Any other mind present in our experience must be occupied with objects; for, as we said, an empty mind is no mind at all. To perceive this mind, I should have at least to perceive the objects it was occupied with: that is, I should perceive certain objects, and know that they were not mine alone but at the same time objects for that other mind also.

Are there any objects in the world which seem to be habitually regarded as shared objects? Certainly *space* is usually taken as common to myself and others; one has to make an effort rather to secure loneliness—build walls, shut doors, etc.—than to secure publicity. So also are physical things in space common objects by nature; we do not have to do *anything* to them to make them public; on the contrary we take their publicity as the sign of their reality,—if we doubt what we seem to see, we call some one else to witness it. If we wish to make physical things our "property," we have to secure them by special marks from theft or seizure by others. If we could find when we *began* to regard space and physical things as common objects, we should there find the beginning of our social experience.

But I cannot find the time when space and physical things were regarded in any other way than as common objects; I doubt whether any such time can be found. And for this reason: space is the minimum physical object any two human minds can have in common. If a minimum is lacking, communication cannot get started: unless two persons have something in common (say space) they cannot so much as approach each other, still less open conversation—how would you address yourself to a being with whom you had no common object? Communication can build from little to more; but it cannot build from nothing to something. Hence there must always have been some minimal object taken as common, and this minimal object seems to be space.

If, then, there is any real social experience at all, it must be that our experience of space (with some content from the sense of touch) has from the beginning the quality of being common object; that is, it is *taken from the first as* a region of experience unprivate in its nature, *already shared* with some other mind than my own, and the invitation and platform for further sharing. And is not this the case? Early sense-experiences are not taken by the infant as purely private facts originating in himself; they are referred by him to an activity arising beyond himself. The sensation is something the mind *receives*; but passivity is the inner side of activity— these are not two facts but one. Just as concave and convex are known in the same stroke, so a knowledge of *being passive* is at the same time a knowledge of some other entity *being active*, a knowledge of receiving is a knowledge of being-given-to. But what kind of being is able to act upon a self? I answer, another self. At the beginning of experience, whatever is other-than-self, acting on self, is other self: the infant's social awareness is contemporary with his recognition of sensation as the inner aspect of an outer action, addressed to him: *his sense-experience is a direct social experience.*

Because of this, sense-experience is referred to a common frame, to space; and sense-qualities are grouped as properties of "things" in space,— objects which the self has in common with that other self. In such a physical world, language is native from the beginning: its physical other- ness is derived from its social otherness, and not *vice versa*. It is because he feels himself to be not alone that he regards space as a common object and a point of beginning for further communication.

Note that the other self will at first be undefined and unlimited, not designated by a "body" but simply the outer side of all the incoming ac- tivity: for the beginning mind, the Other will be simply the world-mind. Particular companions, associated with "bodies," will be, so to speak, carved out of the total social environment by the experience of response.

Thus in answer to the question whether an experience of the world- mind is possible, I conclude that our experience of nature is, at its founda- tion, an experience of the world mind. Nature is not first experienced alone, and then tied-up with other observers. We are born social. We gradually acquire the capacity of abstraction: we learn to think of ourselves apart from others, and of nature as apart from all of us. The independent, non- social object is a high achievement of abstraction. In its true and original character nature is *between* minds: to experience nature is to experience the world-mind in its creative activity.[4]

---

[4] The argument here presented is given more fully in Hocking, *The Meaning of God in Human Experience*, Chs. XVII–XXII. It is always possible that the fuller form is easier to grasp than a severe condensation.

26.5. The effect of this argument is simply to recall an elemental intuition which is only concealed from us by its omnipresence. It is not in rare and irregular experiences of high emotional tension that we have to seek a vision of the world-mind; for that mind is present to us in the permanent stream of plain physical sensation.

Take sensation as a mere fact—something present—a spot of color, a noise—then it remains a mere fact; it means nothing, and nothing can be made of it. But we never take it that way. We take it as a sign of an object; and the idea of an object is of something which it is our business to know more about. The noise calls for a look into its "cause": it has a history, a line of connection with other possible experience. To the beginning mind as to the mature mind every sensation calls for an activity of exploration. It may be a "stimulus" in the biological sense, calling for or stirring up a "reaction," as a flash of pain brings the instant impulse to withdraw. But in addition to the biological response there is always the response of the knower: "I must recognize this sensation as the signal of a *thing*, which summons me to investigate it." This is an aboriginal generosity of the mind, an act of faith if you like, attributing to the sensation a context in a being which requires attention: it is, I think, the acceptance of the most primitive of all *duties*, the duty to live *out*, to live in a world of objects, not of sensations. And note that unless this aboriginal sense of duty were there, and were followed, neither knowledge of natural objects nor of the social world which has them in common could so much as get started. It is an obligation which each mind must meet alone, since by hypothesis there is no one there to explain its purport to him—it is the most crucial decision that the mind makes.

But I propose this: that the *awareness of an obligation to know*, which is at the root of all further experience, *is at the same time an awareness of other mind*, since we can have no obligation to a lifeless universe. It has often been argued that God is present to the human mind in conscience; and conscience has been thought of as very different from sense-experience. But I am here pointing out that there is an element of conscience or moral obligation in the way we at every moment meet sense-experience; we feel bound to treat it as a fabric not of fancy but of "truth." And then I point out that this instinctive prescience of a summons to the tracing of objective truth in sense-experience is the perpetual awareness that the world-mind is there present to us.[5]

It is this very perception of obligation which later on makes scientists

[5] There are some critics of subjective idealism who also acknowledge the necessity for an original social consciousness but who prefer not to call the resultant philosophy "idealism." Among these are, for example, the adherents of the *Existenz*-philosophy of Heidegger. See Ch. 38.

of us, and sets the standards of naturalism. Thus we see that that which in partial light makes naturalists of us is the very thing which, taken with more complete self-consciousness, should make of us objective idealists.

26.6. With this insight, we have at the same time another answer to the question why nature exists. Nature exists in order that we may be social beings. To build up this intricate and endless network of give and take, co-operation and conflict, agreement and clash of judgment, there must be some neutral, colorless, lifeless, stable, indifferent base in the form of a common object: this base is nature.

CHAPTER 27:
APPLICATIONS OF IDEALISM

The meaning of any type of philosophy can only fully appear in its consequences or applications to specific questions. One of the applications of objective idealism we have considered at length—its answer to the question why nature exists. We shall now trace its application to a few of the metaphysical questions which we have had before us,—the relation of mind and body, the problem of freedom, the destiny of human selfhood,—and then devote a separate chapter to its application to human life and conduct.

27.1. *The connection of mind and body.*

The body is a physical object among physical objects; but it is apart from all other objects in having a double rôle to play. It is a part of physical nature, and it is an instrument of the self, so closely incorporated with the self which uses it that they are often identified.

Corresponding to these two rôles, the body appears to us in two ways: first, as an organism, a complex system of causes and effects, an object of all the physiological sciences; and second, as a city of meanings, every line of which, and every motion, is read for what it signifies. For naturalism, the first character is the reality of the body; for idealism, the second is the real, and the first is derived from it.

As a part of nature, the body has for idealism all of the causal relations which science discovers, and in addition whatever meaning belongs to nature. Nature is an assemblage of common objects, aiding minds to communicate: the body is accordingly a common object; by way of the body each self is visible and accessible to other selves, can be seized and injured by them, can be aided and benefited by them. Through the body the self communicates with other minds and receives their communications: it forms part of that bridge of connection whose whole span is nature.

But the body could not serve as the peculiar instrument of language unless it were more instantly commandable than the rest of nature. It is the *sphere of my immediate control.* Detached objects may defy me: my body cannot help obeying—except in the sense that it may register my feelings when I would prefer to keep them covered; it obeys my subconscious and habitual self rather than the conscious self of the moment. The wolf can never quite successfully assume sheep's clothing because the body presents a public confession of the instinctive dispositions of the self. It is, according to Schopenhauer, the external expression of the will ("objectivation of the will"); the bodies of animals showing the whole pattern of their ways of living, moving, fighting, eating, mating, protecting themselves and others, conversing, hiding. The body becomes the most available *symbol* of character, as well as the bearer of the will-acts of the moment.

But how does the body appear to its owner? It could hardly serve as the sphere of immediate control if it were not more intimately united with the self than other objects. If I break a leg, the break is in the common world, and the surgeon can treat it: but the pain is my private property. I have an uninterrupted stream of sensations from my body, of temperature, of comfort or discomfort, of position and muscular strain, of well or ill being (cœnesthesia), the vague general awareness of life-processes going on and the more explicit reports of what my muscles are doing,—all of which no one else enjoys or suffers. This total sensible awareness of the body is the body as "within my mind," and so *an integral part of the self*. Our consciousness of bodily action so closely fuses with our decisions to act that we cannot say we first decide and then perform the appropriate muscular activity, but rather the decision and the action are one experience: I throw the ball,—I am not conscious even of swinging my arm as a separate part of the action, my mind is on the effect, the thrown ball, perhaps on the target itself, and all the intermediate links drop out of sight. In this sense the experience of body-action is an integral part of my will,—not my body as seen by others, but my body as felt by myself: without that experience of physical translation of desire into deed, will would not be will, and the human self would not be itself.

For the idealist, therefore, the question whether and how the mind acts upon the brain, whether there is interaction or parallelism, does not arise. Body and brain are not *another reality*, such as could act on the mind or be acted on: they *are the mind* made visible, translated into the language of space and physical event. If the external observer gets so far as to observe the brain of a living person, all that he sees is the more intimate and exact external symbol of what the person is feeling and thinking. The mind is not acting upon the brain as one bit of nature upon another: the whole natural picture is a consistent expression of relations within the world of consciousness. The law of relation between the world-mind and nature—its external self-announcement—determines the particular form which the physiological pattern shall take. The idealist is ready to learn all that the physiologist has to teach about nerve and brain action. He adds to these observations the two theses which interpret the physiologist's findings: first, that the mind is not identical with the brain-action; and second, that in the order of reality, the mind is first, and the brain-action a derivative. When we say, for example, that the world is acting on a given mind by way of nerves and brain, the fuller and more accurate statement is that the wills which are expressed in the world-phenomenon are acting on that mind, and the brain records the transaction in its own physical language.

This agrees very closely with what we ordinarily feel about the body. It is not *identical* with self: it is more like a piece of property,—we speak of "my body" as of "my house." Yet it is for many purposes *equivalent* to the self,—we say "Here I am," not "Here is my body." The body is, for others, the visible agent for self: it is, so to speak, legal tender for the mind of the owner. But especially it is a magazine of meanings, and we so instantly read these meanings that we seem to be in presence of the self which has them, and we frequently forget the physical characters which carry to us those impressions. For instance, how true a picture can one draw of the physical appearance even of a close friend, in his absence?

This does not mean that the individual mind originally produces its own body. The body comes to each one, like the rest of nature, from beyond himself. We inherit our bodies as we inherit ourselves. But here also the mind is first passive and then active: what it receives it recreates. Only, the body while less plastic than imagination is far more plastic than the rest of nature: it cannot resist the print of the owner's choices. Thus at birth we have the body (and the mind) bequeathed to us: at forty we have the body (and the mind) built by our own wills.

27.2. *Freedom.*

If the mind controls and builds the body, the body does not control and build the mind: this position of control is what is meant by "freedom of the will." The capacity for self-building is the concrete expression of freedom.

The obvious criticism of freedom we have already met: [1] when I say "I choose; I decide," the observer can see that the self which chooses is a definite character for whom that choice was a necessary consequence. His desires being what nature and environment had made them, a shrewd scientist could have predicted the decision. There is no "I" which stands outside the network of causes and gives an original bent to behavior.

Idealism replies that the "I," the self, is always outside the network of

[1] See §3.2.

causes which *it observes:* when it is aware of being played upon by causes it is at that moment free from *those causes:* it is like one who has over-heard a plot against himself—"We will tell X this tale, and he, being a credulous soul, will take it all in." He ceases instantly to be the credulous soul, gullible by that tale. If governments (following a suggestion playfully put out by Bertrand Russell) should discover how to control by drugs or diet the internal secretions of their citizens so as to make them by turns pacific or belligerent, tolerant or irritable,—and if the citizens knew of the method, it would be in their power to accept or reject that invasion of their person by "causes." This is the history of propaganda: it works as a cause of mental attitudes until it is found out, no longer. Freedom, in short, depends on the power of the self to become aware of the causal nexus in which its physical self is enmeshed, and in being aware of it to *be more real* than that causal scheme; to use it, rather than be used by it. All sorts of causes act upon and invade the self: an empty stomach causes hunger, a sudden noise causes alarm, a blow causes anger. There is a natural mechanical procedure in each of these cases, a "reaction" which is no more free than the fall of the apple. But let me become *aware* of this process, able to say "I am becoming angry": then I am no longer absorbed in the anger, and the causes can continue only in such direction as shall carry out my deliberate purpose. The power of self-survey, acting at the "threshold of consent" in the course of emotion,[2] is the thing which puts distance between the history of a mind and the history of any purely mechanical process.

Many a habit establishes itself in the mind, more or less mechanically, and drops out of consciousness,—let us say a habit of evasion, of steering around a difficulty instead of facing it. It becomes a part of one's character, one's "style." The chances are that such a habit will persist and determine conduct until something or somebody makes the owner conscious that he has it. This is bound to happen in time if only because one's mental style is taking bodily shape and becoming visible to the public eye. At the moment one becomes clearly aware, "I am evasive, cowardly, soft," at that moment he has put a distance between himself and the evasive self: he has gained the beginning of freedom. Kant was right in saying that the mind is aware of its superiority to whatever is merely "natural" in itself, its instincts, desires, habits; its task is not to destroy them but to use them. Self-consciousness deposes nature from master to servant of the free self.

27.3. *Human destiny.*

Freedom applies immediately to the sphere of one's own choices. It gives no absolute mastery of nature outside of self: we can directly control

[2] Hocking, *The Self, Its Body and Freedom,* Ch. III.

nothing but the meaning we make our deeds carry. There remain countless things not within our power; [3] there are tides of physical and social circumstance, age, disease, which no man can row against. Death conquers idealist and non-idealist alike.

But the objective idealist, who recognizes that nature with its apparent indifference to his purposes, and its resistance to his thought and will, ought to be there, has certain assurances about his own place in the doings of the universe. If everything is subordinate to mind, then four inferences are to be drawn:

a. *Nothing in the world can be meaningless;* for mind acts always in view of meanings.

b. Then, too, *human beings,* as among the things in the world, *must have a meaning;* and perhaps it would not be straining too far the apparent work of the evolutionary process to say, human beings have a presumptive importance.

c. It would then further follow that *human valuations,* however relative to human limitations, *are not contrary to absolute valuation.* Our way of judging values must be essentially consistent with that of the world-mind; for there could be no more meaningless situation than the production by a cosmic process of a race of valuers whose judgments were at odds with the true judgment of values. Our interest in knowledge, in beauty, and in rightness cannot be entirely off the target. Or, to put it positively, in these appreciations of ours, we must come close to an immediate grasp of the ultimate sense of existence.

d. If this is true, we may perhaps assume, further, that *nothing is foreclosed as impossible,* in the direction of our profoundest will, though we have no inkling as to the manner in which such desire is to be realized.

As to death and survival: death, we have said, conquers idealist and non-idealist alike. Only, to the idealist, it is not a lifeless Nature that conquers: it is the law of the world-order, which is a significant order. If it is significant that his own life should survive, the death of the body need not carry with it the disappearance of his finite personality nor of his consciousness. Death, in this view of things, is the destruction of the body, that is—as we were saying—of the *bridge of connection* with this particular group of fellow minds. Death proves nothing as to whether there are other groups of minds in the universe, and other links of connection to be established with them. Whether one survives may well depend on whether one is fit to survive. The less real can in no case destroy the more real.

[3] Epictetus, *Discourses,* Bk. I, Ch. I.

CHAPTER 28:
IDEALISM AND ETHICS

28.1. We have been discussing idealism as metaphysics, not as ethics. We have forgotten (I trust) that the word "idealism" seems to put in a proprietary claim upon "ideals": no type of philosophy has a monopoly of ideals nor of their championship. But the time has come to ask whether idealism has something distinctive to say about the art of living. As a matter of history it has had much to say: most of the great ethical teachers among the classical philosophers have had an idealistic strain in their metaphysics and so have shared with idealist philosophers of modern times the sense that eternal and divine purpose is the ground of human standards.[1]

Since the opening of the nineteenth century, numerous thinkers have put forward systems of ethics professing to stand on their own feet, dependent on no theology nor metaphysics, idealistic or other. They raise the question whether ethical standards are not, after all, a natural phenomenon of human life; a product perhaps of our social instincts, or of our natural sympathy, or of the disposition to mutual aid (which Kropotkin has celebrated),—traits which even among the lower animals can be observed to mitigate ferocity and egoism. The rise of the modern empirical science of psychology, spreading from eighteenth century England in all directions, would promote this view of ethics; likewise the experience of France since the Enlightenment and the Revolution. Before going on to consider what practical wisdom the idealists have to offer, let us, then, raise the critical question whether ethics is not an independent human interest, without legitimate tie to any type of metaphysics.

28.2. Practical life is occupied—to put it summarily—with two concerns, the adoption of ends, the selection of means. All the issues between wisdom and folly, or between right and wrong, can be put in these terms: what goods do you seek? what means do you use in obtaining them?

But goods or values are matters of experience, not of speculation; and

---

[1] This can be said of Plato and Aristotle, Epictetus and other Stoics, Augustine, most of the Schoolmen, Kant, Fichte, Hegel, and more recently T. H. Green, F H. Bradley and Josiah Royce.

the best ways to reach them are likewise pointed out by experience, sharpened by scientific knowledge. The qualities of things which make them seem good or evil to us, harmful or beneficial, are matters of fact—i. e., of the relation between human nature and its surroundings—not of metaphysics. How could the qualities or values of things be changed by believing the universe as a whole to be living or dead? Colors, tones, odors, and their combinations will be pleasant or unpleasant, harmonious or clashing, according to the laws of their own natures and of psychology, in every conceivable universe.

How could the belief that some all-knowing mind is the author of nature make beauty more beautiful, or human kindness more beneficent, or justice more noble? In any kind of world, materialistic or other, health and liberty are worth having, disease and poverty are evils to be banished, self-control brings self-respect, treachery disorganizes life. These are matters of cause and effect. The dialectic of experience teaches these things to the race; [2] they get embodied in proverbial wisdom; every new generation receives them from its elders, more or less disbelieves, experiments for itself, and finds out their truth at its own cost. The *ends or values* whose attainment constitutes human happiness remain eternally fixed in the nature of the quality itself; and the *means* to their attainment, the wise ways of life, are governed by the given order of nature and society. Metaphysics does not enter the calculation.

On this account, many thinkers have held that metaphysics, and theology likewise, so far from aiding ethics, tend to spoil it, by introducing alien and uncertain considerations. An ethics based on experience and reason stands firm, and recommends itself. An ethics based on the command of God or upon the supposed ultimate nature of things will shake with every doubt that assails our metaphysical capacity. Hence in France, the most rationalistic of modern nations, the prolonged political struggle to release the state from the church has been accompanied by an effort to establish a *natural* moral education as the only sort which can promise to be durable or socially safe. Russia, Mexico and Turkey are following the example of France. What kind of ethics can be set up without metaphysics?

28.3. An ethics is not a set of prudential rules indicating the most expedient ways of getting what we want: if it were, it would be a branch of economics. An ethics is concerned with the difference between right and wrong: it is concerned with a *standard*, or "norm," of some sort for our behavior, toward which we stand in the relation of "ought," obligation, duty.

[2] See Hocking, *Human Nature and Its Remaking*, Chs. XXII, XXIV.

Now human nature is no doubt capable of yielding standards of this sort, especially in social groups. Beginning our lives as impressionable members of the small community of the family, we find standards ready made for us in the kind of behavior and habit which our elders require or approve. And inasmuch as these elders, and our associates, commonly profit by and tend to approve unselfish behavior on our part, and to condemn the more outbreaking sorts of self-assertion, we grow up in the shadow of a certain demand to diminish our natural sense of self-importance, our ego-centric morality, and to count ourselves as surely not more than *one* in the group and possibly a little less than one. No human group can fail to beget the standard which consists in reminding us that "other people exist too"; though no human group, merely by its natural authority, fully succeeds in overcoming our self-centred perspective and making the existence of others as weighty a value for us as our own. The standards of the group, be it noted, never become ethical standards merely by being required or approved by others: they are not *my duty* until I personally see them as such. But every normal human being does, in time, come to recognize that his group has some claim on him, and that he "ought" to be a serviceable member of it. He adopts what we may call a natural *social ethics*. Beginning with conformity to the trend of opinion in the group, he may go on to an independent and intelligent effort for the welfare of that group, even at the cost of some opposition to the prevailing sentiment and some sacrifice of his personal welfare.

Thus social ethics becomes a part of the ethics of *self-expression*; because the self which we have to express is, in part, a reasonable and social self. No normal man is happy in complete moral isolation or self-enclosure: hence a sensitive regard for the after-taste of our pleasures is capable of lifting us a long distance above the level of the brute. It is these decent natural sentiments of regard for others and for common interests upon which the secular educators of France have been inclined to rely:

"A respect for the human person, our own as well as that of the stranger; a respect for science, an admiration for its conquests, a hope that it will make still greater ones; a love of humanity, a confidence in its progress, a desire to contribute thereto; and to this end a love of *la patrie*,—'car la France, le pays de la Révolution et de la démocratie, travaille pour le bien de tous.' " [3]

28.4. If a civilization relies on such sentiments, it relies on something actual and authentic: but it becomes a matter of the utmost gravity for the future of such a society, how strong these sentiments are, and how much education can do toward making them *strong enough*. Education is not om-

---

[3] G. Weill, *Histoire de l'idée laïque en France*, p. 359.

nipotent; moral education is the most backward of our Western arts. It is not sufficient that these sentiments exist merely to the point of dramatic registration; and patriotism itself is not enough!

But beside the social standard, there are other standards present in some degree in all human nature. There is the *aesthetic* standard. Our acts have qualities of beauty or ugliness; and when we become aware of these properties, our personal pride and sense of dignity are involved. No one desires to be ugly, repulsive, awkward or ungracious in the eyes of others, nor yet of himself.

As a strong ally of this aesthetic sense of inner personal quality, there is a natural law (we become constantly more aware of it) whereby these qualities become physically manifest in personal appearance. Swinishness makes its mark on the features. Hardness, worldliness, laxity, coarseness of feeling, become evident in trait, carriage, and gesture of the visible man. Personal vanity comes to the aid of ethics. In recent years it has led multitudes into a kind of physical discipline and restraint—the new asceticism! It has a future of unlimited magnitude!

This vanity is but the outer shell of the true aesthetic standard which is capable of forgetting the outer observer. Grace and amenity of conduct have intrinsic satisfactions of their own. They have contributed to form the vanishing ideals of the "gentleman" and of the "lady," compounded, as these were, half of aesthetics and half of the sentiment of honor. The third Earl of Shaftesbury thought that he could derive the entire code of morals from the standard of harmony.[4] And we remember the noble prayer of Socrates at the close of the *Phaedrus*:

> Beloved Pan, and all ye other gods that haunt this place, give me beauty in the inner man; and may the outer and the inner man be at one.

28.5. The standard of *honor*, just mentioned, marks, I think, the highest reach of an ethics without metaphysics. It is a standard which implies a fine sensitiveness toward unenforceable obligations, such as the "debt of honor." In its history it has had a not wholly fortunate connection with aristocratic orders of society as if it were only for those whom *noblesse oblige*: the honor of the knight or of the officer as it has been interpreted in Continental military circles tends somewhat to a superstitious concern for the show of respect to one's person. But there is a more genuine essence of honor, as in the pride of a Cyrano de Bergerac or in the laws of a reasonable contemporary chivalry.[5] It is still founded on distinction, a sense of superiority to vulgar selfhood: but that vulgar selfhood is one's

---

[4] Shaftesbury, *Characteristics of Men, Manners and Opinions*, 1711.
[5] See Alfred de Vigny, *La canne de jonc*, Ch. IX.

own, and the sentiment of honor carries with it a scorn to take advantage of the many opportunities for feeding the material greeds of that self at the expense of a scruple. Honor is simply the flower of self-respect. It may lead a character into regions where neither the social standard nor the aesthetic standard alone would suffice.

28.6. These standards, we say, do not depend for their existence on any metaphysical theory. They seem to be spontaneous products of human nature,—at least of some human natures; and we find germs of them in animals. Now our question is, Does a metaphysical belief, when it arrives, make any difference to them?

It is evident that, as we find them, these sentiments are both variable and vulnerable. We cannot assume that, merely by the mechanics of heredity, they will be generated in constant and adequate quantities. We may regard them as admirable and reasonable. But what if, in any group of persons, they do not exist, or only feebly exist? Can we beget them? A person may say, "I am not interested in honor nor in personal aesthetics; I find my happiness on the more vulgar plane. I make no apologies, for this is the way nature has made me." Such a person would seem to be in a fairly impregnable position.

Education cannot "inculcate" sentiments the germ of which is not present. A student of mine once said, commenting on a course in ethics, "You can't prove that a man ought to love his neighbor. And if you could, that *would not help him to do so!*" Put it this way: you cannot prove to the unmusical that music is beautiful; and if you could, that would not help him to enjoy it. There is the central difficulty. And the actual situation is that while most of us love a few of our neighbors to a certain extent, very few of us love more than a few: the actual force of the sentiment of brotherhood toward "mankind" is hardly more than that of a mathematical expression, an imaginary picture of a non-existent limit. Well-disposed toward mankind,—yes; glad to help, too, so long as the cost is not too great: the good-natured spirit of the prosperous; fair-weather benevolence. But capable of heroic sacrifice? Or of steadfast loyalty at all costs? Yes also; so long as one listens solely to the native impulse, and does not attempt to rationalize one's behavior. He who deliberates is likely to be lost. If metaphysics cannot create these liberal sentiments on which civilization depends, there are types of metaphysics which can, apparently, *undermine them* by exposing them as irrational. And if this is true, metaphysics is certainly not irrelevant to them.

28.7. In fact, the proposition that ethics has no need of metaphysics runs close to absurdity: it is as much as to say that ethics is indifferent to the nature of reality. Admit that ethical sentiments come out of natural human instincts; but remember that instincts are ways of dealing with reality. Instincts have no theories; but they have at times a wisdom which is deeper than available theory; they are attended by intuitions of the nature of the world wherein they operate.[6] The social instincts and inhibitions out of which our ethical standards arise are active long before we know what these intuitions mean: but when scientific and metaphysical thought arises it will either corroborate or refute these intuitions; it will either sustain or discount those sentiments.

It is simply *not true that the values and qualities of things are fixed in independence of our thoughts about their natures.* Even in regard to tastes and odors, belief about the substance affects the flavor: the squeamish have a need to know what a dish is—whether oyster or snail—before they can eat it with relish. Still more with the value we ascribe to our neighbors. We are bound in the long run to treat things and men according to what they are. As for these fellow men of ours whom we are expected to regard as brothers and equals, the question is *What are they?* Answer that without metaphysics if you can. If they are biological organisms and nothing else, subject to the laws of cause and effect, they must be so treated. In that case, their worth varies through a long gamut, and there are "many too many" of them: it is no use pretending any sentiment of universal respect or fraternity; the principle of "equality" is either a falsehood or a pragmatic assumption for small homogeneous communities, quite inapplicable to humanity at large. Obversely, if that sense of fundamental equality which is the basis of justice as well as of benevolence is to be given a lease of life, we must be assured that men are something else than biological organisms.

Now experience does something to indicate that the cause-and-effect view of human nature is unsatisfactory: it shows that the view does not work. Study human psychology; find the "laws" of human behavior; then try to apply them in the management of men, and see what happens. Let them but get the suspicion that you are trying to practise a cause-and-effect policy on them, and they will spoil your game. Society cannot be worked out on the plan of causal-dealing. Our mechanical "organization" enthusiasts sometimes assume that it can be; they take for granted, let us say, the docility of labor, the predictable working of the "economic motive"; and labor is likely to prove both indocile and uneconomic, capable of a self-sacrificing fury of resentment. Organization and pathology approach the criminal tendencies of men with cause-and-effect remedies, environmental and chemical; and crime continues to increase. We shall learn in time that *we can only motivate other men by what motivates ourselves;* by

6 See §11.5.

value-thinking, not by causal-thinking. The only successful way of treating them is to assume that they are rational, free and responsible; assume that they participate in your appreciations and sense of duty; stop trying to "work" them, as you would work a machine, and begin discussing your mutual rights and obligations. Then you are no longer treating them as mere means to your ends; you are not trying to *cause* them, but to *reason* with them. You are showing "respect"; and respect must stand at the beginning of any honest fraternity. Thus far experience takes us; and we can say that no metaphysics will sustain a modern social structure unless it can justify this mode of treatment.

28.8. Now it is here that idealistic metaphysics strikes in. Confronted with modern naturalism, it declares that man *is* something different from the causal or biological machine, and that by virtue of what he is, he is worthy of respect. It puts a necessary foundation under the centre of the whole ethical and social business.

Kant was the first modern thinker to perceive and to state in unmistakable language this situation. He puts the matter dogmatically: "Now I say man exists as an end in himself, not merely as a means." [7] We call rational beings *persons*, he continues, because "their very nature points them out as ends in themselves." Whatever is a *thing*, as distinct from a person, we are at liberty to use as we like: it has a value just so long as we desire it; its value is relative to our wishes, and if we cease to care for it, that value declines. Things are not ends in themselves; and for this reason, their authority over our conduct is conditional: *If* we desire wealth or preferment, we must be diligent in our business; if not, we may be as lazy as we like. Such rules, Kant suggests, we may properly call "*hypothetical imperatives*": they remain binding only so long as one continues to value the object. But the value of persons has a different status: their worth is objective, independent of our variations of mood because based on what a person is, namely, a free being, capable of seeing an ethical point, and so of being a member of a society of rational creatures. The existence of persons, as ends in themselves, thus imposes on us a requirement which is unconditional, or as Kant phrases it, a "*categorical imperative*," a command without an "if":

"So act as to treat humanity, whether in thine own person or in that of any other, in every case as an end withal, never as means only."

This is one of the most impressive formulations of our moral common sense that has ever been made. We recognize at once its force and its effect.

---

[7] Kant, *Fundamental Principles of the Metaphysic of Ethics*, trans. T. K. Abbott, 10th ed. (London and New York, 1934), p. 55.

Besides defining accurately that element of underlying equality, running through all the inequalities among men, which is the basis of all legal right, and therefore of all equity and justice, it forbids all forms of what we call "exploitation." It clearly excludes slavery;[8] for slavery is the literal treatment of persons as things, treating them as means to the ends of others and not as ends in themselves. In so far as honest contract relations, including the wage relation, supplant relations based on compulsion, men continue to use each other as means to their ends, but they also respect each other's freedom; so that the Kantian principle is complied with.

It also abets and clarifies the sense of honor: for it forbids that the personal principle in myself shall ever be prostituted to the service of material inclination. Don't make the mistake of supposing, Kant admonishes, that the element of free value-thinking in yourself is there purely for the sake of leading you to the satisfaction of your natural desires. It has its biological functions, no doubt: intelligence, like eyesight, has evolved as a means to all sorts of practically valuable ends. But having arrived, rationality, like eyesight, takes rank as an end, and not as a means only, and indeed as the chief good of life: to be a rational being is second to nothing in the satisfaction it gives; and no sacrifice of the personal quality, which constitutes the dignity of man, could be compensated by any amount of the tangible gratifications of the organic self.

28.9. From this categorical imperative we may draw certain direct inferences. To treat all persons as ends is to that extent to treat everybody alike: it introduces a principle of equality into human dealings. But wherever equality appears, logic can be used in ethical reasoning. I may and must think of my own action as if any other person were to act on the same principle—"Would I approve if all others were to do likewise"? That is, I must consider my action as if its principle or "maxim" were to become a general rule for all; as if, in short, to act were at the same moment to make the spirit of my action a law for the entire community of persons (as through the imitative propensities of mankind it actually tends to do). The categorical imperative can thus assume this form:

"Act only on that maxim of which thou canst at the same time will that it should become a universal law."[9]

---

[8] Kant's treatise was published in 1785.

[9] *Ibid.*, p. 46. If the word "maxim" proves troublesome here, as it should, recall that it is not the literal behavior which the neighbor tends to imitate, but the general motivation which he perceives in it. If I drive through a red signal, he may have no inclination to drive through a red signal; but perceiving that I take traffic rules lightly when the police are absent he may be emboldened to use this "maxim" in disregarding speed limits. The "maxim" is the general animus of my act: I may not have it clearly formulated in my own mind. Kant's rule requires we first get clear what our maxim is.

In other words, cease making exceptions in your own favor; eliminate those modes of action which would show themselves self-contradictory if they became general. Do not allow yourself to lie, when the whole effect of the lie depends on that general habit of truthfulness which allows your language to be received at its face value. Do not allow yourself to steal, when the whole advantage of your theft depends upon having your stolen goods respected as your property. Do not kill, when the only value to you of your deed requires the continued protection of your own life by the standards of the community.

Does it seem to you that these rules, which in some form or other appear in the codes of all societies, belong to the abstract and formal side of ethics? It would certainly be a poor ethical theory which could not account for their prevalence. And the logic which Kant proposes is very much the course of thought through which they are arrived at by the ethical common sense of mankind. For all societies have the same problem, selfishness of the human individual: and all have to induce in him the same idea of "justice," that of applying to himself the rules he would recommend to others.

28.10. In Kant's treatment of ethics we have the sense of getting close to the centre of moral life. It has had, and continues to have, a profound influence on the modern conscience, in the field of law as well as in that of personal morality.[10] Like every great formulation of human intuition, it is an approximation rather than a finality; and it must meet a criticism which is keen in proportion to its importance.

On the one hand, it is sometimes said that Kant's imperative is too empty, that it requires nothing specific. One might as well say of the Golden Rule that it also commands nothing specific; yet few have had the folly to suggest that this rule commands nothing merely because it mentions nothing in particular. We have not found Kant's principles devoid of application. On the other hand, it is said that it is too rigorous, and that it requires an impossible standard of human behavior. These two criticisms evidently tend to cancel each other.

The chief defect of Kant's theory is the absence of an independent metaphysics. Kant has argued that the moral law depends on a metaphysical belief for its validity: [11] but at the same time that the only ground for such metaphysical belief is this demand of the moral law. But metaphysics cannot sustain ethics if ethics is the only support of metaphysics. Kant himself is not an idealist in metaphysics; he is rather a mystic, standing on

---

[10] See the contribution by Roscoe Pound to the volume, *Kant 1724–1924*, edited by E. C. Wilm.
[11] §9.4, above.

the threshold of idealism. For this reason, the essential propositions of his ethics can only be stated in the dogmatic way we have noted: they lack theoretical support. Three dogmas form the pivots of his doctrine: "There is nothing good without qualification but a good will"; "Now I say that man exists as end in himself, not merely as a means"; "Now I say that every being that cannot act except under the idea of freedom is really free." [12]

These dogmas are probably true, or nearly true: they make connection —as Kant intended—with the common moral sense of mankind. But they can hardly be exactly true as stated, because they do not agree with each other: if we assert the sole absolute goodness of the *good* will, how can we assert the absolute worth of every person whether his will is good or not? And is it clear that the worth of any person is purely intrinsic, without reference to the world in which he lives and his action in it? Kant wished to find those ethical principles which hold good *a priori*, without reference to the specific consequences of action. He was quite right in thinking that a will does not cease to be good because some unforeseeable accident prevents its carrying out: but it is not clear that a will could be good without any effects whatever, for in that case it would not be a will.

Our own sense of personal worth is certainly variable, and dependent in no small measure on the conviction that we fulfil some function in the cosmos. (Mark, I do not say a social function; but a function having an objective worth of some sort, in the processes of the greater world.) The worth of men comes in part from their cosmic relationships. The "proof that a man ought to respect or to love his neighbor" must come, if at all, from recognizing that this neighbor has, or can have, the interests of the *whole* in his keeping, and is in fact affecting them, if only by the direct contagion of his "maxim."

It certainly will not do at the present moment in history to assume the worth of humanity as a dogma. The weakness which attends the "lay" or autonomous ethics attends also the ethics of Kant: each depends on a native impulse to treat the neighbor as an equal: the impulse is there, but without rational support it gives way. Slavery is out of countenance, but there are various modern substitutes which build upon the evident inequalities of mankind. There has never been a time when the disposition to make use of weaker brethren or of backward races as mere means for national or private ends was more wide-spread.[13] And while professedly democratic peoples are rightly incensed at the rude rejections of all the slow-built respect for the rights of free peoples shown in the series of brutal

[12] *Fundamental Principles of the Metaphysic of Ethics*, p. 80. See also pp. 10, 55.
[13] These words were written in 1921. Since 1945, vast and violent changes in the pattern of dependency have been taking place.

conquests from those of Manchuria, Abyssinia and Czechoslovakia to those of Latvia, Lithuania and Hungary, these same democracies even yet conduct empires in which the usefulness of inferior to superior seems to be the primary principle of organization. If we ought to treat all human beings as ends in themselves, there must be some metaphysical justification for doing so which we do not find in human impulse, nor in the dogma of Kant. We may find it in the thought of his successors.

28.11. Hegel [14] sees human individuals as immersed in the living process of the world, which is at once the history of civilization and the history of a developing thought. Persons get both their freedom and their worth through participation in this universal process.

Our freedom is less an intrinsic and invariable quality, Hegel teaches, than something which develops and whose meaning we learn by various experiments more or less mistaken. The spirit of these experiments may be rendered as follows. We are likely to try (a) the freedom of *aloofness.* Since by entanglement we lose freedom, we seek liberty in detachment, absence of restraint, refusal to engage in common causes with imperfect comrades in an imperfect world. Regarding all inherited institutions, parties, churches, traditions as compromising at best, and at worst as corrupted and corrupting, we are ready to abandon them or if need be to destroy them in the name of liberty. The aloof man is free—and footless: he is not compromised by any party-ties, but without his imperfect fellow citizens he can accomplish nothing. We find this sort of liberty vainly negative, impotent and destructive of selfhood. Seeing that liberty must be something more positive than freedom *from,* that it must be freedom *for* an object, we may swing to an opposite policy, trying (b) the freedom of *capricious self-assertion,* satisfying desires when and as we please, finding the good of life in living, exercising our functions without too much of that pain of criticism which separated us from biological and social realities. We find ourselves still unsatisfied and unfree. For the self is one and not many: in the multitude of satisfactions one thing remains unexpressed and unsatisfied, the total person. An unintegrated self can enjoy nothing: in this finding modern psychiatry reaffirms the discernment of Plato.[15] And impulse itself dies by being too much examined and consulted: no question becomes so tedious when it is constantly reiterated as the question, What do I most desire to do today? We betake ourselves at last (c) to a concrete *freedom,* a freedom which accepts the bondage we at first spurned, that of taking one's part in the institutional life of

---

[14] G. W. F. Hegel, 1770–1831. His ethical theory is best expressed in his *Philosophy of Right.* See also Rayburn, *Hegel's Ethical Theory.*
[15] *Republic,* Bk. IV; also Bk. IX.

mankind. For these imperfect forms of common life do, after all, embody at their core an element of reason without which we cannot come to ourselves, any more than without the imperfect family we could have come into the historical scene at all, or without the imperfect traditional language of our group communicate a single thought. They have the vast merit of *existing*, whereas those ideals we held against them in criticism lack that virtue; and until they have established themselves in general practice remain mere sentimentality, that unrealistic mooning which makes the name "idealist" a practical reproach. There is much alloy in any institution, but each survives by what is sound in it. Hegel intends to say that what is real in it is reasonable because whatever is reasonable becomes real. We find that all laws, conventions, institutions can be, like language, either bonds or wings, according to one's degree of mastery. It is like the rules of poetic form which weaker abilities find it frees them to discard: poetic power uses them. Coventry Patmore symbolizes the whole Hegelian principle in his lines:

> They live by law, not like the fool
> But like the bard who sweetly sings
> In strictest bonds of time and rule,
> And finds in them not bonds, but wings.

The art of life is to discern what is universal in the laws and institutions, and to ally ourselves with that. Our highest ethical law is, *Identify thyself with objective Reason, as found in the institutions of mankind.*

28.12. Hegel has not contradicted Kant: he has supplemented him. And his argument is one of those bits of philosophy so convincing that it has become part of the mind of our age: the ethical will must have its formal rectitude and freedom; but it is equally its duty to *act*, to come out of its self-enclosure and participate in the common efforts of men. Hegel goes as far as an idealist can go toward being a realist in ethics, one who works with things as they are. Royce [16] builds on this foundation. But he finds that objective Reason not necessarily in the established institutions of society. Hegel is right in attributing to them a core of soundness; but Hegel also—conservative—saw that institutions were capable of decay: not every state is a good enough state to keep alive,—the drastic processes of war and revolution clear history of the decaying cultures: history becomes the world's court of judgment. Then it is not to institutions as such that we should attach ourselves, Royce judges, but to those "causes" which at any time embody the *rationality to come*. These causes are likely to come forward because some element of Reason is *not* embodied in the

[16] Josiah Royce, 1855–1916. His *Philosophy of Loyalty* contains the discussion here epitomized.

actual order, and requires our service in order that it may be realized. Loyalty to causes is the primary ethical principle. And though equally conscientious men may conflict in their judgment and find themselves serving with equal loyalty opposing causes, there is one cause in which all can unite; for each opponent can respect the loyalty of the other. The absolute rule is, *Be loyal to loyalty wherever found.*

28.13. Kant and Hegel, in the interest of showing ethical conduct as reasonable conduct, bring all men under the same law (as indeed they must be brought) and appear to recommend to all the same behavior. This is not actually the case, since the same principle applied to different circumstances must give different results. But duty is even more deeply individual than this. I ought indeed to act on a maxim I am ready to defend—this is my tie with the general reason of men: but I ought to do in the concrete what *no other person* in the universe can do.

This requirement, which comes by degrees to light in the ethical writings of Fichte, Bradley, and Royce, we may express in a rule which, I believe, includes the various principles that have come out of idealistic ethics: *Universalize thyself;* that is, Consider thyself a unique being, having a view of reality granted to no other, which it is thy destiny to express: express this latent idea, make thy private feeling or intuition of the world the universal sense; incorporate it in action; build it into the ongoing common life.

The ethical life begins, as we saw, with the summons to take experience as something more than a subjective pantomime; sensation itself I know I "ought" to take as a sign of a common world of objective truth. My first duty is to gain and keep a common footing with the rational life around me through regard for the truth. Such "truthfulness" or "objectivity," taken widely enough to include the artist with the scientist, occupies a peculiarly central position in the moral life. Gandhi, for example, identifies Truth and God. It is the condition of any further moral progress: how far any two minds can get in mutuality depends directly on the degree of their sincerity toward each other. The liar or deceiver deliberately breaks the common ground between himself and the one he deceives. As Montaigne said: "How much more sociable is silence than falsehood!" The common ground has to be made and kept by moral effort. That is, we can serve men only by first serving what appear to be the more abstract elements of reason in the world,—truth and justice, very much as Kant saw them.

But on this foundation must be built our individual contribution to the concrete stuff of existence, our "service of objective Reason." This service has three stages. First, *alliance* with what is there; and this is Hegel's insight. Second, *criticism* of what is there, but from within, not as detached outsider. The discovery of defect is usually easy enough, yet taken seriously it is an indispensable moral function. Anyone can complain; but to see precisely what is wrong is a gift: accurate diagnosis comes from a unique power of vision and indicates the likelihood of an equally unique capacity to remedy the fault. Third, *re-creation*. The highest good of the individual life is not in the acceptance, nor in the criticism, but in the remaking of ideas and thereby of institutional life; [17] affecting a change in the world which will last because it deserves to last; revising a law, painting a picture, building an arch, educating a child,—acting in such wise that your deposit of truth finds its way into the universal current of life. In this way the instinctive "will to power" is given its due scope and satisfaction; and at the same time the sense of obligation to the hidden life of things is honored. A man's worth lies not solely in the fact that he is a person: nor does it lie in his good will alone, considered as good intention: it lies in that concrete good will so to conceive his life and to fulfil this responsible function, a will which is never without its due effect. This is at once the law of duty and the law of happiness.[18]

28.14. *A possible idealist code.* Suppose now that a man were minded to live by such ethical standards as these. Would it make no difference to him if he had some assurance about the nature of the world in which his work has to be done?

Suppose he were convinced of the metaphysics of idealism, and were to carry this out to the consequences we have already drawn: [19] that every human being has a presumptive meaning in the cosmic order; that our judgments of worth must be essentially valid; that our most universal standards, including those ethical standards of honor, beauty, loyalty, cannot be indifferent to the nature of things.

If one had carried his deduction so far, would he not also infer that since these standards are not alien to reality, it *cannot be a matter of cosmic indifference whether we observe them?* And could he any longer doubt whether his metaphysics were relevant to his ethics? Even if the content of the good life were not altered, the obligation to seek it would acquire a new importance. Or rather, obligation for the first time would find its genuine meaning: for in an indifferent world, the idea of obligation is a

---

[17] An approach to this principle of remaking is to be found in John Dewey's principle of reconstruction. See *Reconstruction in Philosophy.*

[18] Hocking, *The Meaning of God in Human Experience,* Chs. XXXI and XXXII; *Man and the State,* Ch. XXI; and *Human Nature and Its Remaking,* Chs. XI and XXIV.

[19] See §27.2.

footless myth. In a living world, the call of duty is the summons to an enterprise in which one can never be ultimately alone.

This metaphysics carried with it a further presumption that the good will, as being in accord with the ultimate power of the world, is succeeding in its unknown cosmic business; whereas neglect of obligation, betaking oneself to shams, and thus, in Carlyle's phrase, parting company with the central realities, is in some unknown way undoing the possibility of such success. For the objective order of the world is not a mechanical but a moral order. It is on this metaphysical truth that idealist ethics rest its case.

Our discussion has been lengthy: yet it has not come to details,—it has been occupied with principles. Personal and social applications have been glanced at in passing. Let us here assemble certain of the principles which emerge, with more definite suggestions for the art of living.

a. *Love life itself*, as a give-and-take with other life; be objective: treat your sensations as signs of a world of objects which you have mentally to build and keep as a common world with such fellow minds as may be there. This is the elemental or sub-conscious virtue: the basis of all character.

b. *Believe in yourself* as having something unique to do in this living universe, namely to universalize what is your peculiar individual perception. Believe that the meaning of life and self-realization lies in doing this thing, and happiness consists in approaching its achievement; whereas the biological pleasures are incidental to normal activity, and are intended to be the tokens, not the substance, of happiness. This is the primary conscious virtue.

c. *Be truthful.* Truth is the chief means of building the common world. Finding, accepting, using scientific truth are aspects of this virtue. Verbal truthfulness is important, otherwise language becomes a debased coinage: but its ethical interest lies in the maintenance of unity with one's fellows, and the avoidance of self-disintegration which deception brings. Where this unity is otherwise destroyed, as in war, truthful language is the empty shell of a departed virtue: its sphere is then limited to the restoration of amity by way of the common ground which always remains beneath the region of conflict. This is the primary abstract virtue.

d. *Be just:* treat no person as a mere means to your ends; recognize the human equality which underlies all inequalities.

Never exploit, and never countenance exploitation, whether for political or for economic ends. Never take advantage of another's inferior bargaining position to depress the living standard whether of the wage earner, or of the employer!

Be just: recognize the inequalities which ride on the underlying equality, and the differences of status which are incident to differences of function. Never envy and never covet: rejoice in the good fortune of others, and hate the swinish use of fortune whether in high or low.

Be just: maintain your rights and the rights of others; and recognize that without good-will there are no rights whatsoever, whether of property or of action. There are no inalienable rights.

e. *Believe in fulness of living;* never cheat for the sake of an artificial fulness.

Fulness of living means the relatively complete exercise of native capacities and functions, including the biological capacities and hungers. There is a duty to enjoyment—not usually necessary to insist on: the enjoyment of life is the route to the unfolding of new appreciations.

Yet there is no principle to the effect that everyone should enjoy everything. Each joy contains the principle of all joy. No joy that is bought at the cost of mental unity is contributory to life; and a joy bought at the cost of another's welfare or at the cost of duplicity of living is destructive of mental unity.

Prostitution and the irresponsible quest of sex-pleasure suffer under both counts. They are, in general, selfish, though under the pretence of affection, and involve using another human being as a means to one's personal gratification. They exaggerate subjective self-consciousness and diminish the natural attraction of pleasures unassociated with sex. Sex is the occasion of the greatest of human illuminations; the demand to have it apart from its natural meaning is the occasion of the greatest human self-befuddlement and divorce from the realities of value.

f. *Understand the uses of friendliness and also of combat.* Seek peace, and never pretend peace when there is no peace.

Peace is assumed to be the name of the ideal condition of mankind. Yet the over-amiable, over-ingratiating soul is everywhere an object of loathing, and the school of opposition is a necessary part of the development of character. To conceal love is wrong; to conceal anger or hostility is equally wrong, a futile type of deception, and a harmful self-suppression. Evil cannot be dismissed from the world by wishing it absent: it can sometimes be overcome by good will, which is the basis of the idea of love of enemy and of overcoming evil with good, and is the highest way to deal with it. But to win the enemy over implies that he is listening to you, and is in personal relation to you: this method is therefore inapplicable to cases in which the self-satisfied aggressor is listening to no one—such evil must be overcome by combat. Failure to define the ethical uses of a just pugnacity is one of the rotting weaknesses of our civilization; and one of the points in which rebels like Nietzsche have scored a telling criticism of the pseudo-idealism which consists in a denial of the profound moral import of opposition when opposition is due.

g. *Believe in the significance of particular circumstance.* Do not demand to be like any other human being in situation, wealth, range of action. The uniqueness of your duty is the sufficient reason for a like uniqueness in your personal history. Your duty is not to be like others, nor yet to be unlike: it is to utilize your circumstance for finding yourself and your own way to universalize yourself.

Hence, never complain of circumstance, never recriminate, never demand the satisfactions which do not honestly come your way—they are not necessary for you. Above all never offer excuses for failure: in your duty as *a human being* (not necessarily as artisan, lawyer, artist),—in *this* duty it is always possible to succeed.

CHAPTER 29: IDEALISM EXAMINED

29.1. Idealism has the advantage of offering affirmative interpretation of those intuitions of the race which dignify the soul of man and give him positive faith in his destiny in the silent mechanism of the cosmos. The essential character is not subjectivism, but the rational expression of those intuitions, and their metaphysical confirmation, in full view of the scientific developments of modernity.

But it has the disadvantage of its advantages. It chimes in too well with our hopes. It is likely to accept the support of human self-esteem where the cool support of reason—which is the virtue of philosophy—falters. Objective idealism does, it is true, attempt to show its primary doctrines as inescapable; but its proofs have so far been less persuasive to mankind than its spirit. Further, it is not possible to proceed in metaphysics without assumptions; the good faith of a philosophy consists in recognizing these initial persuasions or presuppositions and avowing them. Being avowed, they may also be questioned.

Hence the situation is that all other types of philosophy, and in particular the several varieties of naturalism, remain as persistent critics of idealism. Since the teleological view of the world, of which objective idealism is a thoroughgoing formulation, is the eternal thesis of philosophy, idealism is the perennial object of philosophical criticism and attack: its arguments are fair targets for analysis or refutation; its substance lives on, aided by the criticism. It is also an object of theological criticism on the ground that an intellectual view of God can be no substitute for the view of religion, involving a contrite heart and an act of decision.

The "examination of idealism" which is here in place in our own program is thus already recorded, in part, in the preceding types. It will be further carried forward in the ensuing studies of realism, mysticism, existentialism. In preparation for these we may here notice an aspect of idealism which has appeared in recent years peculiarly objectionable and vulnerable, the doctrine of the Absolute Self,—or briefly, of "The Absolute."

29.2. Objective idealism has taken for granted that the phenomena of experience might be regarded without contradiction as presented to us by another mind, free from our human limitations. This world-mind of idealism is in some way the philosophical equivalent of God or some part of it. "Creation" becomes a continuous process, since the activity of the world-mind is not considered as that of establishing an independent physical world, and then leaving it to develop its inner possibilities: its activity is rather a direct dealing with persons,[1] the persons who appear to themselves to have come out of a long antecedent nature.

But is such a world-mind a consistent object of thought? Are we not attributing to it ideas, purposes and feelings too much like our own?

29.3. We have already pointed out [2] that an all-active mind must be profoundly different from any mind that is so largely receptive as our minds are, and so completely dependent on what it receives for its grist. We can reproduce images that have once appeared to us: we have little power to devise images which have no prototypes in experience. It is a good exercise, to try to conceive a new sense-impression as different from sound and sight as these are from each other. Hume thought our powers of invention in this direction limited to imagining intermediate shades in a sensory scale. Modern sculpture and architecture play with unheard-of shapes and curves. But most so-called invention is simply new combination of given materials.

To an all-active mind all images would be originals, the word "creation" would be appropriate. But would such an active being be properly a "mind," since "mind" in our sense is largely made up on one hand of received stuff and on the other of an *effort to think*, on the part of beings largely ignorant? Or could it be, in Royce's terms, a "purpose"; for is not "purpose" a confession that the good we seek is not present, and that we suffer delay in time because of our limited powers?

Mentality and personality thus seem to imply limitations of various sorts; and if any being is limited that fact requires to be accounted for; the cause would lie either in the being itself or in something else. But if the world-mind is the One real being, there is nothing else to limit it: there could be no reason for its having to "think" or to "purpose" except from within itself. Hence, reflection on the nature of the world-mind has led to the idea of a *self-limiting being* whose ultimate nature is unlimited or infinite. To such a being the term "mind" could apply only by dint of our own human need for some aid to imagination,—"mind" being the nearest thing to the unlimited that we know.

---

[1] If "creation" means the bringing into being out of nothing of a substantially distinct material world, idealism has no original creation, but only manifestation or epiphany. This from the point of view of theological realism is a fatal defect.

[2] See §24.3.

The technical name for the unlimited being is *The Absolute*. The word has an air of finality which is intended: it is used as in contrast to everything that is "relative," i. e., everything that "depends" for its character on this or that external condition, everything that is bounded by an environment, everything that has about it the marks of time and place, and of particular existence which is always irrational and factual. Whatever has *grown* in the course of evolution out of preceding conditions is in the current of change: it has only a "relative" stability and reality. The Absolute being must therefore include all time; there can be nothing before it nor after it; evolution and history take place within it; itself has no history. Such a being could not be supposed subject to emotion, an inner agitation in view of external happening; it could neither be angry, nor pleased with prayer and praise, nor be moved by any sentiment of love for finite creatures—it would certainly not be identical with the God of historical religion.

29.4. Another step: The world-self is to us an "object," other than ourselves. It is to me "another self": am I then "another self" to it? If so, it is still a limited being: it omits *me!* The most real being could accept such incompleteness only by way, again, of self-limitation: I can be an "object" for it, only by its own act: I can be a free being only as it freely wills my freedom. I must fall *within* its being as it does not fall within mine; it must have the whole extent of my otherness within itself. In the most real being, subject and object must be united, both being contained in the absolute unity.

For the Absolute, we finite persons would constitute a society of minds with whom it could maintain quasi-social relationships; yet it would *include* that society, much as the subjective idealist found that his companions must also be "his ideas." For the Absolute, solipsism would be true, although we, its other-selves, would have whatever reality and independence we appear to ourselves to have. "Absolute idealism" would thus unite the characters of subjective and objective idealism: it would be their synthesis,—though at the risk of losing its right to the term "mind," and so ceasing to be idealism!

29.5. These reflections can be generalized in a way which is verbally very simple:

All limited being is relative being.

All relative being implies absolute being.[3]

---

[3] To say that anything is "relative" is evidently an unfinished phrase: it is relative *to* something, as the measure of motion is relative to the position and motion of the observer: the formula

From this we may derive the corollaries:

All partial being, including partial truth, partial goodness, implies a whole of being, truth, goodness.

All error implies the reality of truth; all evil the reality of goodness.

All oppositions and contrasts are partial views, partial errors, and must be overcome in an absolute unity of being.

All relations between distinct terms imply a unity of the terms related.

If these principles are taken as a guide to the outline of world-structure, we have a method of thinking which would in time lead us to absolute truth. We would simply use such partial truth as we have, allowing it to reveal—as in the course of experience it would do—its own error, and so from stage to stage push us on to that position to which every departure requires our return. This is the general conception of dialectical reasoning, which we find in Plato, and which in Hegel becomes the cornerstone of philosophical system.[4] The absolute truth which stands at the end of the journey—and whose denial implies its reaffirmation ("When me they fly, I am the wings")—does not reject the partial insights which have led to it: it includes, explains, and places them. And for Hegel, the Absolute being includes also the whole journey with its various accidents and errors, since they also enter into the significance and quality of the Whole: the Real includes all the appearances, now known to be appearances, and so no longer deceptive.

29.6. I have said that these principles are verbally simple. They are simple; but they leave the mind troubled by their extreme abstractness. They show the direction to finality, and suggest to the seeker that he has the Absolute in hand: for is it not implied in every relative, and has he not the relative before him? At least, one is assured that there *is* an absolute truth, and an Absolute Being: and that in It every conflict is settled, every apparent ugliness absorbed in beauty, every evil and defect entered as an episode in a total triumph. In this state of mind the form of completion seems to do duty for its substance; and the soul enthralled by perceiving the principle of perfection tends to rest from the labors of realizing the goal.

Is there not something specious in the very simplicity of these principles? In their vast generality is not some structural feature of this gnarled actual universe overlooked?

---

for that relativity is an absolute formula, unless it, in turn, is relative to something further. Where the term of reference is no longer relative, we have the absolute of that series. The discovery of relativity is only possible by the discernment of the corresponding absolute. For example, the physical theory of "relativity" is an effort to attain a formula which will hold good under all physical transformations, i. e., an absolute formula for physics.

[4] See pp. 284 ff.

29.7. Since the mere idea of finality has its psychological dangers for mankind, an age which made much of the Absolute invited a period in which the very conception of the Absolute was decried. The ideal of the All-One was seemingly impregnable, and the assault required the energies of a courageous if not a reckless spirit. William James was qualified to lead the revolt.[5]

James' intuitive objection to the Absolute lay in its tendency to devour the independence and freedom of the finite, particular beings of the world. He doubts whether every fact is so connected with every other that its being leads to the Absolute. The connectedness of the world is loose: no strand leads through to the end. There is causality, determination, systematic interdependence in the world,—which is only to say that it is not a chaos: but it is not *all caused*, all determined; it is not a "block-universe"; there is room for novelty, freedom, absolute beginning. Of all our systematizations we have to say "Ever not quite!"

The Absolute threatens the reality of time and change: for it englobes all of time, the future with the past, in its single glance, a *"totum simul."* If the future can be seen with the present, the future is denatured and robbed of its amenableness to our wills; hence freedom also disappears.

Such a world is too safe: its perils and adventures will terminate as they are foreordained, and the summation of all is the absolute repose and security,—no danger is genuine.

On the other hand, the Absolute is barren in the sense that no inferences can be drawn from it *by us* as to what will happen. Its being has been compatible with the miseries and calamities of sensitive finite beings during all past time; it may, so far as we can see, be compatible with them throughout the future. It "functions retrospectively only." And even so, it does not function *for us* in transmuting evil into good, for we have not attained nor can we attain the absolute point of view.

29.8. Since the Absolute is not identical with the God of religion, may it not be after all a logical ideal illegitimately foisted on a reality too rich to fit its scheme? In the order of classified knowledge every part is, indeed, defined in terms of the higher genus, and so at last of the whole. But being always overflows knowledge. It may be truer to the whole range of our intuitions—rational, aesthetic, ethical—to abandon the Absolute, and return to a God who is confessedly not the whole, who is outside of evil and against it, who is a possible partner in a struggle whose outcome is not pre-

---

[5] See James, *Varieties of Religious Experience*, Lects. XVII–XX; also *A Pluralistic Universe*. James' temper is exemplified in his gay taunt to Royce as his daughter was preparing to make a snapshot of the two philosophers sitting on a stone wall in Chocorua: "Look out, Royce! I say, damn the Absolute!"

determined, and in which our participation may make an actual difference, —a finite God. Such is James' proposal.

For after all, why must finitude always give a further account of itself? What exists about us is finite, plural, partially involved in its neighborhood, partially satisfied and complete in its limited being. It is factual, and it *is*: it accepts itself; let us accept it and decline the artificial responsibility to trace its being to the Whole.

29.9. James' revolt is in part a temperamental reaction, oblivious of much that the absolutists, especially Royce,[6] had already written in view of just such difficulties. But he did the work of the genial innovator: he lured out the latent discontent under the pall of absolutism; he released the pent-up stream of a renewed pluralism and finitism, encouraged a reassertion of freedom and of the reality of time,[7] and if not a parent at least aided in the delivery of the "New Realism," which will shortly engage us.

Meantime, a few comments on this indictment of the Absolute.

29.10. First, it is not an indictment of idealism, but of monism. So far as it applies at all, it applies equally to the monism of Parmenides, of Plotinus, of Spinoza, and of Feuerbach, none of whom are idealists. It would apply to an idealism of the Absolute, just so far as it was an absolutism, not so far as it was an idealism. It is for this reason that I have not treated "absolute idealism" as a peculiar variety of idealism.

29.11. Second, the argument seems to me valid in calling for an internal disconnection among facts as well as for a degree of connection. There are loose joints in the world, and many a strand of connection which runs out. There are moral discontinuities also; otherwise forgetting and forgiving would be impossible, and the whole ethical vista would be mechanized. The proponents of absolutism have failed to see that these two features of the world may both be valid. A ship is at the wharf, then again in mid-ocean: it is the same ship, and the same wharf—their relations are casual, not intrinsic to either. For purposes of commerce, one can argue from ships to wharves, and from wharves to ships on the basis of "internal relations"; but one could not argue from the wharf to *that* ship, nor from the ship to *that* wharf: such unconnectedness, or "external relation," is presupposed in all free motion, travel, intercourse in the world. At the same time, a shrewd detective might be able to infer from minute scratches and spills what particular ship had been tied at the particular

---

[6] Josiah Royce's chief work, *The World and the Individual* (1900–1901), is directed, as its title indicates, to showing the reality of individual life and freedom in the world of the Absolute.

[7] See especially the works of Bergson.

wharf: the independence is not complete; the endless underlying sensitivity of part to part has still to be assumed; there are no traceless happenings: there is a Whole. Freedom and Wholeness are both to be held.

29.12. But, third, it is as useless to tilt against the Absolute, as to tilt against the most real: these terms indicate the same entity: for unless the Absolute is real it is not absolute. "The Absolute" is simply the name for the unattained solution of an inescapable problem: if you have any dependent beings—and you have—then there is that on which each dependent depends, i. e., the independent being. If the word "absolute" is offensive, call the unknown quantity "X." It is well enough to remind the absolutist that his term is not an answer to the metaphysical problem, but merely the place for an answer. But the conception "X" can be abolished only by abolishing the metaphysical enquiry itself. It is perhaps through a very obscure inkling of this truth that the latest school of fact-and-form worshippers, "logical positivism," tries to banish the metaphysical enquiry by so defining meaning that the enquiry becomes meaningless! [8] It is a simple device, but it deludes many an unwary soul, especially such as on other grounds are disaffected to metaphysics (or metaphysicians).

We turn to the criticisms which more directly concern the idealistic position.

[8] §8.10.

CHAPTER 30: REALISM

30.1. Modern idealism has become an imposing system of thought. Its principles have been applied to every department of life, to history, to art, to religion, to politics and law. After Aristotle and Thomas Aquinas, the greatest of all system-makers was the idealist Hegel (1770–1831). His lectures on the Philosophy of History,[1] the Philosophy of Art, the Philosophy of Law, the Philosophy of Religion not only affected subsequent thinking in these special fields but remain as unexhausted treasures of thought (protected by a forbidding terminology!).

Part of the influence of Hegel lay in provoking vehement reactions. In the retrospect of over a century we find two of the most vehement associated with the names of Karl Marx and Søren Kierkegaard, the founders of dialectical materialism and existentialism (which is a renewal of dialectical theism). Both Marx and Kierkegaard are Hegelian antihegelians. Dialectical materialism [2] affirms that being is matter, but finds matter, not by way of Newton's atoms, but by way of Feuerbach's "food" (*man ist was er isst*)—the economic basis of life and of the commodity-making of mankind. The *Existenz* doctrine of Kierkegaard [3] affirms that being is God; but denies all intellectual access to God, and stakes life on grace alone. These cleanly opposite revolts against the Hegelian system and synthesis express distinct forms of realism in the sense that mind, as known to us human beings, is belittled *vis-à-vis* something vaster, from one quarter by the historical sweep of cosmic matter, and from the other by the fiat of the hidden God. So evident is the debt of each of these movements of thought to the Hegelian form of objective idealism that the full force of the idealistic tradition can only be felt when the student has followed its principles into these diverse directions.

The genius of the idealistic thinkers of Germany combined with the influence of Berkeley to light new flames in England in Coleridge and Carlyle, in the Cairds, T. H. Green, F. H. Bradley, Bernard Bosanquet; in America, via Coleridge, in Emerson, the St. Louis school of philosophy, James and Royce; in France in Victor Cousin, Lachelier, Renouvier and Boutroux; in Italy in Croce and Gentile.

---

[1] This is an excellent and readable introduction to his thought.
[2] Marx and Engels, *Communist Manifesto;* Engels, *Origin of the Family* and *Ludwig Feuerbach.*
[3] Kierkegaard, *Philosophical Fragments,* and *Concluding Unscientific Postscript.* See also Ch. 38.

Idealism for a period appeared as simply another name for philosophy itself. For philosophy in seeking to understand the world must assume that the world is intelligible; that thought can penetrate the opaque screen of nature,—which is to say that the reality which explains nature is not itself opaque in turn, but is understandable by thought as thought is understandable by itself. Idealism would thus be simply the philosophical form of that fundamental belief of all human aspiration that while "the things which are seen are temporal," the unseen reality which animates them is both eternal and intelligible.

But it is dangerous for any philosophy to become consciously identified with all philosophy, i. e., to become an orthodoxy. For as it becomes a convention to assume that its case is made out, the mind of an age which acquiesces by habit finds itself no longer with a philosophy but (in J. S. Mill's phrase) with "one prejudice the more." It is for the health of idealism that naturalism, in wider or narrower currents, has remained side by side with it; and in recent years two other rivals have taken a new lease of life, realism and mysticism. These two, widely contrasted with one another, propose to amend idealism in radically different ways.

30.2. Realism as a general temper of mind is a disposition to keep ourselves and our preferences out of our judgment of things, letting the objects speak for themselves. If we can say of idealism that it has a tendency to read the mind into nature, realism is in this respect its precise opposite. In the interest of allowing every object its full distinctive flavor, realism, at least in its Anglo-American forms, has been inclined to depersonalize or de-mentalize the world, to see things starkly and factually in a spirit which it conceives to be at once more objective and more scientific than that of idealism.

Such a modern realist is likely to feel in idealism some taint of human conceit, as if it were making man again "the measure of all things." Santayana scores German idealism for its "egotism" in interpreting the universe as a grotesquely magnified Self. The modern realist more often sees the mind as a fragment of the world—and very likely as a minor fragment whose first step in wisdom is to learn to keep its place. Realism in this respect is in the vein of naturalism. Its position was well stated by Irwin Edman: "Thinking is the very late achievement of an uneasy animal in a precarious and changing environment"—to interpret the universe by thought is "as if the tail should think it had invented the procession of which it is the tail." [4]

Realism is a word frequently applied to tendencies in literature and art,

[4] Irwin Edman, *Four Ways of Philosophy* (New York, 1937), p. 85.

and to certain disillusioned or unillusioned policies in politics. Realism in philosophy has perhaps something in common with these trends. All realisms agree in their interest in objects as they are, in their confidence that we can know them as they are, and in their hostility to every impulse to substitute our wishes or ideals for the facts, or otherwise to make our conscious selves the centre of importance in the universe. Idealism in art, for example, insists that the essence of the object is its meaning or spirit, and that the function of art is to convey that quality; it may be less particular about accuracy of drawing. Realism insists on faithfulness of detail, and rather goes out of its way to offend squeamish sentiments or preferences if it suspects them of shielding us from the all-important ugliness of the facts. Likewise in philosophy, modern realism is chary of all optimistic intimacy with the heart of the world, and insists on the necessity of careful, minute, unbiassed and unshrinking analysis as the way to get nearest the reality of things. It puts facts plus reason into the saddle, and unlike the pragmatistic chooser of belief is prepared to find the world, thus examined, very far from what we would wish it to be.

So far, the various realisms agree; but beyond this general harmony in temper, they follow divergent lines. To avoid confusion the student would better at the outset forget realism in art or politics while thinking of realism in philosophy.

30.3. *The tradition of philosophic realism.* This general temper of realism is evidently not enough of itself to constitute a philosophic type. Letting the facts speak without intruding ourselves and our wishes upon them is an attitude we have all had to strive for (and which empiricism especially cultivates); it is thus a form of intellectual virtue which no one would willingly admit himself to be without, and to this extent *everybody is something of a realist.*

There are, of course, differences of degree. Aristotle, for example, is *in this respect* more of a realist than Plato. He is less of a poet, and more of an observer. He rests on the hard nubbles of fact with a certain relish which Plato lacks; he enjoys the quirks of individual things; he likes to study the various kinds of thing in the world and to learn the different sorts of law they observe; he runs less quickly to sweeping generalities which embrace the universe; he appreciates secondary principles and partial generalizations. In brief, Aristotle is a good deal of a positive scientist as well as a philosopher; he lives happily in those border-lands where science and philosophy meet. On this account he becomes the great divider of the sciences, writing separate treatises on mechanics, astronomy, botany, physiology, genetics, psychology, ethics, politics, rhetoric, logic, metaphysics. He is the outstanding system-maker among the Greeks, delighting in significant distinctions and capable of leaving himself and "the mind" out of account while he is occupied with things.

30.4. But beneath this temperamental contrast between Plato and Aristotle is there a difference of principle which deserves to be brought into the open? Such contrasts carry in them at least the germs of divergent types of philosophy.

Aristotle takes the uniqueness and difference among things as a real and important character in the world. For Plato the type-character, or "Idea," which a number of things of a kind have in common as their ideal is the real and important thing about them. Plato describes things of a kind as "participating" in the same Idea, and holds that the Idea exists apart from its copies, unaffected by their appearance or disappearance. The Idea of perfect circularity is real in independence of any transitory circular things which participate in this perfect Idea. Aristotle, in the name of common sense, protests at such a separation between the Idea, or "Form," of a thing and its "Matter."

"It would seem impossible that the substance and that of which it is the substance should exist apart; how, therefore, could the Ideas, being the substances of things, exist apart?" [5]

Things of a kind have their common Form primarily in these very things themselves. Circularity is first and foremost in the multitude of things which are circular. The Form is real as embodied Form. Only by a subsequent act of thought do thinkers "abstract" the common Form from its many embodiments for purposes of thought and science. Their first being is in things; their apprehension by the mind is subsequent.

In consequence of this difference of principle between Plato and Aristotle concerning the relative reality of Ideas "existing apart" and particular things embodying Forms, Aristotle finds himself more able than his great teacher to consider the genera and species of physical nature for their own sakes, in their various degrees of mutual independence, and in independence of the observing human mind. It does not occur to him, within a physical science, to lug the knowing human mind into the picture. And being able to consider things and minds independently, Aristotle calls them all "substances" in the sense of individual beings.

These are the traits in the tradition of Aristotelian common sense which furnish the background for the modern and more technical movements of philosophical realism.

[5] *Metaphysics*, Bk. I, Ch. 9.

30.5. Prior to the arrival of modern idealism, this simpler stage of realism was the prevailing philosophical attitude. It was quite consistent with a belief in God, so long as God was not thought of as the whole universe, but simply as among many beings the most high Being, from whom we must distinguish the world of nature and of men with their myriad separable entities.[6] Thus Aristotle thought of God as the "final cause," an eternal self-contemplating Reason who does not create the world, but toward whom, as the essence of goodness, all things in the world strive.

Thomas Aquinas (1227–74), the great scholastic systematizer, bringing together Aristotle's metaphysics and Christian theology into a vast synthesis, was more comprehensively realistic than Aristotle. God both creates and attracts the world. God is not the world which he has created, nor does he strictly speaking include the world. Each may be thought of and studied for itself without reference to the other. We need not be surprised that the form of theological reasoning which we have met as the cosmological argument [7] accompanies realism in the history of thought. The relation between God and the world is not that of a thinker and his thought, but that of an original substance and a derivative, yet separate, substance or group of substances.

The created things are real in the sense that they exercise real powers. They have the "efficient causality" [8] which is capable of bringing about regular and therefore reliable consequences in other things. And living things have, in addition, the capacity to transmit being to other things. God did not create and then hold in leash, but he authorized his creation to do for itself. The majesty of the creator is not shown in the feebleness of what he creates, but in its strength; hence it is a false piety which would detract from the inherent power of created beings in order to enhance the glory of God.

On the other hand, it is true, according to Thomas Aquinas, that whatever is done in the world is done by God; and this appears at first sight inconsistent with the proposition that the apparent causal activity of created things is real. But Aquinas insists on both statements. Everything is done by God: for the creature continues to depend on the creator for its very existence,—if God should cease to maintain what he has created, it would vanish. God could not consistently create a being who could do without him, even for an instant; for were there such a being it would be at that instant its own god.[9] Hence God, in maintaining the beings

[6] For a history of this general conception, see A. O. Lovejoy, *The Great Chain of Being.*
[7] See §4.2.   [8] See §§ 6.7, 7.1.   [9] *Summa Theologica,* I, 104, i.

that act, maintains the action, and in this sense does everything that is done.

The relation between God's action and that of the creature is imperfectly analogous to that between the driver of the car and the motor of the car. The car is driven by its own power, not by that of the driver; yet unless the driver maintains the stream of fuel to the engine, the car can do nothing. The car moves itself and yet it is the man who moves the car. So God maintains the condition without which there could be no "things" and no "causes"; under this condition, the things exercise the powers which define their being. These powers actually belong to the creatures rather than to God, for they are marked with the distinctive characters of these creatures,—different objects regularly produce different effects. This diversified lawfulness implies that the single power of God is, as it were, vested in and refracted through their several and individual agencies.[10]

In this way, St. Thomas criticizes the extremer Platonic tradition which attributes true being only to the timeless and changeless Ideas; and for which the whole arena of physical and human action is a mere shadow of the real. Even more does he rule out in advance the doctrine of "occasionalism" [11] to the effect that all the apparent activities of men and things are in reality the single continuous operation of God. And he would evidently have had none of that phenomenalism which, flowing from Berkeley and Hume, would make of the world an eviscerated system of "experience," devoid of inner substance and energy, even if it were added that this system of appearances is sustained by a divine will to produce these appearances in us. What God sustains is not a set of images, but a set of beings. And what we perceive, when we take cognizance of this created world, is not a procession of ideas or impressions, but these very beings, with just those autonomous powers which they have whether we perceive them or not.

It is not true of God's creatures that "to be is to be perceived": to be, for a created thing, is to receive and use powers conferred and maintained by God. The being of creatures is contingent being, since it continues to depend on God; but this limitation does not reduce it to a dependency upon the observer, not even upon God as observer. For it is not God's picture-consciousness which sustains them, but God's love. And the great-

[10] Summa Contra Gentiles, III, 69.

[11] See Nicolas Malebranche, 1638–1715, a follower of Descartes, who denied interaction between the mind and the body. God continuously intervenes to bring about the appropriate response in the body on the occasion of any event in the mind, and vice versa. This school was accordingly called Occasionalist.

est of the powers which his love confers is the power in turn to love and to beget, i. e., to confer, in love, being on still another.[12]

John Locke also (1632–1704) is a realist of this type; though the difficulties he faced and candidly described, while trying to answer the question, What *substance* is—the substance which gives the core of reality to these many individual beings—led directly to Berkeley's idealism.

Thus to the verge of modern times realism appears as a sort of direct, unfettered, compendious acknowledgment of a pluralistic world, with the same satisfaction in its variety as we find in William James, or poetically in Shakespeare or Tolstoi. And one may be pardoned for surmising that the loose-jointedness of the world-picture given by an Aristotle or an Aquinas may be after all less a matter of principle than of deferred inquiry, due to the immense descriptive burden under which even their encyclopædic minds now and then visibly staggered. Realism had not yet become a conscious philosophic type: it required the shock of modern idealism to pull it into self-awareness and self-definition.

30.6. *Modern realism.* Since idealism burst upon the modern world in its subjective form, modern realism first took shape as a polemic against *subjective* idealism. And since this idealism came in the form of a new intuition, namely, what we have called the "subjective revelation," realistic resistance naturally first took the form of insisting on opposing intuitions. This was Doctor Johnson's method,—the foot-stamping episode was simply a case of *intuition versus intuition,* a perfectly legitimate way of expressing one's lack of confidence in the adversary's logic, while waiting for one's own belated logical artillery to come up!

Thomas Reid (1710–96), founder of the Scottish School, built a system of philosophy about a group of such intuitions, which he called "the principles of common sense." [13] Chief among them is the immediate intuition of the reality of an external world. They are the clear ancestors of those early stated anti-subjective intuitions of Whitehead, above mentioned,[14] to the effect that the self is enclosed in, and surrounded by, a world which is on its own basis without that self; and that this independent status of physical nature is confirmed by the meaning of every voluntary physical action, for in acting I intend to change a reality beyond myself. To these we may add another conviction, not precisely intuitive but belonging to common sense,—that what is true for me and for others like me is presumably true for all of us together, namely that the world of nature extends

---

[12] It is the unifying principle of God's creative love which justified our earlier reference to scholastic theism as akin to idealism. See §19.3.

[13] Reid, *Enquiry into the Human Mind on the Principles of Common Sense,* 1762.

[14] *Science and the Modern World* (New York, 1931), pp. 125 f.

beyond the mental reach of the whole conscious family of minds, and will survive our disappearance.

According to idealism, there could have been no world before mind appeared: there never was a time when there was not the world-mind, and without that mind nothing else could exist. For the same reason, nothing could exist wholly unknown,—no stray disconnected fragments of being, gradually encountered and picked up by the central organizing focus of history,—no undiscovered matter or energy eternally existing on its own account. As the modern realist sees it, an object can perfectly well exist without being known; to any object, it is a pure accident whether it ever becomes known. And if all mentality in the world could be obliterated, there would be many things in the world—perhaps most things—to which that event would make no manner of difference. If there have always been minds alive in the world, that is a pure matter of fact; in principle it would be quite possible to conceive the universe as existing forever without any mind to know it; and with all the mentality now alive much of the universe may still remain forever unknown to any mind. So far, realism would be in full accord with naturalism, and both would be in the agreeable company of common sense as against the idealistic paradox.

30.7. But realism is rationalistic, and recognizes that these metaphysical intuitions, if they are to hold their own, must be sustained by logical argument against the logic of idealism. It must find the weak point in idealistic armor, and set up an opposing theory of knowledge. This was what Thomas Reid essayed to do. He thought he had found the root error of idealism in the theory of Descartes, "that all the objects of my knowledge are ideas in my own mind." Against this he pointed out that *knowledge reaches beyond our minds:* for knowing is something more than having ideas and impressions,—knowing is *judging,* and judging is referring an experience to an object beyond oneself. I *have* the sensation red light; I *judge* that there is a fire: the sensation may be my idea, but the act of judging refers this idea to a non-mental reality.

This was a good preliminary analysis of the subjectivist's error, and a good beginning of cure; but Reid was hardly logician enough to carry his theory through. Thus his school stands chiefly as a school of protest, waiting for the appearance of more skilful and persistent reasoners. It remained for the modern realists, whose work begins with the opening of the twentieth century, a group chiefly of American and British thinkers, to work these beginnings out into coherent form, and to avoid the pitfalls into which naturalism and the naïver or less critical forms of realism had fallen.

CHAPTER 31: MODERN REALISM

31.1. In the development from traditional realism to recent realism in England and America (North America), the common sense convictions we have discussed in the preceding chapter receive a more careful study and formulation. Of recent realism we may say that it is primarily *a way of knowing*, a variant of rationalism roughly describable as a preferential confidence in the thinking which analyzes and dissects, finds the lines of cleavage among things, finds the units; and this way of knowing carries with it secondarily a metaphysical belief that the *objects we observe are in reality independent of us*, and of each other, essentially as they appear to be. We might summarize its principles in the phrase, What seems to be separate *is* separate.[1]

Thus, to the modern realistic eye, the joints of the world are loosened. The effort to describe the whole of things from one centre, whether material or ideal or any other, is abandoned as an artificial and unnecessary *tour de force*. All monisms are too hasty. We are bound to trust reason: but when reason "seeks unity,"[2] the realistic watch-dog in us scents danger,—the human wish for unity is all but certain to falsify the facts. Plain observation shows the world not as one thing, nor yet as two things— though evidently dualism has a realistic motive—but as many things of many kinds. And while it is true that a closer scientific observation shows these things to be connected in various ways, there is still a radical difference between connection and unification. The ingredients of the world, each one a substantial reality, work together without being fused into one substance.

As compared with traditional realism, contemporary Anglo-American realism has a disadvantage and an advantage.

The disadvantage is that, having modern idealism to contend with, it is mainly preoccupied with polemic. Its chief concern has been negative, that of attacking the logic by which idealism has supported its intuitions, an attempt which, even if wholly successful, would still leave idealism unrefuted, since the intuitions remain.

[1] E. G. Spaulding, "A Defense of Analysis," and R. B. Perry, "A Realistic Theory of Independence," in *The New Realism*, by E. B. Holt *et al.*
[2] §16.1.

The advantage is that it arose at a time when logic was experiencing a veritable renaissance, making rapid advances and placing new instruments of intellectual analysis and precise thinking in our hands. Logic, in important areas of its modern development, has come into close connection with mathematics, more especially the analytic disciplines of mathematics like algebra.[3] This aspect of logic is sometimes referred to as "mathematical logic." Logic as the ally of mathematical analysis is particularly helpful for stating the realist's case. In stressing the mathematical side of logic, however, we are liable to overlook the importance of logic as an "organon," that is, as instrument or discipline which governs thinking. Strictly speaking, logic taken as a whole is a non-partisan instrument of precision. The new logic has simply enabled modern realism to give an added clarity to its fundamental positions, namely:

a. That the objects of knowledge do not depend on any knower for their existence or character; and

b. That the world is many, and not one; it is analysis which leads us most surely to reality.

Aside from the newly stated arguments, the chief distinction of modern realism is a new account of the status of objects of knowledge, an account which owes much to the careful reasonings of Hume, reflecting upon the subjective idealism of Berkeley. Hume saw that if we accept Berkeley's dismissal of material substance, perceptions naturally attach themselves to the perceiver. But what evidence, he asked, have we of perceivers? Hume's scrupulous analysis of perceptions yielded nothing but perceptions and their interrelations,—no trace of an active perceiver. His conclusion: "mind" can mean only collections of unit perceptions which come and go. But then why call these units "perceptions" at all? He tentatively opened the question whether the units of experience need to be attached to anything, or need anything but themselves in order to exist. Perhaps the self-same units, in a mental context are called "perceptions," and in a non-mental context are called "objects." Modern realism, sharing Hume's doubts about allowing perceptions to be embedded in matter or mind, developed and strengthened this supposition, sometimes referring to the unattached perceptions as "neutral entities," since they are neither physical nor mental.[4]

We shall consider these positions.

31.2. *The first proposition:* the objects of knowledge do not depend on any mind for their existence or character.

[3] See B. Russell and A. N. Whitehead, *Principia Mathematica.*
[4] We follow here the views of the American New Realists. See also W. James, "Does Consciousness Exist?"

Berkeley, having found his perceptions ensconced in his mind, assumed that they belonged there, and further that they could not belong anywhere else. He hardly argues the case, since to him this mutual lock-and-key fitness so leaps to the eyes that it is a "repugnancy" to suppose that a perception could exist out of relation to a perceiver. A percept is strangely and uniquely fitted to be perceived!

But (asks the realist) does this phrase "fitted to be perceived" mean anything? Is there anything *not* fitted to be perceived? The human hand is a specific something to which other specific things, like jug handles, can be fitted; but perception is no such specific thing; it requires no adaptation to itself on the part of the object it prehends. Nothing surely can be unfitted to be *known*; for knowledge is so hospitable, un-self-intrusive, "diaphanous" as to entertain or consider (either through sense or through idea) everything that exists and many a thing that does not exist. Hence the fact that we know, or think of, or perceive a thing implies exactly nothing about its character, or its capacity for independent existence.

Neither Berkeley nor common sense are altogether appeased by this. At least on naturalistic assumptions there are many things, such as light waves, not fitted to be perceived; we do not perceive them; they stir up in us, by way of the eye-nerve-brain machinery, perceptions of color and shape. On this score, little if anything in nature as it is in itself is fitted to be perceived; it has first to pass through the transformers we term our sense-organs, and the mind then makes of the effect something *sui generis*, the sense-datum: this sense-stuff, as the mind's own version, must be peculiarly "fitted to be perceived." If we hold to the causal theory of perception, Berkeley's position is thus strongly sustained.

Hereupon the realist is forced to a severe decision: if he keeps his essential point that we perceive things as they are apart from perception, he must part company with this scientific account of perception, root and branch. He does it reluctantly [5] because he likes to be on the side of the scientists. But he is forced to the conclusion: sense-perception is not an effect, but "an act in which the object is given or disclosed": [6] the object is just this bundle of colored, sounding, odorous stuff I open my senses to, *and* just this is not at all "fitted to be perceived," but there in its own right!

This, he maintains, is what we mean by "knowledge." If knowing were a process which made, transformed, or in any way altered its object, it would cease to be knowledge and become illusion: it is the business of knowing to report things as they are. That is, in the order of existence,

---

[5] Several, like R. B. Perry and W. P. Montague, try to hold both positions,—in vain!
[6] R. B. Perry, *Philosophy of the Recent Past* (New York, 1926), p. 199.

objects first are, and then become known. Knowing is a peculiarly transparent relationship: objects happen into the field of knowledge as snow-
flakes drift through the light from a window, without significant change.
The process of knowing is hardly an activity at all: [7] the object is simply
"there," and we are effortlessly taking note of its presence. We attend, we
focus our eyes, but we do not "construct" what we see; we admit the
sense-datum, accept it as now part of our mental history, forever woven
into memory, whereas it, the sense-datum, goes its way as a part of the
living world of physical things. Knowledge is a sort of *tangency* between
a personal history and a physical system of events: it is a relationship which
acknowledges and enjoys but does not claim.

31.3. On this view, as on Berkeley's view, we are spared the necessity
of believing that the "secondary qualities" of things, their colors, odors,
etc., exist in the mind, while the real objects possess only the "primary
qualities." [8] This ungracious divorce of the qualities of nature from her
quantities Berkeley got rid of by taking both primary and secondary qualities into his fabric of "ideas"; realism gets rid of it by allowing both
of them independent extra-mental reality. The color of the sunset is not
due to the eye, nor the sound of Niagara to the ear, nor the warmth of
the fire to the sense-organs of the skin. These qualities are in nature, just
as they seem to be. We might say that they are in the objects, or belong to
the objects, but most of the realists, fearing to admit the spectre of
"substance" into their account of experience, would prefer to say that the
object is simply an assemblage of these qualities. "The principle of substance betrays realism into the hands of its enemy." [9] For if we say that the
extra-mental thing to which knowledge refers as its object is the "substance" of things, the qualities remain in an uncertain halfway status
between the mind and the external substance, in danger of capture by the
mind by having confessed their incapacity for self-subsistence.

A dissenting group of realists, the Critical Realists, demonstrated that
this fear is well-founded; for maintaining the tradition of an extra-mental
substance, they allow that sense-qualities are subjective appearances. They
deviate from New Realism in the direction of Kant's theory of knowledge.
They are thus less typical than the New Realists, and we regretfully omit
the discussion of their views.

31.4. It begins to appear that the realist is trying to walk a rather
narrow plank. The fire is surely hot; but we find it a little hard to believe

[7] For a classic formulation of this miracle, turn to Aristotle, *De Anima*, Bk. III, Ch. 4.
[8] §21.5.
[9] R. B. Perry, in *The New Realism*, by E. B. Holt *et al.* (New York, 1925), p. 103.

that it feels hot to itself [10] in the same way that it feels hot to us: the warmth as an experience would seem to belong to the mind. Naturalism, as we found, itself requires this interpretation of the feeling of warmth. But realism, having dissociated itself from the causal theory of perception, is not at one with naturalism on this issue.

Allow, then, that the color, the shape, the sound, the warmth exist as qualities in nature, not dependent on being perceived by us or by any other mind. What now shall we do with dreams, mirages, illusions, hallucinations, errors of judgment? Are these "unreal" objects also "there" and independent of being thought of? And what shall we do with objects which we usually regard as objects of thought *par excellence*, namely, mathematical conceptions, numbers, perfect circles, logical rules, hypotheses, our tentative and variable "ideas" about what natural law is,—all the abstractions of reason, the world of "universals"? Common sense would say, these at least are mental, or, as Aristotle held, acquire their standing as objects of thought through a mental activity of abstraction.[11]

But if we allow these to be mental, we compromise the independence we have already granted to the objects of sense-perception. For these thought-objects mingle with them, and are inseparable from them. It would be impossible to draw a line between sense-objects and thought-objects without creating another bifurcation, as objectionable as that between the primary and the secondary qualities. Modern realism, therefore, takes the courage of its convictions and accepts the unplausible alternative: all these objects are likewise independent of being thought about.

The truths of logic and of mathematics certainly remain valid whether any one thinks of them or not. If the perfect circles, straight lines and the like, together with the eternal truths about them, do not exist in nature, they may *be assigned to a realm of their own*, a realm of "subsistence," or "essence," where our thoughts may find them without pretending to create them.[12]

31.5. Here modern realism may claim the support not alone of its own logic, but of a notable strand of the history of thought which we have not hitherto noticed, likewise called "realism," and hailing especially from Plato. For to Plato, the "ideas," as the universal perfect prototypes of defective particular things,[13] are real; and this reality implies that they

---

[10] The realist will object to this phrase, and rightly in so far as feeling implies apperception. But reduce feeling to the "given," and I think we have what *must be meant*. In what other way can heat exist than (1) molecular vibration in space or (2) feeling?

[11] Aristotle, *Physics*, Bk. II, Ch. 2.

[12] See, for example, Santayana, *Scepticism and Animal Faith*, Chs. VII, IX; also *The Realm of Essence*. Santayana is a Critical Realist.

[13] §16.4.

have an eternal and changeless being, not only in independence of the
material stuff which takes on their semblance, but also, as he maintains in the *Timaeus*, in independence of any mind which thinks them.
Existence in time and space is certainly not their way of being; for the
particular things in time and space are transitory; nor yet do they depend
on our thinking them, for we also come and go: they have a different mode
of being to which the questions where, when and how do not apply, and
which can best be indicated by a figure such as Plato resorts to when
speaking of the ideal city:

"I understand; you speak of that city of which we are the founders, and which
exists in idea only; for I do not think that there is such a one anywhere on earth?
In heaven, I replied, there is laid up a pattern of such a city, and he who desires
may behold this, and beholding govern himself accordingly." [14]

This thought of Plato's found a strong echo in various mediæval philosophers, impressed by the absolute claims of logic upon the human mind.
There was evidently a realm of universals having an order of its own which
we neither determine nor control, but obediently observe. The *genus*,
including several species, was not alone logically "higher" than the *species*,
but of a higher degree of reality: the species is derived from the genus.
Then the highest universal, Being, is the most real entity in the system,
including them all and binding them all together. To some of these mediæval thinkers, this whole system of ideas, so far as it had being apart
from temporal things, could only be conceived as existing in the mind of
God, as his eternal thoughts.[15] To others, the highest universal *is God*; or to
put it conversely, God is no other than the highest of all universals, including in itself all the rest.

Modern realism is quite free from the theological preconceptions of
the great scholastics, and would particularly repudiate the notion that
the universals need the mind of God or any other mind to confer reality
upon them. It finds itself more immediately at home in the Platonic world
of thought, where the ideas "subsist" in their own right.

31.6. It seems somewhat anomalous to intrude into this realm of perfect and eternal order those other objects of mental vision,—dream, fancy
and mistake. Yet they must not be taken into the mind. Are not they "objective" in the same sense that actual things are? The monster that pursues
me during a nightmare is not of my intentional fabrication, otherwise I
would have an end of him; and the scenery of my dream is of such detail
as I would be at a loss to paint, if I were commissioned to do it. It is

[14] *Republic*, Bk. IX, 592.
[15] See, for example, Bonaventure, *The Itinerary of the Mind to God.*

not my deliberate self who produces this concrete environment. Shall we then assume another region or regions for these illusory objects, which are certainly not "eternal" like the circles or numbers, and say of them, with E. B. Holt, that "unreality is no more subjective than reality; for a thing may be objective and yet unreal"? [16]

To an uninstructed mind a vivid dream may be taken, not for a "mental" experience, but for an actual excursion into another world. But even a savage ordinarily ascribes a mistake to himself; and to more sophisticated minds, error and dream alike are distinctively "my" ideas. Charles Peirce goes so far as to say that it is chiefly through error and ignorance—which must be ascribed to something—that one gets an idea of himself in the first place. In any case, for common sense and for philosophy alike, it would seem that if the word "subjective" is to mean anything it must apply to these private and unsharable visions which mislead my judgments of the "objective" facts.

But common sense can be no final criterion of truth. If realism is to be thorough with the view that the objects of mind are not mental, it must make up its mind to part company here with common sense whose friendship it could claim at first with such good effect. From the difficulty we have here reached we can see that realism needs much ingenuity to make out a tenable theory of error.[17] Modern realism, however, is an intricate philosophy. It is rather striking that beginning as it does in a sturdy alliance with common sense against idealistic paradox, it ends by being peculiarly a professional development of philosophy. It pays the penalty of all such intricacy in philosophy: its members reach vastly divergent results. We cannot here follow them into these, as yet unfinished, developments. We have traced as far as we may the bearings of the first proposition, that the objects of knowledge do not depend on the mind for their existence.

31.7. *The second proposition:* The world is many and not one; it is analysis which leads us most surely to reality.

The reader will have observed that the arguments of realism under the first proposition affect only the subjective form of idealism. There are few idealists to-day who would say that "things owe their existence to being known." Most of them would say that "things owe their existence to being *willed*," or that they owe it to their value or meaning; and they would add that the source of the existence of natural objects is certainly not the will of the finite human knowers. To the objective idealist, most

---

[16] *The New Realism* (New York, 1925), p. 367.

[17] The fifth and sixth essays in *The New Realism*, by W. P. Montague and E. B. Holt respectively, are devoted to this enquiry.

human knowing, all "empirical" knowing, is receptive first and reproductive or re-creative only as response to the outer action, and he would agree with the contention of realism that we know what is beyond ourselves. In so far, then, as the realist confines himself to refuting the proposition that "things owe their existence to being known" his quarrel is with subjective idealism only.

But objective idealism requires that the world be conceived as a teleological unity; and that this unity, which is mental, shall be understood as the original source of the many things in the world, not as built up by these many things into a compound which is *their* product. If the second proposition of modern realism is true, objective idealism becomes untenable.

31.8. Now analysis in physics discovers molecules, atoms, electrons: these, according to the realist and the common convictions of science, come successively closer to reality. We are nearer the truth when we think of a gas as composed of separate molecules than when we think of it as a continuous fluid; and still nearer the truth when we carry our mental microscope to the last frontier of minute dissection. Likewise in biology one may analyze an organism into cells; and in psychology, the mind may be analyzed into sensations or minute shocks of experience.[18] Are these units also nearer the reality than the whole organism or mind taken as a unit? The realist fears that we are continually misled by what appears simple to our apprehension,—the fallacy of "pseudo-simplicity"; [19] and that the idealist is especially the victim of this fallacy when he assumes that the self or mind can be taken as an original unity.

31.9. Now the idealist has been prone to make much of the fact that analysis discovers something else beside the elements, namely, their *relations* to each other, their types of connection, their modes of interaction which we call "laws." These arrangements and laws have a reality of their own; they are not nothing. The space in which atoms play is not nothing. The attraction or repulsion which one atom has for another is an important part of what an atom *is*. Two atoms whose essence it is to attract one another are not two separate things, but two members of a single thing. And since everything in the universe is related to everything else, the universe is ultimately one being.

To this the realist recalls that we must distinguish between *two types of relationship*. There are relations which are an integral part of the being of an element; there are others which are so far accidental that they may

---

[18] See E. B. Holt in agreement with Herbert Spencer, *The New Realism*, p. 351.
[19] *The New Realism*, p. 13.

come and go without making any difference to the element. A molecule of gas may be taken away from the other molecules and remain (approximately) the same molecule; a cell cannot be taken away from the other cells of an organism and remain the same cell. Its "life," we say, goes out of it. In other words, it is a part of the being of a cell to be in an organism: its relations to its neighboring cells are called "internal" relations, because they make up a part of what the cell is. The relations of a molecule to a molecule, or still better, of a brick to a brick, are called "external"; because it is indifferent to the being of the brick whether it is or is not with other bricks.

The reduction of the main issue between realism and idealism to the one of the status of "internal" and "external" relations is a deed of idealist analysis, especially of F. H. Bradley and Josiah Royce. This aspect of the new logic of relations is especially pertinent to the metaphysical issue of unity and plurality here raised.

The modern realist does not deny that all things in the universe are related—this is what makes them a universe; nor that relations are real— he asserts this. But he maintains that many relations are purely external,— especially those frame-relations which might tie the universe together, such as the relation between thought and its objects,—so that what we have is a group of independent entities, independently related,—an ultimate plurality of reals.

31.10. If this is the case, we must understand the world from the parts to the whole, not from the whole to the parts; and whatever the *mind* is, it must await the results of analysis to determine whether it can pose as anything original and simple or whether it must be regarded as a composite of numerous simple elements. On the face of it, the realist is disposed to accept the naturalistic evidence that mind does not occur until we have organisms with nervous systems; and what results from such an assemblage of non-mental reals is presumably itself composite and not simple.

A satisfactory analysis of the mind must be regarded as a piece of unfinished business for modern realism. But the general plan on which its description would proceed has been sketched along lines suggested by William James.[20]

The elements of mind, whether perceptions or sensations or something more elementary, are just those "*neutral entities*" which also aggregate themselves into physical objects. When they enter into causal relations

---

[20] See his article, "Does Consciousness Exist?," 1904, reprinted in *Essays in Radical Empiricism*. See E. B. Holt, *The Concept of Consciousness* and *The New Realism* (New York, 1925), pp. 372 f. Also Bertrand Russell, *An Analysis of Mind*.

with other such entities they constitute the world of physical nature; when they are combined in the order of memory continuity and cumulation, they constitute minds. Just as the square at a cross-roads belongs to both roads and to neither, so these elements become ingredients of mind or of nature according to their patterns of relatedness. Mind is a mode of relationship among contents which are not peculiarly mental.

So far from supposing that the knower makes or qualifies his objects, it is in this view the objects which constitute the knower—or such knower as there is. For in this view of mind, there is no Ego aside from these "contents" and their interplay; there is no "conscious-ness" as a distinct entity in the world; there is no distinctive activity which is to be called mental [21] and attributed to a self. The mind is a selection from all of the infinitely numerous neutral-entities of the world—a selection indicated in some way by the capacity of a nervous system to react to its environment—according to a law of world-organization as objective as any other law of nature. Dreams, fancies, erroneous judgments are no more subjective than the rest: they are good neutral stuff, shreds of imagery, let us say, which do not happen to connect with other neutrals in the order of causation. And where they live when not entering a mental context is not yet determined.

The mind itself, being a relatively unstable and transient union of elements which are relatively permanent, is thus secondary, derived, composite,—eminently unfit to serve as creative principle of the universe.

31.11. The realist critique is directed as much against monism as against idealism: its pluralism has no room for an absolute one. American realism continues the campaign of William James against the Absolute [22] but with certain emphases of its own. The unity of the world is in one respect meaningless; in another respect immoral.

It is meaningless: for whatever can be said of all things can logically make no difference to anything. Mind as we find it in the world is in contrast to things that are non-mental, and gets its distinctive meaning by this contrast. When we try to make mind the substance of everything, we lose this contrast, and therefore the significance of the proposition. The reference of everything to "mind" becomes in the end tedious and unprofitable; the more so since we can never be quite sure what an absolute and all-inclusive mind would be like.

It is immoral: since it must assume that in the absolute mind good and evil, which are present in the world on equal terms, are reconciled or made consistent with each other. If the absolute mind is held to be all-good, then

---

[21] Here schools of realism disagree, the English school inclining to advocate a specific mental act,—a non-interfering observing whereby object-stuff is admitted to relation with memory.
[22] Ch. 29.

the evil of the world must be an illusory appearance which vanishes from the absolute point of view,—and from ours, in proportion as we succeed in attaining that outlook. This to the realist is an encouragement to indifference and moral laxity; an apology for the abominable. "There is always one remaining philosophy," says E. G. Spaulding, "that allows evil to stand at its full face value, and that finds all methods of arguing it out of existence to be invalid. . . . Evil is evil, and it cannot be transformed or argued out of existence." It lies in the nature of the Whole that it cannot be partial to any side; but the moral life is a partisanship and a combat.

We now have before us the elements of a position which may be taken as typical of modern realism.

CHAPTER 32: REALISM EXAMINED

32.1. Modern Realism is a system of thought which presents itself to us with the strange but candid admission that it is incapable of being tested. It necessarily accepts the fact that in the nature of the case no object independent of thought can be found or thought of. It can only urge us not to build hasty inferences on what may after all be a mere incident of our ego-centric mode of knowing.

It does indeed propose to analyze the process of perception, and professes to find that the object perceived is independent of the perceiver, meaning thereby not "out of relation" to the perceiver but out of any relation which would imply dependence on the perceiver for existence,[1] such as being then and there caused or created by the perceiver. And the realist is undoubtedly right when he reports that we do not find ourselves in perception creating our own objects. But this does not prove what he needs. For (in order to be sure that there is not some kind of dependence he hasn't thought of) he would have to show that the perceived object is capable of existing apart from the mind. And this he could only do by a physical or mental experiment, such as trying whether we can conceive objects as existing apart from all thought, an experiment manifestly incapable of execution, though unabashedly countenanced by no less a thinker than David Hume! Analysis cannot show that the object is independent of, that is to say, externally related to the knower: it can only indicate that dependence is, in its judgment, not as yet made out. As important collateral evidence for this proposition, note that such springs of realism as we find in Brentano, Meinong, Husserl rest the independence of the object on an "intention" of the mind; while Alexander bases it on a "conviction," Santayana on "animal faith." Most American realists are satisfied with the absence of a proof of dependence.

What positive grounds, then, does realism offer us? Essentially but two: those intuitions of common sense to which, it alleges, idealism does not do justice; and the possibility of making a consistent theory of the world on other than idealist assumptions.

[1] *The New Realism*, p. 117.

32.2. These grounds are pertinent, so far as they can be established. As to the second, I shall undertake to show that it lends no support to realism in any present form, inasmuch as no consistent realistic system is yet forthcoming. The first ground is more substantial. We thus have the interesting situation that a type of philosophy which prides itself particularly on its rationality is chiefly recommended by intuitions,—the intuitions which determine its revolt against idealism.[2]

To my mind the most important element in modern realism is its renewal of a direct and naïve view of the world of objects in a spirit of return to these intuitions of common sense. Try the assumption that objects exist when we are not looking, just as we see them. Try the assumption that there is no bifurcation in nature. Try the assumption that mind is in a greater world, and not the world in any mind. Try thinking of the world as a lot of independent reals. Allow, with Perry, that "the human mind is instinctively and habitually realistic, so that realism does not so much need to be proved as to be defended against criticism," [3] a most fortunate thing, if true, for a system which foregoes proof. Take these as your postulates and see what you can make of them. This is the essence of modern realism, an invigorating experiment in re-interpreting experience.

32.3. Of course, these intuitions, like all other intuitions, need themselves to be interpreted. We ought not to let pass without scrutiny the general impression just noted that the instinct of the human mind is clearly realistic:—we recall that Berkeley thought he was speaking for the common man against the philosophers! What does the intuition of common sense say about independent objects?

Chiefly this, I think: that I can shift objects without substantially altering myself, and that the objects can shift observers without themselves being altered. When I am attending to a brick wall or a tree, I am not expressly attending to myself; hence when my attention flits from the brick wall to the tree, I am not observing any change in my "self,"—*self being a constant in the flux of sense-objects*, something I carry around with me. Likewise when I cease attending to the brick wall and another observer takes my place, he sees what I saw,—*the brick wall being a constant in the flux of observers*. Thus the observers and the objects are relatively independent. But there are two things common sense does not say. It does not report that when I attend to myself I have no physical object at all in the field,—for this is not true: I can dispense with any particular physical object and still be myself, but *not with all* of them, not with "nature." Nor does it report that the physical object which can dispense with my mind

<hr>

[2] §28.6.   [3] Perry, *Philosophy of the Recent Past*, p. 201.

or yours can dispense *with all minds,* and still be itself; on this point, which is the point at issue, common sense has nothing to say.

But there is one intuition which does bear on this point. It is mentioned by Whitehead as an additional reason against subjectivism. "I do not understand," he says,[4] "how a common world of thought can be established in the absence of a common world of sense." This common world of thought he assumes we have; for do we not converse? But why not appeal at once to the intuition *that our world of sense is a common world?* For surely we all take this for granted. The same brick wall may be seen by a multitude of observers, not alone successively, but at the same time. I do not so much as need to see these other observers to know that the wall is thus sharable. How do I know this? It goes with what I mean by the "objectivity" of the wall: it is not subjectively mine, because it is in the nature of the thing to be observable-by-many. If this is common sense— and I believe it is—then common sense does say with realism that in knowing I reach beyond myself,—the object is independent of *me;* but it also says that in getting beyond myself I get into a world in which mind other than my own has an established concern,—and this is no longer distinctively realism. Objective idealism comes nearer to common sense at this point.

It remains logically possible that the object is capable of belonging to many minds because it first belongs to itself alone; that is the doctrine of realism. But the intuitions of common sense cannot be appealed to as favoring this view. For what we have on the surface of experience as we spontaneously take it are two aspects of the objectivity of the wall, either of which can be inferred from the other. Assume that the object is independent, belonging to itself alone (or to nature apart from all minds), and it follows that it will be open to all observers on the same terms, if it is open to any. Assume, on the other hand, that the object is primarily a common term in many minds and it will follow that it must appear relatively independent of any of them, as the hub of a wheel in rapid motion seems to exist in independence of its spokes though it may be cast in one piece with them. As between these alternatives, common sense does not trouble to decide; though the realist has still to make out that any one knows by intuition or otherwise what is meant by an unperceived physical object in the full glory of its secondary qualities.

And there is still a third alternative, to which I, for my part, subscribe. Namely, that no empirical knower, and no group of empirical knowers, can supply all the necessary conditions for the presence of any physical object in experience: the object being, in its substance, "given" to all such know-

[4] *Science and the Modern World,* p. 126.

ers. But it is not given by a physical world: it is given by an active will, which intends to communicate that experience. On this teleological view, the object has a certain being in independence of all mere observers, yet its being is not a dead and absolute fact which somehow bursts into a mysterious relation of being known. This view seems to me the only one fully just to our native intuitions. All empirical knowers know realistically, as knowing beyond themselves; but they know nothing independent of all mind. Nor is there any such thing.

If then we appeal to intuition alone to decide this issue, it would give no unequivocal verdict for realism. But we are committed at present to entertaining the realistic alternative, and to considering it, not on its intuitive, but on its logical merits.

32.4. *Is the realistic analysis of perception valid?*

Is knowing an inactive relation, in which an independent object is simply disclosed? I cannot agree that it is. Knowing is too evidently active.[5]

"I open my eyes, and the world is there: this is knowing! No activity on my part except the muscular effort of opening the eyes." The whole fallacy of realism is comprised in these plausible words. They contain one item of truth: the activity of knowing is not a muscular effort, and they who can conceive no other kind of effort will never find it. It is an effort of judging. Nothing is known unless it is *judged*; experiencing is getting answers to questions which the mind is putting to the world; if there is no questioning activity, there is no knowledge. It is not sufficient to open the eyes, even to see what is there, as any one who has looked long for something "in plain sight" ought to know; as all the failures of "eye-witnesses" to see what happens before their noses amply testify. For a totally unquestioning mind, the brick wall itself may not be there; for the completely "absent-minded" person, the wall begins to exist only when he begins to ask why he can get no farther along that line,—"O yes, a brick wall!" A man knows as much as he judges; he judges as much as he questions, and no more. Knowing is acting.

It is this activity which gives me both truth and error. Colors and shapes, as simply present facts, say nothing, and therefore cannot possibly be erroneous or illusory. And I can never be wrong if I confine my judging to noting, this color or shape is present to me. But if a spider on a window-pane is taken to be a mile away and I seem to see a monster in the sky, there is an error; the error lies in my active contribution to what is there. I can be in error only if I act and because of my own act; the erroneous contents of my judgment are of my private fabrication. And I am equally

[5] §24.2.

acting if I truly judge the object to be on the windowpane two feet away, and a spider. Knowing is never mere transparency: it is always doing something.

But does this activity change the object? And if so, is it not, as the realist charges, false to the meaning of knowing?

There is confusion in this question. Suppose sense-qualities are subjective, in the sense that the brick wall is not red until some one opens his eyes to see it: then is my knowledge falsified if I observe, "Here is a brick wall; I must change my course"? Not at all. I am at that moment asking no question about the conditions which make the object before me seem red; I am not judging that point, and therefore not misjudging it! No matter to what extent the mind may be implicated in the nature of what it perceives, there is no falsification so long as my questions are confined to such as these: "What color is this, vermilion or orange? How far to the top of the hill? What shall I do about it?"—questions of the relations within experience. Evidently, the question "What color has the foliage when there is no eye to see it?" is not one which the ordinary business of living raises, and which that business never answers, whether right or wrong. There can be no falsification where there is no answer to a question that is not raised!

But if I do, as a metaphysician, raise the question, What are the conditions under which I perceive a red color? then there is indeed a chance for error. The realist, who believes that analysis leads toward truth, might be expected to follow the analysis of physiological science, which leads straight to the conclusion that there is no red color at all in the world until there is an eye and a mind. If, in order to keep the red in the object, he rejects the whole causal theory of perception (as he must), he would seem to reject the method of analysis at the same time. He is then at liberty to say "I see a red color when there *is* a red color; there are no other conditions calling for analysis." But having thus closed off a scientific and philosophical question, he cannot complain if some one else regards the question as significant, and answers that the mind is one factor in the appearance which nature presents,—an answer in which judgment, and therefore knowledge, remains intact.

32.5. We have just now declined to allow the realistic theory of error, on the ground that the erroneous contents of my judgment are demonstrably my own private production.[6] We must also decline to admit that the "universals" can either exist (as embodied in a world of physical laws

---

[6] See §29.7. Holt and others would say "private selection" from the realm of universals or essences. The following argument deals with this mode of interpretation.

and classes) or subsist (in an eternal realm of their own) in abstraction from every thinker.

The reasons for this are twofold: First, as an elementary consideration which since it is *the* consideration, we can't avoid mentioning, a universal must be *thought* for the same reason that a purpose must be *purposed*, or roughly for the same reason as that a frown must be frowned. The frown without the face will be allowed to be an abstraction; and an abstraction is an object which ceases to be viable by itself when we cease thinking about it. I agree with Aristotle here.

Second, if we allow any universals an independent existence, we must allow them all: and there are too many of them! Every conceivable idea must subsist in that realm, every shade of meaning being flanked by the next barely distinguishable shade, till as we consider it the whole mass fuses into a homogeneous plenum. With such a world of ideas our thought can do nothing. It resembles a storehouse stuffed so full that no access can be had to anything; or better, a library of music containing all possible compositions written and unwritten, every combination of tones that can be made on any instrument. Thus the very notion of a composition, which implies the rejection of innumerable possibilities, is destroyed, an infinite resource rendered useless and meaningless by its unselective totality. This pseudo-realm would include well-ordered series, like the series of real numbers, which while infinite have a known and usable law. But it must include, beside such series, all possible variations upon all possible objects from all possible points of view, that is, in all respects about which questions might be asked. But there is no such manifold as "all possible respects"; and such respects as there are imply the questioners. Such an independent realm of universals or "essences" appears to me, with all respect, as a piece of modern mythology without Plato's excuse, an ironical reversal of the realist's resolve to be supremely matter-of-fact.

William James objected to the absolute mind that it contained too much, since it must be aware of every actual detail of the world, and why it is so and not otherwise, an endless "superfœtation of useless information." [7] If this be said of a mind, whose nature is selection, and which has only the actual world to consider, what shall we say of the realist's substitute for the absolute mind, the realm of eternal essences, which omits nothing?

32.6. *Is analysis the way to reach reality?*

The ultimate units which analysis finds are certainly not unreal. The

---

[7] "Along with what everything is it must also be conscious of everything which it is not. . . . Furthermore, if it be a fact that certain ideas are silly, the absolute has to have already thought the silly ideas to establish them in silliness. The rubbish in its mind would thus appear easily to

realist is quite right in pointing out the absurdity of supposing that the more we think our way into the structure of things, the farther we get from final truth. The ultimate atoms, if we ever get to them, are undoubtedly things to reckon with! The question is, Are they self-sufficient and final?

If they were independent, self-existent beings, are we to accept with "natural piety" the fact that there are so many of a kind, struck, so to speak, out of the same mould, and ask no further questions as to origin? The modern realists have done little, so far, in cosmology; but what they have done takes the inevitable direction of referring these multitudes of minute beings to some relatively simple generating process or auspices, like the primitive space-time of Samuel Alexander.[8]

32.7. Realism is justified in rebelling against the notion that all relations are "internal." There are external relations, such as make no significant differences to their terms. As we have pointed out, all motion and exchange and substitution in the world are based on external relationships.

But with every external relation, there is an internal relation. It is nothing to the brick that it lies beside or above another brick. But it is something to the brick that it is in space: and therewith has the possibility of being beside or above another brick. And this spatial character, inseparable from the being of each brick, relates them internally. The external relation is a specification of a prior internal relation. These internal relations are inescapable, and unify the world.

32.8. If analysis is the way to reality, it must, in theory, lead us at last to objects ultimately simple and unanalyzable. And when we analyze the same thing in different ways, we should reach the same ultimate units. The mind, for example, being regarded as a combination of the same elements as those which make up physical nature—the neutral entities—should reveal to analysis the same irreducible simples as are found by physics. Does it?

The ultimate simple for the mind must be something in the nature of sensation, a spot of color, a nervous shock. But these, if physics is right, are the outcome of processes highly complex. And a complex cause, we are told, cannot produce an absolutely simple effect. Shall we then revise our view that the spot of color is simple? Or shall we say that the simples of mental analysis are not the same as the simples of physical analysis?

---

outweigh in amount the more desirable material. One would expect it fairly to burst with such obesity, plethora, and superfœtation of useless information." *A Pluralistic Universe* (New York, 1920), pp. 127 f.

[8] *Space, Time and Deity.*

Either alternative is embarrassing for realism; but in any case the second is inevitable. It is impossible to regard the ultimate units of physical analysis, say electrons, as in any sense elements of mentality. Thus, the view that the mind is a cross section of the world-collection of simple neutrals is hopelessly inconsistent with the doctrine of analysis as the revealer of reality.[9]

32.9. Under these circumstances, it might be advisable to abandon this conception of the mind. For, except Bertrand Russell's, it is very nearly the most skeletal and eviscerated formula of human nature that has yet been put forward. And it has the additional disadvantage of being inconsistent with another fundamental principle of realism.

For the degree of independence which exists between thought and its objects is best brought into evidence when we note, as above,[10] that the same self may have different objects and the same object different observers. That is, the self is something which remains substantially the same while the objects change. But if the self were a collection of objects, it would necessarily change as the objects changed. It could have no permanence except the relative permanence of the more persistent groups of independent objects, such as, say, the objects of memory and body-sensation. The only possibility of setting those objects free from mind is to recognize in the mind another sort of thing, such as the activities we were speaking of.

32.10. But it is also necessary to modify our trust in analysis. For there are objects in the world which are *both simple and complex*, simple from one point of view, complex from others. The spot of color may well be such an object. The mind itself is another. With such objects, analysis will give us part of the truth, but runs the danger of leaving out of account another part equally important. The false assumption in the theory of analysis is that simplicity is to be found *in one direction only*, the direction of the microscope. The simplicities of the world are presumably bipolar, microscopic and telescopic. It remains possible therefore that the entire universe, with many varieties of external relation among its parts, much loose play and independence, has also its ultimate unity and simplicity.

32.11. *Is it true that the unity of all things, if there were such a unity, would be an indifferent and meaningless fact?* In particular, is the idealistic disposal of evil immoral?

The realist is right in pointing out that no concrete problem is solved

[9] Professor J. W. Miller, in view of this difficulty, has devised a theory in which mental simples are superimposed on physical complexes.
[10] §29.6.

merely by the assertion that all is one in the Absolute. But it is a fair question, whether any one can avoid the acknowledgment of such unity; and whether it is not involved in realism itself. For the universals of the world, whether they form an independent realm, or whether they exist only as in the facts and as thought of, are at any rate a *system*, not a loose-strewn chaos. The genera do include the species; and there is a highest genus which includes them all. This highest universal may be lacking in differential connotation; but it cannot be meaningless, for it means whatever is included within it, namely, the universe.

This was the conclusion drawn by the great Platonic realists following Plato, such as Plotinus and John Scotus Erigena, in the line of ancestry of modern realism on one side of the house. From their realism of universals, they deduced a type of monism, which as we shall shortly see is called *mysticism*. These thinkers are of the same view with the realists in their antipathy to such propositions as All is mind; not because they wish to escape unity, but because they distrust hasty descriptives. The modern realist, when he is consistent with his own premises, will discover himself, if I am not mistaken, as a mystic in disguise. For the unity which logic requires in the realm of ideas is for him a metaphysical unity also.

32.12. The ethical difficulty remains. No doubt it is this question of the relation of good and evil in the world which chiefly leads the realist to distrust all philosophies referring to the Absolute or the One.

Realism accepts good and evil as distinct and opposing qualities, externally related to each other. Evil is evil and good is good. Good is to be made in the world, a human enterprise to be carried on by human effort and instruments. Evil is to be eradicated, not excused; and this battle is also a human responsibility. The method is scientific analysis, not prayer. The ethics of realism, so far as it has a distinctive ethics, is *humanism* in the sense that human good is to be achieved by human effort.

Now no one can doubt that evil is evil. Nothing can be gained by calling evil illusory; for an illusion of evil is an evil illusion. The only question is whether evil is evil *and nothing else*, incurably external to all goodness; or whether it can also be something else, or a member of something else, and as such member change its character. Many evils we know to be thus transmuted by the whole to which they belong. Danger, for instance, when an ingredient of adventure becomes a source of pleasurable excitement. A fright or a *faux pas*, when looked back on in memory, may be an occasion for laughter rather than pain. Transmutation is a fact of experience, not a theory; a fact which it would be absurd to call immoral.

Good and evil as objects of experience are the least independent of all objects; for they most sensitively change with every change in the experiencer. And since the experiencer is always changing with time, these qualities never stay precisely what they were. The chains are removed from Socrates' ankles; and as he rubs his shins he wonders whether there is any pleasure so great as the pleasure of relief. But a pain which one would willingly accept as the price of pleasure is no pure evil: it is evil and something else. "Call no man unhappy"—we might reverse the saying of Solon —"until he is dead," i. e., until you know the end of his story.

But suppose you know the end of his story. And suppose the story closes, as many stories do close, on a retrospect and a present experience of misery or humiliation or injustice unrelieved. Suppose there is no further experience to transmute this evil. Then you have pure evil and nothing else. Thus the realist may point out that the transmut*ability* of evil is of no use in acquitting the universe, if it is not *in fact transmuted*.

However, we may reflect that, on realistic grounds, one moment of time is not another. Analysis shows that they are separate. The past is past. If the quality of the present is externally related to the quality of the past moment, the death of any sufferer closes his account. His sufferings are over; and the past evil no longer exists as a debit against the universe. Wait until all the sufferers die, and the universe will have cured its own evil! Thus analysis, carried to the extreme.

Graveyard logic, we say. The realist rejects it explicitly. It is he who has been holding this untransmuted evil up against the Absolute, as a moral debit, an evidence of the futility of the One. Thereby he is himself assuming a responsibility for past evil; he is accepting the past as a living part of the present. He is rejecting the atomic, over-analytic, view of time, and making its parts into a moral continuity: the unity of his own mind is doing a work which he reproaches the Absolute for not doing. But in so doing he admits that the case of the untransmuted evils is a hopeless case *only if there is no absolute mind*, to create a moral continuity beyond the reach of human loyalty, and to ensure that the apparent end of the story is not final. It is only on realistic or naturalistic grounds that any such evil must remain untransmuted. This being the case, one could hardly say that the mental unity of the whole of history and of the world would be an insignificant fact if it were true, and certainly not an immoral fact.[11]

32.13. So the argument stands at present. I cannot reach the judgment that modern realism has as yet supplied a consistent system of metaphysics. I do not believe that a consistent system can be built on the *uncorrected*

---

[11] This argument is given a more adequate statement in *Journal of Religion*, Nov., 1923, pp. 582–589.

principles of analysis, external relations, and the independence of object from subject.

Nevertheless, realism has performed a great service to philosophy. It has destroyed over-ease and over-simplicity in the idealistic outlook. It has proposed a variety of new alternatives. It has made emphatic the reach of knowledge beyond the self. It has called due attention to the actual complexity of the world, the prevalence of external relations, the futility of reiterating the reference of things to Mind without the heavy logical labor of showing *how* they relate thereto, and what difference it makes. It has broken up the indolent habit of solving philosophical problems by a uniform method, encouraging thinkers to take them individually and for their own sakes, as if the world had its local habits and a freedom of play between province and province.

And no doubt there will be a transfiguration of naturalism as one of its results. In attempting to take the world out of the mind, the realist will succeed in reading part of the mind into the world, its qualities and its universals. He fights idealism, as we have seen, in part with idealistic weapons: he accepts the dismissal of Newtonian material substance. The world composed of his "neutral entities" cannot persist in its neutrality; it bears on its face a pertinence to experience; it is alive with the stuff that thought is made of.

The weakness of the realistic way of knowing is this: that in his preferential trust in analysis, the realist forgets that the human organ of knowledge is bi-focal, as befits a world in which the complex may be also simple. He has the right focus for the one, but not for the other. If there are characters of the universe which are hidden from the wise and prudent and revealed unto babes, the realist will not find them. The other focus is that of the mystic.

CHAPTER 33: MYSTICISM

All that is not One must ever
Suffer with the wound of Absence.—JELALU'D DIN

This, therefore, is the life of the Gods, and of divine and
happy men, a liberation from all terrene concerns, and
a flight of the alone to the Alone.—PLOTINUS

33.1. The realist in us looks at things with analytical eyes: "As you believe in reason," he admonishes us, "you must believe in the results of reason; the atoms or other plural elements of the world are its realities, they are independent of each other and of the knowers." The idealist, he believes, is too much of a monist; and he is such because he allows too little finality to the findings of analytical intelligence.

But the idealist has another critic within us who declares on the contrary that he, the idealist, *analyzes too much!* For he still distinguishes between himself and his objects, between himself and other selves, between the Great Self and all the finite selves of the universe. It is true, he is a monist; he believes that all the finite selves, and nature also, depend on the Great Self: but the finite selves are free, and value their independent separateness of being and action; and nature is a common object, distinct from all of them. Perhaps the idealist is *not monistic enough*; and for the reason that he relies too exclusively on reason for the last word in his relationship with reality.

For we know that the kind of knowledge we call "objective" is in some respect imperfect: there is something arm's-length about it. The objective knowledge of charity "cases" may be entirely accurate without being entirely important: it may miss the heart of the matter. "Scientific management" will not make a man a good manager of men. Even intuition, which perceives the whole unique being of its living object with sympathetic intelligence, may still hold the object as something different from the one who knows it. Idealism—even with the intuitions which lead to it—leaves us unsatisfied, suffering "with the wound of Absence." There is, so to speak, another stage of intuition, in which the sense of other-ness drops away and the knower realizes that he is identical with the inner being of his object. At least, such is the view of our final type of philosophy, mysticism, which, in contrast with realism, teaches the *absolute unity of reality*. If reality is one, we can only know it truly when we merge with it; that is, when knowing, in the "objective" sense of knowing *something not myself*, ceases.

"To see and to have seen that vision is reason no longer. It is more than reason, before reason, and after reason, as also is the vision which is seen. And perhaps we should not here speak of *sight*: for that which is seen—if we must needs speak of seer and seen as two and not one—is not discerned by the seer, nor perceived by him *as a second thing*. . . . Therefore this vision is hard to tell of: for how can a man describe as other than himself that which, when he discerned it, seemed not other, but one with himself indeed?" [1]

Realism separates object and knower; idealism holds that all objects belong to some knower; mysticism holds that the objects and the knowers belong to each other,—they are the same reality, they are one.

33.2. On account of its common uses, the name "mysticism" is more misleading than any other of our type-names. As a form of philosophy, mysticism is not to be associated with occultism or superstition, nor with psychical research, nor with an application of the fourth dimension to psychology, nor with a cult of vagueness, nor with a special love of the mysterious for its own sake.

Mysticism does indeed assert that after our best intellectual efforts there remains an element of mystery in reality: in this respect, mysticism is more allied to scepticism or agnosticism than to credulity. But the mystic, in the history of philosophy, is the *initiate*, one who has attained a direct vision of reality, a vision which he is unable to describe. Like the initiate in the old Greek mysteries, after the sacred drama has been shown to him as a pictorial symbol of metaphysical truth, the mystic is silent not because he does not know, but because he cannot explain. The word mysticism is related to the word "mum,"—the condition of one who knows but must not or cannot speak.

We recognize his "way of knowing" here as that of the intuitionist, carried as we suggest to a further stage.[2] But in spite of the difficulty he finds in expressing his belief or his vision of reality, he seldom accepts the rule of complete silence which this situation would seem to require. Lao Tze, the Chinese mystic, draws this conclusion:

One who knows does not talk.
One who talks does not know.
Therefore the sage keeps his mouth shut and his sense-gates closed. . . .

[1] Plotinus, *Enneads*, VI, 9, 10.
[2] Mysticism is, of course, not the same as intuitionism; because it is more than a way of knowing: it is a definite metaphysical doctrine, and an ethics or way of life.

The holy man abides by non-assertion in his affairs and conveys *by silence* his instruction. . . .

To be taciturn is the natural way.[3]

Nevertheless, Lao Tze was persuaded to record his thoughts in a brief book, the famous *Tao Teh King*. Mystics have indeed been unremitting in their efforts to express the inexpressible. The results are, as consistency would lead us to expect, enigmatic or paradoxical. Mystics frequently abound in the language of symbol or allegory to express what cannot be defined in strict conceptual form. Consider William Blake, Dante, Jacob Boehme (German mystic, 1575–1624), Dionysius the Areopagite (pseudonym of an unknown writer of about 500 A. D.). The immortality of many of these writings, as the *Enneads* of Plotinus or the cryptic *Tao Teh King* itself, indicate that the mystic is not wrong in making these efforts. For in terms of our more mechanically conceived ideas, there no doubt *is* an element of paradox in experience; and the paradoxical statement about the experience means something to the person who has himself had it: the mystic can understand the mystic,—and, if I am right, there is an element of mysticism in all of us. And further, he can at least tell us what reality is not, as an indirect way of indicating what it is, thus:

"The Reason that can be reasoned is not the eternal Reason. The name that can be named is not the eternal Name. The Unnamable is of heaven and earth the beginning. . . .

"Thirty spokes unite in one axle; and on that which is non-existent—the hole in the axle—depends the wheel's utility. Clay is moulded into a vessel; and on that which is non-existent—its hollowness—depends the vessel's utility. By cutting out doors and windows we build a house; and on that which is non-existent—the space within—depends the house's utility. . . .

"We look at Tao (reality) and do not see it: it is colorless. We listen to Tao and do not hear it: it is soundless. We grope for Tao and do not grasp it: it is bodiless. . . . Forever and aye, Tao remains unnamable: and again and again it returns home to non-existence.

"The world's weakest overcomes the world's hardest (as water overcomes the rocks). Non-existence is at the heart of the impenetrable. Thereby I comprehend the advantage of non-assertion, and the lesson of silence. Tao always practises non-assertion; and there is nothing that remains undone."[4]

33.3. We may now form a summary picture of mysticism as a philosophy. It holds:

a. That reality is One, an absolute unity, as against all atomistic or pluralistic metaphysical doctrines;

---

[3] *Tao Teh King* (Paul Carus's translation), §§56, 3, 23.
[4] Lao Tze, *Tao Teh King*, adapted from translation by Paul Carus.

b. That reality is ineffable (indescribable); whence, all the predicates or descriptives which we apply to it are somehow in need of correction,—including the predicates which now follow;

c. That reality (as we seek it in the world outside of ourselves) is identical with the equally indescribable essence of the human self,— we may find reality, therefore, either by looking without or by looking within, and what we find in either case is the same, not merely alike in kind, but identically the same thing: the extremes coincide;

d. That it is possible (and vitally important) to reach an intuitive knowledge of, or union with, this absolute One;

e. That the way to achieve this is by an effort which is primarily moral rather than theoretical.

In each of these respects, it is evident that mysticism is the precise counterpart of realism. Where the realist affirms a thesis, the mystic affirms the corresponding and completing antithesis. The spirit of this type of metaphysics, in its "mystical" identification of the outer reality and the inner reality, may be seen in this passage from one of the classics of ancient India:

" 'Bring hither a fruit from yonder tree.'—'Here it is, venerable one.'—'What seest thou therein?'—'I see here, venerable one, very small seeds.'—'Divide one of them.'— 'It is divided, venerable one.'—'What seest thou therein?'—'Nothing at all, venerable one.'—Then said he: 'the subtle essence which thou canst not perceive, from that truly has this great tree arisen. Believe me, dear one, that which is this subtle essence—of its being is the universe—that is the Real, that is the Soul,—*that art thou, O Çvetaketu.*' "

" 'Here, put this piece of salt into water, and come back to me to-morrow.' He did so. Then said he: 'Bring me the salt which you put in water yesterday.'—He looked for it, but did not find it.—'Try on this side!—How does it taste?' 'Salt!'—'Try it in the middle!—How does it taste?'—'Salt!'—'Try on that side!—How does it taste?'— 'Salt!'—'Leave it alone and sit down near me.' He did so, and he said: 'It exists still.' —Then he said: 'Truly, so also thou canst not perceive the Existent here (in the body) but it is nevertheless in it. That which is this subtle essence—of its being is this universe—that is the Real, that is the Soul,—*that art thou, O Çvetaketu!*' "

"If a man cuts this great tree at the root, it drips because it lives; if he cuts it in the middle, it drips because it lives; if he cuts it at the top, it drips because it lives: it stands penetrated through and through by the living Self, exuberant and joyful. But if life leaves one bough, it withers. . . . Thus also shalt thou know, said he: this body certainly dies when the living one leaves it, but the living one does not die. That which is this subtle essence—of its being is the universe—that is the Real, that is the Soul,—*that art thou, O Çvetaketu!*" [5]

33.4. Mysticism has had a long history: it is older than realism, older than idealism. No age, not even our own, has been without notable representatives of this type.

[5] From *Chândogya Upanishad*, VI, trans. Deussen, in *System of the Vedanta*, pp. 265 f.

While appearing in China, and reaching a high development in India as Brahmanism and Vedantism, it had a remarkable burst of popularity about the Mediterranean basin from the sixth century B. C. onward. We hear of the "mysteries" of various deities, of Osiris in Egypt, of Adonis in Syria, of Demeter, Dionysus, Orpheus in Greece, of Mithra in Persia and the Roman world. These mysteries were off-shoots of current religions; and were perhaps due to the break-up of great national religions in the political turmoils of the time, leaving the individual no longer able to identify his religious loyalty with his social loyalty, and giving him a strong motive to seek without reference to race, nation, sex or caste, a direct personal relation with reality in the form of an accessible deity, thereby willing moral stability in this life and a hope of personal immortality in another life. They had in common with philosophical mysticism chiefly this cult of personal union with the god, in states of enthusiasm, after moral preparation. There was much crudity, superstition and folly in these popular cults, —often downright barbarism. But the vital elements of the movement were so great as to command the interest of the greatest thinkers, as well as of the state. Athens established the Eleusinian mysteries as a public institution. Plato in his Dialogues made fun of the Orphics, and adopted certain of their ideas. Christianity in its early spread into Asia Minor found various mysteries in vogue; the theology of Paul is strongly influenced by that fact. The gospel of John is a mystical document: "I am the vine, ye are the branches . . . I and the Father are one." Plotinus (204–270 A. D.), a disciple of Plato, by the power of his thought and the nobility of his character lifted mysticism for the classical world into a clarified philosophical expression.

The influence of Plotinus was enormous. It spread, via the later Neo-Platonists—as his school is called—from Alexandria through the whole world of fading classical antiquity. It was transmitted to Arabic philosophy, and came to life again in a series of Mohammedan Persian mystics. One of these was Al Ghazzali (1058–1111) who, falling into scepticism while teaching philosophy in Baghdad, abandoned his chair and his family, betook himself to asceticism, and ultimately reached a mystical philosophy. It influenced the Pseudo-Dionysius of whom we have spoken, who in turn became the progenitor of a long line of Christian mystics (John Scotus Erigena, Bernard of Clairvaux, Meister Eckhart, Tauler, Suso, Teresa, Nicolas of Cusa, Bruno, Silesius, Boehme, Dante, William Blake, Coleridge).

Spinoza and Schelling have much in common with mysticism in their doctrine that the One, the absolute substance, cannot be described, since all description is limitation (*omnis determinatio est negatio*). The absolute Being is beyond the distinctions of mind and matter, of good and evil, of finite and infinite, even of the numerical one and many.

Mysticism is evidently often the product of an intensely philosophical spirit discontented with the mere rationality of philosophy, and of an intensely religious spirit discontented with the dogmatic systems of theology in every creed. It is inspired by the insatiable ambition of individual spirits to know reality by direct acquaintance, rather than by rumor or description. Relying on the "inner light" rather than on tradition, it has a constant tendency to heterodoxy. It may produce the heretic, as Joan of Arc, as Bruno, as Spinoza. Or it may produce deviations within tradition, such as the "Quakers," the Pietists out of whom Kant came, the Anabaptists, ancestors of the Puritans.

In any case, the mystic's confidence that the divine principle is identical with himself, and that he may for himself gain direct access to ultimate truth, is well calculated to produce great and independent characters, as well as not a few fanatics and mystified spiritual wastrels. Our concern, however, is not with the failures. For if there had been but one genuine mystic in the course of history, a Mohammed, a Buddha, a Saint Francis, there would be, corresponding to that person, a true mysticism which would reward our utmost effort to recognize and distinguish it from its counterfeits.

CHAPTER 34:
THEORETICAL MYSTICISM

34.1. Mysticism has two aspects, its metaphysics and its way of life, its theory and its practice.

Theoretical mysticism, the metaphysics of pure unity, is supported by all the considerations which, in the discussion of dualism, we were urging in favor of monism. But if this unity cannot be described, the corollary is that we ought not to call it either mental or material, either idealistic or naturalistic. This doctrine requires further study.

34.2. The great mystics, though relying on intuition for the final leap of knowledge, have commonly been keen reasoners. They have given something like a demonstration that the Real can have no attributes. They have used the same argument we found appealing to the realist,[1] namely, that what is true of all things cannot be a mark characteristic of anything. Every possible predicate, such as "great," excludes something, the "not-great." If then we say "The Real is great" we are denying that the Real can be small. But this limits the Real. The mystic is persuaded that the Real can be whole and entire in the minutest being, just as the salt-quality can be complete in every smallest drop of sea-water, or as one who is injured, however slightly, may truthfully say, "I am hurt,"—I, the whole Self, am identified with the part that is injured. The Real, then, cannot be called either great or not-great: these quantitative and relative ideas do not apply to it.

For the same reason, we could not call the Real good nor evil, nor a mixture of the two: it would be beyond the distinction of good and evil, this distinction being relative to our finite human point of view. It would likewise be beyond the distinction between mental and non-mental. It might fairly be said that the neutrality which the realist finds in his analytical elements of experience tends to reappear in the mystic's Unity,—a "neutral entity" of cosmic proportions!

But if we are persistent in our logic, we shall remind ourselves that to describe the One as "neutral," or as "cosmic," or even as "one" in the

---

[1] §30.6.

rdinary numerical sense would be to exclude from it the characters of "non-neutral" and the like; for these too are descriptives. In all consistency, we should find ourselves reduced to silence! Are we not, in fact, reviving from another angle the considerations which led certain thinkers to ag- nosticism and the doctrine of the Unknowable? It is indeed true that the agnostic is, in this part of his philosophy, on ancient mystical ground: Kant and Herbert Spencer are, in so far, mystics. But there are two or three re- marks to make about this logic.

34.3. First, the mystic does not pretend to be neutral, *in the sense of indifference,* as between the various opposing predicates which we may try to attribute to the Real.

We may refrain from calling the Real "good," for fear of limiting it to our conceptions of goodness, and yet believe that "good" comes *nearer the truth* than "evil."

"The cause of all things is not any one of them. Hence it must not be called good in the sense of that good which it imparts to others. But in another sense it is *the good* itself, in a way transcending all other goods." [2]

And while hesitating to assert that the Real is "mental" or "personal" —for the mentality we know requires a non-mental environment to live and grow in, and the personality we know needs a society of other persons around it to play its very partial rôle in—the mystic still im- plies, when he identifies the Real outside us with the ultimate self within us, that "mind" or "spirit" would come nearer the truth than "matter" or any non-mental thing. Thus, while mystics have commonly been in trouble with an orthodox tradition which insists on the literal personality of God, they have commonly referred to their Real as "God." And Spinoza, who maintained a stricter neutrality than most, used the expression "*Natura sive Deus*"—Nature *or* God.

34.4. Second, there is some reason for the mystic's judgment that it is more important to believe *that* the One exists than to know *what* it is like. To use a barbarous philosophical mode of speech, the "That" is more im- portant than the "What," in this case. Let me illustrate:

A recent novel represents a Mr. Fergus and a Mr. Saber playing at chess problems. Mr. Fergus has a notion that every man has a mission or purpose in this life imposed upon him by the universe: he does not in the least know what it is, but if he goes honestly ahead working toward it it will some day appear to him. He believes in the "that" of his mission, without any "what." Saber is sceptical. He asks a pointed question:

[2] Plotinus, *Enneads,* VI, 9, vi.

"How can you work toward a purpose if you don't know what it is?"

Fergus answers: "How can you work toward a (chess) solution, if you don't know what it is?"

"Yes, but you know there *is* a solution."

"Well, there you are. And you know there *is* a purpose." The "that" is enough to keep you going.

Other instances—Walter Bagehot, thinking of the formation of the first large national groups of men, said there was a time in history when it was more important that there should be law than that there should be good law. The mere "that" of a law, recognized by all, helps a society to hold together; the "what" of the law could be attended to after the authority of law itself was established.—In the conduct of battle, Scharnhorst's maxim is frequently cited: In war it matters not so much *what* is done, as that something is done, and done with unity and strength.—If a person is freezing, it is of the utmost importance that he keep moving; what movements he makes is unimportant. Metropolitan police sometimes distinguish in the same way between the "that" and the "what" in telling bystanders to "move on." In all these cases, the distinction is relative. There can be no "that" without some "what"; i. e., there must be enough "what" to identify your object. Thus, if you know a law to be a law, or a motion to be a motion, it already has some "what." So, if I know "that" God is, without knowing "what" he is, I already know some "what" about the One, enough to identify it as God. But though relative, the distinction does not lose its meaning.

Suppose then that we could know, as the mystic says, that God exists, without knowing what God is. This would be a sort of middle ground between theism and atheism. The atheist says there is no God. The theist says, God exists, meaning thereby a personal deity. The mystic says, the atheist is right: the God of theistic imagination does not exist; the theist is also right,—that God is. Thus the person who cannot accept the theistic deity, and yet cannot believe the negation of atheism may find a secure, even if tentative, position in the mystic's "that."

The importance of such a position is that, as in the chess problem, one can keep going. The atheist necessarily stops thinking about a supernature or adjusting his life thereto. The mystic has something beyond nature to keep thinking about, to gain approximate or symbolic conceptions of, and to live by. The "that" of God's existence thus operates as what Kant called a "regulative" idea; one whose meaning was not in any picture we could form, but in what it led us to do.

34.5. Third, the mystic believes, as the agnostic does not, that the quality of the Real, though not describable, can be *experienced* in a sort of direct knowledge which is far more satisfactory than the remoter knowledge of concepts, just as acquaintance with a person is a more satisfactory knowledge than the best description.

This immediate experience of the Real is regarded by the mystics as an unusual and privileged state of being. It is a sort of initiation, after which one is no longer an *outsider* in the world. They would, on the whole, agree with Bergson's language when he describes, we remember, the difficulty in reaching an intuition of the *élan vital*. So the vision of, or unity with, the Real, is difficult and exceptional: but, if the mystic is right, it is an experience which satisfies both the intellect and the will. It is often referred to as the "beatific vision"; and the words of the great mystics— Plato or Plotinus, St. Bonaventure, Dante or Eckhart—imply that it shows the Real as transcending in value what our commonplace descriptives can convey. It solves—or rather dissolves—for them the problem of evil; and establishes in the mind not merely a reconciliation to the difficulties of ordinary experience, but, as it were, a certain appetite for them.

Plato gives in the *Symposium* an allegorical picture of this experience:

"For he who has been instructed thus far in the things of love, and who has learned to see the beautiful in due order and succession, when he comes toward the end will suddenly perceive a nature of wondrous beauty—not growing and decaying, or waxing and waning; not fair in one point of view and foul in another . . . but beauty only, absolute, separate, simple, and everlasting, which without diminution and without increase or any change is imparted to the ever-growing and perishing beauties of all other things." [3]

Plotinus puts the matter thus:

"Now often I am roused from the body to my true self, and emerge from all else and enter myself, and behold a marvellous beauty, and am particularly persuaded at the time that I belong to a better sphere and live a supremely good life and become identical with the Godhead, and fast fixed therein attain its divine activity, having reached a plane above the whole intelligible realm; . . .

"Nor did he (who has had such a vision) concern himself with the beautiful, but had passed beyond beauty and had transcended the series of virtues as one might penetrate into the interior of the holy of holies, leaving behind in the temple the statues of the gods. These he would not see again until he came out after having had the vision of what lay within, and communion there with what was no statue or image but the divine itself—of which the statues were but secondary images. And perhaps his experience was not a vision but some other kind of seeing, ecstasy and simplification and self-surrender, . . . a thought centred upon being merged in the divine." [4]

In this report of the mystic, however much or little we can make of it at the cold distance of our own description, we find corroboration of a surmise which must have come to every one at some time or other,—that

___
[3] *Symposium*, 210 f.
[4] Fuller's translation in Bakewell, *Source Book in Ancient Philosophy* (New York, 1907), pp. 386, 392.

the inherent value of the world is unlimited; that the reason for the apparent piebald mixture in our experience of moderately good and bad ingredients into a mongrel potpourri of so dubious a resultant value, that we can dally between optimism and pessimism, is a result of our dulness of sight rather than of the nature of things. The mystic is a radical, without caution, trimming, or compromise, in his assertion of the essential worth of life. And some mystics, at least, have lived as though that perception of worth, received in the rare moments of exceptional insight, had become a constant factor of their ordinary consciousness, altering judgment and action.

"Now since in the vision there were not two, but the seer was made one with the seen . . . , he who had been united with it might, if he remembered, have or keep by him some faint image of the divine." [5]

Thus it would be far from the truth to say that the mystic's One because ineffable is therefore characterless and neutral.

But the attainment of this privileged insight into the nature of things cannot come from purely thoughtful exertion. It is the result of an effort primarily moral. We turn, therefore, to consider the practical aspect of mysticism.

[5] *Ibid.*, p. 391.

CHAPTER 35:
PRACTICAL MYSTICISM

35.1. From the words of Plato and Plotinus above quoted, it is evident that the mystic's experience of the Real is closely allied to our perception of beauty in Nature. Perhaps the simplest and most wide-spread form of mystic experience is that which finds in these occasional glimpses of beauty something more than an interesting play of form and the superficial qualities of things, namely, an indication that there is within Nature a reality akin to ourselves and as it were an invitation to realize our union with that inner reality. These words of Arthur Balfour would be significant to many who have no other conscious share in the vision of which the mystics speak:

"But when we look back on those too rare moments when feelings stirred in us by some beautiful object not only seem wholly to absorb us, but to raise us to the vision of things far above the ken of bodily sense or discursive reason, we cannot acquiesce in any attempt at explanation which confines itself to the bare enumeration of psychological and physiological causes and effects. . . . However little, therefore, we may be prepared to accept any particular scheme of metaphysical æsthetics—and most of these appear to me to be very absurd,—we must believe that somewhere and for some Being there shines an unchanging splendour of beauty, of which in Nature and Art we see, each of us from his own standpoint, only passing gleams and stray reflections. No such mystical creed can, however, be squeezed out of observation and experiment; nor can it be forced into any sort of consistency with the naturalistic theory of the universe.[1]

In such a mystic as Rabindranath Tagore, beauty becomes the chief guide to metaphysical initiation, and art the chief means of conveying metaphysical truth.[2] But as Plato's words indicate, for the attainment of their privileged knowledge of the Real, even through the sense of beauty, the mystics with singular agreement have held that some kind of moral preparation, or discipline of the will, is needed.

35.2. In the more popular forms of mysticism, this discipline consisted in certain abstinences and ceremonies of purification. The Orphic rule forbade the eating of flesh, of certain kinds of fish, of beans; pre-

[1] *The Foundations of Belief* (New York, 1897), pp. 65 f.
[2] See Tagore, *Sadhana*, esp. Ch. 2. See also Charles Bennett, *A Philosophical Study of Mysticism*, Ch. XV.

scribed a peculiar garb, and in various ways required an ascetic habit of life. The more rational forms of mysticism required a searching self-examination, a review of one's habitual ways of thinking and wishing, and a mental enactment of rejection of whatever could be found partial or untrue in them. This often took the form of repudiating the objects of ordinary natural interest and ambition, not as essentially evil, but as something less than the supreme good, and therefore as more or less obstructive to the free flight of the mind. According to Plotinus,

"he, I say, will not behold this light, who attempts to ascend to the vision of the supreme while he is drawn downwards by those things which are an impediment to the vision. . . . He, therefore, who has not yet arrived thither . . . may consider *himself* as the cause of his disappointment through these impediments, and should endeavor *by separating himself from all things* to be alone." [3]

In general, the mystic prescribes a sort of "flight from the world" in a vein of renunciation little sympathetic to our prevalent present temper. His way of moral preparation has been called, accordingly, the "Negative Path."

35.3. To give a foreshortened picture of this Negative Path, we may describe it as a "world-flight" or retreat, physical, intellectual and moral.

The *physical* world-flight: In all concentration of thought there must be some leaning away from the distractions of the senses. Socrates in the *Phaedo* makes a whimsical comment on this fact in the phrase "the true disciple of philosophy is likely to be misunderstood by other men; they do not perceive that he is ever pursuing death and dying,"—a remark which he explains in the dialogue as follows:

"What shall we say of the actual acquirement of knowledge? Is the body, if invited to share in the inquiry, a hinderer or a helper? Are not sight and hearing, as the poets are always telling us, inaccurate witnesses?—When does the soul attain truth? Must not existence be revealed to her in *thought*, if at all?

Yes.

And thought is best when the mind is gathered into herself, and none of these things trouble her—neither sounds nor sight nor pain nor any pleasure—when she has as little as possible to do with the body, and has no bodily sense or feeling, but is aspiring after being?

That is true." [4]

Likewise in that particular form of concentration known as worship or prayer, there seems to be an instinctive turning-away from the ordinary currents of sense-experience,—the modification of light and sound in the interior of the mosque, the incense, the checkage of physical activity, the

[3] *Enneads,* VI, 9, iv. Taylor's translation.   [4] Plato, *Phaedo,* 65.

postures which still further close the organs of sense. The mystics have developed this sort of procedure into a technique for concentration, or "recollection and quiet."

The *intellectual* world-flight: A process of systematically reminding oneself that all the concepts which we are accustomed to apply to reality are incompletely true, and must be rejected. It, the Real, is not Nature; it is not matter; it is not energy; it is not power; it is not space, nor anything in space; it is not society nor the state. This process is called by some of the mystics, "laying aside the creatures"—i. e., the secondary realities. Meister Eckhart puts it:

"If a man will work an inward work, he must pour all his powers into himself as into a corner of the soul, and must hide himself from all images and forms. Then he must come into a forgetting and a not-knowing. He must be in a stillness and silence where the ineffable word may be heard. When one knows nothing, it is opened and revealed." [5]

Especially, we are advised, is it important to remind ourselves that the *distinctions and divisions* which our concepts make in the world of objects are misleading, since in reality all things are one. We must deny the boundaries which separate thing from thing, person from person, level from level, race from race, nation from nation. Wherein it appears that the mystic, by way of his negations, is reaching for a sense of the uniting element in things, a realization of the fraternal and equalitarian groundwork of the cosmos.

The *moral* world-flight: In like manner one enacts a denial that all partial goods are *the* good: none of them, passed in review, contents that Faustian element of our spirit which demands an object in which it can remain forever satisfied. So the mystic requires himself to consider his various objects of desire and ambition, and to reject each one in turn: "this is not the good." Especially his invidious desires,—his rivalries, competitions, antipathies, must be put down. Even his virtues he must suspect as not being altogether good, and renounce all satisfaction in them. For the very fact that a virtue can be consciously known and named shows that it is somewhat corrupted by self-satisfaction, or warped away from that elemental simplicity of will which alone is absolutely right. Old Lao Tze says:

"If beauty makes a display of beauty, it is sheer ugliness; if goodness makes a display of goodness (even to oneself) it is sheer badness.

Superior goodness resembleth water (transparent, pervading everything without self-assertion): the water's goodness benefiteth the ten thousand things, yet it quarreleth not (raising not its voice).

[5] Underhill, *Mysticism* (New York, 1912), p. 381, or R. Blakeney, *Meister Eckhart* (New York, 1941), p. 107.

Superior virtue is unvirtue: therefore it has virtue. Inferior virtue never loses sight of virtue; therefore it has no virtue. Superior virtue is non-assertion and without pretension. Inferior virtue asserts and makes pretensions.

Abandon learnedness, and you have no vexation. Abandon your saintliness; put away your prudence (and the people will gain a hundredfold). Abandon your benevolence; put away your justice (and the people will return to filial piety and paternal devotion).

He who seeks learnedness will daily increase. He who seeks Tao (the Real) will daily diminish; he will continue to diminish until he arrives at non-assertion. With non-assertion there is nothing he cannot achieve." [6]

This moral world-flight is sometimes spoken of as a cultivation of *poverty* in a broad sense, poverty of possessions, of mind and of heart. In some cases poverty means an actual renunciation of goods, as in the numerous monastic orders, Christian and Buddhist. In other cases, it means a practice of dis-attachment from all emotional bonds and pride.

"I am not here speaking of the absence of *things*,—for absence is not detachment if the desire remains,—but of that detachment which consists in suppressing desire and avoiding pleasure. It is this that sets the soul free, even though possession may still be retained. . . . In detachment the spirit finds quiet and repose, for coveting nothing, nothing wearies it by elation, and nothing oppresses it by dejection. . . . That thou mayest have pleasure in everything, seek pleasure in nothing. That thou mayest know everything, seek to know nothing. That thou mayest possess all things, seek to possess nothing." [7]

35.4. It is evident that the Negative Path of the mystic is negative chiefly in form. He uses a negative method to reach a positive goal. He seeks to get rid of the misleading fascination of subordinate goods in order that the absolute good may appear unimpeded to his mind: in putting away what is partial, he hopes to become directly conscious of what is complete.

"All those other things in which the soul once took pleasure—power, strength, wealth, beauty, science,—it now says that it holds in contempt. It would not say this if it had not come upon something better than these." [8]

For as Spinoza said—and Spinoza was very close to mysticism, both in his personally heroic life of renunciation, and in his idea of happiness as *amor intellectualis Dei* [9]—it is impossible to expel any passion from the mind except by a greater one.

According to some mystics, if your renunciation is sincere, the absolute good appears to you, as it were automatically:—"when the half

---

[6] *Tao Teh King*, adapted from Carus's translation, §§2, 8, 38, 20, 19, 48.

[7] St. John of the Cross, *Subida del Monte Carmelo*, Bk. I, quoted by Underhill, *Mysticism*, pp. 255, 249.

[8] Plotinus, *Enneads*, VI, 7, xxxiv; quoted by Charles Bennett, *A Philosophical Study of Mysticism* (New Haven, 1923), p. 29.

[9] Spinoza's philosophy has been described as a mystic completion of a rationalistic base. See R. McKeon, *The Philosophy of Spinoza* (New York, 1928), p. 27.

gods go, the gods arrive." According to others, the culminating experience of "illumination" is a gift which has to be waited for, with complete passivity and without demand. There is a transition in the will which cannot be effected by will,—for will operates upon something outside itself,—by which one passes into identity with the One which is also the Good. It is as if one who has been saying "You" to another person, now begins to say "We": in this transition from the second person to the first, there is a new element of identification, without change in the objective facts of the world. The ineffable reality has to be adequately discerned by an ineffable will-attitude.

Here lies an essential difference between idealistic philosophy and mysticism. The idealist believes that the world is a Self. The mystic holds that this knowledge is accurate without being adequate, or quite deserving the name of knowledge. Idealism can never serve as a substitute for religion: and only in religion is metaphysical truth truly known. In the classic philosophy of India, Brahmanism, the universe is Brahm, and each person is Brahm. But the judgment "I am Brahm" must be something more than believed,—it must be "realized." To realize it is *ipso facto* to attain absorption in Brahm. But one cannot by a violent stroke of will *resolve to realize*, any more than he can by great resolve realize the beauty of a symphony. The *right* to say "We" cannot be taken by force; it must be given, or, as it were, *happen* to one. Hence the necessity for this careful, perhaps life-long, discipline of the Negative Path,—the Yoga of the Hindus, the asceticism of the religiously ambitious in all great religious systems, the "worship" of the multitudes. For common worship is a much abbreviated epitome of the Negative Path.

35.5. But what kind of practical living can come out of such a direction of energy into the quest of a perhaps unattainable realization of absolute Being and absolute Good? Is this not a deliberate cult of alienation from this world and its proper business which might have harmonized with mediæval romanticism, but which we have now finally dismissed? Contemplation of the Real or the Good in their abstract perfection seems an idle occupation: was not Plato, as John Dewey suggests, after all a misleader of the race in teaching that there is some peculiar value in the pure vision or contemplation of an ideal essence? Ideals are to be embodied, not to be gazed at.

Further, there seems to be something fallacious in the mystic's conception of what he has achieved. If he comes into actual consciousness of the absolute Good, there is nothing more for him to wish for; no reason for return to any other kind of consciousness, or for doing anything else in the world. Perhaps he returns not because he wishes to, but because he cannot help it, being unable to sustain the vision. In that case he must still return with regret, and with averted sympathies, as one whose true interests are elsewhere.

As a matter of experience, this alienation does not as a rule take place. The Hindu mystic, it is true, is traditionally counselled to continue his worldly affairs, but *without desire!* This is the theme of the *Bhagavad Gita,* the most influential of Hindu poems, in which a prince on the eve of battle is represented as enquiring of the Deity whether, on strict philosophical grounds, he should fight or not fight. He is counselled to continue the combat, but as one looking alike on victory and defeat.

"Having regard to your own duty you ought not to falter, for there is nothing better for a Kshatriya (one of the warrior caste) than a righteous battle. . . . Looking alike on pleasure and pain, on gain and loss, on victory and defeat, then prepare for battle, and thus you will not incur sin. . . . He is wise among men, he is possessed of devotion, who sees inaction in action. Forsaking all attachment to the fruit of action, always contented, dependent on none, he does nothing at all though he engages in action. Devoid of all expectation, restraining the mind and the self, and casting off all belongings, he incurs no sin. . . . To whom pleasure and pain are alike; to whom a sod and a stone and gold are alike; to whom what is agreeable and what is disagreeable are alike; to whom censure and praise of himself are alike; who is alike in honor and dishonor; who is alike towards the sides of friends and foes. . . ." [10]

Such a state of mind would seem to promise something less than an enthusiastic battle! But the typical mystic is not thus neutralized: he is one to whom action in the world has become more rather than less engaging. What he has gained from his discipline is not disaffection, but inner certainty, originality with stability of character, courage, a moral invulnerability which appears to be superior to ordinary fears but not at all superior to the positive objects in behalf of which he is courageous. Joan of Arc may serve, in this respect, as the typical mystic.

Is there not, then, something wrong in the theory which supposes that the whole and absolute Good can be realized in a temporary experience, from which all consciousness of other things is excluded?

Let us answer first by enquiring whether mysticism can give us an *ethics*—that is to say, a code for action in the world—or whether it must limit its practical counsels to its Negative Path of retreat from the world.

35.6. When we consider that most, perhaps all, of the original moral codes of the world have been propounded by mystics, there can be no doubt about the fertility of mysticism in this direction. Perhaps a clue to this paradox may be found in the fact that successful action requires *a union of attachment and detachment.* There are two kinds of temper not likely to succeed and not deserving to succeed in any important

[10] *Sacred Books of the East,* VIII, ed. F. Max Müller (Oxford, 1879 f.), pp. 47, 48, 60, 110.

undertaking: the temper which cares nothing about it, and the temper which cares everything. A man who was completely indifferent to public office would not deserve to win such office; nor would he deserve it if it would break his will to lose it. A man is right in his efforts, and we respect him, if he does his best to succeed and yet retains an inner immunity to success or failure because he is greater than any of his particular aims. What the mystic is doing in his discipline of negation is to secure that this inner immunity is a genuine fact of character and not an assumed pose. He is attending, not to the whole of happiness, but to one indispensable condition of happiness.

35.7. The principle of all mystical codes of ethics may be stated in this simple form: *Be what you are.* That is, be in action what you are in reality. In reality, you are Brahm; you are identical with the most real; act, then, with the confidence, the freedom, the simplicity, the emancipation from petty sense allurements and social bribes, which belong to one who knows absolute values. To Lao Tze, Tao is the "law of heaven and earth"; and the code of life is simply—Act according to Tao; express Tao in your conduct. As Tao is non-assertive, so be you non-assertive; as Tao is not revengeful, be you non-revengeful, requite evil with good.[11] Remember that all of the conventional virtues are *not enough*; "patriotism is not enough," neither is benevolence enough nor justice. Tao sets a simpler but a higher standard:

If one loses Tao, virtue appears;
if one loses virtue, benevolence appears;
if one loses benevolence, justice appears;
if one loses justice, propriety appears.
Propriety is the semblance of good faith, and the beginning of disorder.[12]

This masterful attitude toward types of conduct which have the name of virtue fits the mystic to be a moral originator, a reformer of laws and customs. He has so often filled this rôle that it would be interesting to enquire whether any great reform had occurred in history without some mystic at the bottom of it. On the other hand, this same superiority to the letter of the law, in the confidence that one has an intuition of its meaning, makes an easy path for a soft-fibred and semi-sincere mystic to antinomianism and self-indulgence in the name of higher liberty,—a tendency which the mystic shares with the "aesthetic temperament." "Many are the thyrsus-bearers, few are the mystics," ran the Greek saying: many, we may say, are the near-mystics, and the spoiled mystics, few the true prophets. But these few are the indispensable men of history.

[11] *Tao Teh King,* §§63, 49.   [12] *Ibid.,* §38.

35.8. How does the ethical innovator know where customary morality, benevolence, justice, need revision? How does he know, for example, that the old saying, "An eye for an eye and a tooth for a tooth," is a mechanical and inadequate way of meeting injury? He knows by way of his "conscience." What is conscience?

When we were speaking of the evolutionary theory, which would make conscience an hereditary relic of ancient punishments, we thought that theory disproved by the fact that conscience grows more sensitive, like a gradually refining aesthetic sense, and rises in some individuals to the point of genius. Thus in the career of Socrates, we have a literary record of the work of conscience—personified as his *"daemon"*—in guiding his decisions at critical junctures. In him, conscience appeared as an unanalyzed sense of wrongness warning him away from certain courses of action which he was inclined to adopt. These actions were *incongruous with some inner standard* of whose nature he was hardly aware. That inner standard, we may suppose, is simply the persistent mystical sense of unity with the Real; and conscience is the intuitive recognition that a proposed course of action is, or is not, consistent with that unity.

If this is a true theory of conscience, we understand how it is that the mystics have been the great adepts of conscience, and the ethical pioneers of the race. We understand also why it is that the qualities of *moral courage* and *honor* are peculiarly associated with mysticism; for both imply a certain superiority to the risks of life and possessions which would naturally come from a belief in which Kant shared,[13] for example, that conscience allies us with a reality deeper than the flow of natural events. We understand also why it is that conscience is variable; for conscience would be clear only as the sense of unity with the Real is strong, and this sense might require renewal from time to time by deliberate acts of attention. The Negative Path, then, would be understood as the process of renewing the sensitivity of conscience.

35.9. To return, then, to our question,[14] there is indeed something wrong in the theory of mysticism when it proposes the end of the Negative Path as an entire and self-sufficient good, the absolute Good. It is unjust to its own function in the world. The mystic vision, taken by itself, tends to vanish into the meaningless. Pure unity, unless it were understood to be the unity of something plural, would be a nondescript unity indistinguishable from nothing. The experience of the mystic, and the discipline that leads up to it, belong somehow in the circuits of a life within the world of nature and human history.

[13] §9.4.   [14] §31.10.

CHAPTER 36:
MYSTICISM EXAMINED

36.1. The mystic, we say, in his direct vision of the Real reaches something which as he defines it ought to be the end and culmination of life,—all continuance an anticlimax.

> "It may not be
> That one who looks upon that light can turn
> To other object willingly his view,
> For all the good that will may covet there
> Is summ'd; and all, elsewhere defective found,
> Complete." [1]

Yet this experience has some function to perform for the rest of life, and works in with it. The explanation lies, I believe, in what I shall call the *law of alternation.*

The law of alternation is a practical principle, perhaps the chief of practical principles. It declares that we cannot make out a good life either by exclusive contemplation of the One or by intelligent management of the Many: but that we must have both, in the form of a rhythm, like the rhythm of work and play or of sleep and waking.

Life requires of us, in the first place, concentrated, realistic attention to business. This specialized attention analyzes its world of objects and affairs; and focuses its best intelligence on each thing in order. Now experience shows that this kind of attention, when prolonged, brings about a decline of power,—not alone to act, but even to see facts and to feel values. On realistic principles, this ought not to be: for facts are facts and values are values, and the knower has nothing to do but open his eyes to them. But for the weary head, these "independent" objects have a way of becoming imperceptible. The value and meaning of a thing prove to be not in itself alone, but in something the perceiver brings to it, some freshness of vision which fatigue has lost. There is a background *with which* I meet experience: disorganize that background,—as, for example, by committing a crime,—and nothing remains the same, none of the familiar objects are quite themselves. The continued strain of attention

---

[1] Dante, *Divina Commedia,* trans. H. F. Carey (New York, 1901), Canto xxxiii, lines 100–105.

in the day's work *runs down* our capacity to see what is there. Chesterton avowed he must leave Battersea in order to be able to perceive Battersea. Life requires, then, a periodic re-charging, in order to win even its most material successes.

This recharging is accomplished in many ways, as by rest, play, sleep; all of them involve the reversal of the direction of attention and the contemplation of what unites rather than what separates. The mystic's moral discipline, his Negative Path, provides the most direct and pertinent technique of re-creation. It involves the breaking of mental habit, release of strained attention in detail, recovery of sense of the whole. Every prepossession being passed in review and rejected, one's individual crotchets, prejudices, antipathies and petrifications are limbered up in such wise that something new may emerge, something nearer what one's perception of the whole would suggest. Thus the mystic experience has for its function the recovery of freedom as well as of the sense of value. And since the contemplation of the unity of things itself *runs down* when it becomes perfect and prolonged, the mystic must turn again to the world and discover it as having regained its lost fascinations, and himself his lost powers.

36.2. We may put the matter this way: the mystic has recovered the power to be realistic, to *face the facts*. Note several ways in which this takes place:

First of all, the power of plain *scientific observation*. What we call the scientific attitude toward the world is clearly the result of a moral development,—a new reverence for Nature (as in Bruno) developing into a new care in recording fact and discerning natural law. It has come to appear to us not merely a scientific but a moral duty to submit our minds to the evidence found in experience: the honesty required for scientific work, the suppression of what one wishes to find in favor of what one does find, have become moral axioms for all students of nature. The mystic, then, is entirely right in his doctrine that the *chief conditions for truth-getting are moral*,—not alone the metaphysical truth of the One, but the truth of physical detail as well.

The discovery of new hypotheses calls for something more than faithful observation: it requires imagination. But not every imagination will do. What distinguishes the successful from the unsuccessful explorer of nature is in the first place *simplicity and open-mindedness*,—freedom from pretence and personal vanity, showing itself in cravings to be different or ingenious or in the haste to gain startling results,—and in the second place a kind of sixth sense about the way Nature works, which can only come from a *love of the thing*. Both of these are moral qualities, and such qualities as the mystic's discipline is particularly fitted to develop. Said Ruskin:

"That virtue of originality that men so strain after is not newness—it is only genuineness, —not very different from what I call transparency. . . . What we call genius is largely extreme genuineness. . . . There are people so fundamentally simple that they are no longer embarrassed by all the irrelevant details which obscure the outlook of the average man; they see the essential at the first glance and go straight to it."

It is thus no accident that we so often find the mystic in the person or in the immediate tradition of the man of scientific genius.

36.3. Further, the mystic recovers the power to appreciate facts of the *qualities of things*, achieving a new innocence of the senses so that flowers, sounds, colors are felt as if for the first time: such, at any rate, seems to be the experience of William Blake, Jacob Boehme, Francis of Assisi and others. And therewith we remember that there is room here also for much new exploration, or perhaps for the exhuming of whole realms of sense-appreciation which man in his realistic march has surrendered from ancient animal inheritance.

And he acquires or recovers the power to face the facts of *social intercourse*, and thus to extend his capacity for friendship. Friendship, among other objects of appreciation, has its own way of running down; largely because, as it develops, there come occasions for saying truths we judge to be unwelcome, and we cannot command the art to say them without offense. We are not able wholly to eliminate the self-interest from our criticism. One needs something like the mystic detachment from self in order to find that common ground with his neighbor which will enable him to denounce him, say to him "Thou art the man," in such wise as to leave the friendship strengthened rather than destroyed.

36.4. If we are right, then, it requires the mystic to be a completely successful realist; and the realist to be a successful mystic. The practical conduct of life falls into a normal alternation between work and worship, each phase sharpening the need for the other.

Only by some such alternation can mankind keep at par, and remain fit for the increasing burdens of an intricate civilization with its growing, and rightly growing, load of material power. For with this material load, the race must grow *pari passu* in its capacity for transparent observation, for artistic sensitivity, and for friendly personal and national relationships.

36.5. And with this practical principle of alternation there goes a corresponding metaphysical truth. The Real cannot be either the absolute

One of the mystic or the absolute Many revealed by realistic analysis. The Mystic and the Realist, each being guided in what he sees by his practical pre-occupation, and believing final what he most effectively deals with, each grasps *half of the truth* about the world. Each therefore supplements and corrects the other.

As against the realist, the mystic is right in declaring the unity of the world, and the infinite worth of that unity. A world of plural substances in external relation is an incalculable, and therefore essentially hopeless world. And a world devoid of any inherent quality commanding reverence or permitting rational worship, must be devoid also of that spring of mental re-creation and fertility, without which nothing is useful.

As against the mystic, the realist is right in asserting the reality of the many. If God is, his life must run into the multiple facts of a differentiated world-order: if he is anywhere, he must be also in those facts. A unity which runs away from diversity, and has no explanation of how that diversity has come to be, cannot be the final truth about the universe. The One we can believe in must be a One which needs and is able to produce the Many.

Both realism and mysticism thus appear as aspects of the world-view of objective idealism, which explains and places them both; while they, in turn, make clearer the practical necessity of rhythm or alternation. An element of supernaturalism, asceticism and world-flight, must be taken together with an element of humanism to make up a working program of the good life.

PART IV

CONSPECTUS
OF THE TYPES

CHAPTERS 37–40

CHAPTER 37: THE STRUCTURE
OF A PHILOSOPHY

37.1. Our business hitherto has been primarily to understand the fundamental types of philosophy rather than to pass judgment upon them. Naturalism and Idealism have been treated more fully than the other types because the tension between them is the prolongation of the original polarity which we saw at the outset as generating the philosophic enterprise itself, and best expresses the creative impetus running through the entire history of human thought. I have made critical comments on various of these types in passing, not as offering a final assessment, but as indicating the motives which lead me in each case to go farther in my own search for truth. It is now our business to consider, each for himself, where he stands; certainly not in the vain hope of finishing one's world-view, but by way of demanding of ourselves what result is left by the working of these types upon our minds, and whether it amounts to a coherent view or direction.

Your philosophy is something more personal than the truths of a science: it must be made, not of things learned, but of your own seeing. The review of these types can only have aided this your seeing, and less by proposing ideas new to you than by bringing clarity to ideas already taking form in your thought, by way of your own experience. It may be that you have recognized some one of these types as your own. On the other hand, it is not likely that any great strand of human thought, such as these types are, is wholly alien to you. It is conceivable that you may find yourself belonging to all types, and to none. Mental hospitality is in danger of finding itself encumbered with an ill-fitting assortment of beliefs, composed of fragments from various types: there is "something in" all of them! This state of mind is intelligent and liberal; but also deficient in strength and decisiveness,—a success, which is a relative failure. No one wants to live with a patchwork philosophy. Without limiting your breadth of view, I should like to put you on the way of escape from this situation.

37.2. You have probably noticed that not many of the greater thinkers are perfectly typical. Spencer is not a pure naturalist; for he believes that there is a reality, though unknowable, beyond or behind nature. Plato is a dualist; yet, since he describes matter as a certain sort of "non-existence," he leans toward idealism,—an idealism of so interesting a variety that one strand of modern realism could emerge from it! Aristotle, with another vein of realism in his temper and way of thinking, inclines strongly to idealism in his metaphysics. Divergent lines of thought go out from Socrates, all claiming their rootage in that great character; and the same may be said for Descartes, Kant, Hegel. A man need be no pluralist to have plural strands in his philosophy. The stimulating and fertilizing force of a thinker is often a symptom of a moral and intuitive vigor which may outrun his logical consecutiveness. Such men take truth where they see it, and as they see it, whether or not their grasp of it achieves perfect coherence; believing that truth is consistent with itself, and that the discovery of its manner of hanging-together may wait. Meantime they defy our classifications; and we think of them as too wide of range to be contained in an "ism," as if in the very conception of a type of philosophy there were something belittling to men of the first order of genius.

37.3. This same unclassifiable quality appears in various contemporary systems of philosophy, in part as a natural result of a more general and extensive knowledge of the history of thought. We are today inheritors of all the types, and also of the cumulative debate which supports their continued existence. Here the principle of all debate holds good: refuting an opponent does not dispose of him; it is necessary to understand why he sees things as he does, and seeing this, something of his view is likely to adhere. The history of thought, thus taken, becomes an important way of enlarging one's own experience: and since breadth of experience has a natural priority over unifying principles, decision as to type-belonging may be, and often is, indefinitely postponed.

It is well to remember that thinking, if it is alive—even published thinking—is always unfinished. Philosophers, they say, are mortal, and their work must some day be called "done"; but how many, dying, have written a conclusive *finis* to their thought? Not Socrates, not Plato, not Kant . . . and certainly not the most germinal of our recent thinkers. Charles Peirce, begetter of pragmatism and of much new life in logic and metaphysics, left a mass of discarded beginnings: the world treasures his fragments. With William James' pragmatism coexist traits of idealism, realism, mysticism, achieving no final consistency. He might well have looked askance at such achievement. Royce sadly saw the curtain fall on an unfinished program. Dewey was reconstructing his concepts to the end.

The work of A. N. Whitehead (1861–1947) is remarkable among all these for what one might venture to call a purposeful unfinishedness.

As a masterful contributor to pure logic and to the mathematical theory of nature, he was temperamentally careful for consistency and completeness; yet few have been so emphatic in rejecting claim to finality. Believing as he did that the universe is a "Process," incessantly creative, the notion of a final description was excluded. Indeed, the earlier stages of his developing world-view seemed more readily aligned with a type than the later stages. I was at first inclined to associate him with the modern realists, in view of the strong position taken in *The Concept of Nature* (1920) to the effect that "nature is closed to mind." [1] But in his *opus magnum*, *Process and Reality* (1929), he rejects in clearest terms the notion that any actual being (or "occasion")—be it person, nation, molecule, atom, proton, quantum—is empty of *awareness* in some degree. "Each actual entity is a throb of experience . . . apart from the experiences of subjects there is nothing, nothing, nothing, bare nothingness." [2] It is not surprising that a scrupulously careful recent historian has classified his work as "fundamentally a form of idealism." [3] As I shall shortly point out, the nobly speculative aspect of his thought, in its courageous attempt "to express the infinity of the universe in terms of the limitations of language"—his view of the task of philosophy [4]—contains aspects of both realism and idealism, and of other contrasting motives. [5]

But if the unfinished and the atypical in philosophy, even though not positive virtues, are common traits of the work of our leaders in thought, what shall we do,—we who also inherit the full gamut of the types,—to win a unity of world-view having a character and integrity of its own?

37.4. *Eclecticism.* The assemblage of beliefs from various sources into a composite philosophy has been frequently enough resorted to in the history of philosophy to receive a special name,—*eclecticism.* The eclectics

[1] *The Concept of Nature* (Cambridge, 1920), p. 4.
[2] *Process and Reality* (New York, 1929), pp. 290, 254.
[3] W. H. Werkmeister, *History of Philosophical Ideas in America* (New York, 1949), p. 343.
[4] P. A. Schilpp, *The Philosophy of Alfred North Whitehead* (Evanston and Chicago, 1941), p. 14.
[5] Alfred Whitehead joined the Harvard Faculty in 1924. In the first edition of this text (1929) I wrote of him: "His thought is still growing; classification is premature . . . his metaphysic is quite too original and many-sided to be squeezed into this type (neo-realism)." In the second edition (1939) I noted the significant change, expressed most concisely in the Chicago Lectures of 1934, *Nature and Life*, in the statement, "We are in the world and the world is in us." He justly described this mutual within-ness as a "baffling antithetical relation,"—one might say a geometrical absurdity. The novel element in it, for Whitehead, is the second proposition, "In one sense the world is in the soul" (p. 40): the strongly anti-subjective position of *Science and the Modern World*, is now cancelled by the discovery that in some sense both propositions are true, a discovery which I believe subsequent to the publication of *Science and the Modern World* (1925).
With this, the third edition of *Types,* we survey the whole of Whitehead's work as printed during his lifetime. In his later essays I find a growing insistence on the responsibility of all philosophical speculation to common intuition,—what I have elsewhere called "the wider empiricism." For example: "All propositions are erroneous unless they are construed in reference to a background which we experience without any conscious analysis." (Schilpp, p. 680.) Mystics will agree.

whose names have been preserved have been thinkers, for the most part, of greater ingenuity than power, and relatively devoid of originality: the inner variety of their philosophy has been due not to an excess of explorative spirit, but to a sensitive docility in appropriating the thoughts of others. They see that different fragments of truth belong to *them*; they assume that they can be made to fit each other; they lack the ability to see how they fit. The name eclectic is thus not a term of the highest honor in philosophy. It has been applied to such thinkers as Philo of Alexandria, Simplicius, Cicero, Horace, Mendelssohn, Victor Cousin.

Victor Cousin (1762–1867), French philosopher and educator, deserves a special place, because in him eclecticism became a consciously avowed principle.

"Each system expresses an order of phenomena and ideas which is in truth very real, but which is not alone in consciousness . . . whence it follows that each system is not false but incomplete, and that in reuniting all incomplete systems we should have a complete philosophy, adequate to the totality of consciousness."

One could adopt such a principle only if he believed that all important truth about the world had already been proposed, so that the work of the philosophic mind of the present can only be one of judicious selection and adjustment. The eclectic has his eye directed to the history of thought; the thinker whose disorder comes from abundant originality has his eye directed to experience,—his observations and intuitions.

Still, the difference between the eclectic and the atypical original thinker is but gradual, since no degree of originality can safely ignore the history of thought, or decline the liberty of taking from whatever source what it finds true. In this respect Aristotle is to some extent eclectic; and St. Thomas Aquinas, who creates a compound of Aristotle with Christian theology, still more so. A realistic attitude toward the world will trust experience for its data; and if experience shows facts, even a single fact, inconsistent with our pre-conceived structure of thought, such fact or facts must be given a temporary roof, until a new roof can be devised to cover the whole of experience. It will favor the eclectic tendency.

Realism and "radical empiricism" alike require respect for the variety of the world, its endless internal richness which calls for perpetual humility regarding our theories: like true art, they never cease to learn from "nature." They also require respect for its possibilities of change: an "open" universe may outgrow our cherished stabilities. Further, they imply a willingness to consider the differing experiences of others, perhaps to try them out, even in points which one's existing world-scheme would exclude. William James was notably chivalrous in his disposition to the deviator who could plead "experience." His *Varieties of Religious Experi-*

ence lends ear to much of the religious mystic's record in which he himself could but dimly share. We recall also that both he and Josiah Royce
made investigations in the field of "psychical research"—now with enlarged scope commonly referred to as "parapsychology," including "extra-
sensory perception"—but without definitive result. Both A. N. Whitehead
and Gabriel Marcel found in their own experiences events apparently inconsistent with the prevalent theory of sense-perception: each independently discarded that theory.[6] It is not often that persons of divergent
religious beliefs actually try out the experiences of their neighbors. It has
been done. Ramakrishna in India and Gerald Heard in America have enlarged their own experiences in this way. Lutoslawski (referred to in
William James, *The Energies of Men*) made notable use of Hindu Yoga.
Deviating experiences or alleged experiences—as in the phenomena basic
to quantum-theory—will naturally remain (as Max Planck's data did for
a time remain) under a certain suspicion. But as the experimental facts
are verified, they may compel—even before a satisfactory unitary theory
is found—a tentative pluralism—"pluralism" being in this case another
name for the eclectic type of accumulation.

37.5. Eclecticism appears to be a preliminary stage of philosophical
construction, the collector-stage. Its spirit is allied to that strange virtue
we call *toleration*, which modifies all our dispositions to strict partisanship with the caution,—Your opponent is worth listening to; there is
some good reason for the way he thinks! Toleration is a difficult and
incomprehensible virtue to those who can grasp their beliefs in clear-
cut outlines, and thoroughly disbelieve what they disbelieve, because they
believe what they believe! Unless it is the virtue of the educator or law-
maker, it is the virtue of the incompletely certain mind, or of the Faustian
spirit ever-seeking.

There is thus a close affiliation between eclecticism and scepticism.
The man who takes something from all sides must discount every side; for
whatever opinion he considers with favor he will have something in common with its opponent also or its possible future critic. Like the sceptic,
he will be too wise to lend himself whole-heartedly to anything. Thus universal hospitality is the affirmative form of a universal reservation of
judgment, akin to universal doubt.

37.6. Eclecticism cannot be a satisfactory resting place for thought;
though it may well be a necessary stage to go through. It does not lie

---

[6] My account of Marcel's personal experience and its result (to which I, on somewhat different
grounds, had come in 1903) is given in an article on "Marcel and the Ground Issues of Metaphysics," *Philosophy and Phenomenological Research*, June, 1954.

within one's will to reject a proposition he believes true merely on the ground that he does not at the time see its connection with his other beliefs. One's first business as a knower of the world is accumulation.

But it is always a self that accumulates: and a self is a unity which cannot forever live, or face the prospect of living, with mental disorder. One must believe that the world of reality is consistent with itself; inconsistency is a subjective condition, not an objective fact. If there is no overt consistency among our beliefs, there must be a *latent* consistency among such of them as are true; and we are bound to find it. For we cannot lead completely rational lives until that latent agreement among our scattered insights can be grasped as a principle giving unity to the whole world-view.

There is but one way to be duly hospitable without being unduly eclectic: that is—since truth itself must be self-consistent whether or not we are—to seek relentlessly the *single principle* which shows how its several parts belong together. When you find that principle, your philosophy ceases to be eclectic—it has an identity and a character. Your philosophy is not your collection: it is your principle.

37.7. *The dialectical method.* Attempts have been made in the history of philosophy to work out a systematic method of discovering such a final principle. Socrates and Plato developed a method of mental experimentation, which Plato called the "dialectic"—a method well fitted for use in conversation or dialogue. It consisted in taking up any belief one of the speakers chose to present, treating it as an hypothesis, and following it ruthlessly to its extreme conclusions. An element of humor, chiefly of irony, entered the treatment of these deductions in the hands of the deft Greek masters of dialectic, through the fact that the sustainers of the hypothesis would occasionally find themselves on the opposite side of the argument from that which they entered.[7] If for this reason, or any other, the consequences of the hypothesis were unacceptable, a new hypothesis must be tried; and the process may be continued until one is found which leads to no error. Thus the dialectic is a progressive thinking process; and in Plato's management of the dialogue, the various hypotheses considered would be those which were upheld in the current philosophies of his day: the various types of philosophy would appear, so to speak, in person, and contribute each one its quota to the final result. The true hypothesis would be the dialectical survivor,—not the survivor in a Darwinian struggle, for the competitors, instead of being killed off, are preserved after correction in their subordinate places.

7 See Plato, *Protagoras*, 319.

It is evident that this method has much in common with the empirical and experimental method of to-day: it is, in fact, a form of induction. It is search for a premiss from which the several partial truths represented by the participants may, in their corrected form, be deduced. Like all induction, it is an attempt to escape from a purely empirical situation, to *understand* the variety while enjoying it.

In modern philosophy this method reappears with a peculiar sharpening of its angles. It was Hegel who most exploited it: in his view, every imperfect opinion, when carried out to its consequences, betrays itself into the opposing camp. Antithetical opinions generate one another, very much as tyranny brings forth anarchy, and anarchy tyranny; they may live side by side for a long time without knowing their kinship, regarding one another as pure antagonists. But when the situation is seen, the thesis and antithesis require a *synthesis*,—a new opinion which shall preserve the truth of each of the hostile opinions, and eliminate their inconsistency. This synthesis Hegel sometimes represents as logically derived from the antithesis; but for the most part it is evidently a new idea, brought into the situation like any other new idea, by a stroke of inductive invention. Any synthesis is truer than its component theses; but it may itself be an incomplete truth, and thus beget its own antithesis, so that a further synthesis is required. The final synthesis is found when we have a proposition which every attempt to deny reaffirms.

This method Hegel applies to the history of philosophy: he finds the various divergent philosophies begetting one another, and giving way to their synthesis when it arrives. In this way, he preserves the valid elements of opposing types—as he modestly puts it, "*all* earlier logic and metaphysics"—in his final result (his own philosophy, of course; for to every man his own belief must be that true belief to which the history of thought, as he reads it, leads). At the same time, the structure of this world of truth has revealed itself to him as he proceeds: he achieves a world-view of vast empirical and historical richness without eclecticism. The final truth at which he arrives, his principle of unity, is that the world is Spirit: understanding that it is the nature of the Spirit to express itself in these dialectical developments in the world of ideas, in nature, and in history.

37.8. *Cosmology.* The universe for Hegel, as we have noted,[8] is the embodiment of an absolute Spirit—we might say, of an absolute Thinking-process—both in its permanent constitution, and in the whole course of its history through Time. In Hegel's day, notions of some kind of patterned development of the world of nature were in the air. Kant had proposed

[8] §25.5.

an embryonic nebular hypothesis on the basis of Newton's *Principia*. Lamarck was bringing out ideas of the development of animal forms by way of inner striving or "appetition." The moment was ripe for philosophy to take over some of the ancient responsibility of religion for First and Last Things, beginnings and ends of creation, and the meaning of what lies between: a *Cosmology*, based on modern scientific suggestions, was possible. Hegel accepted the responsibility, and worked out what I think we may regard as the first modern Cosmology, not the first philosophy of Nature's unfolding—that is Schelling's deed, and from it Hegel learned—but the first to include with the astro-physical background the whole history and destiny of man as part of the cosmic story and of its dialectic.

The ruling conception of this cosmology is that physical and biological Nature yield Man as a product because they already contain as their essential being, not purposeless law, but a striving toward consciousness and self-knowledge. The idealism of Fichte had understood Nature as a needful resistance for developing the human sense of duty; Schelling proposed to understand it as the germinal source of human life: "the way from nature to spirit must be as possible as the way from spirit to nature." [9] We may see in nature, apparently passive to strict law, a sleeping giant laboring toward consciousness and freedom:

> Within it a giant spirit doth dream,
> But his soul is a frozen lava stream;
> Yet . . . mightily stirs in his dungeon-keep . . .
> To know his will and to free his wings.[10]

And Hegel proposed to show this same Spirit, disguised in the garb of Nature's externality, as following a necessary course of dialectical self-discovery. He translates the romantic poetry of Schelling into a sober argument, whose firm order can be demonstrated.[11] It is through this his Cosmology that we may best grasp the character of Hegel's achievement in bringing unity into an immensely comprehensive plurality of types.

He was not one to overlook the stark factuality of fact, the accidental and non-rational aspect of particular circumstances whether in nature or history. In interpreting history he was not unaware that human affairs

[9] Royce, *Spirit of Modern Philosophy* (Boston, 1931), p. 185.

[10] Quoted in *Spirit of Modern Philosophy*, p. 188.

[11] This firm order is not inconsistent, in Hegel's view, with a rich breadth of exemplification: the divine life, even in nature, has its release into a certain play of variety, and its enjoyment of emotion. Hegel's *Phenomenology of Spirit* (1807) leads what-it-means-to-be-particular-fact through various stages and forms of the human condition, and ends with a diptych borrowed (with modification) from Schiller:

> Aus dem Kelche dieses Geisterreiches
> Schäumt ihm seine Unendlichkeit.
> (Out of the chalice of this Spirit-realm
> Foams up to him his own Infinitude.)

present far greater resistance to rational understanding than the phenomena of the exacter sciences. Yet he saw this time-struggle-through-the-
irrational as a necessary part of the journey of the Spirit toward complete
self-knowledge, which is at the same time a journey toward realizing freedom: the Orient (he said) knew that one, the despot, is free; the Mid-
world that some are free; the Modern world that all are free! It is easy,
looking at history, to see the accidental particular, of which we must report simply the "once-upon-a-time-it-happened," *das Einmalige*. What
Hegel requires us to see is a buried thread. There is a hidden *Wirklichkeit*
(working-reality) which is *vernünftig* (rational). Not (as he has been
accused of saying) that "Whatever is, is right," but that whatever is right
has a deeper hold on being, a certain working toughness which in due
time shapes the actual to its intention.

We may be helped to picture this working (*Wirken*) by the informal philosophy
of Walt Whitman's lines:

> Through angers, losses, ambition, ignorance, ennui,
> What you are picks its way.

Whitman as poet was interested in the circumstances: Hegel as philosopher, was interested in the adventuring seeker, What you are, What the Life-force is. *That*, the buf-
feted, thwarted and hidden rationality, *that* has *Wirklichkeit*: that "picks its way."

And because the right and rational have this concealed pertinacity, one
may write much accurate historical narrative and yet, failing to see
Reason at work there, miss the truth of history. Hegel's interpretation
of history, passé in many points, is not without lasting validity in
others. His account of the modern era, the rise of the doctrine of human
rights, the democratic revolutions, perceptive and not uncritical, must be
reckoned among the most durable of historical insights.[12]

Hegel knew too little of physical science and of biology to be reckoned
among the philosophers of Evolution—the next important stage of Cosmology. He did, however, anticipate much of the spirit of Herbert Spencer's *motif* of "differentiation and integration"—analysis and synthesis—
and of the "Process philosophy" which dominates Cosmology today
(Bergson, Alexander, Whitehead). He differs from contemporary views
chiefly in the logical rigor he hoped to achieve in his dialectic. His system
of categories, intended to serve as a sort of constitutional law for the
entire course of world-events through time, must obviously be itself

---

[12] The elder Arnold Toynbee, writing on the Industrial Revolution, explains the repudiation
by the English worker of the appeal of the Humanists, especially of Carlyle, for a return to the
personal relations of the feudal system as against the impersonal "cash nexus," by the principle
"Men must separate in order to unite"; they must be detached from the remnants of the family-
order in order to unite on the basis of rights and duties. This, of a piece with Henry Maine's
concept of a movement "from status to contract," is a clear illustration of the Hegelian dialectic.

eternal. They constitute a necessary group in a necessary order; no Creator could devise a different set. Hence Kant's dream—Kant, who first called for a "deduction of the categories," and who criticized Aristotle's variable list (beginning with ten, and moving toward three—"substance," "condition" or "attribute," "relation") as "swept together"—was here most completely realized. The dialectical linkages in this ambitious enterprise remain a standing example of philosophy in its most formidable guise, uncannily penetrating and incredibly obscure. If for this reason alone, I should be remiss if I failed to offer a glimpse of Hegel's architecture.

This eternal constitution, the system of the categories, is the theme of the *Logic*, the most thorny of Hegel's writings, yet in broad outline the key to his entire system. For the adventurous reader I may here sketch the opening stages of its dialectic, since they indicate how Process becomes a necessary element in Hegel's system, and how his thought comes therefore into immediate bearing upon contemporary cosmologies.

There is, thinks Hegel, a necessary beginning of thought. It is not anything so explicit and concrete as Descartes' I-am. It is simply "Being," Being-in-general. Of "Being" we may say, with at least as much assurance as that of Descartes, that "Being" indubitably *is*. As the highest genus, "Being" includes everything that exists. It excludes nothing. Or, let us say, it excludes "Nothing"—allowing that we have a concept of the "Nothing" which borders the totality of what is. "Being" is what we find as "there"; it is the factual population within an infinitude, within an ocean of the possible-but-not-extant plus the impossible-and-therefore-not-extant.

"Being" is therefore distinguished from "Nothing." But *by what mark*?

Wherever you assign a definite mark you outline a class of beings. In that same act you define a class not having that mark, which class "Being" must include. In Spinoza's phrase, "All determination is negation"; what you define, you finitize. And what is finite is less than all: "Being" can therefore have no mark.

And if it can have no mark, our effort to distinguish it from "Nothing" fails. In Hegel's phrase—who conceives himself as observing and reporting the self-development of an idea—it has "passed into its opposite." The thesis (Being) has "passed into" the antithesis (Nothing).

There is a certain logical violence in this phrase, obnoxious to the contemporary semantic susceptibility. That it is not, however, pure logomachy may be indicated by the history of religion. Religion has at times defined God, the Absolute, as pure "Being": "I am that I am." So also Plotinus, so Thomas Aquinas, and in our own day Étienne Gilson. Yet the mystical phase of religion, impressed by the ineffable character—or characterlessness—of the Absolute, has often identified it with "The Void" (as does Ch'an or Zen Buddhism, and at times Taoism). This position, adumbrated in Schelling's Absolute Indifference (called by Hegel "the Night in which all cows are black"), reminiscent of Silesius' "*Gott ist ein lauter Nichts*," is approached in the contemporary invocation of the Subconscious in the guise of "the Unconscious" (for what could be more Nothing than a disembodied Unconsciousness?).

Yet "Being" and "Nothing" melt into one another not meaninglessly, but with a significant *belonging together*. They have a "synthesis," the category of *Werden*, "Becoming." If anything happens—and who can doubt it?—something becomes which was not. "Becoming" is the precise conjunction of "Nothing" (*Nichts*) and "Being" (*Sein*).

We try to evade this mystery by saying "From nothing nothing comes": *Ex nihilo nihil.* But this is to assert the absence of true "Becoming" in an eternal identity of substance: it is the negation of novelty, the denial of creation. The given world is a world not of static fact, but of incessant passage: "Nothing" merges into "Being"; "Being," forever perishing, merges into "Nothing." All that Is "takes place" in Time. Change is one of the unchanging categories: the Real is Process, playing in dialectic bounds. Thus Hegel's first and fundamental triad: thesis, *Sein;* antithesis, *Nichts;* synthesis, *Werden.*

37.9. The earliest cosmologies of the race were speculative; and as philosophy entered the picture,—with such touches of science as were available to the thinkers of China and India, to the early Greek cosmogonists, to Plato of the *Timaeus,* to Augustine—the outer frame of time was commonly still provided by epic, by myth, by religion. With the era of Hegel, Schelling, and Goethe, biology had begun to contribute decisively to the outlines drawn by astro-physics. There could be no longer a doubt that cosmology, with a scientific basis, is an essential part of the philosophic task. Even those who like Feuerbach and the Marxists rejected the career of a World-Spirit as a clue to the possible meaning of world process, felt responsible for providing materialism with a dialectic! For the nineteenth century, Evolution was the revealing topic: Darwin's work lent an inner direction,—a vector quality without over-all purpose,— to the biological picture of struggle and survival. We have noted Herbert Spencer's valiant attempt to provide a general law of evolution valid for all spheres of science within a vast cosmic rhythm of evolution-dissolution-and-repeat. Important modifications of this picture have been suggested: Bergson we have seen insisting on the factor of creative novelty, as cancelling the Hegelian proposal of a dialectic of history; Lloyd Morgan and S. Alexander have pointed out the fallacy of the continuously unfolding germ, maintaining the actual step-wise advances through which new qualities "emerge,"—the world grows *via* unpredictable saltations.

All of these themes have been brought together in the philosophy of Alfred N. Whitehead, who, as the first since Spencer, has proposed a cosmology comparable with that of Hegel in its synthetic range. He has brought to the task a mastery of the mathematical aspects of science such as neither Hegel nor Spencer could command; but at the same time a flexibility and a respect for intuition providing a sharp contrast with the dialectical scheme of rationally controlled process. It will materially help our enquiry at this point to note this contrast, and to feel the fresh vigor that Whitehead brings to the task of cosmology.

37.10. The task of philosophy, according to Whitehead, is to *interpret* the given world. As directed to something given in experience, the task is empirical: it must begin with an "adequate" description. But interpretation is more than description. The scheme of most-general ideas used in description must indicate the *organization* of experience, each aspect being interpreted by its place in the whole scheme. The scheme itself must be "coherent" and "logical": here the rationalist factor declares itself.

Where, then, are we to find these most-general ideas,—the "categories"? Here we encounter a pronounced contrast with Hegel, and indeed with most prior metaphysics.

Hegel, like Kant, accepts the categories as staples not only of logical tradition, but of common speech,—"being," "nothing," "change," "causality," "substance." Language as the universal tool of thought will not fail to reveal the most needful general terms as standard coinage. Whitehead demurs. Language-habits may be snares as well as aids: if there are current illusions, language will tend to embody and perpetuate them. The categories now needed cannot be picked up by the common roadside: Whitehead seems to say, *we must devise them.* The method is "to frame a scheme of ideas, the best that one can, and unflinchingly to explore the interpretation of experience in terms of that scheme." [13] We are familiar with the necessity of new technical terms in the sciences; but new categories are a different matter; they strike hard against the bent of our minds. To set up a new frame of categories is an immense task; in Whitehead's case, it is one of unexampled extent and avowedly experimental: "philosophers can never hope finally to formulate them." [14] The careful reader soon discovers that he must learn a new elementary language: he reads of "prehension," "concrescence," "nexūs" etc., and when the terms are familiar, as "actual entity" or "occasion" or "togetherness," he finds them clothed with new meanings. This hurdle is a part of the exhilaration of the great enterprise in hand, which requires the warning-sign against traditional sources of metaphysical shipwreck and disrepute. Among the causes of error which he proposes from the start to repudiate are "the trust in language as an adequate expression of propositions," and in particular "the subject-predicate form of expression," [15] which guards the illusion of "substance."

---

[13] Whitehead, *Process and Reality* (New York, 1929), p. x. Quoted by permission of the publishers, The Macmillan Co.

[14] *Ibid.*, p. 6.

[15] *Ibid.*, p. viii. The sentence-structure of languages of the Indo-European stock,—subject, copula, predicate,—tends to assume and confirm the mental habit of interpreting events as changes in the attributes of underlying "substances." The grass turns brown, the grass was green; the grass was succulent, it is now dry; it was almost odorless, it now has the smell of hay. What we experience of the grass is its attributes, including its shape and location; the underlying substance we do not find, the attempt to define it has haunted modern philosophy (see above, p. 159). Whitehead proposes to dismiss the effort as mistaken: the world is a world of qualities, considered as the "prehensions" entering into "occasions," the only "actual entities" there are. It is chiefly this which gives him a sense of kinship with Locke and Hume; though the "occasion" has something in common with Locke's mental substance, as contrasted with Descartes' physical substance (*ibid.*, p. 29).

The test of any such experimental scheme of categories is simply its capacity to interpret the given world; and this means not primarily its ability to propose hypotheses which sense-data can verify—the business of the sciences—but rather what Whitehead calls "the elucidation of immediate experience,"—enlightenment, the removal of confusion, the liberation of the persistent convictions of common sense. Profound changes in empirical science will certainly affect our scheme of categories; but scientific method taken as standard procedure would be the death of philosophy, which must proceed by "imaginative rationalization": "philosophy is the welding of imagination and common sense into a restraint upon specialists"; and what chiefly impedes progress in philosophy is "deficiency in imaginative penetration," a penetration aided not infrequently by "the poetic insight of artists." [16]

Imagination as a source of new categories for cosmology! Does this mean a return to primitive beginnings? [17] It does set Whitehead's method in sharp contrast with all the rationalists, including Hegel, who find their beginnings in *a priori* certitudes; but also with all these empiricists and positivists who rely on induction for their major generalities. For Whitehead there is no *a priori* certitude: "rationalism never shakes off its status as an experimental adventure,"—James and Dewey in hearty agreement. We begin not with axioms, but with "tentative formulations of ultimate generalities"; [18] and such certitude as we can reach comes at the end. Hegel's order was precisely wrong! On the other hand, these tentative formulations are not working hypotheses of the inductive order: the imagination which bears them is responsible to the facts, but also to the intuitions by which human living is commonly guided,—intuitions embodied partly in common sense, and partly in the esthetic, moral, religious qualifications of factual experience,—aspects of what we have called the wider empiricism. Whitehead sets up an extraordinary "metaphysical rule of evidence," a rule that has not so far entered into any canon of induction or deduction: "we must bow to those presumptions which, in despite of criticism, we still employ for the regulation of our lives," [19]—the presumption, for example, that in our ordinary actions we are dealing with a real world, and not with a subjective illusion. This rule admonishes him that we cannot include in our scheme of ideas any that involve the "bifurcation of nature": the sensationalist doctrine of perception must be banished,[20] however firmly founded in the facts of physiological psychology.

By this same rule, Whitehead disposes of the problem of solipsism, likewise a corollary of the current causal theory of perception. For common sense, he holds, this problem simply does not exist; and by his rule of evidence we must "bow to the presumption" we always make that we

---

[16] *Ibid.*, p. 26.   [17] §37.3.   [18] *Ibid.*, p. 12.   [19] *Ibid.*, p. 229.   [20] *Ibid.*, p. viii.

live in presence of our fellows in a world common to all. Hence Whitehead can say "Our datum is the actual world, including ourselves," [21]
or informally (as in one of our joint seminars), "*Here we are: we don't
go behind that, we begin with it!*" He can daringly pronounce empiricist
Hume to be unempirical on this point: we do not "dance with (Hume's)
'impressions of sensation' and then proceed to conjecture a partner"; [22]
the partner, he implies, is as much a part of the experienced fact as the
dance or the music!

This does not imply, however, that our current intuitions are to be
accepted as they stand. They, too, require to be interpreted by our categories; if they criticize our tentative ideas, these ideas in turn criticize
them. For example, there is a very widely held intuition, perhaps universal,
to the effect that not everything passes; "in the inescapable flux there is
something that abides (quite as much as) in the overwhelming permanence there is an element that escapes into flux." [23] In making room in
cosmology for that intuition of the enduring, Whitehead distinguishes
between the finer intuitions of higher civilizations and the cruder myths,
and *finds a place for permanence* in accord with the finer. Intuition must
interact with rational thought; it can admonish, but not dictate. For its
very language must be supplied by the categorial scheme.

Once the scheme of primary ideas has been devised, its consequences
must be followed through with the utmost rigor; only thus can schemes,
always defective, be replaced by schemes less defective. In this working
union of the empirical with the rational, Whitehead sees the prospect,
long hoped for, of a continuous progress in speculative philosophy, hitherto
the prerogative of the empirical sciences.

The admission of imagination and intuition to a position of importance for knowledge, in a carefully systematic work like that of Whitehead, is a major contribution to the resources of speculative philosophy.
As a basis for beginning, we now have not two proposals, but three: the
a priori certitudes; the widest inductive generalities; the persisting convictions of mankind, as discerned in imagination, intuition, common sense.
Of these, imagination is a natural function of exploration, and thus of
growth; and as Whitehead points out, not alone in philosophy but also
in science. This appeal to responsible imagination gives the work of
Whitehead a poetic drive and to his language an untranslatable fascination: to expound him is to quote him. As with his master, Plato, mathematics passes into exalted myth, and myth into mathematics, without
sense of discord; and one perceives as in no other writing of our time their
essential kinship.

[21] *Ibid.*, p. 6. (I cannot say that he solves the problem of solipsism.)
[22] *Ibid.*, p. 481.   [23] *Ibid.*, p. 513.

For our present purposes, Whitehead's vitally living method of thinking is his primary contribution to our enquiry. It is a synthesis of rationalism and empiricism, by way of intuitive feeling,—a radical addition to
both which (I believe we can show) contains germs of both. We recall
that Kant also undertook to unite the empirical and the rational strands
of philosophy in his time; he retained the Cartesian *a priori* as limited to
the sphere of experience. In my own judgment, Kant's *a priori*, with
modifications, has still something to contribute to the cosmology of Whitehead; for the guide of induction, often felt as an undefined necessity, may
be an *a priori* laboring to be born. With this comment in passing, let us
turn to a brief sketch of the unifying principles in Whitehead's world-
view.

37.11. We have classed Whitehead with the philosophers of Process,
or of The Flux. We have also pointed out that he finds a place for permanence in his world-scheme. How does he do this? Passingness he emphasizes as the primary empirical description of the world; with Locke he
sees Time as the "perpetual perishing" of what is, and in the interest of
a veracious report he proposes to dispense with "substance" as a changeless
substratum of changing attributes. But there must still be identifiable
entities with careers in time. Hence Whitehead's use of the term "actual
occasion" or "actual entity" conceived on the pattern of a finite life-process
that arises, matures, perishes, transmitting something of its mature fulfilment to subsequent occasions.[24] Substance is, as it were, biologized.
Hegel had declared that "Substance must be raised to Subject"; Whitehead's reinterpretation of substance as living process, with a trait of subjectivity throughout, is on ground not wholly alien. And with this trait
of subjectivity, there enters the more tangible factor of durability, since
the identity of the occasion is chiefly signalized by continuity of *aim*.
There is a "static vision" as well as a "dynamic history"; and "This development is nothing else than the Hegelian development of an idea." [25]
The element of permanence in the world is to be found, not in conserved
physical substrata, but in the *metaphysic of ideal aims*.

Since Plato it has been a common persuasion that some Ideas, including certain standards of value, have a permanence superior to that of
things; though non-existent they are in some sense eternal. In recent years,
this Platonic realism-of-ideas has occasionally flowered into a "realm of
essences" or "of ends." Whitehead conceives a totality of such "eternal
entities," in infinite totality including all possible aims of all possible
"occasions." Clearly no individual occasion could be aware of such an

---

[24] "The notion of 'substance' is transformed into that of 'actual entity.'" *Ibid.*, p. 28.
[25] *Ibid.*, p. 254.

ideal totality; nor could it—if it were aware—single out from this com-
pactly infinite multitude the particular aims relevant to its own fulfilment.
To pass from the universal infinitude to the particular possibilities relevant
to individual careers Whitehead invokes a mediating activity, an actual
Subject who judges and orders "the entire multiplicity of eternal objects,"
and who brings them into the horizon of each occasion, not as imposed
choices, but as persuasion or "lure" toward its own fulfilment. For this
subject, as a necessity of his scheme of categories, he uses the name "God";
and says of him, that "apart from the intervention of God there could
be nothing new in the world, and no order." [26]

For the existence of God Whitehead offers no proof [27] and no evidence
beyond (a) the systematic necessity just mentioned, and (b) the corroboration of experience thus given interpretation. This God is "the eternal
urge of desire," felt by each actual entity not as a self-begotten impulse
but as an appeal from the nature of the world, carrying the sense of "re-
freshment and companionship at which religion aims." [28] In other words,
our natural desires, as they work their way toward an intelligent life-plan,
have the character, not of organic impulses from a subconscious under-
ground but of weighted images of potentiality as from the enduring magazine of the world's meanings. And this God, who in his inviting function,
(his "primordial nature,") must be eternal as the continuing need of the
occasions, will also cherish the responses as a "reaction from the world"
(his "consequent nature") so that from the perishing occasion, not all
perishes: "the perfect moment is fadeless in the lapse of time." [29]

This God is obviously not the God of tradition, nor the Absolute Spirit of Hegel.
He is not the creator of the world, nor self-created. He is himself the creature of a more
fundamental factor in Whitehead's cosmos, the "principle of creativity." God in his
primordial nature is said to be an "accident" of a non-actual creativity. The question
might be raised how the non-actual can create the actual. It might also be considered
whether, as between the creative principle itself, and the two natures of God, the
primordial and the consequent, we have not a trifurcation of God not less difficult
than the bifurcation of nature. In presence of such questions, Whitehead brings the
disarming comment that "the system is confessedly inadequate"; [30] its only support is
"the elucidation of somewhat exceptional elements in our conscious experience . . .
religious and moral intuitions." Its main point is clear: that "realms of essences" are
inoperative abstractions apart from actual selective relevance secured for the individual
by a subjectivity present as guide in his environment, most concretely as group interpretation of the generalities of instinct, ultimately as an element in the constitution of the
world.

As a totality of numberless finite occasions, Whitehead's universe has
apparently only the unity of the Subject who grasps the realm of eternal

---

[26] *Ibid.*, p. 377.   [27] *Ibid.*, p. 421.   [28] *Ibid.*, p. 47.
[29] *Ibid.*, p. 514.   [30] *Ibid.*, p. 521.

objects in their relevance to passing lives. These occasions recall the monads of Leibniz in their subjective structure. But Whitehead chooses for his cosmology the name "organic philosophy," indicating first that each unit-occasion has an organic structure, and second that each occasion enters into organic relations with all the rest, by way of its aims. An organic structure is one which brings about a certain union of opposites,— a permanence of identity with a continuous metabolism of ingredients, and also an incessant passage of moments within the stable unity of a time-epoch; in this sense an organism illustrates Whitehead's translation of Plato into contemporary terms: "The things which are temporal arise by their participation in the things that are eternal"; [31] and with this further comment that in such participation (another term for "prehension") the eternal element is not simply something received: it has an active part. "The ideal, itself felt, defines what 'self' shall arise from the datum." It is not simply, as Descartes assumes, that the ego as thinker creates the thought; it is also that *the thought creates the thinker.* And here, says Whitehead, lies "the final contrast between a philosophy of substances and a philosophy of organism." [32]

Few systems of thought not dialectical in structure have so powerfully united contrasting factors. Within the dominating pluralism there is yet another aspect of unity. There is indeed no Supreme Being; there is no explanation for the odd particulars constituting the actual universe. Yet the world thus empty of sponsorship remains an identifiable total. It is not merely that all are related through interaction with each other: it is also that each one of the multitude, while prehending its predecessors, prehends also the whole: each organic occasion from its unique center organizes the whole universe. The identity of the total thus held in common constitutes the solidarity of which we are immediately aware.

And there are other "ideal opposites," freedom and necessity, greatness and triviality, God and the world—all are "elements in the nature of things, and are incorrigibly there. The concept of 'God' is the way in which we understand this incredible fact—that what cannot be, yet is." [33] There is indeed, no divine plan; nor is there, as with Hegel, a definable goal: the common belief that every series must have a terminal member is dismissed as "a prevalent fallacy." [34] Can a process be said to have a meaning, if it has no *ad quem?* Whitehead answers that even though (or just because?) the total significance of things is not reserved for a final consummatory moment, there may be at all points a satisfying intimation of cumulative sense in the time-order. "In place of the Hegelian hierarchy of categories of thought, the philosophy of organism

[31] *Ibid.,* p. 63.   [32] *Ibid.,* p. 228.   [33] *Ibid.,* pp. 518, 531.   [34] *Ibid.,* p. 169.

finds a hierarchy of categories of feeling." [35] And where there is hierarchy there is at every point a sense of direction, and of achievement in kind.

37.12. *Polarity.* In Hegel and Whitehead, we have contrasting illustrations of our thesis that "your philosophy is not your collection, it is your principle." Each of these vastly different cosmologies brings into a synthesis various types of philosophy, and indeed, much the same types. They shared a conviction not uncommon in our time that traditional oppositions of belief are seldom pure contradictions, such that we must choose *either A or B.* The opposition may have the character of a *polarity,* such that each pole derives part of its meaning from its contrast with the counter-pole; and thus we can have neither A nor B unless we have *both A and B.*

Such polarity is first recognized not in oppositions among ideas, but as a matter of observation, in nature. We have met it in the Yang and Yin of Chinese lore, and in various ancient dualisms. It appears in the male-female differentiation, in the relation of positive and negative electrical charges; perhaps also in the still problematic tension between quantum and wave in the phenomena of radiant energy, a tension giving rise to theories of "complementarity" in the school of Niels Bohr.

In philosophy, the effort at synthesis through polarity tends to the dialectical form, especially among the early idealists whose aim was to make intelligible the opposition of mind and body and of form and matter. Synthesis through polarity is likewise developed in terms of naturalist principles. Dialectical Materialism, for example, during the nineteen-twenties, developed in the Moscow schools the doctrine that matter is "autodynamic," and as such contains in itself both the mental pole of spontaneity and the physical pole of conserved quantity. In our own day the concept of polarity has been developed with powerful originality by W. H. Sheldon,[36] who credits Thomas Aquinas with having achieved principles of synthesis valid for all time.

Departing from Whitehead's terminology, and perhaps from his thought, let me express in terms of my own views what I see as the implied principle of unity in Whitehead's cosmology. It is certainly not a dialectical argument-and-goal. But it is a cumulative organizing process, an *interorganizing* let me say, in which thought and feeling alike find increasing at-homeness in a given Nature. Nature, in this case, is the physical counterpart of the "eternal entities," corresponding in contemporary terms to the Aristotelian "matter," whose endless resistance is endlessly revealing to the selfhood engaged in the contest, and thus an end-

---

[35] *Ibid.,* p. 252.   [36] Especially in a notable work, *God and Polarity.*

less potentiality. With this understanding, the dangerous term "substance" loses its power to harm!

37.13. *Analysis and Synthesis.* There are signs that the present moment in philosophy is one of recovered energy of Synthesis, after a considerable period of Analysis, logical and linguistic. To some extent the constructive power is due to the analytic restraint. For if the demand is made, Choose either A or B, a more careful analysis may reveal that the alternative is spurious. For example, Is the world One or Many? Choose either Monism or Pluralism. Confronted with this issue, William James chooses *both*: he writes A *Pluralistic Universe.* The alternative is spurious on the ground of a simple analysis of meanings. An aggregate can be counted as "many" only if it has a definable togetherness or "oneness," the character of cardinal numbers; and again, the "one" as predicate is significant only if there is a "many" to be taken together. So with many of the pairs which find themselves in polar relationship. The conjunctions of universal and particular, of the ideal and the actual, of form and matter, give us what we mean by the "concrete." The growth of logical insight and of semantic clarity can be ends in themselves; but they also serve—not to supplant speculative metaphysics, but to promote it by bridging artificial hostilities between seekers of truth. The "Age of Analysis" is transitional.

At the same time, Synthesis is not—cannot be—the last word in the structure of one's personal philosophy.

The great syntheses are indeed achievements of the first rank; they have brought to an end unnecessary conflicts and have refuted the charge that philosophy has no advances to its credit. In the field of political philosophy, individual freedom and a firm public order stand as opposed ideals; in the representative and democratic constitutions we have the promise of a workable synthesis, and therewith a new era in the political life of mankind. Likewise with the Kantian synthesis of the empirical and the *a priori* in knowledge; it may or may not be final,—we have raised that question in examining Whitehead's work,—but all future advance must take it into account.

At the same time, it is not true that *all opposites* belong together. In politics, if the ideal of synthesis were to mean universal compromise or appeasement, a lying-down of good with evil or of truth with falsehood, it would deserve the reproach that has come upon those terms. To adopt a policy in which there is *nothing to exclude* as untrue would be to invite defeat in the moment of victory: to make a principle of "the relative truth of all principles" is to surrender principle. The area of synthesis is always finite: the area of conflict remains. The function of synthesis may be that of cancelling spurious alternatives in order that the genuine issues may become more salient. As between the One and the Many, we reject the demand to choose; the world is both: but *is its unity purposive?* There is a Yes or No to be entered here; and gradations from biological appetitions upward to full self-awareness do not meet the issue. If such intentionality as we can verify in the cosmos emerges from a non-intentional background, we are still in the grip of irresponsible actuality,—the central problem of metaphysics remains.

Beyond the great cosmological synthesis, then, lie further labors. Character, whether of men or of philosophies, is shown as much in what one denies as in what one affirms. Preachers of pure peace by the Both-And route (commonly dubbed Hegelian) have but half the gospel: Hegel, too, was a fighter! We must again enter the area of conflict and decision— with courage.

CHAPTER 38: SYSTEM AND
ANTI-SYSTEM: NIHILISM;
THE EXISTENTIALISTS

38.1. It may be taken as a near-axiom that the great systems of philosophy survive only because we, the people, want them to survive. They have no inherent power to oblige our attention. This does not mean that we accept any one of them as it stands: it means that we need something of the sort, and that we continue to hope. It has been said (and Whitehead quotes the saying) that a system is never refuted, it is only abandoned. A careful look at the facts suggests a different report: most systems are refuted, the major systems many times; but they are not abandoned. Hegel is perhaps the most thoroughly refuted of all philosophers, unless it be Aristotle or St. Thomas; and even more often, Hegel is rejected out of hand. Bergson refused to know more of him than the curriculum required, for the reason that "Hegel taught that there is a dialectic in history; but there *can be no dialectic in history*"—the time-movement is incessantly creative of novelty.[1] Whitehead dismisses Hegel unread, because Hegel's remarks on mathematics appeared "complete nonsense."[2] Yet Hegel survives. And William James' experience with this redoubtable obscurantist may be typical. In his early years, writing a scathing diatribe "On Some Hegelisms," he comes in his maturity to a qualified admiration. Hegel, he suggests, "like Byron's corsair . . . has left a name 'to other times, linked with one virtue and a thousand crimes'—the virtue (being) the vision . . . that things are 'dialectic' . . . the dogging of everything by its negative, its fate, its undoing . . . the hegelian intuition of the essential provisionality, and consequent unreality of everything empirical and finite."[3] "Merely as reporter of certain empirical aspects of the actual, Hegel, then, is great and true";[4] and the ground of this judgment, we may note, is the same as that on which Bergson excludes him from consideration!

The reason for this apparently unreasonable situation may be in part

---

[1] In answer to a question I put to him in 1913.
[2] Schilpp, *The Philosophy of Alfred North Whitehead*, p. 7.
[3] James, *A Pluralistic Universe*, pp. 88 f.   [4] *Ibid.*, p. 100.

this: that refutation is a private enterprise, whereas the judgment of a significant system is a world enterprise—its thought must be tested by thought equally competent; it may have to wait through the ages for its competent appraisal. But there is another reason more fundamental. A system of philosophy however impressive in its architecture—the cosmologies we have been reviewing may serve as examples—does not rest its case on technical judgment alone. It appeals also to the untechnical intuition of thoughtful mankind, sensitive less to its argument than to its vision, its veracity, and its relevance to the human situation. The judgment of analysis is indispensable; but the judgment of *feeling*, as nonanalytic intelligence, has a wider and more durable justice.

The judgment of feeling may conserve what analysis at any moment appears to condemn. The continuing pursuit of metaphysical system, for example, proceeds against the current of analytic diagnoses of its "nonsense." [5] On the other hand, the judgment of feeling may be averse to what analysis approves. The most brilliant construction will not survive if it is felt artificial or ungenuine. The mark of ingenuity, of contrivance, of a dominant ego in the "I-think" which must be present in all speculative thought, will be against it. And especially, any felt irrelevance to the total human situation. This matter of relevance deserves particular consideration.

38.2. Any system of metaphysics must concern itself with the situation of man-in-his-world, that universal "finite situation" (as Royce termed it) of the limited being in presence of infinite Nature. But the judgment of relevance will consider also its concern for what I will call the *existing human burden.*

The often quoted comment of the Marxian tradition contains a halfvalid intimation of this point: "philosophy reflects on the world, whereas the task is to change it." The alternative is spurious; for any worldchanging, not preceded and shot-through with reflection, can only be mischievous. But the demand for concern with the human burden is always in order. The actual engagement of man in the actual world gives the inescapable empirical basis for his judgment of the character of that world, which metaphysics must deal with. Philosophy differs from science in this respect, that philosophy is always being generated afresh from the ground level of experience: every man, every thinker, has to begin

---

[5] Bertrand Russell has now clearly separated himself from "the new philosophy," most carefully analytic, which has arisen between the two world wars through a ripening Logical Positivism and Wittgenstein's later investigations, which Russell identifies as Wittgenstein II. He does so on the ground that the business of philosophy is "to understand the world, not merely to understand sentences" (*Hibbert Journal*, July, 1956). In brief, metaphysics cannot be reduced to semantics.

anew with zero, even while fully aware of cumulative tradition. Each phase of history reverts, in this sense, to philosophical innocence; and is prepared to wipe the slate clean of whatever tradition shows itself irrelevant to the existing burden.[6]

In the world situation of today there is a human burden such as no age has hitherto borne. Though its incidence is variously felt, the burden itself is universal. It is not simply the fact of the limitless capacity for mutual destruction now resting in human hands; it is that with this capacity there goes a degree and kind of hostility between human groups that rejects rational solution. In earlier eras, rational man stood against non-rational Nature: the victories of science and technique were in principle common victories. Today, rational man stands against rational man as ultimate group-will *versus* ultimate group-will: this non-rational crux in human history turns the scientific advance, by nature a common good, into a common peril. We have still with us the naturalistic cosmology, according to which human life is set within a meaningless universe: to this abyss, we now add the abyss of a meaningless history, a factual power-balance triggered to accidents of political clash, in the absence of a common ethical groundwork.

And in so far as a common ethic can only coexist with a common world-view, this burden, felt by every sentient being as a menace to the security of his own existence, translates itself—as it should—into philosophical attitudes expressive of distaste toward irrelevant systematic structures, of a will to reduce speculation to its barest minimum, and not seldom in a revolt against system-making itself, a Nihilism.

38.3. To appreciate the status of philosophy in the world today, it would be necessary to trace the descent of confidence-in-thought from its high point in the eighteenth century, on the ground of the new light of science, its faith in human nature and in "progress," through the era of the democratic revolutions and the nineteenth century which have brought something far less than the Millennium, to the present pass. With a disturbed disillusionment, our western self-criticism in philosophy has often taken the form of a call to Return—Return to Kant, to Descartes, to Plato—or if Rousseau or Walt Whitman are our prophets, to Nature.

---

[6] The great ages of philosophical construction have tended to run out into periods of scepticism and barrenness. This may be due to an inner defect in the presuppositions of the prior tradition, as Prof. Gilson proposes in *The Unity of Philosophical Experience*. It is seldom, however, unrelated to alterations in the social frame of individual life. Loss of stable bearings as in the decay of Greek life may lead to what Gilbert Murray has called a "loss of nerve," and thus to a pervasive tendency to take refuge in emotional mysticisms rather than to build farther upon the magnificent foundations then at hand. I suggest that this tendency, even in its cruder forms, was not wholly unphilosophical; it was rather a reversion to philosophical innocence, disposed to begin afresh with an empiricism truer to the wisdom of feeling.

Such appeals are always pertinent—if there are any eternal truths we have frequent reason to return to them in a gaunter simplicity.

But Return has no peculiar lifting power for the present burden. It is for this reason that "Ideologies" arise, another factor in noting the present status of philosophy. An Ideology is not a philosophy nor a type of philosophy; it is a philosophically tinctured program for action. Some philosophical attitude (say Materialism) shorn of complexity is applied to presently insistent human interests (say property, labor, distribution, liberty)—an attempt to be tangibly burden-lifting. And if, like the Soviet Ideology, it merely shifts the burden, and by temporarily relieving sore muscles breeds illusion of cure, it may still allure through the circumstance that it has occupied itself with the burden's existence. Ideologies sensibly recognize the pertinence of metaphysics to the business of living. At the same time they threaten destruction to the spirit of philosophy through the assumption that a specific philosophy, regardless of individual enquiry, may become *parti pris* for political groups aspiring to dominance. Philosophical debate, leaving the academy and the privacy of the thinker, becomes part of the struggle for public power, and the search for truth has lost its soul.

But Returns and Ideologies are *placebos*.

38.4. The root of trouble within the philosophical spirit is biographical: it cannot be defined apart from personal experience. I have recently come into the presence of this spirit of despair-of-philosophical-thought in the student life of a destroyed and defeated Germany. In 1948 the universities of Bavaria were crowded with students whose future was undecipherable: their normal world had crumbled; they were living on nothing, devoid of prospects, chary of all ready-to-hand solutions, indisposed to any world-view not beginning, as they must, with chaos. One of them, third-year law, ex-Hitler-soldier, wrote me his views. I quote some of his words:

"We shall shiver through the third winter in unheated rooms. But why? . . . Many are saying, 'Let come what will, it cannot be worse.' Many become Nihilists, because with fair professions all remains phrases, and no one shows the substance. The word 'Democracy,' offered (by the Military Occupation) as the trump card, is daily so abused in practice that it becomes its own dirge . . . For myself, I believe in spite of everything in the triumph of Christianity, in the unchanging mission of a man and of a people, in a future Freedom, in a Peace, and in an understanding among the peoples. (But) perhaps I am wrong. Who knows?"[7]

"Many become Nihilists": the temper of No-belief became widespread in Europe, and not alone among students nor alone in the defeated

[7] This experience has been related in detail in Hocking, *Experiment in Education* (Chicago, 1954), pp. 147 ff.

countries. The reason lay largely, I believe, in this matter of *relevance*. If the victors were disposed to conduct a world-rebuilding, what had they to offer, either to the needed-vision of those who must struggle upward through the ruins or to the wider situation demanding new thinking? As my student-friend later wrote me:

"I do not doubt the capabilities of America. But in all the western lands does there not seem to fail *die tragende Idee*—the Load-lifting Idea?"

Is the phrase precise? Had anyone a right to expect of the Ideas under which we carry on our work that, beside being true, they shall also lift the burden, or at least be relevant to it? I believe the answer is Yes. Philosophy under the spell of the scientific spirit has in modern times commonly considered its theme, "reality," as a matter of dispassionate Fact. Fact it must be. But never *indifferent fact!* If it is the finally Real we are talking about—not clean "Objects" about which we are bound to be "objective," but the source of the Subject-Object mixture we call the world—I am prepared to say that the alleged "truth" that has in it no disturbance of feeling is not true:

"If (such a 'truth') lowers the capacity of men to meet the stresses of existence, or diminishes the worth to them of what existence they have, such a theory is somewhere false . . . A proposition that falls on the mind so dully as to excite no (emotion) has not attained the level of truth." [8]

In brief, if what is offered in metaphysics is of the purely dispassionate type, and if the generation in crisis to which it is offered should "spue it out of its mouth," the reaction may possibly be from the root of a truer metaphysic! The student's challenge is pertinent: have we or have we not a Load-lifting Idea?

38.5. Literal Nihilism, as a rejection of all metaphysical judgment, is an unachievable limit. The rejecting reaction I have just mentioned is itself a metaphysical reaction: it contains the (unproved) postulate that the world, whatever its make-up, *must give some sense to human living.* When Nihilism is professed, what is meant is a direction, not a terminus. It is precisely an attempt to reach the unrejectable postulate, to dive beneath the Cartesian limit of doubt, in order to get a more primitive hold on livingness itself—let us say, on raw "Being." [9]

There are few radical Nihilists; but the Nihilist direction, in this sense of Reduction-of-philosophy-to-a-new-minimum, is widespread. Reductionism—if you will allow me the momentary use of the unappetizing but more accurate term—is the common element in a number of noteworthy move-

[8] Hocking, *The Meaning of God in Human Experience* (New Haven, 1912), p. xiii.
[9] The precise argument of Albert Camus' notable work, *L'homme révolté*, translated as *The Rebel* by Anthony Bower (New York, 1954).

ments. The Logical Positivists (and most Semanticists) would relieve us at once of the whole metaphysical enterprise. The "Phenomenology," proposed by Edmund Husserl in Germany, invites us to distinguish in experience the "that" and the "what," i. e., the particular and the general, or the existential and the conceptual; and to discard from attention the existential element in order to note with precision the meaning or intention of the *concepts* there involved. This act of essence-viewing he calls *Wesensschau*; and its purpose is to rehabilitate the *a priori* character of fundamental thought-elements of experience, as against the prevalent psychologizing of the thinking process. A third group of Reductionists gives the place of honor to the stone which the Phenomenological builders rejected, that of *particular existence:* it looks away from the concepts, to concentrate on the pure mystery of Being. If Husserl could be called an "Essentialist," these should be—and are—called "Existentialists."

It is they who have judged most keenly the gravity, and the location, of the philosophical crisis. They, too, seek a minimum, through a clean-sweep of complexities, for a fresh beginning of reflection. They find that minimum, not by "doubt"—Descartes' intellectual instrument of Reduction; nor by "suspension" of the metaphysical impulse, Husserl's abstraction or *"epoché,"* equally intellectual. They proceed directly to *Being-as-felt*, the immediate awareness of existing which underlies all reflection—primitive livingness, we called it, the rawest of raw-material.

38.6. As a starting place for thought, this may appear unpromising. For what can be said about *existing*, except that it Is? When Descartes reached "I-exist," he seems to have struck bottom; he attempts no analysis nor description of what is elemental. For the logician, as we have seen, Being, as *summum genus*, cannot be defined: it has no differentiating marks—nothing (as Hegel observed) to distinguish it from Nothing. And to the stone, indeed, non-existence would "make no difference." But to the self-conscious being, the difference between Being and Nothing is *everything*. It is upon this ultimate difference that Existentialism finds much to say. Of all contemporary movements, it is most literally true to Aristotle's view of metaphysics, "the study of Being as be-ing."

In the nature of the case, Being cannot be clarified by concepts: it can only be pointed to, and only to one who exists, and who already knows what it is to exist. The Existentialist is obliged to be autobiographical: G. Marcel, intending to develop a "system," found it necessary to express his early thought in a "Metaphysical Journal," and later through drama. The (unintentional) originator of the movement, the Dane, Søren Kierkegaard (1813–1855), administered a shock to his time by assaulting the

Hegelian system for its faith in concepts. Hegel, still under the spell of Plato, for whom the pure Idea is the perfect mode of being, made the general ideas, *Begriffe*, the vital and growing element of experience and history. The irrational particulars could only participate in this dialectic. Kierkegaard championed the irrational particular in the form of the individual self. To him, only the particular, individual, personal has true Being. It was as though he had rediscovered the *infinite importance of the non-rational factor* in all that is. There is no reality except what the private, non-deducible individual finds valid in his biographical journey.

As prophet of that shock, administered about 1840, and transmitted at long intervals by Ibsen and Unamuno, and to some extent paralleled by Nietzsche, he becomes again an influential factor in the human outlook, especially in the post-war world, whose "lostness" and whose burden seeks something more radical than conceptual relief.

But what does the Existentialist find?

38.7. At least this, that existing, for a person, is not identical with existing, for a stone: it is not plain factuality, plain thereness. To exist for a person is to be *concerned about existing*, to regard the ever-possible passage from existing to non-existing as first-order peril. It is striking that the Existentialist here does precisely what Hegel does at the beginning of his *Logic*, he confronts Being with Nothing. But not in order to note their conceptual kinship. It is to recognize their omni-present interplay in Feeling. In presence of the incessant boundary-setting of Non-existence on Existence, of Death on life, of Infinite Nothingness on the finitude of Being, existence for a person is *passion-filled awareness*. And since apart from feeling, value is non-existent, only personal existence is truly "concrete." The swimmer, struggling against an ebb-tide, is more truly concrete than the tide, which is unaware of its own power. As charged with feeling, personal existence might well be given a special term: the name *"Existenz"* clings to it, because with Kierkegaard it was impressed into this usage.

It would be fair to say that for this group of thinkers, existence loses its neutrality and acquires emotional meaning through assimilation to an *élan vital* permanently tangent to non-being, to death. It is thus colored by an undercurrent of anxiety, *Angst* or Dread. And if, in revulsion against system, we surrender that conceptual enterprise in which traditional man has attempted to think out his destiny, what can we find in immediate Existence to dispel the shadow of meaninglessness which the enveloping cloud of non-being casts on our time-finitude as individuals or as human race? Where Husserl seeks *intentions*, and of them builds structures, the Existentialist seeks *intensity*—emotional intensity—and the underlying dread not seldom verges toward despair. Despair is the nihilism of emotion: it may be inspired by the invasion of our being by the total irrationality in which that being appears to be set; it is not of itself irrational. It may well be an experience of greater, not lesser, veracity of sight.

It is also conceivable that this deeper veracity, if we could attain it, would be a path toward assurance at a deeper level than that of Descartes. Despair is never, like the doubt of Descartes, a deliberate and semidramatic exercise. It involves the whole man. It is a completer and more genuine negation. If, in its dialectic it reveals, as with Descartes, an absolute affirmation, that affirmation would be the more firmly founded.

CHAPTER 39:
REBIRTH OF PHILOSOPHY

39.1. It is not every pain that is a part of joy. But there is an integration of pain into joy, whose understanding is elementary to the account of human experience. Let us widen our field of view.

The despair of the truth-seeker is of a piece with the pain of the artist, with the pain of all creative workers. The artist's work—is it a joy or a suffering? It is both. That he finds joy in his subject needs no saying: he has chosen it. Yet his experience is one of suffering in so far as he knows himself falling short of what he wills to achieve. The pain exists because, and only because, of the perfection he contemplates. Reject the vision and the suffering disappears. Then why not get rid of it? Get rid of the vision? But this vision is what life has come to mean! Strange that something apparently accidental should leap to a place of such necessity: the world need not have contained that thing, it need not have come his way, it is life's unsought gift. Its renunciation would leave all things as before. Yet renunciation has become unthinkable; the accident has become a commitment; and the price of the gift is this pain.

So with other fields of effort. Men cling with a strange perversity to their most pain-costly visions. They have beaten their way to the Poles; they have climbed their Annapurnas "because they are there." So we explore the universe—because it is there—pursue retreating galaxy-fields, as if revelling in the growing sense of our insignificance. The stages in that unfinishable task of knowledge are none the less conquests. And if the race is, as Heidegger puts it, "for Death," we hope to know the How of it before it closes in on us.

It begins to appear that despair is possible only in situations in which we ourselves insist on a certain greatness inseparable from human nature. The animal is incapable of it, having no traffic with totality, nor with perfection. We certainly do not insist on frustration; but we are unwilling, perhaps unable, to purchase freedom from its pain by lowering our sights. We prefer not only to be "man dissatisfied rather than a pig satisfied," but also to be man in pain because of his limits rather than man relaxed within those limits. We take to ourselves Nietzsche's dictum regarding

Spirit—it is life carrying out its own surgery on itself: *"Geist ist das Leben, das selber ins Leben schneidet."*

And this is not Stoicism nor Titanism: it is there in the centre of the "will to live," in the simplest moment of waking to the active Be-ing of a new day. Analyze it or not, pleasure itself is a being-burned, and the measure of our joy-in-being-alive is the measure of our being consumed. Here we catch a glimpse of the dialectic by which despair at its limit touches a certitude. As Descartes could say, "I doubt, ergo I think, ergo I exist," so we may say "I despair, ergo I aspire, ergo I enjoy existence as Spirit," and this joy can not be taken away while I am I: it is the central fact of my Be-ing.

39.2. But the despair incident to striving is not the full story of the despair that leads toward the root, the philosophic minimum. It is not the encounter with cosmic Nothingness, the encounter which marks the heaviest point of the contemporary burden. By itself, this encounter may seem to entail surrender of the great world beyond self to meaninglessness and a taking refuge in one's subjectivity.

In truth, it is part of the mission of current Existentialism to arouse human nature to an appreciation of the resources of its own subjectivity, the inexhaustible miracle of "I exist as conscious and caring." And in so far as this movement is atheistic, as with Sartre,[1] accepting the ultimacy of Nothingness as human destiny, subjectivity and its freedom must be the resort. But all human action deserts pure subjectivity: and part of its joy-in-pain is an awareness, all but subconscious, that its simple aliveness to qualities, apparently of the world, is no mere passivity, but is literally changing "the face of nature."

We observe these qualities as "in the objects"; and yet, if our scientific analysis of perception is valid, there are certain qualities which, apart from our awareness, the world would not have. And though that analysis is at best but a half truth, our activity in the world's endowment of quality is evident: it is only for the living self that the world has good and evil, beauty and ugliness, the affective aspects of color, sound, taste. Bring a magnet into a bunch of listless iron fragments, and at once all are polarized as minor magnets. Bring a mind, as passion-charged, into a world of neutral fact, in which nothing is "important"; and instantly every item of that world takes on positive or negative importance. The polarized world, with its implications of joy and suffering, is in some degree our own creation.

---

[1] Though Sartre as playwright is capable of using an imaginative mythology of an "other world" with striking effect, as in *Les jeux sont faits*.

We have thus passed beyond ourselves, though only into the realm of quality; we have not dispelled the final Nothingness. There is a further step to be taken.

39.3. We have spoken of the artist's pain in work—his occupation being perhaps at its best the happiest, and at the same time and for the same reason the unhappiest, of human callings. But the principle of joy-through-despair need not be looked for solely among exceptional passages of human experience. It belongs to the day-by-day developments of human concern.

Every wakening of the mind to love, every opening of the eyes to beauty, brings evidence of it. So also every act of devoted labor. Everyone who undertakes to create with hand-and-mind knows the deliberate and joyful adoption of pain. Gerald Heard once remarked to me that in earlier England a master workman was often referred to as "a very painful man." The Biblical curses on the pair expelled from the Garden—sweat of brow for man, travail of childbirth for woman—become traits of blessedness when joined with the consciousness of sharing in the work of creation.

But here the word "sharing" must become literal, if the integration of pain-in-joy is to take place.

And at this point our experiences of love and beauty have a decisive word to say. We speak of them as "feelings": what if they are also *knowings?* I suggest that they are such: that they afford an initiation into the nature of objective reality—in brief that they are, of themselves, not emotions only but moments of metaphysical insight. Love, an admission into identity with Being-other-than-self, the human-other in the foreground, includes the world-other in its natural sweep: it is our most direct partnership with the life-within-nature, our most immediate awareness of the Real. Its most familiar form, that of ordinary human communication, is an experience of receiving-and-invading in which the solitary I-think of Descartes becomes spontaneously a We-think—so simply that we fail to note the momentous transition. In it, we directly share the object-world. It is "our" world; it is universal. "Here we are," its most spontaneous language, contains the rejection of solipsism, that spectre which modern philosophy, held by Descartes' I-think, has been unable to shake off.[2] In this, our normal "inter-subjectivity," we recognize, without analysis, that the "objectivity" of this object-world is something more and other than alien stuff. The silent, impersonal "It" retains its abstraction *for a purpose:* the "It" discloses itself as a "Thou."

With this disclosure, the bleak and qualityless universe, the ultimate

[2] More detail in Hocking, *The Coming World Civilization*, Study II.

Nothingness which the sober Realisms of our time (with most of the Nihilist and Reductionist tendencies) have accepted as the Fact any honest man should face, is transformed. And not by intricacy of argument! What we discover is only what is included in the nucleus of human experience, the irreducible "root" to which, in despair of prodigious thought-work, we seek to return. The decisive truth of metaphysics is there at the beginning, simple and inescapable: in our loneliness we cannot be alone. The "flight of the alone to the Alone" is the escape from solitude; and the escape from solitude at that level is the escape from Death.

39.4. We are thus spared some natural errors of those who have similarly sought the rebirth of philosophy through return to the root.

We are spared a certain *alienation* from reality as infinite and meaningless. What Max Planck calls the "World of Physics" is seen to be an abstraction, and as such never the whole of Fact. The "World of Values" is not a private creation of the sentient fraction of existence. We men do indeed "make our own values" in the sense that we choose our part, and also that we contribute to creation: but value, too, has its universality. What we make is neither solitary, nor the perquisite of a human enclave-of-conscious-being. We make value, and make ourselves, on the basis of an original gift-of-self: we are created first, and creators afterward.

The enclave-feeling implies the huddling-together for warmth on the part of value-seeking beings within a nescient universe: a sense of alienation from that reality is inescapable. We find its note in Plato, in Plotinus, in Vedanta, in Buddhism, in much of the other-worldliness of early Christianity, in Berdyaev, . . . It is inconsistent with the whole-hearted "engagement" in the world which is also a part of our nuclear attitude. A genuine Existentialism should relieve us of it entirely. The mission of that 'ism is to recover the glory of the particular; to cure all scorn for the oddities and irrationalities inherent in Factual existence. When an Existentialist expatiates on the "absurdity" of bodily details, of the "nauseating" in life, of circumstance generally (as do Sartre and the earlier Camus), he is false to his own insight. The unique givenness of every particular thing, feature, person, contains the anchor-catch for all recognition, memory, affection, individuality itself. The particular body is the signature for the universal, yet time-and-space-engaged, mind.

Among the Existentialists, it is Gabriel Marcel who has most clearly discerned this function of the particular and of the body. It is he, too, who has most clearly—and almost alone—discerned the mission of the existential to the metaphysical; that it is only the biographical that can be truly universal; that it is only in the intimate detail of individual being that our solitude reveals its inter-subjective character, and our private actions become participants in universal creativity.

39.5. Whatever the factual world-picture revealed by the cosmological advances of astro-physics, the world in which we are entangled is a world in which "the irrational particular" is the carrier of the entire mesh of being and becoming which we call the real world. It is, at the same time, a world in which loving and being loved are both possible and actual, as expressions of the inner being of certain irrational particulars, presumably indicative of the nature of things. With this foundation as origin of a reborn philosophy, our human engagement rediscovers the scope of its own will—what we sometimes call our conception of happiness. Happiness requires a *will to create through suffering*, a suffering which alone can express its love.

With this perception, mankind loses the absoluteness of its intolerance of pain, without losing its sympathy and its will to concrete health of living. It becomes capable of a cosmic patience, for which pain has an intelligible function, such that were we world-creators we would not wholly banish it from the picture. And this cosmic patience can sustain a possible political patience wholly different from mass-opiate, a patience for which, without relaxing purpose, the strife for power ceases to be the ultimate issue among men. Thus the releasing idea in a reborn philosophy becomes also the Load-lifting Idea in human relations.

And herewith the dialectical journey is completed, with a fuller scope, needing no aversion from the disclosures of an advancing physical cosmology. We must face the occasion for despair, in order to discern the meaning of that occasion. One could not despair, we said, if he did not aspire: that is true. We can now say, One could not despair if he did not at the same time hope (*désespoir* contains *espoir*); and one could not hope if he did not love. Thus we undergird and revise the Cartesian dialectic:

> · I despair, ergo I hope, ergo I exist as loving, ·

and to exist as loving is to *co-exist* with the real, as Thou art. The dialectical journey completes itself in an unshakable Affirmation.

39.6. If our interpretation of the present era is just, we have experienced, as a necessary condition for the rebirth of philosophy, the dissolution of the characteristic outlook of what we call "modernity," the period governed by the antithetical insights of Descartes. The present century has seen the extreme assertions, both of the subjectivity of the I-think, and of the objectivity of the purposeless physical world. It has been a period of split mentality, not knowing how to unite these insights, and unwilling, indeed unable, to surrender the riches flowing from each.

That this division-of-mind should bring confusion and dismay in public affairs as well as in the world of thought was to be expected. Yet it is not the disarray itself that has brought the solution. That solution could come only through pursuing each antithetical insight to its limit, until subjectivity, finding inter-subjectivity at its center, could rejoin objectivity. It is only through reaching the depths that the solving idea gains acceptance: it is the nature of the dialectic of experience, as of thought, that the radical reassurance arrives *de profundis*.

And with this reassurance, not only is philosophy reborn, but the present century, if I mistake not, has passed beyond Modernity.

CHAPTER 40: CONFESSIO FIDEI

40.1. In saying so much, I have already made, in germ, a statement of my own philosophic creed,—a statement which, on various counts, I owe you. The judgment of philosophies is from a philosophy; in those judgments which we have made, the judging philosophy is fractionally revealed as by convergence of reflections. An explicit bringing-together of these reflections will give the reader the clue whereby to estimate, perhaps discount, the judgments themselves.

Working out a philosophy is, as we said at the beginning, an inevitable activity for a rational being: it is an expression of his own integrity of thought. If it is, in addition, a "duty" and also a "source of happiness," that interesting conjunction indicates something about the nature of the universe in which philosophizing takes place. For in a dead or meaningless universe there could be no such thing as a *duty* to reflect about the whole; it might rather be a human duty to forget it and attend to the day's business. There is only one *internal* source of duty, that is, the way to one's own "fulfillment." This means, in practice, the way to one's next stage of growth (if one is growing), or to those satisfactions with which living is chiefly identified. (Thus one says of a particularly good play or book or important occasion or journey, "You ought not to miss that.") Only one thing could make philosophizing a duty of this sort, and that is that the universe has *an intrinsic meaning* which one ought not to miss, and desires not to miss.

In fact, unless the universe has some meaning, in its being and direction-of-process, philosophizing becomes a meaningless occupation; for we might define philosophy as the effort to interpret experience as a whole, that is, to find the meaning of things. If things have no meaning, philosophy is ideally futile.

It follows that every philosophy of whatever type is bound to assume that the universe has a meaning (or a system of meanings); a meaning which is objective, in the sense that it is there whether or not you or I discover it, but which can be discerned by us.[1] And since meanings are

---

[1] For a further development of this idea see Hocking, "What Does Philosophy Say?", *Philosophical Review*, XXXVII, No. 2 (March, 1928).

something more than the bare facts of the natural order, all philosophy is, in its assumptions, contradictory to naturalism, taking naturalism strictly as the negative doctrine that Nature is all there is.

40.2. And since meanings are abstractions unless they are somehow known or felt or appreciated, the existence of objective meaning in the world implies some kind of mental life at the core of reality. To this extent, I believe that idealism is not so much a separate type of philosophy as the essence of all philosophy, an assumption whether recognized or unrecognized of the philosophic enterprise itself. I take idealism, then, so far as this argument carries us, as the centre of my metaphysics. And I take this as a point of certainty, established by the dialectical method of which we were speaking. One who should say "The world has no objective meaning" would, as I see it, contradict himself.

40.3. This amount of idealism one may regard as a sort of philosophic minimum. The mystic, I believe, is much more adequate in his judgment that the world is an almost untouched reservoir of significance and value, whose quality we sense in passing perceptions of beauty in nature; or in love, which always comes as a surprise strangely reflecting on our previous inability to see, so that we say of ourselves, "Atheists are as dull Who cannot guess God's presence out of sight"; or still more continuously in that vague but inescapable sense of impending possible good for which we continue to hope while we live. What is living? Striving? Yes: incessant striving, but not "dumb striving." Living is reaching out to the reality of things as a region in which the discovery of value need never end. In philosophy, this conviction counts as the mystic's; but in this respect, I believe, again, that every man is an avowed or unavowed mystic,—even the Schopenhauers.

40.4. But why not be content with the minimal judgment that the world has a meaning (and that the old teleological argument was essentially right after all)? Why believe in such a plenum of meaning? Is this not, surely, an *a priori* prejudice? It is not "optimism" in the sense that good has to happen to everybody in the long run: the good has to be found, and we all run a chance of missing it. More than that, every one does, as a matter of fact, miss much of it, perhaps most of it. That is the essential and pervasive element of tragedy in the world. But I believe that the meaning is there. Yet, how does that agree with our intellectual duty to take things as we empirically find them, the meaningful and the meaningless mixed together in experience?

There is, to be sure, something matter-of-fact in all discoveries of good. We could never deduce music, for example, from any previous knowledge about sound; and certainly not from any general theorem to the effect that objective values exist. We have to be as empirical as you please about the flavors of olives, a boat race, the Syrian desert. Values "emerge." Does not this pure unanticipatable discovery of quality carry with it an equal requirement to be empirical toward the meaningless? There is much in the world we can only accept: it is blank datum,—there it is! The realistic temper in us demands that we rub our noses against such facts, and acknowledge them.

Willingly; but for how long? Philosophies which run into a wall of blank datum and end there are either tentative or lazy. They dare never say, These things have no meaning, but only, We have not found any, and regard it as not worth while to try. Such terminal empiricism toward the meaningless is but a personal confession: it implies nothing about the world, but only that the speaker should make way for the poet or the artist, who can see. Empiricism can set up no negatives: and we know this of the world, that values *keep emerging* as we enlarge our capacity and learn the adjustment of our instruments of vision.

40.5. I should go farther with idealism, and say that the world is a self. And I should immediately add, in explanation, that the self, so far from being a wholly evident and graspable being, as Descartes and Berkeley seemed to assume, is infinite in its depth and mystery. It is only with this understanding that it can be used as a concept for the whole of things: the infinite is measured by the infinite and the unknown by the unknown. Here again mysticism is nearer the truth than much current idealism.

When I speak of what the mystic knows of the self, I am distinctly not referring to an element of semi-occultism which runs through contemporary psychology under the head of the "subconscious." The subconscious is a veritable fact, and a vastly important fact in mental life. That is no reason for making it the home of a host of mythical complexes, and ghosts; or speaking of it as the "unconscious" and imagining one understands an unconscious mental state, as something half-way between mind and body.

The "subconscious," under the veiled and mechanized form which it has assumed in contemporary psychology, following the lead of Schopenhauer and von Hartmann, has been the means of concealing from view all the fertile (though weirdly expressed) inquiry into the self as ethical agent, as judge and creator of art, as logician and philosopher, which the idealists after Kant were chiefly concerned with. These activities represent far more nearly what the self is than do either laboratory reactions or subliminal cravings.

The word "self" indicates chiefly that the mental life within the world has its unity, and that all the meanings of things cohere in a single will. But may not all the selfhood in the world be a manifestation of something more profound or higher? No. For there is nothing higher than selfhood, and nothing more profound. Spinoza's Substance, with an infinitude of attributes, unless it were conscious and self-conscious, would be lower in being than the simplest of mankind. Within the Selfhood of substance there is room for all the unfathomed majesty of reality.

40.6. The human self, which we take as an imperfect image of the whole cosmos, is a thing of nature and also something more than that.

This human self must be made an object of scientific study, in its relations to its environment, as the naturalistic program requires. There are laws of learning, of habit, and the like which (since they are not used to "manage" us), we have no reason to disown or to break across. Psychology, as a natural science, may explain a great deal about ourselves; provided we understand by "explaining" not deriving one thing from another, but simply showing a law of variation. Thus vibration does not explain color in the sense that color is derived from vibration; but differences in vibration-rate may explain variation in color. The physical fact does not produce the mental fact; but changes in the one correspond with changes in the other.

The human self is more than a thing of nature, because it is more than a fact: facts are not conscious of facts,—the self is; facts are not values,—the self lives on values and is a value; facts are particulars, not universals,—the self is both; facts are present,—the self spans past and future. And because of these things, while facts are as they must be, the self is free: it determines, out of a matrix of plural possibilities, which one shall be the fact of the next moment.

The self is thus a union of opposites. And because precisely the same opposites are discernible in the composition of the larger cosmos and must somehow be united there, we may transfer the problem of this "somehow" in part to the world within, as we do when we recognize that the whole is a self. The ultimate evidence for the selfhood of the whole is not primarily the evidence of argument, however, nor of analogy, but that of immediate experience, interpreted by the dialectic. We, as a group of human selves, know that we are not alone in the universe: that is our first and persistent intuition.

40.7. This proposition, that the world is a self, I regard as a point of certainty in philosophy. And therewith I confess another belief,—the belief that *philosophy aims at certainty*, and can be content with nothing less. If one wishes to be emphatic, one may say absolute certainty,—there is no logical difference between certainty and absolute certainty. Some such certainty is necessary to give structure to our system of knowledge, as well as to the experimental business of daily life. The life of knowledge as well as the life of action swings, I believe, in irregular rhythm or alternation, between this pole of certainty and the region of exploration, tentativeness, probability, hypothesis.

"Absolutism," I know, is a word of reproach for the present age of thought. Rigid codes of truth and law and morals are recognized as deadly: it has been the genius of our age to get away from their shackles. The scientific spirit is open to the perennial revision of ideas: we must be ready to accept a new hypothesis to-morrow. Yes: but *by how much* is your hypothesis new? By all that you have believed to-day? Then you are no longer the same self from day to day, and your mental world has become an insane place not worth living in.

There is a certain illusion in our estimate of the degree of change that is going on: it is the fascinating aspect of experience, also the aspect which requires our *qui vive* and so holds attention. But the history of all social revolutions reminds us that there is a law of continuity in history: there is a similar law in the revolutions of thought. There is more than continuity: there is a *principle of changelessness* in the basis of things, on which certainty can take hold and remain certain. That is the objective counterpart of the changelessness of the self which apprehends and enjoys change.

It is true that we must be ready to revise our hypotheses: that is why we call them hypotheses. We must likewise be ready to revise the laws of our life. But what if in doing so we dismantle also the spirit of lawfulness and the "rule of law"? Then the change of laws becomes nonsense. We rely—when we talk about changing laws—on the stability of the "that" while we experiment with the "what." When a contemporary prophet, urging "the transitional character of our times" (all times are transitional), admonishes us that "as nothing is permanent either in institutions or in thought, we must stand ready to revise all the old rules of religion and sex, art and letters, politics and law," we hear what is in a sense a truism rather excitedly proclaimed; but what, if presented as the whole truth, is an exemplary untruism. It can never be a question for religion, sex, art, letters whether all things change. It can only be a question what things are changeable, what are relative to time and place, and what things are stable. It is the first business of philosophy to make evident what is stable, in order that change may go on with freedom of conscience and success. Instrumentalism, in the interest of its polemic, neglects the one thing needful.

The true experimental spirit is that of the mystic, who regards every fixed habit as tentative, and every conceptual standard as provisional, not because there is nothing absolute, but *because there is:* and because—since there is this absolute standard—every conceptualized mental property must recurrently be brought to court to bear comparison with it. By renewing from time to time his perception of that absolute real and good he prepares himself for those fresh contacts with reality in social and natural experience, which are destined to revise no one knows how much of the crusty shell of our assumed axioms and prejudices.

The scientific method itself (which every contemporary philosophy hastens to claim as its own peculiar ally, realism, naturalism, pragmatism in particular) is no partisan of unlimited relativity and change. For the scientific method would be nothing without the logic and mathematics it persistently uses. Probability itself must be reckoned by a calculus which is beyond the reach of probability. The realists have done well in asserting for this aspect of truth a certain independent finality. The pragmatic declaration that the experimental method is the only method, and that therefore all truth must be held tentatively, is a prime example—in so far as it regards this thesis itself as permanently true—of a self-refuting position.

Thus realism also agrees that there is certainty in philosophy; but certainty of an abstract sort; whereas the intuitionist adds to this abstraction the effect of experience, making it a concrete certainty. This concrete certainty however must be rationally—in this case, dialectically—established. It is this which makes the distinction between philosophy and art. Rationality is the genius of philosophy: and in this sense *all philosophy is rationalism.*

40.8. As on the side of epistemology, so on the side of practical philosophy, I believe in a mystical realism, which is the only tenable sort of realism.

We must treat things in the day's work as if they were independent, naturalistic, over against us and *against* us, or at least, not for us. Struggle to build a human habitation in the midst of an alien universe; unremitting effort to expel by the aid of science whatever is evil from our point of view; expecting no good from the universe other than what we human beings construct in the face of nature, except the universe itself; and admitting no wrong as inherent in the constitution of things:—this is the program in which we join the realist.

But who has the eye for this humanistic work, and the endless patience and energy for it, in view of the fact that the task defined is nothing short of infinite? Who can wait until the end of evolution for an achievement which only remote posterity can ever see? Only one who in some way already is at the goal, as the mystic is (who for us represents the religious spirit). For him, reality in its fulness is always accessible where he is: he is always in the middle of time and space and history; he is never neurotically anxious to catch the *dernier cri*, nor hurried on to a remote goal. He alone can labor with endless resources and patience for what may yet be; for he knows that the nature of things is with him. He knows that there can be no incommensurable relation between the task and the power to deal with it. He knows that what is in him is the same substance that has set the object and established its over-againstness. He is assured, with Confucius, that the "good man is a ternion with Heaven and Earth."

40.9. It was one of the strengths of naturalism that it had an explanation for the propensity of the race to religion. The mystical-realism which we are here presenting has its corresponding explanation of the propensity of the race to naturalism, as the mode of thought fitted to the out-swing of the alternation of life.

But this is naturalism on its positive side, not on the side of its negations. It is, let us say, a *transfigured naturalism*, which enlarges physical nature by making it a province within a greater nature.

Of this enlarged conception of nature we may say what we say about the self: it is not in reality a scheme of mathematical phenomena shifting lawfully through endless space and time. It is infinite with an inner life of its own. The reality of Nature is the sum of all the meaning that can be found in it. Taking Nature as Schelling took it, or Bruno, or Royce; not reading its inner being from the atoms upward but from consciousness in all directions:—taking nature in this way, it and its laws become the expression of an ultimate purpose and significance. And nature in turn, with its vast impersonality, removes that taint of arbitrariness which is likely to cling to our usual conceptions of "mind" and of God.

Thus, in Dante's *Inferno*, the literal element of the allegory presents the punishments of the damned as having been inflicted by the will of God. In the deeper sense of the poem there is nothing arbitrary or conventional in the fortunes of these spirits; but the poet is working out, in pictorial symbols, the inherent logic of various forms of vice, wrong, or simple absence of positive good. He is considering the lots of these souls as a working of a natural law; only, a type of law which like the Hindu law of Karma, applies to ethical distinctions, and so works out perfect and invariable justice. Such a conception is akin to naturalism; but a naturalism so transformed that the inner mechanism of nature is not a lifeless, but a moral lawfulness; and the destiny of the self is not limited by the exigencies of any single time-space order.

Some such naturalism as this, so far from being inconsistent with an idealistic metaphysics, is an essential part of the world-picture. It is only the mystic-idealist who is justified in exploring all the "hard facts" and facing all the risks of a naturalistic system of experience, neither defying them nor running away.

40.10. Humanism, some one said, is a sort of "class consciousness,"— we men banded together in solidarity against the universe outside. Yet to fix our mind upon the human interest is to lose the best things that have come to mankind. These have arrived by way of a love of art or of science, as we say, for its own sake, with humanity relatively out of the focus. How can you do good to individual men, each of whom contemplates eternity, unless you yourself contemplate eternity? Consider a man as a group of instincts hailing from animal ancestry, best understood by looking backward, and you can do him a limited amount of good, and that at the cost of his humiliation. Consider him as a group of impulses tending forward to a will to be immortal, and you find material interests taken care of as incidents. Humanism can be fulfilled only in a world that sustains the zest of doing one's human job as a religious observance. This can continue only if the world is worth that kind of devotion. Humanism depends on a transfigured naturalism which is idealism.

40.11. This view does justice also to the pragmatic outlook. For the unfinished part of the world, in which the will to believe has its rightful play, is vaster than idealism usually represents. Human life as we find it *is* not free, sacred, immortal. It must be made free; its sacredness must be conferred upon it; its immortality must be won. In these respects we are the creators of our own destinies: even beyond the humanistic limit, the world of our destiny shall be what we believe and make it.

BIBLIOGRAPHIES

CHAPTER 1
WHAT PHILOSOPHY IS

ON THE HISTORY OF
PHILOSOPHY

Every student of the Types, just because he is not studying the history of philosophy, would do well to have at hand some good book on this history, so that he may turn to it for light on the persons who interest him, and their setting.

Rogers, A. K. *Student's History of Philosophy.* A markedly readable and reliable book for beginners.

Royce, J. *The Spirit of Modern Philosophy.* One of the few modern books in which the aspiration and ageless charm of the philosophic quest are conveyed, with profundity, learning, and mastery of language.

Durant, Will. *The Story of Philosophy.* Conveys something of the essential spirit of philosophy, without being reliable in detail. To my mind, the chapters on Spinoza, Spencer, and Nietzsche are especially good.

Weber and Perry. *History of Philosophy.* A sober and full account for maturer students.

Gilson, E. *History of Christian Philosophy in the Middle Ages.* A masterly account of the intellectual side of the "mediaeval synthesis."

Fuller, B. A. G. *A History of Philosophy.* Particularly helpful on Greek and Hellenistic thought.

Russell, B. *A History of Western Philosophy.* Very readable but uneven in excellence.

Perry, R. B. *Philosophy of the Recent Past,* and Rogers, A. K. *English and American Philosophy Since 1800,* give valuable accounts of several of the recent writers, as Bergson, James, Royce, with whom we shall be concerned.

Ferm, Vergilius, ed. *A History of Philosophical Systems.* Although a Type is a much broader entity than a System, there is a rough relationship between them in the sense that Ferm's Systems usually gather together a group of thinkers about some leading idea. The prominent 'isms are there: Idealism, Materialism, Pragmatism, Naturalism. The reader of Types will readily find supplementary discussion in Ferm.

Werkmeister, W. H. *A History of Philosophical Ideas in America.* Arranged similarly about ideas, not exclusively about persons. An excellent chapter on Current Tendencies gives a clue to the present issues in this country, with some reference to the situation in Europe.

Radhakrishnan, S., ed. *History of Philosophy Eastern and Western.* For the purpose of restoring balance, the philosophies of western lands here fall into the rear of the philosophies of Asia, especially of India: Chinese thought receives mention, and there is a word for Japan.

WRITINGS OF THE
PHILOSOPHERS

Among source books of readings the following are useful:

Bakewell, C. *A Source Book in Ancient Philosophy.*

Nahm, M. C. *Selections from Early Greek Philosophy.*

Rand, B. *Classical Philosophers* and *Classical Moralists.*

Robinson, D. S. *Anthology of Modern Philosophy* and *Anthology of Recent Philosophy.*

An excellent series of selections is published by Scribners, the Scribners Philosophy Series.

Numerous inexpensive editions of philosophical classics are to be found in Everyman's Library, Modern Library, Library of the Liberal Arts, Open Court Publishing Co., and in other series.

CONTEMPORARY AUTO-
BIOGRAPHY

Contemporary British Philosophy, J. H. Muirhead, ed.

Contemporary American Philosophy, G. P. Adams, W. P. Montague, eds.

Contemporary Indian Philosophy, Sir S. Radhakrishnan, ed.

CHAPTER 2
ENDURING PRE-PHILOSOPHY: SPIRITUALISM

ON PRIMITIVE WORLD VIEWS

Brelsford, Vernon. *Primitive Philosophy.*
Hopkins, E. W. *The Origin and Evolution of Religion.*
Malinowski, B. *The Foundation of Faith and Morals.*
Marett, R. R. *The Threshold of Religion.*
Moore, George F. *The Birth and Growth of Religion.*
Radin, P. *Primitive Man as Philosopher.*
Rivers, W. H. R. *Medicine, Magic and Religion.*

EARLY RELIGIOUS OUTLOOK
OF THE GREEKS

Cornford, F. M. *From Religion to Philosophy.*
Fuller, B. A. G. *History of Greek Philosophy*, Ch. II.
Murray, G. *Five Stages of Greek Religion.*

RELATIONS OF SCIENCE
AND RELIGION

Dewey, J. *A Common Faith.*
Jevons, F. B. *Introduction to the History of Religion.*
Needham, Joseph, ed. *Science, Religion and Reality*, London. Essays of extraordinary merit: those of Malinowski, Singer, Eddington, and Needham are especially valuable.
Otto, R. *The Idea of the Holy.*
Planck, Max. *The Universe in the Light of Modern Physics.*
Simpson, James Y. *Landmarks in the Struggle between Science and Religion.*
White, Andrew D. *Warfare of Science and Theology.* Still the standard history of this special topic.
Whitehead, A. N. *Science and the Modern World.*

See also the histories of philosophy for the period of the sixteenth and seventeenth centuries, giving especial notice to the work of Copernicus, Kepler, Bruno, Galileo, Newton.

TYPE I: NATURALISM

BOOKS REPRESENTING THE
NATURALISTIC OUTLOOK

For brief descriptions of some of these works, see section 3.10.

Lucretius. *De Rerum Natura.*
Büchner, Ludwig. *Force and Matter.*
Haeckel, Ernst. *The Riddle of the Universe.*
Huxley, T. H. *Lay Sermons.*
Spencer, H. *First Principles.* Also *Data of Ethics.*
Nietzsche, Friedrich. *Beyond Good and Evil.* Also *Thus Spake Zarathustra* and *Genealogy of Morals.*
Romanes, G. J., *Examination of Theism.*
Ostwald, Wilhelm. *Natural Philosophy.*
Dewey, John. *Reconstruction in Philosophy.* Also *Experience and Nature.*
Russell, Bertrand. *What I Believe.* Also *A Free Man's Worship.*
Santayana, George. *Skepticism and Animal Faith.* Also *Three Philosophical Poets* (on Lucretius).
Edman, Irwin. *Four Ways in Philosophy.*
Sellars, R. W. *Evolutionary Naturalism.*
Moore, B. M. *The Origin and Nature of Life* (Home Univ. Lib.).
Watson, John B. *Psychology from the Standpoint of a Behaviorist.*
Huxley, Julian. *Religion without Revelation.*
Krikorian, Y. H., ed. *Naturalism and the Human Spirit.*

BOOKS CRITICISING NATURALISM

Note that most of the types of philosophy later considered will be more or less critical of the foundations of naturalism. The following books are especially pertinent to our argument at the present point:

Eddington, A. S. *The Nature of the Physical World.*
Haldane, J. S. *Philosophical Basis of Biology.*
Hartshorne, C. *Beyond Humanism.*
Henderson, L. J. *The Fitness of the Environment.* A biological chemist argues that causal explanation cannot close the door to teleology in nature.

Hocking, W. E. *Science and the Idea of God.*

Jennings, H. S. *The Universe and Life.*

Millikan, Robert A. *Evolution in Science and Religion.*

Oppenheimer, J. R. *Science and the Common Understanding.*

Perry, R. B. *Present Philosophical Tendencies,* Ch. IV. Excellent analysis; somewhat advanced. Discusses Büchner (p. 68), Spencer (p. 70), Haeckel (p. 72).

Thompson. J. Arthur. *Concerning Evolution.* A biologist in a popular summary of the present state of the argument.

Ward, James. *Naturalism and Agnosticism,* 2 vols. Elaborate, but clear and forcible.

Weyl, H. *Mind and Nature.*

Whitehead, A. N. *Science and the Modern World.* Difficult but inspired.

TYPE II: PRAGMATISM

James, William. *The Will to Believe* and *What Pragmatism Means.* (As in Everyman's No. 739, Ch. X).

LITERATURE OF PRAGMATISM

Protagoras. In Bakewell, *Source Book in Ancient Philosophy,* pp. 67, 78–84.

Kant, *Critique of Practical Reason,* Bk. II, Ch. II.

Fichte, J. G. *First Introduction into the Science of Knowledge* (esp. §5).

Nietzsche, Friedrich. *Beyond Good and Evil,* Preface and Ch. I.

Peirce, Charles. "How to Make Our Ideas Clear," *Collected Papers,* Vol. V, pp. 248 ff.

Balfour, A. *Foundations of Belief.*

James, William. *Pragmatism.* Also *The Will to Believe* and *The Meaning of Truth.*

Schiller, F. C. S. *Riddles of the Sphinx,* Chs. 5, 6. *Humanism.* Also "Axioms as Postulates" in *Personal Idealism.*

Dewey, John. *Influence of Darwin on Philosophy.* Also the following works, *Reconstruction in Philosophy; Quest for Certainty* (esp. Ch. X); *Studies in Logical Theory; Logic: The Theory of Inquiry.*

CRITICISM OF PRAGMATISM

Boodin, J. E. *Truth and Reality,* Chs. IX, X.

Hocking, W. E. *The Meaning of God in Human Experience,* Preface and Parts II and III.

Lovejoy, A. O. *The Revolt against Dualism.*

Macintosh, D. C. *Pilgrimage of Faith,* Chs. VII, VIII.

Montague, W. P. *The Ways of Knowing,* Ch. V.

Perry R. B. *Present Philosophical Tendencies,* Part IV.

Pratt, James B. *What Is Pragmatism?*

Royce, J. "The Eternal and the Practical," *Philos. Rev.,* Mar., 1904. Also "The problem of truth" (in *William James and other Essays*) and *Philosophy of Loyalty,* Lecture VII.

DEVELOPMENTS OF PRAGMATISM

Bridgman, P. W. *Logic of Modern Physics* (Operationalism).

Lewis, C. I. *Mind and the World Order* and *An Analysis of Knowledge and Valuation.*

Pepper, S. C. *World Hypotheses.*

TYPE III: INTUITIONISM

Bergson, Henri. *An Introduction to Metaphysics* (Putnam's), pp. 1–43. Also *Creative Evolution.*

LITERATURE OF INTUITIONISM

Plato. *Symposium; Republic,* Books VI and VII.

Plotinus. *Enneads,* I, vi, and VI, vii.

Boethius. *Consolation of Philosophy,* v.

Spinoza. *Short Treatise on God, Man, and Human Welfare,* Part II, Chs. I, II, XXI, XXII.

Kant. *Critique of Judgment,* Introduction, and Part II.

Schelling, F. W. J. *System of Transcendental Idealism,* §§3, 4. Also *Philos. Briefe,* VIII.

Schopenhauer, A. *World as Will and Idea.* Bk. II, §§17, 18.

Bergson, H. *Time and Free Will,* Chs. II, III; *Creative Evolution,* Ch. II; *Laughter,* Ch. III, §1.

CRITIQUE OF INTUITIONISM

Aliotta, A. *Idealistic Reaction Against Science*, pp. 115–150.

Bennett, C. A. "Bergson's Doctrine of Intuition," *Phil. Rev.*, January, 1916.

Hamilton, Sir William. *Discussions on Philosophy and Literature* (Criticism of Victor Cousin).

Hocking, W. E. "The Significance of Bergson," *Yale Review*, Jan., 1914.

LeRoy, E. "Science et Philosophie," in *Rev. de Métaphysique*, 1899.

Maritain, J. *Creative Intuition in Art and Poetry*.

Mill, John Stuart. *Examination of "Sir William Hamilton's Philosophy."* Chs. IV, V, XXIV.

Montague, W. P. *The Ways of Knowing*.

Spencer, W. W. *Our Knowledge of Other Minds*.

TYPE IV: DUALISM

Plato. *Phaedrus*.

Balfour, A. *Science, Religion and Reality* (edited by Jos. Needham), Introduction.

Needham, Jos. "Mechanistic Biology" (in *Science, Religion and Reality*).

LITERATURE OF DUALISM

Anaxagoras. Burnet, J. *Early Greek Philosophy*, pp. 272–300. Gomperz, T. *Greek Thinkers*, Bk. II, Ch. IV.

Plato. *Phaedo*. Also *Phaedrus* and *Timaeus*.

Descartes. *Passions of the Soul*, §§XXX–XXXIV.

Pratt, J. B. *Matter and Spirit*.

McDougall, W. *Body and Mind*.

Driesch, Hans. *Science and Philosophy of the Organism* and *The Problem of Individuality*.

Bergson, H. *Mind-Energy*. Also *Matter and Memory* and *Creative Evolution*, Chs. 1, 2.

CRITIQUE OF DUALISM

Plato. *Symposium*.

Augustine. *Confessions*, Book VII.

Descartes. *Principles of Philosophy*, §§45–70.

Spinoza. *Ethics*, Book I.

Bergson, H. *Creative Evolution*, Ch. 3.

Hocking, W. E. *The Self, Its Body and Freedom*.

Moore, Jared S. *Rifts in the Universe*.

Lovejoy, A. O. *The Revolt against Dualism*.

Dewey, J. *The Quest for Certainty*.

DEVELOPMENTS OF DUALISM

Kierkegaard, S. *Philosophical Fragments*.

Cohen, Morris R. *Reason and Nature*.

Sheldon, W. H. *Strife of Systems and Productive Duality*. Also *God and Polarity*.

TYPE V: IDEALISM

*Berkeley, G. *Of the Principles of Human Knowledge*, omitting §§118–134.

(Metaphysical aspect of idealism)

Plato. *Phaedo*.

Fichte. *Vocation of Man*.

Royce, J. *Spirit of Modern Philosophy*, Lecture XI "Reality and Idealism."

(Ethical aspect of idealism)

Epictetus. *Discourses*, Book I, and *Encheiridion*.

Kant. *Foundations of the Metaphysics of Morals*.

Bradley, F. H. *Ethical Studies*.

Royce, J. *Philosophy of Loyalty* (omitting V and VI).

Jones, Sir Henry. *Idealism as a Practical Creed*.

(Idealism and Fine Art)

Hegel, G. W. F. *Philosophy of Fine Art*.

(Idealism and the interpretation of History)

Hegel. *Philosophy of History*, Introduction.

(Idealism and Religion)

Royce, J. *Religious Aspect of Philosophy*.

Hocking. *Meaning of God in Human Experience*, Chs. 17–20.

Brightman, E. S. *Person and Reality*.

FURTHER LITERATURE OF IDEALISM

The literature of idealism includes also the work of the following, among others:

* Read Berkeley and study at least one other work from one of the subgroups.

Leibniz, Schelling, Schopenhauer, Carlyle, Coleridge, Emerson, T. H. Green, Gentile, Bosanquet, Bowne, Howison, Hoernle, M. Sinclair.

HISTORY AND CRITIQUE

OF IDEALISM

Ewing, A. C., *Idealism: A Critical Study.*
Hoernle, R. F. A. *Idealism as a Philosophy* (the best summary appreciation).
Höffding, H. *Modern Philosophers.*
Montague, W. P. *Ways of Knowing.*
Perry, R. B. *Present Philosophical Tendencies*, Part III; also *Philosophy of the Recent Past*, Part III.
Rogers, A. K. *English and American Philosophy*, Chs. V and VI.
Royce, J. *Lectures on Modern Idealism.*
Santayana, G. *Winds of Doctrine.*
Sheldon, W. H. *Strife of Systems.*
See also literature under Realism and Mysticism below.

TYPE VI: REALISM

PROGENITORS OF MODERN

REALISM

Plato. *Timaeus* and *Parmenides.*
Aristotle. *Metaphysics*, Chs. I, VII, VIII.
Augustine. *On the Free Will.*
Aquinas, Thomas. *On Being and Essence* and *Summa contra Gentiles*, Bk. II. (Chs. XV ff. on the order of creation.) See also E. Gilson, *Philosophy of Thomas Aquinas.*
Reid, Thomas. *Enquiry into the Human Mind.*
Hodgson, Shadworth. *Philosophy of Reflection.*

NEW REALISM (AMERICAN)

(Precipitating the American discussion)
Royce, J., *The World and the Individual*, Vol. I, Lect. II, ii–iv, Lect. III.
James, W. "Does Consciousness Exist?" in *Essays in Radical Empiricism.*
The New Realism: E. B. Holt, W. T. Marvin, W. P. Montague, R. B. Perry, W. B. Pitkin, E. G. Spaulding. (See esp. pp. 2–35.)
Perry, R. B. "Royce's Refutation of Realism," in the *Monist*, 1901–1902; "The Egocentric Predicament" in

Journal of Philosophy, 1910; *Present Philosophical Tendencies*, Parts III and V.
*Montague, W. P. *Ways of Knowing.* (Read esp. the concluding dialogue for literary as well as dialectical skill.)

NEW REALISM (ENGLISH)

Moore, G. E. "The Refutation of Idealism," in *Philosophical Studies.*
*Russell, B. *Scientific Method in Philosophy.* (See esp. Lects. I, III, IV.)
Alexander, S. *Space, Time and Deity.*
Laird, J. *Study in Realism.*

CRITICAL REALISM

Essays in Critical Realism: D. Drake, A. O. Lovejoy, J. B. Pratt, A. K. Rogers, G. Santayana, R. W. Sellars, C. A. Strong.
Broad, C. D. *Mind and Its Place in Nature.*
Pratt, J. B. *Personal Realism.*
Santayana. *Skepticism and Animal Faith.*

NEO-SCHOLASTICISM

Gilson, E. *The Unity of Philosophical Experience.* Also *God and Some Philosophers.*
Maritain, J. *Introduction to Philosophy.* Also *Preface to Metaphysics.*
Pegis, A. C. *St. Thomas and the Greeks.*

METAPHYSICS AS TREATED BY

MODERN REALISTS

Alexander, S. *Space, Time and Deity.*
Boodin, J. E. *A Realistic Universe.*
Hartmann, N. *New Ways of Ontology.*
Santayana, G. *Realms of Being.*
Sellars, R. *The Philosophy of Physical Realism.*
Woodbridge, F. J. E. *An Essay on Nature.*

ABOUT MODERN REALISM

Montague, W. P. "The Story of American Realism," in Muelder and Sears, *The Development of American Philosophy*, pp. 420 ff.
Perry, R. B. *Philosophy of the Recent Past*, Part V.
Riley, J. W. *American Thought.*
Rogers, A. K. *English and American Philosophy*, Ch. VIII.

* For an introductory attack read these passages.

Russell, B. *Skeptical Essays*, pp. 68 ff.

Schneider, H. W. *History of American Philosophy.*

Wahl, J. *Pluralistic Philosophers of England and America*, Ch. IV.

Werkmeister, W. H. *History of Philosophical Ideas in America.*

TYPE VII: MYSTICISM

*Lao Tze. *Tao Teh King* (tr. Carus).

Deussen. *System of the Vedanta.* (Outline, by J. H. Woods.)

Al Ghazzali. *Confessions* (Wisdom of the East series).

Plotinus. *Enneads.*

Bonaventure. *Itinerary of the Mind to God.*

Theologia Germanica (tr. S. Winkworth).

Meister Eckhart (tr. R. Blakeney).

Dante. *Vita Nuova* (tr. D. G. Rossetti).

Spinoza. *Ethics*, Parts I and V.

Tagore, Devendranath. *Autobiography.*

*Tagore, Rabindranath. *Sadhana* (Essays 1, 2, 3, 4, 6, 8).

DISCUSSIONS OF MYSTICISM

Bennett, C. A. *A Philosophical Study of Mysticism.*

Bergson, H. *Two Sources of Morality and Religion.*

Hocking, W. E. *The Meaning of God*, Parts V and VI, esp. Ch. XXVIII, "The Principle of Alternation"; which may be followed by Chs. XXVI, XXIV, XXXII.

Hügel, F. von. *Mystical Element in Religion.*

James, William. *Varieties of Religious Experience*, Lectures XVI, XVII.

Leuba, James. *A Psychological Study of Mysticism.*

LITERATURE OF MYSTICISM

Enc. Brit., 13th ed., Vol. II, p. 1013, gives valuable references to recent literature.

Jones, Rufus M. *Studies in Mystical Religion.*

Underhill, E. *Mysticism.* Appendices give a good sketch of the vast literature of this subject.

---

* Accompany your reading of these with the reading of one of the discussions of mysticism.

INDEX

INDEX OF NAMES

SUBJECT INDEX

Absent Objects, 165

Absolute, 16, 86, 217–223, 241, 251f., 318; and relative, 87, 138, 219

Absolute Knowledge; see Certainty, Knowledge, relativity of

Abstract, Abstraction, 121, 314

Activity, 192, 197, 308; moral, 186; see also Passivity

Actual Occasion, 281, 290, 293

Advertising, 58

Aesthetics, 11, 90, 118, 203, 265

Agnosticism, 69, 82, 85, 87, 88, 92, 94, 95, 112, 117, 128

Alienation, 310

Alternation, 132, 273, 275f., 317, 319

Altruism, 9, 118; see also Egoism

Analysis, 82, 89, 91, 121, 135, 139, 226, 232f., 239f., 248f., 253, 254, 276, 297, 300

Anger, 155, 215

Animism, 154f.

Anthropology, 154

Anti-intellectualism, 69

Antinomy, 45, 170f.

Antithesis, 180, 187; see also Dialectic

Anxiety, Angst, 305

Appearance, 118, 128; and Reality, 6

A priori, 70, 80, 81, 82, 83, 85, 94, 95, 144, 209, 291, 304

Art, 20, 38, 110, 265, 307, 315, 318, 320; and religion, 38; organon of philosophy, 118; realism in, 225f.

Asceticism, 118, 266, 269, 276

Asymmetry, 63

Atheism, 117, 262, 308

Atom, 50, 52, 153, 165, 224, 239, 249, 319; see also Analysis, Simplicity

Authority, 4, 6, 10, 73

Axiom, 61, 83; see also Certainty, Postulate

Beauty, 118, 137, 155, 183f., 199, 201, 203, 220, 263, 265, 267, 309, 314

Becoming, 289; see also Change, Event, Being

Beginning, 221, 286, 288

Being, 43, 137, 148, 149, 152, 219, 224, 228f., 237, 259, 269, 303f., 308; and being perceived, 163; self limiting, 218; contingent, 229; as felt, 304f.; see also Becoming, Event

Belief, 3, 4, 5, 6, 10, 37, 66, 94, 95, 98; examination of, 3, 14f.; in primitive society, 14; cash value of, 101

Body, 40, 76; and mind, 139-146; an organ of the mind, 145; a symbol of mind, 196; see also Mind, Brain, Matter

Brahmanism, 9, 152, 258, 269

Brain, 54f., 139, 140, 144, 166, 180, 196f.; see also Body

Buddhism, 9, 152, 268, 288, 310

Categorical Imperative, 99, 206ff.

Category, 17, 139, 287, 289ff., 292; makes experience possible, 171; deduction of, 288

Causality, Cause, 25, 29, 59, 60, 61, 63, 78, 79, 80, 81, 84, 129, 143, 144, 162, 166, 171, 193, 197, 205f.; vs. creation, 44; vs. reason, 58, 69; and purpose, 60, 62, 155, 180, 182; anomalous causation, 143; see also Efficient Cause, Final Cause

Certainty, Certitude, 69, 78, 79, 82, 156, 292, 314, 317; and doubt, 76, 156; subjective and objective, 78; see also Knowledge, Absolute, Dialectic, Axiom, Rationalism

Change, 9, 14n., 50, 109, 120, 121, 125, 126, 182, 221, 289, 317f.; see also Permanence

Christianity, 48, 96, 105, 152, 258, 268, 310

Class, Classification, 120, 135; see also Likeness

Code, 3, 16, 208, 213, 270f.

Coincidence of Extremes, 257

Common Sense, 30, 39, 124, 227, 230, 232, 234, 238, 243ff., 291f.

Communication, 179, 191, 195, 309

Complementarity, 51, 296

Concept, Conception, 126, 267, 304; see also Perception, Idea, Intellect, Universal

334